"WHORES AND THIEVES OF THE WORST KIND"

"WHORES AND THIEVES OF THE WORST KIND"

A Study of Women, Crime, and Prisons, 1835–2000

L. MARA DODGE

NORTHERN

ILLINOIS

UNIVERSITY

PRESS

DEKALB

Published by the Northern Illinois University Press,

DeKalb, Illinois 60115

Manufactured in the United States using acid-free paper

Design by Julia Fauci

Library of Congress Cataloging-in-Publication Data

Dodge, L. Mara

"Whores and thieves of the worst kind": a study of

women, crime, and prisons, 1835–2000 / L. Mara Dodge.

   p.   cm.

Includes bibliographical references and index.

ISBN 0-87580-296-6 (alk. paper)

1. Women prisoners—Illinois—History. 2. Female

offenders—Illinois—History. 3. Sex discrimination in

criminal justice administration—Illinois—History.

I. Title.

HV9475.I3 2002

364.3'74'09773—dc21

2001056213

CONTENTS

LIST OF GRAPHS AND TABLES

ACKNOWLEDGMENTS

My family, friends, colleagues, and students provided the emotional, social, intellectual, and political support without which this project would never have been possible, even as they wished I made more time to spend with them. My mother, Judy Webb, deserves special acknowledgment for her unfailing love and support. Margaret Power acted as friend and critic through years of activism and graduate school. Christine Harrison saw me through the final year of dissertation writing, providing much-needed laughter. Ezra Upshaw contributed years of patience and encouragement. Hossein Massoudi deepened my understanding of the world during many years of juggling (often unsuccessfully) competing personal, political, educational, and social commitments. I owe much of who I am to him. Staff and students at the Pedro Albizu Campos High School and the Puerto Rican Cultural Center, especially Marvin Garcia and Felix Rosa, taught me the true meaning of liberatory education. The original "Spaulding Street Collective"—Ellen Finkelstein, Darlene Gramigna, Janie Hoft, Merryl Geffner, Mark Perry, and Jan Susler—provided inspiration and role models of comrades in struggle. Joan Darvish Rohani helped me to endure (and even to thrive during) two years in Delaware. Maurice Taylor (a.k.a. "Soulfighter") was my best friend during the final year of revisions, sharing poetry, politics, laughter, love, and many heartfelt struggles.

This study was originally inspired by my experiences teaching prisoners in college programs at Stateville and Joliet penitentiaries, and later at Dwight Correctional Center. I owe most of my understanding of prison life to them, even though they remain anonymous here. Barbara Echols and Carlos Vega of the Chicago Prison Action Committee deserve special recognition for their uncompromising activism. Don T. helped guide me through my first encounters with prison life. Fameeda Veal generously shared her life story during hours of interviews. Luis Rosa, Alicia Rodriguez, Jerry Kavinsky, Thomas B. Harris, and dozens of other current and former prisoners touched my heart and shaped this work in profound, if indirect, ways.

Numerous colleagues and friends generously shared their time over the years, reading chapters and offering invaluable feedback. Although I cannot list them all here, I would especially like to thank Elise G. Young, Nicole Hahn Rafter, Anne M. Butler, Catherine Reid, Anne M. Boylan, Beverly A. Smith, Margaret Power, Robin Semer, Carl Nightingale, Meg Cox (my editor), and fellow teachers at Westfield State College for their thoughtful reviews. Leo Schelbert and Margaret Strobel, my dissertation co-chairs and committee members at the University of Illinois at Chicago (UIC), encouraged and advised me throughout my long and winding sojourn through graduate school. Both provided unfailing enthusiasm for the project and an unwavering faith in my ability to complete it.

Marion S. Miller offered an illuminating comparative perspective from European social history. Darnell F. Hawkins, Eric Arnesen, and Shelley Bannister provided critical feedback and support during its final stages.

This study would not have been possible without the full cooperation of staff at the Illinois Department of Corrections (D.O.C.) and Dwight Correctional Center. D.O.C. Director Odie Washington generously granted my request to access all primary sources, including restricted-access files. Director of Research Robert J. Jones enthusiastically supported the project from its beginning stages. Dwight Warden Lynn Cahill-Masching and Jean Fairman, Director of Family Services, both went out of their way to facilitate my research, even when it led in unexpected directions. Dozens of former employees who worked at Dwight Correctional Center between 1930 and 1980 graciously opened their homes to me for extensive interviews. I apologize that so many of their stories did not make it into this book. Special thanks to Dr. Lois Guyon for her many hours of interviews. Finally, staff at the Illinois State Archives deserve special recognition for the hours they spent helping me track down and locate materials (many of which were not catalogued). They carted many volumes of convict registers and file drawers full of inmate jackets to my desk from their sixth-story locations, all with no complaints over my extended use of their time and resources. Finally, I must thank the librarians and computer center staff at Westfield State College for their indispensable help in locating obscure bibliographic materials and printing out numerous rough drafts as I revised this manuscript for publication.

This study could not have been completed without significant financial support during its early stages. A dissertation grant in women's studies from the Woodrow Wilson Foundation and a Littleton-Griswold Research Grant in legal history from the American Historical Association inspired me during the early phases of research. A university fellowship and the Robert A. Remini Dissertation Award from the UIC Department of History provided critical financial aid. Teaching assistantships from the history department, education department, and women's studies program at UIC paid my rent. A King Hostick Award from the Illinois State Historical Society allowed me to return to Springfield, Illinois, for a second summer of research. Finally, an extraordinarily generous award from the American Association of University Women provided invaluable support during my final year of dissertation writing.

"WHORES
AND THIEVES
OF THE
WORST KIND"

INTRODUCTION

This study explores the treatment of women in Illinois prisons from the early nineteenth to the late twentieth century. Although it focuses on a small minority of women—convicted felons—it asks far broader questions: Who were these women? What were their crimes? How and why did patterns of criminality, prosecution, conviction, and sentencing shift over the decades? How did factors such as race, class, ethnicity, age, marital status, reputation, and social standing influence the chain of official decisions that led from arrest to prosecution to conviction and, finally, to sentencing? Once women were sentenced, what was the character of their prison experience, and how did that experience evolve over time? How were women affected by shifting philosophies of punishment and rehabilitation; by changing ideologies of prison superintendents, psychiatrists, sociologists, and parole board members? What was the nature of discipline, surveillance, and social control within women's prisons? And finally, how did women resist, subvert, or accommodate prison regimes?

Female convicts were a diverse group of women. Among them were habitual shoplifters; domestic servants who stole from their employers; prostitutes who robbed their clients; impoverished women who forged checks out of economic necessity; and women who assaulted or killed husbands, lovers, or other women in fits of rage or after many years of abuse. Their ranks also included abortionists, bigamists, burglars, con artists, drug addicts, embezzlers, forgers, grand larcenists, and a handful convicted of infanticide. After 1930, over half were sentenced for misdemeanor offenses, such as public drunkenness, prostitution, adultery, fornication, and vagrancy. Whatever their alleged crimes, nearly all were poor, working-class, immigrant, or minority women. Even though most were first-time offenders, within their local communities many had already earned reputations as improper, immoral, or disreputable women.

Despite the marginality of this small group of outcast and "outlaw" women, their experiences illuminate the many ways in which the bonds of "respectable" womanhood imprisoned all women. A woman who strayed too far from the conventions of proper femininity risked being stripped of her gender-based protections and cast into the role of the fallen woman. As women's prison files reveal, the bounds of proper femininity were vigilantly policed by family, friends, church, community, local institutions, and the state. Throughout the 137-year period of this study, behaviors and circumstances that were defined as improper, including alcoholism, promiscuity, illegitimate births, disorderly living, venereal disease, interracial relationships, homosexuality, and common-law marriages, emerge as central to the narratives of female prisoners. Above and beyond their legal offenses, and well into the 1960s, it was officials' estimates of women's character, particularly their moral and sexual reputations, that often determined their fate within the criminal justice system.

This carefully contextualized analysis fills in a significant gap in the historical study of women's experiences of criminalization and incarceration. As a large, urban, industrialized state with an ethnically and racially diverse population, Illinois offers a particularly illuminating case study for analyzing the interactions of gender, race, and class in the criminal justice system. Illinois women's prisons have clearly reflected the dominant models and historical trends in the development of women's prisons nationally. The Joliet Women's Prison (1896–1933) was among the nation's largest custodial-style women's prisons. Likewise, the Illinois State Reformatory for Women at Dwight (1930–72) was considered a model reformatory, fully embodying the domestic-cottage ideal of Progressive Era female reformers. Whereas nearly all recent historical studies of women's prisons have focused on the pre-1930 period, this study traces the evolution of the Illinois State Reformatory for Women from its opening in 1930 to its transformation into a co-educational "correctional center" in 1972. By examining this complete history, this investigation challenges many popular assumptions regarding the character of mid-twentieth century women's prisons. Although never as violent as men's prisons, women's reformatories were equally as repressive and oppressive, if not more so.

The sources for this case study are exceptionally rich, although they vary for the different time periods. Information from convict register books (1835–1933), individual inmate "jackets" (prison files that were preserved for the years 1920–1963), and superintendents' statistical reports (1945–1970) enabled me to construct a complete demographic profile of female convicts based on every woman incarcerated in Illinois between 1835 and 1970. This quantitative data base (including such variables as crime, age, race, nationality, marital status, prior criminal record, and so on) allowed me to carefully examine shifting patterns of prosecution and criminality over the decades.

Qualitative sources proved even more illuminating. Women's pardon petitions (1848–1911), along with confiscated letters and notes they wrote family, friends, and each other (preserved in their prison jackets) poignantly and powerfully reveal their own voices and perspectives. The inmate jackets also contain a wide range of staff reports written by prison psychiatrists and sociologists (including admissions, classification, mental health, pre-parole, and parole reports), verbatim transcripts from women's parole board hearings, and occasional letters from prosecuting officials (judges and state's attorneys). A second set of inmate jackets (1937–1968), preserved only on microfilm, includes a wealth of additional material: daily conduct records, disciplinary tickets, incident reports, prisoners' letters to staff, letters to family and friends that failed to pass the mailroom censors, and notes women wrote one another. Male wardens and female superintendents chronicled the official version of institutional histories in their annual reports, while newspaper coverage exposed unacknowledged scandals and hidden controversies. Oral testimony further deepened my analysis. I conducted interviews with forty-four employees who worked at the Illinois State Reformatory for Women between 1930 and 1980, as well as with eight former prisoners who served time between 1936 and 1980.[1]

This study is further informed by my personal experiences. For five years I taught college-level history classes at Illinois prisons, including Joliet, Stateville, and Dwight Correctional Center. I am thoroughly indebted to my prison students for the many insights they shared. As I walked the corridors, observed interactions and routines, and experienced the delay and cancellation of classes due to lockdowns and missing count checks, the nature of prison life became real to me in a visceral way. I hope that this work, although historically focused, will enable readers to think more critically about the role prisons play in contemporary U.S. culture and society.

• • •

Part I, "Women in the Nineteenth-Century Male Penitentiary," traces the evolution of the Illinois prison system and the shifting physical and ideological place of women within this masculine world. For most of the nineteenth century, female convicts were imprisoned alongside the state's male prisoners at Alton, Joliet, and Chester penitentiaries. Chapter 1, "She Will Benefit from Further Disciplinary Treatment," offers an introduction to nineteenth-century definitions of respectable womanhood, attitudes toward female criminality, and competing interpretations of the creation of the penitentiary and the position of women within this new institution. The chapter concludes with a survey of the two distinctive types of women's prisons—the custodial and the reformatory—that emerged in the nineteenth century.

Chapter 2, "One Female Prisoner Is of More Trouble than Twenty Males," explores the experiences of women at Alton penitentiary from 1835 to 1858. Female convicts endured the same degrading conditions as men while their gender exposed them to added indignities and abuses. Prison officials complained bitterly about the burden female convicts posed and the greater difficulties they experienced in managing and disciplining them. Chapter 3, "The Most Degraded of Their Sex, if Not of Humanity," examines women's treatment at Joliet and Chester penitentiaries from 1859 to 1896 within the context of evolving penal philosophies, new management practices, and more sympathetic perceptions of and responses to female criminality. Despite the amelioration of prison conditions, the profit motive continued to dominate the state's prison policy. Officials praised the value of women's labor within the penitentiary, but none expressed any interest in their reformation. Chapter 4, "For God Sake Your Honor Let Me out of Here," offers a rare glimpse into the world of nineteenth-century female convicts as disclosed through their pardon petitions. These petitions—which include equally revealing letters from prison officials, judges, prosecuting attorneys, family, and friends—expose the many injustices and prejudices that women faced in their confrontations with the legal system.

Part II, "The Social Construction of Crime and Criminality," interrupts the chronological narrative to analyze the broader criminal justice system. Chapter 5, "An Act Becomes a Crime According to the Community in Which It Is Committed," examines the complex social and legal processes through which an event becomes defined and constructed as a criminal act. Before a sentence could be imposed, authorities had to choose whether to arrest, prosecute, and convict. This background allows us to understand the critical events that took place long before a woman ever arrived at the gates of the penitentiary and to explore the many extralegal factors that biased prosecution.

Chapter 6, "Lured Traveling Salesman to Her Room," analyzes the character of the crimes for which women were sentenced. Although their offenses ranged from the trivial to the heinous, most fell far closer to the former than the latter. Between 1835 and 1890 the majority (78%) were convicted of larceny, although this percentage fell to roughly one-third (37%) by the 1910s. Between 1920 and 1950, 33 percent of women prisoners were committed for larceny, 29 percent for murder or manslaughter, 16 percent for monetary crimes (mostly check forgery), and 14 percent for crimes against persons (robbery or assault). After 1954, when the Illinois General Assembly passed a new narcotics-control act, one-third of women were incarcerated for drug offenses, nearly all (92%) of whom were African American.

Chapter 7, "Whores and Thieves of the Worst Kind," provides a collective portrait of Illinois's female prisoners. Race, ethnicity, nativity, age, marital and maternal status, along with more subjective assessments of a woman's degree of social respectability, morality, and conventionality, shaped the response of police, prosecutors, and judges to women's legal transgressions. Foreign-born women (particularly Irish) were overrepresented among female prisoners throughout the nineteenth century. After 1890, however, race became more central to the ideological construction of female criminality. African-American women, a bare 2 percent of the state's female population between 1890 and 1920, averaged almost one-half (46%) of women incarcerated during these years, and 70 percent after 1954.

Part III, "Doing Time at Joliet Women's Prison, 1896–1933," returns to the chronological narrative. In 1896 a separate, one-hundred-cell women's prison was constructed across the street from the male prison at Joliet, yet this new institution remained under the authority of the male warden. Chapter 8, "Defective Degenerates" versus "These Poor Unfortunates," examines daily prison life, relations between female matrons and their charges, and competing theories regarding women's rehabilitation. Ideological constructions of female criminality were complex and contradictory. At the same time that some Joliet prison staff were expressing increasingly positive and sympathetic views, there existed a widespread eugenics discourse that characterized female offenders as depraved, defective, and degenerate, beyond any hope of reformation. Ironically, such views were most openly voiced by staff at the Illinois State Training School for Girls, a reformatory-style institution that incarcerated much younger, and presumably less hardened, offenders.

Chapter 9, "The Rottenest Hole in the Whole Prison System in Illinois," examines an explosive scandal involving allegations of rampant homosexuality at the Joliet Women's Prison in 1926. This controversy prefigured a growing conflict between college-educated superintendents and their patronage-appointed subordinates (matrons and warders) that deepened over the next four decades. The second half of the chapter chronicles the campaign launched by women's groups for an entirely new institution for female offenders. The Illinois State Reformatory for Women, opened in 1930, reflected a qualitative increase in the state's ability to police, penalize, and punish female offenders. Whereas 343 women were sentenced for felonies during the 1930s, nearly one thousand were incarcerated for misdemeanors. Women in Illinois could now be committed to prison for offenses such as petit larceny, prostitution, vagrancy, public drunkenness, adultery, and fornication. Misdemeanants ranged from three-quarters (73%) of female prisoners during the 1930s and 1940s to one-fifth (19%) in the 1960s.

Part IV, "Finding a Cure: Psychiatrists, Sociologists, and the Parole Board, 1917–63," returns to a thematic approach. In the 1920s progressive legal reformers championed the introduction of modern psychiatric and social work techniques into the state prisons. Chapter 10, "We Seem to Be Dealing with a Psychopathic Personality," examines the evolution of both psychiatric discourse and the role of clinical staff (psychiatrists, psychologists, sociologists, and social workers) from the 1920s to the 1960s. Even as clinical staff constructed female delinquency in increasingly psychiatric terms, they continued to draw upon highly moralistic criteria. Most female prisoners were branded as immoral, sexually promiscuous women who had led "improper" lives.

Chapter 11, "Success Upon Parole Is Doubtful," analyzes women's experiences before the parole board. Prison officials were rarely satisfied that any reformation had taken place. After 1920 the parole board tightened release procedures, doubling the amount of time women were required to serve for every category of crime. Even though the parole board was not legally empowered to retry women, that is essentially what it did. Unconstrained by the legal rules that limited courtroom interrogations, board members routinely questioned women on their histories of premarital sex, adultery, illegitimate births, alcohol use, venereal disease, homosexuality, and common-law marriages, heavily weighing such "crimes" in their decision making.

Part V, "Managing Wayward Women at the Illinois State Reformatory for Women, 1930–1972," traces the reformatory's history from its idealistic origins through its transformation into an oppressive, custodially oriented institution woefully lacking in resources, treatment programs, and trained personnel. Chapter 12, "Discipline and Morale Have Not Been Satisfactory," documents the decline that began during the reformatory's very first decade. Although the cottage-style women's reformatories appeared less punitive and confining than fortress-style men's prisons, female prisoners were often subjected to much more intensive levels of surveillance and control in their "homelike" settings than were men in their far larger and more anonymous cell houses. Women's disciplinary reports reveal daily struggles and contests for power between female prisoners and their cottage matrons. Female prisoners were held to strict standards of proper language, behavior, attitude, and feminine attire while staff vigilantly monitored all friendships for the smallest signs of affection or homosexuality.

The late 1940s was a particularly troubled period. In 1949 Superintendent Helen M. Hazard (1930–1949) resigned in despair. Four superintendents came and went between 1949 and 1954. In 1954 Ruth L. Biedermann, whose background lay in policing rather than social work or education, accepted the post. Chapter 13, "I Have Trouble Getting Her to Live by the Rules," analyzes her administration's extraordinarily tight levels of surveillance and control. Relying on both staff and inmate informants, Biedermann zealously investigated and punished every infraction of prison rules (or suspicion thereof), no matter how trivial. Lesbianism was the greatest violation of all. In 1962 Biedermann resigned amidst newspaper accusations of "brutality" toward inmates and of creating an "unbearable atmosphere" for staff.

Chapter 14, "Punished for Vulgarity and Unladylike Behavior," examines the institution's final decade as a reformatory (1962–1972). Although the atmosphere of paranoia declined considerably under Margaret Morrissey's administration, discipline remained strict. Security and custodial concerns continued to take precedence over rehabilitation goals. In 1972 the institution was transferred to the jurisdiction of the newly established Illinois Department of Corrections. Shortly thereafter it was transformed into a coeducational "correctional center," although this experiment was terminated in 1978. The vision of the reformatory's founders, entailing a specifically feminine form of "disciplinary treatment and care," even though inherently flawed and never realized in practice, was officially abandoned.

The book's concluding chapter analyzes the lessons of this history and examines national trends and issues in women's imprisonment at the end of the twentieth century. Even though today's women prisoners share many similarities with those of earlier eras, they are being incarcerated in historically unprecedented numbers. In almost every year since 1970 the number of women sentenced to prison has increased at a faster rate than that of men. In 1972, the year this study ends, there were 6,269 women and 189,823 men incarcerated in all state and federal prisons. At mid-year 2000, there were 92,688 women in prison and nearly 1.3 million men. Although often regarded as marginal institutions, for the last two hundred years prisons have been central to U.S. policies of race, class, and gender control. They are even more central today.[2]

PART I

WOMEN IN THE NINETEENTH-CENTURY
MALE PENITENTIARY

CHAPTER ONE

"SHE WILL BENEFIT FROM FURTHER DISCIPLINARY TREATMENT"

The Historiography of Women's Imprisonment

On September 11, 1835, an Illinois prison clerk recorded the following entry in the first Alton Convict Register:

> No. 23. Received the body of Sally Jefferson in the penitentiary at Alton. Said convict is 5 feet 4 inches high, black eyes and hair, fair complected [*sic*], about 24 years old. Her left hand and arm considerably seared by a burn when young. Sentenced for Arson to twelve months confinement in the penitentiary, two weeks of said time to solitary confinement. Done at the Peoria County Circuit court on the 11th day of September, A.D. 1835. Pardoned by the Governor, 23rd October, 1835.[1]

Sally Jefferson has the distinction of being the first woman sentenced to prison in Illinois. This brief entry, the only extant record of her case, raises as many questions as it answers. Arson was an extremely unusual crime for a woman. Jefferson's severe treatment by the court suggests that her deed was regarded as willful and premeditated. Yet the convict register offers no clues as to her motive, the amount or type of property damaged, or to whom it belonged. Her arson could not have resulted in any fatalities, or she would have been charged with murder or manslaughter. The condition of Jefferson's hand and arm, "considerably seared by a burn when young," offers a possible clue. Had she engaged in numerous other acts of arson in the past?

Was she regarded by her neighbors as a dangerous or deranged woman, a community nuisance or local troublemaker? Did she have a history of aberrant or antisocial behavior? Such questions are purely speculative. Jefferson's burned hand and arm could have easily resulted from a childhood accident. Nevertheless, the convict register hints that Jefferson defied traditional gender roles in other ways as well. Even though she was twenty-four, she was unmarried and reported no children. Physically scarred, unmarried, and childless, Jefferson garnered little community sympathy or judicial leniency for her legal transgressions.

Regardless of the true motives or underlying reasons for Jefferson's conviction and unprecedented sentence to the penitentiary, the prison warden had no place for her. During the 1830s the state's fledgling penitentiary was on the verge of physical and financial collapse; one-third of male inmates escaped at least once, as would two women in the following decade. Prisoners were supplied with only the barest necessities, and these were often inadequate for survival. Jefferson was quickly pardoned by the governor and released after only six weeks; Illinois judges sentenced no more women to prison for the next five years.

In 1835 the penitentiary represented a radical new form of punishment. At the end of the eighteenth century a transition from corporal and capital punishment to incarceration had taken place in the United States and Europe. The first half of this chapter examines this transition and analyzes the place of women within these novel institutions. Separate and autonomous women's prisons were not established in the United States until the end of the nineteenth century. The second half of this chapter provides an overview of the two types of women's prisons—the custodial and the reformatory—which emerged at this time. The custodial prison incarcerated only women committed for serious felonies, but the reformatory institutions imprisoned both misdemeanants (minor offenders) and felons, significantly enhancing the state's ability to police and penalize deviant behavior. Although only seventeen states established women's reformatories, the reformatory model influenced the treatment of female prisoners throughout the twentieth century.

· · ·

A study of changing definitions of, attitudes toward, and penal responses to criminal—or criminalized—women reveals much about the shifting perceptions and boundaries of proper femininity. Neither seventeenth-century Europeans nor eighteenth-century American colonists viewed women as the frail, fragile, and ennobling creatures of nineteenth-century Victorian ideology. Instead, religious doctrine portrayed women as a dangerous source of evil, corruption, and depravity. A woman's acting out meant that, by definition, the female offender threatened patriarchal authority at the same time that she defied legal and religious codes. Even when she committed the same offense as a man, her actions were often seen as more threatening. During most of the nineteenth century, and well into the twentieth, criminal women were widely regarded as more hardened and depraved than their male counterparts and consequently beyond any hope of redemption.

In the seventeenth and eighteenth centuries, before the birth of the modern penitentiary, women figured prominently in European criminal and penal populations. In English courts, women ranged from one-tenth to one-third of the accused. In jails and workhouses throughout Europe they made up 20 to 40 percent of prisoners. Women were whipped, pilloried, and hung next to men. They were burned at the stake as witches by the tens of thousands, and they constituted one-quarter to one-third of convicted felons transported from England to the Americas and Australia.[2]

English settlers brought English laws, penalties, and beliefs with them to North America, including the concept that women had greater potential for evil than men. Although the Calvinist religious doctrine of the Puritans held that both men and women were born in original sin, religious leaders frequently singled out women as the most dangerous and uncontrollable source of evil. Historian N. E. H. Hull argues that in colonial Massachusetts the punishment of women played a unique symbolic role. Because Puritans thought that "the crimes of women could be traced back to sexual breaches," they believed that "once [women] had 'fallen' into the snares of 'lust' and 'uncleanness,' they were ripe for thefts, homicides, and arsons." Public, corporal punishment served as warning to all women regarding the grave danger of even small acts of immorality and sexual deviance.[3]

During the colonial and revolutionary periods (1607–1776), women were subjected to the same punishments as men: fines, public shaming in pillory and stocks, ducking stools, whipping, banishment, fines, letter wearing, branding, mutilation, and occasionally execution. The nineteenth-century prison represented a fundamental shift in penal practices. This shift from corporal forms of punishment to incarceration had a contradictory impact on women. Championed by its proponents as a "monumental leap forward in the rational and humane treatment of criminals," the penitentiary "reflected a new environmental theory of criminal behavior." Whereas American colonists had equated crime with sin, Enlightenment theorists such as Cesare Beccaria (1738–1794) and Jeremy Bentham (1748–1832) viewed criminality as the product of corrupting external influences.[4]

The modern prison was designed to reform offenders by segregating them from bad influences and instilling new habits through a regimen of total seclusion, silence, work, and religious instruction. The goal was complete isolation from the corrupting influences of both other prisoners and the outside world. Yet those who championed the penitentiary never hinted that women might be incarcerated within, or reformed by, its new disciplinary practices. Enlightenment philosophers viewed women as incapable of full rationality, doomed by their defective biology and inherently sinful natures.[5]

None of the nation's first penitentiaries was designed with space set aside for female convicts. Nevertheless, women were incarcerated in American prisons from the earliest years. An 1840 survey of fifteen state penitentiaries revealed that all but three housed female prisoners. In 1850 the federal census reported that 3.6 percent of the nation's convicts were women, of whom 43 percent were African American. These women were incarcerated in the most makeshift and wretched of quarters.[6]

At New York's model Auburn State Penitentiary, women were housed in a cramped and windowless attic room with no female supervision. According to historian W. David Lewis, "The result was a dark, stifling, nauseating atmosphere in which as many as thirty women were crowded together without supervision or proper exercise facilities." Food and water were carried in daily and refuse carried out, but "otherwise the unredeemable were in a limbo all their own." A New York prison chaplain writing in 1830 best captured their ordeal: "To be a *male* convict in this prison would be quite tolerable; but to be a *female* convict, for any protracted period, would be worse than death." As another New York prison official explained: "The opinion seems to have been entertained that the female convicts were beyond the reach of reformation, and it seems to have been regarded as a sufficient performance of the object of punishment to turn them loose within the pen of the prison and there leave them to feed upon and destroy each other." The women, branded as incorrigible, were provided neither supervision, work, recreation, nor religious instruction.[7]

As in New York, throughout the nation female convicts endured wretched conditions, including overcrowding, lack of supervision, neglect, enforced idleness, corporal punishment, and sexual abuse. For most of the nineteenth century female prisoners remained social outcasts and pariahs, incarcerated alongside males in separate annexes, wings, or units within their states' male penitentiaries. However, by the end of the nineteenth century states began to remove female convicts from inside their male prisons to separate, adjacent buildings. Yet these new units remained under the authority of male wardens, and their architecture and internal regimes were entirely custodial in character. The units were designed to warehouse rather than reform. Only New York, Indiana, and Massachusetts broke with this pattern and established totally separate prisons for women during the nineteenth century.[8]

Attitudes toward female criminality and female prisoners have always reflected broader social views regarding the nature of "respectable" womanhood. The early nineteenth century, which witnessed the birth of the penitentiary, represented a period of rapid social and economic changes. Expanding market forces and incipient capitalism undermined traditional sex roles. As men entered the wider public world of paid labor, politics, and professional life in rapidly growing numbers, middle-class women's realm was increasingly restricted to hearth and home. These changes in status and roles were accompanied by an equally profound shift in gender ideologies. Religious, cultural, and social authorities portrayed women as the weaker sex, uniquely suited to domesticity—to the raising and nurturing of children and to a more restricted life overall. Historians have offered several labels for this new ideology, calling it the "cult of domesticity," the "doctrine of separate spheres," and the "cult of true womanhood." Although such beliefs are deeply rooted in the Western tradition, they took on new power in nineteenth-century America precisely when women began organizing to demand greater freedoms, opportunities, and rights.[9]

Concurrently, social attitudes toward female sexuality underwent dramatic transformations. The early American colonists, including the Puritans, regarded women as fully sexual beings. Women were commonly portrayed as more licentious, lustful, and insatiable than men. Indeed, they were regarded as the source of all evil and temptation. By the 1840s, however, female passion was replaced by "passionlessness." According to this new doctrine, proper women had little or no sexual desire. William Acton, a popular medical writer, explained: "The majority of women (happily for them) are not much troubled with sexual feeling of any kind." By mid-century the medical establishment had fully endorsed this perspective, which was widely promulgated in medical manuals and advice literature aimed at middle-class women. Although the view was never monolithic, Nancy F. Cott argues that in early nineteenth-century America the "traditionally dominant Anglo-American definition of women as *especially* sexual was reversed and transformed . . . into the view that women . . . were *less* carnal and lustful than men."[10]

Within this new ideology, sexual purity became the defining feature of a woman's virtue. As Barbara Welter observes, without purity "she was, in fact, no woman at all, but a member of some lower order." The "fallen" woman was vilified as a woman who relinquished her claim to femininity and the respect and deference due to all true women. As one novelist explained, "Even as woman is supremely virtuous, . . . when once fallen" she became "the vilest of her sex." Indeed, nineteenth-century literature conveyed the message that death itself was preferable to dishonor. Loss of virtue became synonymous with a living death. The dishonored woman, cast out of respectable society and forced to fend for herself, was inevitably portrayed as suffering an early demise from sickness and poverty.[11]

At the same time, earlier beliefs about feminine nature, which held women to be the source of all evil and temptation, still exerted a powerful influence. Lucia Zedner contends that while late-nineteenth-century women were depicted as the source of all moral virtues, they were also "feared to be deceitful, designing, avaricious, and dangerously susceptible to corruption." Zedner argues that it was this very duality that necessitated such an elaborate system of social and ideological controls: "This gap between the feminine ideal and the feared potential for female immorality could only be breached by enforcing an elaborate code of prescribed feminine behavior which might suppress the 'darker self' beneath."[12]

This highly restricted definition of proper womanhood shaped and limited penal responses to women's law breaking. The woman who violated the law threatened not only legal norms, but the boundaries of femininity itself. Because women were now held to be inherently purer and more moral than men, any woman who strayed from her elevated pedestal fell a greater distance than an offending man. Such women, whose actions defied feminine nature, were literally beyond any possibility of reformation. In W. David Lewis's words, "Especially if she had been sexually promiscuous, the female convict was a veritable pariah" viewed with "a special degree of aversion and despair." Historians Russell P. Dobash, R. Emerson Dobash, and Sue Gutteridge similarly observe that nineteenth-century Victorian theorists of female criminality "are quite *breathtaking in the ferocity* with which they depict such women as depraved, desperate and degraded." Criminal women were portrayed as the "very negation of the feminine ideal." Because their "crimes" transgressed sexual and cultural as well as legal boundaries, in the public imagination such women represented a moral menace, evoking horror and disgust rather than sympathy or pity.[13]

Lucia Zedner points out that, unlike women, male offenders "could be seen as displaying attributes not too far removed from Victorian notions of masculinity: entrepreneurial drive, initiative, courage, physical vigor, and agility." Although male criminals earned social disapproval and punishment for their law-breaking activities, they did not bear the added guilt of either defying or negating "accepted notions of 'manliness.'" Even as they ignored the prospects of women's reformation, the penitentiary's champions expressed great hopes for rehabilitating errant males.[14]

The first generation of female prison reformers themselves despaired over the possibility of reforming "fallen" women. After their first visits to the penitentiary, many middle-class "lady visitors" expressed more shock and outrage over the behavior of the female convicts than over their wretched living conditions. After a visit to England's Newgate Prison in 1813, penal reformer and Quaker activist Elizabeth Fry recoiled at the "dreadful proceedings that went forward in the female side of the prison; the begging, swearing, gaming, fighting, singing, dancing, dressing up in men's clothing." She concluded that such "scenes [were] too bad to be described." Behavior that was considered normal when engaged in by male prisoners evoked only horror and disgust when exhibited by women. As another English Quaker explained: "the reformation of these women, lost as they were in every species of depravity, was scarcely an object of consideration, much less expectation." Characterizing the female prisoners as "of the lowest and worst description," she described them as "the very scum both of the city and country, filthy in their persons, disgusting in their habits, obscene in their conversations, and ignorant, to the greatest degree, not only of religious truth, but of the most familiar duty and business of common life."[15]

Scholars fully subscribed to and widely promulgated these popular prejudices. In his influential 1895 work *The Female Offender,* Italian theorist and physician Cesare Lombroso, known as the father of criminology, advanced the concept of the "born criminal." Arguing that criminality was a biologically determined, masculine trait, Lombroso and his coauthor William Ferrero concluded that criminals were less highly evolved than law-abiding citizens. In their schema, female offenders were degenerate, atavistic monstrosities, throwbacks to an earlier evolutionary stage. Thus, their very biological nature placed them beyond any hope of reformation. Caricaturing them as more violent, aggressive, and sexual than normal women, Lombroso and Ferrero asserted that such biologically distinct females could be identified by their "primitive" and allegedly more masculine physical traits: they had darker and coarser features, an overabundance of hair, shorter stature, less discriminating senses, and assorted skull abnormalities. Perpetuating the view that a female offender was far worse than a criminal man, Lombroso and Ferrero argued that "women are big children; their evil tendencies are more numerous and more varied than men's but generally remain latent. [However], when they are awakened and excited they produce results proportionately greater."[16]

Lombroso and Ferrero's purportedly modern, evolution-based theories fully reflected popular views. These deeply-rooted prejudices help explain why there was no widespread reform movement on behalf of female convicts in the United States during most of the nineteenth century. Before female reformers could reach out a helping hand to their fallen sisters, they had to overcome deep divisions between the pure and the impure, as well as even deeper divisions of class and race: nearly half of the nation's female convicts were African American, while the other half were overwhelmingly destitute, uneducated, working-class, and immigrant women. The tiny number of women incarcerated in state penitentiaries (barely 4 percent of the prisoner population) provides another reason for their near total neglect. Offending women were far more likely to be sentenced to local county or city jails, workhouses, or houses of correction. To the extent that reformers expressed any interest in female offenders, they tended to focus on these larger populations that were incarcerated for less serious offenses.[17]

Public attitudes and academic discourse regarding criminal women remained contradictory and ambivalent throughout the twentieth century. In his 1928 book *The Criminal and His Allies,* Chicago judge Marcus Kavanaugh warned his readers that "evil women" were the most important, although rarely recognized, criminal agents. Contending that every male criminal "has at least one woman partner," Kavanaugh openly voiced his deeply misogynist views:

> The number of crimes committed could easily be cut in two but for the evil influence of evil women. The evil power of a bad woman reaches further, presses harder and lasts longer than the power of a wicked man. Her influence is more insidious. Her poison is as pervasive in the veins of a man's heart as that of a snake.[18]

Like Lombroso and Ferrero, Judge Kavanaugh believed that female criminals were "bolder and crueler than men," and "so much harder to reform." His views, recorded in the 1920s, fully echoed nineteenth-century conceptions of criminal or "fallen" women. Kavanaugh concluded: "No man can be so bad as a wicked woman. He hasn't the same genius for evil. A woman is always more hurt by her fall than is a man by his fall, for the reason that a man drops from the first-story window, while a woman tumbles from the roof."[19]

As late as the 1950s academic criminologists fully subscribed to Judge Kavanaugh's unabashedly sexist theories. In his 1951 study *The Criminality of Women,* Otto Pollak, one of the few male scholars since Lombroso to focus on female offenders, argued that women were as criminal as men but that they were far more successful at hiding their crimes. Like Lombroso, Pollak rooted female criminality in women's biology: he offered the absurd hypothesis that women were more skilled at covering their crimes because they had long experience concealing their monthly periods and hiding their orgasms. If their crimes were detected, he contended, female offenders often escaped prosecution because of the "misplaced gallantry" of criminal justice authorities. Pollak fully endorsed the conception that women were more deceitful and cunning and "fundamentally less honest" than men. He approvingly quoted FBI director J. Edgar Hoover, who argued that women were often the masterminds behind criminal organizations. However, because women were more likely to act as instigators or accessories, rather than direct perpetrators, Pollak claimed that they were unfairly shielded from prosecution. Chapter 10 analyzes in greater detail these derogatory twentieth-century representations of female offenders, which dominated mainstream criminology through the 1970s.[20]

. . .

As Lombroso and Ferrero were promulgating their biologically deterministic, evolutionary views, some female reformers began challenging their theories. In *Their Sisters' Keepers: Prison Reform in America, 1830–1930,* Estelle B. Freedman traces the history of the women's reformatory prison movement that emerged in the United States at the end of the nineteenth century. Women reformers charged that because male officials regarded fallen women as beyond redemption, their predictions became self-fulfilling prophecies. Freedman quotes Elizabeth Chace, a Quaker activist from Rhode Island, who wrote to the first national prison congress in 1870 criticizing the public sentiment that "pronounces [women's] reformation hopeless" while male prisoners are "constantly influenced by the expectation . . . [of becoming] virtuous and useful members of society." Without a similar belief in the possibility of women's reformation, she argued, female convicts returned to society "hopeless for themselves."[21]

After the Civil War, Chace and a handful of women leaders began to campaign for entirely separate and autonomous women's prisons. Although unable to fully counter the view that criminal women were monsters of depravity, these reformers succeeded in championing a new image of the female offender as "childlike, wayward, and redeemable, a fallen woman who was more sinned against than a sinner herself." Reforming women were convinced that under the maternal guidance of an all-female staff and a distinctly feminine correctional regime, "this new female offender could regain her place on the pedestal of true womanhood." Rejecting Lombroso's characterization of criminal women as more masculine than normal females, these reformers portrayed female offenders in quintessentially feminine terms: they were childlike in nature, more impressionable, more easily led astray, and in need of greater protection than male prisoners.[22]

In 1873 Quaker activists in Indiana succeeded in establishing the nation's first completely independent, female-staffed women's prison. Galvanized by public exposés of rampant sexual abuse of female convicts incarcerated in the state penitentiary, they had campaigned for a separate "Reformatory Institution for Women and Girls." Their efforts were reinforced by male prison officials' equally strong desire to rid themselves of female convicts whose presence they regarded as "annoying" and whose labor they viewed as "altogether unproductive." Concurrently, women in Massachusetts won legislative approval for the Massachusetts Reformatory Prison for Women, which opened in 1877. Although both employed all-female staffs, these institutions were constructed according to a traditional cellblock design.[23]

Ultimately it was reformers in New York state who achieved the greatest penological innovations in women's prison regimes. Modeled after juvenile reformatories, New York's House of Refuge at Hudson (opened in 1887) and

Western House of Refuge at Albion (1893) were the first women's institutions (albeit, for younger women) to incorporate cottage units in remote rural settings. Designed to foster women's rehabilitation by promoting the "idea of family life," each cottage contained its own kitchen and dining room and a sitting room where "the family [i.e. female prisoners] assemble in the evening for diversion." In these idealized domestic settings, female convicts received training in sewing, cooking, serving, and other domestic arts. From the beginning, the fostering of "appropriate" gender roles was a central component of women's prisons' regimes. Rehabilitation meant teaching offenders to be proper women. Reformatory advocates further championed the curative powers of outdoor exercise and unspoiled natural surroundings. Viewing urban life as a source of sin and corruption, they established most reformatories on large, remote tracts of land where female prisoners labored at gardening, farming, and animal husbandry.[24]

Thus, by the end of the nineteenth century, female reformers had developed a model of a distinctive, gender-specific women's penal institution. Yet this ideal was barely implemented in actual practice. Although rooted in nineteenth-century conceptions of Victorian womanhood, most women's reformatories were not established until after 1910, and slightly over half did not open until the 1920s. The majority were established in response to women's groups' World War I–era campaigns against prostitution, promiscuity, and venereal disease. The movement died during the 1930s, its rehabilitative failures obscured by the fiscal crisis of the Great Depression.[25]

The ideology behind these twentieth-century women's institutions (associated with the Progressive Era in United Sates history, roughly 1900 to 1920) differed in important ways from the domestic philosophy of the nineteenth-century reformatory pioneers. Although domesticity and the inculcation of norms of proper femininity remained central components, the medical model became critical to Progressive Era ideology and rehabilitation programs for female offenders. This emerging medical model embodied a faith in scientific classification, psychiatric diagnosis, intelligence testing, and eugenics doctrines. Progressive Era reformatory administrators represented a new generation of college-educated, professional women, who viewed their charges not so much as "sisters," but as difficult clients in need of segregation, medical and psychiatric treatment, educational and vocational training, and, at times, sterilization and permanent institutionalization.

Women's reformatory prisons broke radically with traditional male prisons in their commitment policies, incarcerating both felons and misdemeanants. Unlike men, women could be committed to state penal institutions for misdemeanor offenses such as disorderly conduct, public drunkenness, vagrancy, adultery, fornication, "lewd and lascivious behavior," and "willful stubbornness." Previously such offenders could only be punished by short terms of incarceration, typically ranging from a few weeks to a few months, in local jails or houses of correction. Now they could be sentenced to a state prison for a period of up to several years in some states. In contrast, the young men's reformatories, which flourished at exactly the same time, only received men who had been committed for felonies.

Women's reformatories significantly expanded the power of the state to police, penalize, and punish "improper" female behavior. The 1923 federal prison census revealed that annually only 20 percent of women committed to penal institutions (reformatories and prisons combined) had been sentenced for felonies; 80 percent had been incarcerated for misdemeanors. Of the latter group, 50 percent had been sentenced for public-order offenses, such as disorderly conduct and public drunkenness; 18 percent for chastity offenses, such as prostitution, fornication, and adultery; 14 percent for vagrancy, which was often the label given to street-walking or prostitution; and 9 percent for violating Prohibition-era liquor laws. As late as the 1950s over one-third of female prisoners in Illinois (38%) were incarcerated for misdemeanor offenses. Progressive Era female reformers initiated these campaigns to increase the scope of formal legal authority over wayward and delinquent women. As criminologists Kathleen Daly and Meda Chesney-Lind observe, "Reform-minded women unwittingly assisted the state in incarcerating large numbers of girls and young women for 'immoral behavior.'"[26]

Not only could women be committed to a reformatory for a wide range of misdemeanors, but they were also often given an indeterminate sentence, such as the standard "one-to-three" years. Reformatory and parole board officials exercised total control over a prisoner's actual release date. Women often served longer sentences for misdemeanor crimes than men did for more serious felonies. Persuaded that women's reformatories were treatment oriented rather than penal in nature, several states adopted sentencing laws that officially endorsed this double standard. Well into the 1970s at least ten states maintained laws permitting, and sometimes even mandating, longer sentences for women than for men convicted of the same offense.[27]

Reformatory advocates offered contradictory justifications for this disparate treatment. Many argued that women were more amenable to rehabilitation than men and thus would benefit from a longer period of "disciplinary treatment and care." Others maintained that short sentences did not allow enough time to reform wayward women, who often proved far more intransigent and resistant than expected. Although historians Nicole Hahn Rafter and Estelle B. Freedman conclude that reformatory prisons succeeded in creating docile subjects and "dutiful daughters," the limited data they present are not particularly persuasive. Recidivism rates remained high at even the most model Progressive Era reformatories. As in any penal institution, maintaining order and discipline proved challenging. After the first few years their founders' optimistic hopes quickly faded. Over the decades, as security and custodial concerns took precedence over treatment and rehabilitative goals, reformatory regimes became increasingly repressive.

Historians' understanding of the women's reformatory prison is severely limited by the fact that research has focused almost exclusively on the Progressive Era reformatory movement that lasted from about 1890 to 1930. No scholar has traced the evolution of a single reformatory institution over the course of the twentieth century. The first sociological studies of women's prisons were not conducted until the 1960s; both focused narrowly on homosexuality, female-inmate subcultures, and the formation of pseudofamilies. As a result, we know surprisingly little about discipline and social control within mid-twentieth century women's prisons. Likewise we know little about the frequency of punishment, prisoners' strategies of resistance and accommodation, staff-inmate relationships, and how these evolved and changed over time. The present study helps to fill these gaps. Well-documented evidence from the Illinois State Reformatory for Women from 1930 to 1972, presented in the last five chapters, reveals inmates' daily and ongoing resistance to the reformatory's disciplinary regime, including its myriad of petty rules and regulations regarding proper feminine behavior.[28]

Prisoners at the Illinois State Reformatory for Women were graded daily on their attitude, work, and "citizenship." In the 1950s and 1960s women were disciplined for such rule infractions as wearing inappropriate clothing ("failing to wear socks to recreation," "not wearing galoshes in rain," "altering jeans"); improper etiquette ("sitting on chair sideways during meal," "coming to breakfast with hair in pin curls," "failing to eat all her French toast"); and poor attitude ("expressing negativity," "talking in an angry tone of voice," "serving coffee in a hostile manner"). These minor violations adversely affected women's chance of parole. More recent studies from the 1980s and 1990s suggest that women prisoners continue to be punished more often and more severely than men for petty rule infractions.

Despite the zeal of its proponents, the reformatory model was not universally realized. Only seventeen states established women's reformatories, most in the Northeast and Midwest, and half of the institutions opened in the 1920s or later. The reformatory movement barely touched the South or regions west of the Mississippi. In an effort to economize, or because corrections officials simply lacked interest in improving conditions for female prisoners, many states continued to build custodial women's prisons that were either physically attached to or a short distance from their male penitentiaries. As late as 1976 fifteen states still "relegated [women] to a corner of the state prison for men." Another five states incarcerated female felons in county jails or boarded them out to women's prisons in neighboring states.[29]

By the 1970s, the ideal of a gender-specific women's prison was in decline. In its place, the model of "coeducational" or "co-correctional" prisons returned. Although most such institutions survived only a few decades, they presaged a rejection of gender-specific treatment models. Architecturally, today's women's prisons are virtually indistinguishable from men's. Once again under the authority of centralized departments of corrections, women's prisons are ostensibly governed by gender-neutral policies and practices. At the beginning of the twenty-first century male correctional officers and administrators, anathema to an earlier generation of reformatory advocates, dominate women's correctional facilities in many states.[30]

• • •

Historians continue to sharply debate the origin and nature of the penitentiary. Early-twentieth-century historians uncritically adopted the views of the penitentiary's supporters, concurring that the prison reflected genuine progress, a humanitarian advance over medieval practices of corporal and

capital punishment. Progressive Era scholars perceived historical develop-
ments as evidencing an inexorable upward progression from barbarism to
advanced civilization. In this view, the penitentiary represented the most enlightened and humane form of punishment yet invented.[31]

The progressive paradigm reigned virtually unchallenged until the 1960s,
when it was rejected by a new generation of social-control theorists. These historians contended that the penitentiary's founders were motivated less by humanitarian concerns than by a desire to impose ever more effective discipline
and control on those whom they perceived as increasingly disorderly and
"dangerous classes." In *Discipline and Punishment: The Birth of the Penitentiary*
(1977) French philosopher Michel Foucault argues that the penitentiary symbolized modernity itself, representing the creation of a "carceral society" with
a network of interrelated penal, welfare, charitable, and educational institutions that employed repressive mechanisms of power, knowledge, discipline,
and control. According to Foucault, these new "disciplinary technologies" represented not a humanitarian lessening of society's power over the individual,
but a radical intensification of that power. Authorities no longer sought only
external control over offenders' bodies, but endeavored to penetrate their psy-
ches as well. In Foucault's imaginative yet deeply problematic conceptualiza-
tion of a new "disciplinary society," the penitentiary is moved from the mar-
gin to the center of modern institutions for social control.[32]

Although Foucault offers a wealth of provocative insights that will be examined throughout this study, his work is deeply flawed. Foucault was oblivious to gender differences. His generic prisoner, the object of the new disciplinary society, was implicitly male. Similarly, Foucault failed to take into
account such attributes as class, race, and ethnicity. His paradigm is limited
to understanding the prison as a metaphor, not as a historical reality. Foucault was entranced with English philosopher Jeremy Bentham's ideal prison.
Bentham's "panopticon" (meaning "all-seeing") offered an architectural design for a perfect penal institution: one that enabled total surveillance of
each prisoner at all times. But this idealized model never succeeded in actual
practice. The nineteenth-century penitentiary never achieved its founders'
dreams of total surveillance, control, and domination; nor did prison authorities ever realize Foucault's metaphor of the "docile body." Prisoners' ongoing
and effective resistance fundamentally shaped the penitentiary's history and
evolution. And during the nineteenth century, prison officials labeled female
convicts as the most unruly, unmanageable, and resistant inmates.

Sherrill Cohen observes that such attitudes toward female inmates are
deeply rooted in the Western tradition. In *The Evolution of Women's Asylums
Since 1500: From Refuges for Ex-Prostitutes to Shelters for Battered Women* (1992),
she argues that "females as a group have been particularly problematic for
western societies." In a bold and sweeping challenge to nearly all histories of
the penitentiary, Cohen traces the roots of the modern prison not to medieval
jails or workhouses, but to women's asylums, including convents, refuges for
prostitutes, and shelters for unmarried women. Contending that prison historians "appear unaware of the existence of an extensive, finely graded network
of institutions to correct, help, and supervise females in sixteenth-century

Europe," she points out that for women "Western patriarchal society has long been a 'panoptic regime,' with females being watched, measured, judged, and corrected when they deviate from prescriptions." Cohen argues that women's asylums provided the "prototypical model" and served as "training grounds for practices in the fields of correction and social welfare that were later applied to men and the populace in general." Ironically, although the techniques of surveillance, conversion, and control pioneered in women's asylums from the fourteenth century onward may have provided the model for the nineteenth-century prison, legal authorities persisted in their belief that female law breakers were beyond rehabilitation.[33]

Drawing from these competing theoretical perspectives, the next chapter explores women's status within Illinois's fledgling legal and penal systems. During the nineteenth century, female convicts were incarcerated alongside men within Illinois's three male penitentiaries at Alton (1835–1858), Joliet (1859–1896), and Chester (1878–1889). Although the circumstances that led a judge to sentence the hapless Sally Jefferson to the Alton penitentiary for arson in 1835 remain obscure, one can speculate that her violations of both legal and gender norms were perceived as sufficiently egregious to remove her from the realm of judicial leniency. By definition, some women already occupied a suspect status. Police, prosecutors, and judges viewed working-class, immigrant (particularly Irish), and African American women as inherently more hardened, violent, aggressive, and immoral than middle-class, native-born, white women. Women like Sally Jefferson, who were considered outside the control of local patriarchal authorities due to their unmarried, divorced, separated, or childless status, or because they were recent migrants to the state and had few community connections, risked harsher punishments for their legal transgressions.

CHAPTER TWO

"ONE FEMALE PRISONER IS OF MORE TROUBLE THAN TWENTY MALES"

Female Convicts at the Alton Penitentiary, 1835–1858

In 1840 Mary Wiser (Alton #198) was sentenced to the Alton penitentiary, charged with the highly atypical crime of "poisoning with intent to kill." She was the first woman to be incarcerated at Alton since Sally Jefferson's brief commitment five years previous. The nineteen-year-old Wiser had journeyed to western Illinois from New Jersey only two years earlier with her husband and young child. Cut off from any long-standing family, kin, or community networks that might have supported her, she was convicted despite her continuing claims of innocence. Unlike the more fortunate Sally Jefferson, Wiser was not pardoned by the governor. She was forced to serve her full one-year sentence, the only woman amidst eighty-five male prisoners.[1]

The "fiendish" nature of Wiser's offense may explain her prison sentence. Poisoning was widely regarded as a particularly horrific women's crime because it represented a perversion of woman's domestic image as loving spouse and nurturing homemaker: perpetrators poisoned the food or beverages they prepared and served in their roles as wife, mother, and nurse. Although female poisoners were rare, their deeds generated attention disproportionate to their numbers and evoked outrage and dread among their contemporaries. Indeed, the only woman executed in nineteenth-century Illinois, Elizabeth Reed, was hanged in 1845 for allegedly "feeding her husband 'white arsenic.'" Whereas a murder by physical violence (using thrown objects, a knife, or a gun) could be defined and perhaps even justified as an "accidental" or "momentary" deed by a woman who had been "overcome by passion," poisoning necessitated premeditation and was thus construed as a far more heinous and cold-blooded act.[2]

Yet only certain deaths generated suspicion. The symptoms of poisoning resembled those of many common gastrointestinal problems and could be easily overlooked or misdiagnosed by physicians or coroners. Only when a woman's prior actions had aroused community mistrust or community ire were allegations of poisoning likely to be made. The ill-fated Elizabeth Reed excited local suspicions by making several other attempts on her husband's life before she succeeded in administering the lethal dose. The careful wording of Mary Wiser's charge, "poisoning with intent to kill," suggests that her attempt also failed. Her intended victim (most likely her husband) survived; it was probably he who brought charges, pressed for prosecution, and demanded the harshest possible punishment.

This chapter examines the place—physical as well as ideological—of female convicts within the state's first penitentiary. It asks several related questions: Who were these women? What were their crimes? Why were they sentenced and how were they treated during their incarceration? Sally Jefferson and Mary Wiser, the first two women committed to prison in Illinois, may well have been singled out because of the potentially fatal and highly unusual nature of their crimes (arson and "poisoning with intent to kill"). By the 1850s, however, Illinois judges were sentencing women to prison for far more ordinary offenses (primarily larceny), and women were becoming a permanent presence in the penitentiary for the first time.

As the number of female inmates grew, officials were forced to grapple with increasingly pressing issues. Where should they be housed? How could they be effectively managed, disciplined, and controlled? Who would oversee them? How could their labor be most profitably employed? What should be done with pregnant, sick, and "deranged" women? At the same time prison officials faced far more daunting and vexing tasks. The reality of prison lagged far behind Michel Foucault's ideal of the penitentiary as the hallmark of modernity and the exemplary realization of the "bourgeois social order." Prisons never fulfilled their founders' panoptic visions of total surveillance or total control. Throughout the nineteenth century Illinois prison officials struggled, often in vain, to master fundamental problems of discipline, management, engineering, sanitation, health, and profitability. Within this broader, masculine context, women prisoners nearly disappeared; their existence was barely even mentioned in official reports. Early legislative debates over the penitentiary made no reference to the inclusion of women or to provisions for their care.

· · ·

Illinois's first penitentiary was built in 1830 at Alton, ten miles north of St. Louis. Its original twenty-four cells immediately proved insufficient. Over the next three decades the state added new stories and eventually erected whole new cell houses within a squalid and grossly overcrowded two-acre compound. At its height in 1858 the penitentiary contained 256 cells housing over six hundred men and a dozen women. During most of these years, the penitentiary and its entire convict body were leased to one Samuel S. Buckmaster, who also served as warden. For an annual sum paid to the state, Buckmaster was to provide for the physical, medical, and spiritual needs of the convict population in exchange for any and all profits he could realize from their labor. Under this system it was in the lessee's financial interest to expend on food, clothing, and medical treatment only the minimum required for bare human maintenance. The arrangement was so lucrative that Buckmaster later bid for and won the lease at the Joliet penitentiary, constructed in 1858. After a series of scandals, the state took over direct control at Joliet in 1867. Yet even under state management, profit was the overriding motive, and the quality of the care and treatment given to prisoners, both male and female, suffered accordingly.[3]

In a sixteen-page memorial to the Illinois General Assembly in 1847, national prison reformer Dorothea Dix condemned every aspect of the Alton penitentiary, concluding that there were "but two prisons in the United States which are so badly supplied, and so comfortless and disorderly, as this." The ground upon which the prison was built was so uneven that the walls were constantly falling down. Rain left rivers of mud flowing through the basements. There was no prison yard and no hospital, chapel, library, or dining hall, standard features of most penitentiaries at this time. The small, dark, damp cells had little if any ventilation. As a result, the prison physician testified, "the moisture collects on the walls to such a degree that it drains from them in warm weather, and in cold completely coats them in ice."[4]

The prison employed no chaplain and made no provision for the moral instruction or education of convicts; not even Bibles were available. Neither the state legislators, the penitentiary commissioners, nor the wardens expressed any interest in the moral condition or reformation of their charges. Instead, their overriding goal was to make the prison financially self-supporting. One early historian concluded: "In the history of the Alton penitentiary nothing stands out more clearly than the fact that the state's prison policy—if it may be said to have had any prison policy at all—was to reduce the cost of prison maintenance to the lowest possible figure."[5]

Between 1835 and 1858, sixty-five women and three thousand men were sentenced to Alton. The nineteenth-century prison never succeeded in providing male convicts with even minimal standards of health care, sanitation, or humane treatment. At the same time female convicts suffered an even greater degree of neglect and were subjected to additional indignities and abuses. Prison officials were hard-pressed to provide even the most rudimentary essentials, such as separate toilet and bathing facilities. As Anne M. Butler observes, menstruation, pregnancy, and childbirth "all created female needs for which the male prison world had no accommodation." Meanwhile, the added security and supervision women required was also lacking.[6]

In 1843 the Committee on the Penitentiary commented upon the existence of women prisoners for the first time, reporting in passing on the final page of its biennial report: "There is [sic] likewise two female convicts that have to be kept in the cook house in the day time and in a cellar at night."

Several years later Dix characterized this cellar as a "wretched den, un-cleansed, unventilated, and utterly comfortless." By day the women worked alongside male convicts, but the cellar's location directly underneath the "Warden's House" may have provided the women with a degree of privacy, security, and safety from sexual abuse at night.[7]

Few penitentiaries employed female matrons before the Civil War. In her 1845 survey Dix reported that only four of nine eastern penitentiaries with fe-male convicts had any female staff. In some states the warden's family lived in an apartment within the prison and the warden's wife acted as unofficial ma-tron. However, in 1843 Warden Buckmaster transferred all of his female pris-oners directly into the male cell house in order to relieve the extreme over-crowding experienced by male prisoners, twenty of whom could be housed in the cellar space previously occupied by the two women. For the next ten years the two to six women unfortunate enough to be incarcerated at any given time were forced to live in cells adjacent to those of several hundred men.[8]

The penitentiary inspectors were deeply disturbed by this solution. In 1844 they demanded, "if females are to be sent to the penitentiary" then some provision had to be made for a female department. "The impropriety of confining them in adjoining cells and working them in the same shops with the male convicts," they argued, "is too evident to be dwelt upon." A minority report of the Penitentiary Committee condemned the intermin-gling of the sexes in even stronger terms and demanded an immediate ap-propriation of two thousand dollars for the construction of an entirely sepa-rate "female department" that "shall be of sufficient dimensions for sixteen convicts." In 1846 the penitentiary inspectors repeated their demand for a separate female department, going so far as to suggest that the state legisla-ture "should relieve the warden, by law, of receiving any women prisoners until after some suitable provision has been made for them." This radical rec-ommendation was carried out on a temporary basis. In 1847 Dix reported that "there are [at present] no women convicts in the prison at Alton, not probably because there are none whose offenses subject them to being sent there, but because there is not the smallest provision for their reception."[9]

Nevertheless, Illinois's judges continued to sentence women to Alton. Pregnant women and mothers of young children posed the greatest problem. When Mary Perry arrived in 1848, Warden Buckmaster immediately dis-patched his assistant to Springfield with a letter for the governor. Admitting that he had no option but to house female convicts "in the Common Prison and Yard with the males," Buckmaster was deeply troubled that Perry, a "re-spectable, married woman, and the mother of several children," was also pregnant. The county officials who had convicted her had other reasons to regret her incarceration. Writing at the "request of several leading Citizens," as well as the very judge who had sentenced her, the state's attorney ex-plained that Perry's husband was "so poor as to be unable to procure any one to take care of his children and their situation is very destitute." Although the state's attorney acknowledged that Perry was guilty of stealing eight dol-lars and a bonnet, he begged for clemency "on the grounds of humanity to-wards her children." The governor bowed to these requests. Perry was released within a day of her arrival, conveniently sparing the warden the burden of her care while simultaneously sparing the county the cost of maintaining her motherless children.[10]

In the following years Warden Buckmaster was faced with a growing number of female prisoners, none of whom were pardoned. The twelve women who entered between 1849 and 1852 were all required to serve out their full one-year sentences. The reasons for this harsher policy are not entirely clear. Certainly more adequate quarters did not exist for them. Despite Dix's denunciations and the penitentiary inspectors' repeated expressions of concern over the lack of "propriety" that resulted from the intermingling of the sexes, the state legislature failed to approve funds for a separate female department. The General Assembly was committed to turning the penitentiary into a profitable business venture and spending as little in additional funds as possible on its upkeep. Nor was the state willing to shoulder the financial burden, albeit small, of hiring a female matron.

The perceived low character and incorrigibility of convict women were major factors contributing to this neglect. In 1878 the penitentiary commissioners complained that "only the most depraved women are sent here," a sentiment that was repeatedly echoed by prison staff over the next one hundred years. The majority of women imprisoned at Alton in the years before the Civil War led lives that lay at the boundaries of social and economic marginality. Three-quarters were foreign born, and over half were Irish immigrants. None had been born in Illinois; indeed, their mean length of residence in the state was barely four years. Although they averaged thirty years of age, less than half were married, and only one-third reported children. Of those who were married, one-quarter had husbands who were also in prison. These women were already marked as beyond the bounds of respectable femininity. The state expressed little concern for either their reformation or their care.[11]

. . .

During the 1850s women became a permanent presence in the penitentiary for the first time. With an average of six female prisoners in the daily population of three to six hundred men, officials were forced to find a more secure and permanent place for them. In 1851 the penitentiary inspectors complained that

> As it is now, this [complete separation of the sexes] cannot be done either by day or night. When out of their cells, in the day time . . . they cannot be prevented from intermingling more or less; and at night, being necessarily confined in adjoining cells, they can converse together without restraint—a state of things that needs only to be stated to show that it should not be permitted to exist any longer.[12]

Again the inspectors declared that if totally separate accommodations could not be provided, then "the law should be so amended that thereafter no female shall be sent to the penitentiary."

The following year the state legislature finally heeded these pleas and appropriated funds to convert the prison's hospital building into a separate female department. Located at the center of the prison yard, the building housed six cells on the second floor and a series of workrooms on the first floor where the women were employed in laundry work. The inspectors claimed that the construction was "of a character which makes this part of the penitentiary all that can at present be desired." However, because men were also employed in these workrooms, the female convicts were still in close contact with male prisoners during the day. The warden's wife continued to provide the only feminine oversight. But because she did not share their quarters as a matron would, the female convicts remained under the purview and control of male guards.

The inspectors' insistence that the women be completely isolated and "kept entirely separate from the men" was not motivated simply by humanitarian concern over "propriety" or the wretched conditions of their incarceration. Prison officials regarded even verbal exchanges between the sexes as highly disruptive. In 1845 the inspectors observed that

> when . . . convicts of both sexes are confined in the same yard, it is impossible for them to be restrained within the bounds of propriety, or their morals reformed; and from past experience, not only in our own State, but in others, one female prisoner is of more trouble than twenty males.[13]

Over the next thirty years, Illinois officials repeatedly complained that female convicts were more trouble than males. Their reports condemned the women as the sole agents of disruption. Similarly, prison officials outside Illinois rarely depicted female convicts as the dutiful subjects of penal regimes. They also portrayed them as more difficult to manage than their male counterparts and blamed them for creating greater problems in managing male prisoners. One of Warden Buckmaster's pardon recommendations aptly illustrates officials' negative attitudes toward female convicts. "Urgently requesting" the pardon of another pregnant woman, Buckmaster added: "You are aware that our accommodations for females are very poor, even when they are in a situation to care for themselves, and I hope you will not consider that it is from a desire to get clear of all female prisoners, as we are still left with two, both of whom are hard cases." Despite Buckmaster's protestation to the contrary, most wardens would have greatly preferred to simply "get clear" of all women prisoners.[14]

Throughout the nineteenth century, women's forms of resistance to penal authority proved particularly troubling to their male captors, who continually found themselves frustrated in their efforts to effectively manage, control, and discipline their female charges. In assessing the historical record, the following questions need to be posed: Were female convicts, in fact, more undisciplined and difficult to manage than their male peers? If so, in what ways? What forms did their resistance to prison authority take, and why did their male captors find them so hard to handle? No Illinois officials detailed the specific behaviors in which the women engaged or described the precise ways in which the "bounds of propriety" were stretched or broken by the women's presence in the penitentiary. Eschewing specific illustrations, the penitentiary inspectors asserted only that the impropriety was "too evident to be dwelt upon." Studies of nineteenth-century women prisoners in other places, however, provide insights into the behavior of female convicts in Illinois.

In her study of women in nineteenth-century Australian prisons, Joy Damousi argues that "women challenged the boundaries that circumscribed their behavior in different ways to men. Their disturbance was perceived in sexual terms and understood in relation to middle-class expectations of feminine behavior, such as passivity, docility, and subservience." Thus, while "sexual immodesty, foul language, and drunkenness were accepted as normal male convict behavior," prison officials viewed these same behaviors as far more disturbing and disruptive when female convicts engaged in them. As chapter 13 discusses, throughout the twentieth century correctional officers continued to regard female convicts as more troublesome, demanding, and difficult to handle than male.[15]

Women prisoners were well aware of the ways in which their presence disrupted penal discipline, and they often deliberately exploited that disruption. Although one must not downplay the brutality and exploitation that women faced in nineteenth-century male penitentiaries, it is equally important to emphasize the ways in which they successfully resisted, subverted, and manipulated prison regimes. Female convicts employed a wide range of strategies in their efforts to negotiate their place within the prison. Whether they acted as wanton, lascivious women who flaunted their sexuality, engaged in brazen and unseemly exchanges with male convicts and prison officials, and deliberately manipulated the contradictions that their presence created within the masculine world of the penitentiary, or whether they acquiesced to a more demure standard of proper feminine behavior, thereby seeking protection based on gender privileges, women's forms of resistance to prison authority confounded male (and often female) officials.

For many officials it was women's demands to be treated as individuals, thereby defying and undermining their status as prisoners, that posed the greatest challenge. One British prison matron reported in 1862 that

> It is a harder task to manage female prisoners than male. . . . They are more impulsive, more individual, more unreasonable and excitable than men; will not act in concert, and cannot be disciplined in masses. Each wants personal and peculiar treatment, so that the duties fall much more heavily on the matrons than on the wardens; matrons having . . . to adapt themselves to each individual case, instead of simply obeying certain fixed laws and making others obey them, as in the prison for males.[16]

This theme—that female prisoners demanded individualized care and attention—has been echoed by prison observers down to the present day. This British matron admitted that female prisoners were often highly successful in compelling prison staff to bend prison rules, offer concessions, overlook routine transgressions, and recognize their individual needs. She acknowledged that "to a certain extent" the staff response was "subversive of true discipline, but a strict observance of the rules would inevitably kill the woman, whose indomitable spirit would last till her dying day." Although Illinois prison officials never offered such detailed descriptions, this "indomitable spirit" was equally present among the state's female convicts.[17]

Male officials were also limited in the range of threats or punishments they could impose. The warden's official reports do not indicate that female convicts were ever subjected to flogging, the standard punishment applied to male convicts who engaged in anything from verbal insolence and profanity to attempted escape. Indeed, Illinois's 1827 Revised Law Code explicitly prohibited the whipping or pillorying of white women, although these punishments were allowed for African American women. Consequently, some female convicts may have felt that they could act with greater impunity because they did not face the lash.[18]

Nevertheless, official punishment records must be viewed with great skepticism. Prison officials were notorious for underreporting or failing to report the full range of punishments and abuses that they inflicted upon prisoners. In his 1892 work *Behind the Bars at Joliet,* Joliet prison clerk and amateur historian Sidney W. Wetmore referred in passing to a "'whipping-post' for female prisoners" at Alton. He claimed it was abolished in 1850, two decades before the Illinois General Assembly explicitly forbade the whipping of male prisoners. Although no official sources corroborate Wetmore's disconcerting reference, his allusion to a "female whipping post" bears serious consideration: all of his other claims proved accurate.[19]

• • •

The failure to inflict the lash on women (after 1850, if not before) exposes the contradictory position of women in the penitentiary. Women's bodies could not be subjected to the same forms of discipline as men's could, while women's unique bodily needs imposed added burdens. This contradiction was most evident in the case of pregnant women, whose increasing numbers (roughly 5–10% of convicted women in the 1850s and 1860s) generated conflicting and ambivalent responses. In 1855 the penitentiary inspectors acknowledged that "the laws passed for the government of the prison do not appear to have contemplated such an event, and no provision has been made for such cases." Noting that the prison had neither a lying-in hospital nor a nurse, they described the convict and her offspring as an "incumbrance [sic] on the warden." Buckmaster pointed out that as warden and lessee he lost the value of the mother's labor, which "could not be profitably put to use," while simultaneously incurring the added expense of caring for an infant.[20]

Other authorities feared that if they adopted a policy of automatically pardoning and releasing all expecting mothers, women would "not hesitate to commit one crime to escape the penalty attached to the commission of another"—that is, becoming pregnant for the sole purpose of escaping their prison sentences. In 1858 a new warden strongly objected to the wholesale pardoning of all pregnant women, proposing instead that a nursery be established within the prison—a novel idea for the time. He admitted that "as at present situated, it is impossible for the officers of the prison to provide the care and treatment such cases demand."[21]

The dilemma posed by pregnant female convicts remained intractable, and officials developed no clearly articulated policy. In 1862 a distraught interim warden at the new Joliet penitentiary wrote a letter to the governor informing him that one Anna Roach (Joliet #1620) was "badly pregnant" and was due within the month. Writing that he was "in a terrible bad fix," he reminded the governor that "our prison is in an unfinished condition" and begged him to "relieve me by granting her a pardon, and doing so *at the earliest possible day.*" Noting that he understood that such had been the practice of former governors, he concluded with a vehement postscript: "If you cannot grant a pardon . . . please tell me what I am to do." Within a week Roach was pardoned and sent home. Although this resolved the warden's problem, his solution did not please local officials. Two weeks later an indignant judge wrote the warden for information "on what ground one certain Anna Roach sentenced . . . for one year for the grave offense of Burglary is permitted to be at large?"[22]

Despite the ambivalence expressed by some officials, by the late 1860s a de facto policy had evolved of summarily pardoning and releasing pregnant women prisoners. It quickly became the standard practice for the prison physician to examine all women upon their entrance to the penitentiary and automatically request pardons for those who were pregnant. These requests were routinely granted, although in a handful of cases (for unknown reasons) women were denied pardons and gave birth in prison. During the 1870s the number of pregnant women sentenced to prison declined. County officials apparently concluded that transporting such women to the penitentiary was not worth the expense, as most would be pardoned and released within a few months.[23]

Given the nineteenth century's sanctification of motherhood, it is rather surprising that judges sentenced expectant women to prison in the first place. It is possible that some women failed to realize their condition at the time of their sentencing. Others may have become pregnant in a deliberate attempt to avoid their prison sentences, as some officials had feared. Of these, a few may have become pregnant during the months they spent in jail awaiting trial. In her study of prisons in the antebellum period, historian Estelle B. Freedman found that "illegitimate births" by female prisoners were noted in nearly every prison and jail report, although it is not clear from her sources whether the women became pregnant before or after they entered prison.[24]

The situation at Alton remains obscure. Both coerced and consensual sexual liaisons could have easily been concealed. However, the official records support wardens' claims that the women entered prison pregnant; their pardon requests all dated from the first months of the women's arrival. Nevertheless, it is possible that prison officials used other pretexts, such as poor health, to secure pardons for women who became pregnant after their incarceration. Moreover, given their short sentences, some women may have given birth only after their release. Yet credit to Illinois prison officials may also be due. No suggestion of sexual abuse of female prisoners ever emerged in Illinois until the late twentieth century. Under the watchful eyes of paternalistic wardens and, after 1863, of vigilant matrons, female convicts in Illinois may indeed have been successfully shielded from the sexual abuse that was common for women in many nineteenth-century penitentiaries.

Expectant women were not the only prisoners whose sentences were routinely commuted. At Alton in the 1850s nearly one-half of the women (47%), and one-quarter of the men (23%), served less than their full sentence. Pardoning was a widespread practice in nineteenth-century penitentiaries. The hope of pardon and the relative frequency of its occurrence were instrumental for maintaining prison discipline, especially in the chaotic early years. Although in the 1850s women received an average sentence of 1.6 years (compared to 2.5 for men), due to the frequency of pardons their average time served was less than a year (11.3 months). The relative shortness of women's sentences helped them endure the deprivations, stresses, humiliations, and abuses that accompanied their incarceration. Such short sentences also shaped the ways in which women responded to prison life. Historian Bronwyn Dalley suggests that in many women's prisons "the rapid turn-over of a small number of short-term prisoners meant that an organized group response was unlikely." Instead, many women pinned their hopes on the possibility of individual pardons.[25]

Wardens also sought to rid themselves of female prisoners who were perceived as overly burdensome due to sickness, advanced age, or emotional disturbances. They frequently categorized such women as "unfit subject(s) for prison discipline." The case of Gertrude Wolfe provides one such example. Warden Buckmaster described her in 1859 as a "great nuisance." Characterizing Wolfe as "a poor old German woman . . . who is at least (or I think partially) deranged," he wrote that in this exceptional case he would "go over my usual rule [of not recommending pardons] and say that I do hope that you will pardon her." Wolfe was soon released. Other women attempted to manipulate such considerations in their efforts to secure sympathy, at times feigning or exaggerating their "weakened state" or "mental anguish."[26]

In some instances wardens admitted that they knew and cared "nothing about [the prisoner's] guilt or innocence." In 1862 a warden wrote of inmate Caroline Meyer, "Her mind is evidently deranged . . . and we have no suitable place for a woman in her condition." The elderly, illiterate, German-born Meyer had proven equally troubling to city authorities. According to one informant, she had "been a burden as a Pauper to the City of Quincy for some years, and for a very small offense sentenced for a long term." Bereft of a husband, parents, or children to support her, Meyer was sentenced to three years. Town officials were disappointed to discover that she was released within eight months.[27]

Poor health sometimes created a common bond among female convicts, but it also generated conflicts. Nursing fellow prisoners represented an added chore for inmates while contagious diseases threatened their own health. A warden wrote the governor that the care of Rose Slocum involved "the constant labor of at least two other female prisoners." Hoping to win her immediate release, he averred that her "incurable" condition was "so offensive that it will endanger, before long, the health of the other female convicts, who can not escape the effluvia in their limited quarters." Not all female convicts were willing to attend sick or dying prisoners. In 1857 Lydia Burke, devoted friend of prisoner Ellen McCarthy, wrote the governor explaining that although "there are two other females in said prison," neither was "willing to stay in the same room with said Ellen and take care of her, on account of the disease with which said Ellen was troubled." Warden Buckmaster suspended prison regulations and allowed Burke to visit and care daily for the sick prisoner. Burke concluded her emotional appeal by noting that the warden was equally "desirous that the said convict shall be released." The governor immediately granted their request.[28]

Even though prison officials expressed some concern regarding the problems posed by sick and pregnant women, female convicts represented barely a footnote in their official biennial reports. From the point of view of wardens, inspectors, and state legislators, far more urgent problems demanded resolution. Alton's male prison population tripled during the 1850s. Despite the assertions of a joint legislative investigating committee that described the prisoners ("both male and female") as "comfortably clothed and abundantly fed on good, well-prepared and wholesome food" and in "excellent health," conditions had deteriorated badly. Even though the committee professed that prisoners "freely declared themselves quite as well treated as they deserved," 12 percent of male convicts died before the completion of their prison terms. In 1857, for the first time in the institution's history, an official investigation concluded that there was ample evidence to support reformers' charges of gross negligence, fiscal corruption, and excessive use of corporal punishment. The investigators closed with a wholesale indictment of the lease system:

> Under the present system, the food . . . clothing, bedding, and medical attention . . . is under the sole care and control of a warden, and the expense incurred in keeping up and properly administering the affairs of each of [these] departments is borne by him. As he is the person leasing the labor of the prisoners for a stated annual salary . . . it is but reasonable and natural to suppose that he will manage them as economically, if not parsimoniously, as possible.

Concluding that with such pecuniary temptations "a man that was honesty itself could hardly resist," this second investigating committee declared that the penitentiary was beyond repair and should be entirely relocated. In 1857 the General Assembly agreed and selected the town of Joliet, forty-five miles southwest of the emerging Chicago metropolis, as the site of the state's new penitentiary.[29]

Because this investigating committee never alluded to the lessee's treatment of his female convicts, we have no way of establishing to what degree they suffered from these same deprivations. However, in planning for the state's new penitentiary at Joliet, officials could no longer ignore the question of accommodating female prisoners. In their original design, Joliet's architects quadrupled the number of male cells over those at Alton from 250 to 1000 and increased the number of female cells fifteen-fold, from 6 to 100 cells, nearly 10 percent of all prison space. It is astonishing that prison officials and state legislators anticipated the need for a 100-cell women's cell house, when no more than 10 women had been incarcerated at any one time in the 6 female cells at Alton. Some officials may have believed that the state harbored a large number of female offenders whom judges had previously been reluctant to commit to Alton. Other officials may have been guided by lessons gleaned from other states. Joliet's architects and inspectors had toured several eastern penitentiaries before designing Illinois's new prison. They could not help but notice the squalid, sordid, and inadequate accommodations that existed for females in virtually all institutions. Although they never recorded their reasoning, Joliet's commissioners and architects were clearly convinced that a far larger cell house was needed for Illinois's female felons.[30]

. . .

Throughout the nineteenth century female convicts' dual status as women and prisoners remained highly contradictory and problematic: their presence challenged ideological constructions of gender, crime, and punishment. Although women averaged a bare 2 percent of the prison population, they were viewed as both more difficult to manage than their male peers and as a threat to the discipline of the entire institution. Despite the complaints of penitentiary commissioners, during the 1840s female convicts (averaging only one or two at a time) were housed inside the male cell house at Alton. Even as they suffered under the same inadequate living conditions as the male inmates, their gender exposed them to even greater degradations and abuses. In the 1850s women became a permanent presence in the penitentiary for the first time, their numbers fluctuating between five and ten. In 1852 the state converted the prison hospital into its first women's department. Consisting of six cells and a laundry workroom, it was located in the middle of the prison compound. Although officials expressed distress over the presence of pregnant women, this concern was motivated more by the financial burden they posed than by a genuine interest in their welfare. Throughout the century financial concerns rather than rehabilitative philosophies drove the state's prison policy, and few exceptions were made in the treatment of female convicts.

Catherine Sweeney's case illustrates their plight. In 1857 the twenty-two year old Sweeney, an illiterate Irish washerwoman who had lived in Chicago for fewer than three years, was sentenced to one year for stealing a five-dollar gold piece from her employer's home. She spent her first eight months at Alton doing the laundry for six hundred male prisoners and their officers. On May 16, 1858, she was one of three women in the second shipment of prisoners transported to Joliet to begin work on the new penitentiary. Not even rudimentary housing facilities existed for these women, but authorities believed that the value of their labor as cooks and laundresses would offset whatever difficulties their presence created among the male convicts. Three months later a fire at Alton destroyed the women's unit and the remaining women were transferred to Joliet. The next chapter explores their fate.[31]

CHAPTER THREE

"THE MOST DEGRADED OF THEIR SEX, IF NOT OF HUMANITY"

Female Convicts at the Joliet Penitentiary, 1859–1896

n July 25, 1864, Mary Brennan (Joliet #2321a) began a letter to Governor Yates:

> Sir, I hope you will pardon my boldness in trespassing on your valuable time but it is with a breaking heart I am going to ask your honor to pardon me out of the State Prison. I have been in here three months. . . . I have been sent here for two years. . . . I have never been arrested before for any crime and I have been severely punished.[1]

The assertion that they were being "severely punished" is a central theme in the pardon letters of many nineteenth-century female prisoners. Most women represented their prison experience as a trying ordeal that tore them away from their loved ones, broke their hearts, and shattered their health. These pardon letters, consciously crafted to arouse sympathy, must be approached with caution. Nevertheless, female convicts' impassioned pleadings bespeak a profound anguish over their imprisonment and a tremendous longing for release. Brennan's appeal clearly conveys their shared sense of desperation. Declaring that she had "gone through severe troubles and trials since this war broke out," Brennan wrote that she had encouraged her husband to join the 90th Illinois Irish Legion to "fight for his country and the Old Flag."

GRAPH 1

Total Female Prison Commitments and Average Daily Population, 1850–1930

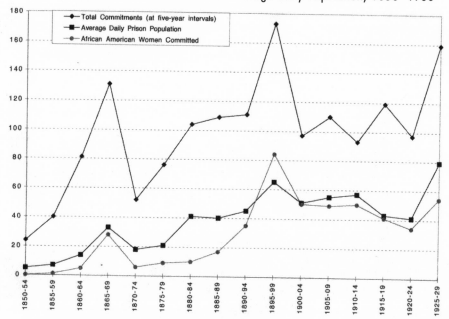

Source: Compiled from the Alton, Chester, and Joliet convict registers.

After his enlistment she had contributed to the cause by volunteering at Union hospitals in Memphis and Vicksburg. Brennan professed, with perhaps only a touch of exaggeration, that "the terror of seeing so many human beings wounded and dying is nothing to this being in prison far away from my husband who does not know where I am and is anxiously expecting me."[2]

Mary Brennan was representative of the growing number of women sentenced to prison during the Civil War. Whereas only sixty-four women were committed to Alton in the 1850s, over two hundred were sent to Joliet in the 1860s, a level that would remain unsurpassed until the 1890s (see graph 1). As in earlier decades, female convicts were disproportionately immigrant (63%) or migrant (31%) women. The majority (87%) had been imprisoned for larceny, often of relatively small amounts. Similar to Brennan, when convicted most were without husband, family, or friends who could protect, advise, or rescue them from their encounters with the law.

Brennan had traveled to Chicago to search for her husband when "wounded members of his regiment were rumored to have been sent back from the battle." She was convicted shortly thereafter of larceny. In her pardon letter Brennan invoked both her patriotism and her forlorn status in the hope of evoking a sympathetic response. She claimed that "I have none of my friends here or would send them down to plead with you for me. My only brother is in the 72nd Ill. and I have no one here in the state belonging to me." She was quick to assure the governor that "the people of the prison will give me a good character." Like many other appeals, Brennan's concluded on a note of utter desperation: "For God sake your honor let me out of here and you will never do a greater charity to a human being."[3]

Although one-quarter of female convicts were pardoned during the 1860s, the governor rejected Brennan's request. Three months later she wrote a second entreaty that was equally long and impassioned. Beginning on a melodramatic note ("It is out of the walls of the Prison I write to your honor"), she described her desperate desire to be reunited with her two small children: "Oh my poor heart is breaking and my children need my care." Reminding the governor of her husband's war service, her own volunteer hospital work, and her friendless status, she again concluded on an anguished note: "I ask you for God sake once more for a Pardon." Brennan drew upon the language of the abolitionists, expressing confidence that "if this letter ever reaches your honor you won't turn aside from the Prayers of the Suffering of those that are in bondage." For a second time the governor denied Brennan's request, and she was forced to serve out her two-year sentence at Joliet. No record of the reason for his refusal has been preserved.[4]

By 1870 Joliet was the largest penitentiary in the United States and the second largest in the world. Its massive size, strict system of discipline, nationally known wardens, and several large-scale riots have drawn the attention of the public throughout its history. Between 1860 and 1896, when a separate women's unit was built, approximately twenty-five thousand men and seven hundred women passed through its gates. At Joliet as at Alton, the story of female convicts begins as a mere footnote in a much larger drama. In the second half of the nineteenth century women constituted only 2.4 percent of those sentenced to the penitentiary.

This chapter analyzes women's experiences of incarceration by viewing them in several contexts. It examines changes in penal ideology, architecture, economies, management, and release procedures; transformations in the demographic profile of the female prison population; and evolving social constructions of female criminality. By the end of the nineteenth century some prison officials began offering more sympathetic portrayals of women offenders. At the national level competing discourses regarding the nature of female criminality emerged. A new generation of female reformers and criminologists challenged popular theories of criminal anthropology. But these debates had little discernible impact in Illinois. Despite the opening of a separate women's prison in 1896, Illinois reformers failed to rally to the cause of female felons. This neglect had many reasons, including the small number of female convicts, their race and social status, the lack of any reported scandals or abuses, and the large number of reform projects closer to Chicago that occupied the energies of the state's most active women's groups.

• • •

Prison architecture reflects competing ideologies of punishment and reformation. At Joliet nothing distinguished the original female cell house, constructed in 1859, from the male. Both were secure, heavily fortified custodial units whose design emphasized security and punishment. The women's building was a two-story structure with fifty cells on each floor in a traditional cell-block pattern. Each cell was four feet by seven feet, the same size as a man's cell. The building was deliberately designed to ensure the complete isolation and segregation of the female convicts. Centrally located inside the prison compound, the women's cell house adjoined the chapel, the hospital, and the dining hall, offering direct yet private access to these facilities (see drawing, p. 83). The women were further protected from the male population by a high stone wall. Adjoining the women's cell house was another large two-story building designated the "female workshop." Although in many states incarcerated women suffered from idleness rather than overwork, Joliet's designers fully expected their female convicts to be as productive and profitable as the male.[5]

The fourfold increase in the number of female prisoners after 1860 suggests that Illinois's judges were far more willing to commit women to the new penitentiary; perhaps they were encouraged by the fact that a much larger and far better designed women's building now existed. Whereas in the 1850s only ten Illinois counties sent women to Alton, and Cook County (Chicago's county) accounted for 75 percent of all female commitments, in the 1860s judges from forty-one counties sentenced women to Joliet. This Civil War–era increase mirrored national trends. As in Mary Brennan's case, the war often disrupted family relationships and exposed women to severe economic hardships. More women may have resorted to crime as a means of supporting themselves and their children. However, the fact that virtually no native-born white women were incarcerated indicates that these women continued to receive preferential treatment within the criminal justice system.[6]

Moreover, despite the original plan for a separate female cell house, women's living conditions at Joliet proved woefully deficient. Because the one-hundred-cell women's building was far quicker to construct than the larger five-hundred-cell male units, Joliet's planners decided to build the women's unit first. For the institution's first five years it was used to house male convicts rather than female. According to one account the dozen women prisoners were "confined in one small room, which was made to serve the three-fold purpose of working, eating, and sleeping, rendering it alike inconvenient and unhealthy."[7]

Throughout the 1860s the penitentiary remained unfinished. It was managed by seven successive wardens and two dozen commissioners, none of whom succeeded in establishing effective control. As at Alton, convicts confronted a violent, degrading, and debilitating environment. Those who entered in poor health, as did many women, found their "symptoms aggravated" by inadequate food; lack of clean water; and dank, unventilated, and cramped living conditions. Women's pardon petitions are replete with references to their authors' weakened state, respiratory ailments, and infectious diseases. Occasionally a warden reported that a woman who was "quite dead" or "could not live but a few weeks" "begs that we will let her out so that she may not die in prison."[8]

Poor conditions for the men stretched official resources to their limit and exacerbated the women's plight. In 1867 overcrowding reached a peak, with over eleven hundred men crammed into four hundred cells. Amid mismanagement and allegations of fiscal corruption, the second five-hundred-cell male unit remained unfinished until 1869. Meanwhile, the prison's lease changed hands several times as various lessees attempted in vain to secure a profit from the growing population of prisoners. Ten wardens served between 1857 and 1874, the first four of whom were also the lessees of the convicts' labor. Effective outside oversight was nonexistent. The penitentiary was supervised by a revolving group of commissioners. Twenty-four served during this period, averaging less than two years each. Official legislative investigations that took place in 1867, 1872, and 1878 documented widespread abuses by prison officials. Yet none of these investigations' reports includes even a passing reference to the treatment, or even the existence, of the state's female convicts.[9]

The earliest mention of female prisoners at Joliet is an obscure reference. An 1861 listing of officers' rules includes the warning: "No guard will be allowed to speak to or converse with any convict woman. Any one so offending will be discharged." This prohibition may have been formulated in response to some particularly flagrant abuses during these chaotic early years. Interestingly, it was not repeated in any subsequent listing of rules, nor were any other explicit guidelines ever developed for the governance of the female prisoners at Joliet. However, a female matron was soon hired. In her 1864 letter Mary Brennan alluded to a Matron Paris, characterizing her as "a good Christian lady who knows how to feel for those who have been deprived of their liberty." In 1867 Illinois's revised Penitentiary Act officially acknowledged the existence of the state's female convicts, mandating that the warden appoint a head matron and "such assistant matrons as shall be necessary, not exceeding one for each twenty-five female convicts in said penitentiary." Head matrons rarely lasted long. At least six served over the next twenty-five years.[10]

In 1864, the female convicts were finally allowed to occupy their original cell house, where they remained for only five years. The daily female population averaged only thirty, far fewer than the one hundred cells provided for them. In 1868 the penitentiary commissioners gave the first of many recommendations for the construction of a separate women's prison, this one to be located completely outside of the male prison enclosure. Echoing earlier remarks from prison officials at Alton, the commissioners complained that "the present female department . . . is a great annoyance to the management, and . . . its removal would be conducive to the general discipline of the institution." That same year Chaplain A. T. Briscoe voiced an even stronger opinion on the necessity of removing the women:

> Situated directly in the midst of the prison premises, are the apartments assigned to the female convicts. Experience has convinced all who have been intimately connected with the prison, that no degree of vigilance secures the great mass of prisoners from the pernicious influence of these females. It is the bane, in fact, of morality among our men.[11]

Prison physician C. H. Bacon heartily concurred and was even more explicit in his allegations regarding the nature of these disruptive influences. Proclaiming it his "duty" to call the attention of prison authorities to the "prevailing habit of self-abuse [masturbation] among the convicts," he judged this habit to be the direct cause of "five-sixths of the disease I have had under treatment" and of the male inmates' purportedly low productivity at work. Holding the female convicts directly responsible for this sad state of affairs, he concluded:

> Convicts are a class of men whose principles and tastes have been more or less debauched from the course of life they have hitherto led. . . . Add to this the presence within the prison walls of a large number of depraved females, who, by secret contrivances, are in constant communication with the male convicts, and you will be at no loss to understand the temptations to this vice are irresistible to natures already fearfully depraved. *At any cost the female prison should be removed from the premises.*[12]

As in earlier complaints from prison officials at Alton, the female convicts were singled out as the agents of depravity: it is they who were accused of being in "constant communication" with the men, rather than the men being held responsible for "secret contrivances" of their own. One can only speculate what impact these attitudes had on the female inmates. Aside from these disparaging remarks, none of the prison physicians or chaplains at Joliet ever again mentioned, much less commented upon, the presence or special needs of the state's female convicts in their official reports. While this derogatory commentary may have reflected an orchestrated campaign by prison officials to convince reluctant state legislators to appropriate funds for a new women's unit, the evidence suggests that these harsh sentiments were deeply ingrained and widely shared. In one particularly frank letter a warden wrote the governor that Mary Kelly's "exemplary" prison conduct was highly atypical. He explained that "she has been very faithful in her performance of her duty" and concluded with a revealing aside, "So much so that my wife and the Matron both declare that if they required help, they would be very glad indeed to secure her, something which they could say of but few other female convicts."[13]

In 1869 the two dozen women then incarcerated were moved from their original cell house inside the prison compound. The following year Chaplain Briscoe reported that "the removal of the female convicts from their old quarters to the fourth story of the Warden's House, thus cutting off every avenue of communication with male prisoners, has been of vast importance to the prison." He added that "to remove them entirely away from here, would prove of still greater importance." Judicial authorities seem to have heeded these pleas. The two-thirds drop in female prison commitments during the early 1870s, from 131 in 1865–1870 to 52 in 1870–1875 (see graph 1), may reflect prison officials' opposition to having to manage female convicts. It may also represent judges' disillusionment with the new institution.[14]

• • •

The difficulties voiced by prison officials in the 1860s over the management of their female charges may be attributable to several factors. As members of the first generation of women sentenced to prison in large numbers, many may have harbored deep resentments. Few women could have imagined that they risked a penitentiary sentence for their assorted petty thefts and rob-beries. According to their pardon letters, few believed their actions warranted such "severe punishment." The prison was a far more masculine and brutal world than the local jails and houses of correction with which they may have been familiar: there women represented 15 to 30 percent of the population. Exacerbating the problem, far fewer women succeeded in securing early re-leases: pardons declined from nearly half (47%) of all prisoners in the 1850s to a quarter (23%) in the 1860s (see table 1). Initially many women probably sought to curry favor with prison officials. Once their pardons were denied, however, they may have channeled their resentment into more open acts of defiance and resistance.

Simultaneously, prison officials confronted a disproportionate increase in the number of African American women inmates, whom they characterized as a particularly troublesome group. During the second half of the 1860s their numbers rose from 2 percent to 25 percent of female prisoners. This up-surge corresponded with the first large-scale migration of African Americans into Illinois. Nevertheless, African Americans still represented a bare 1.1 per-cent of the state's population in 1870. The case of one young African Ameri-can woman exemplifies the harsh treatment these new migrants experienced within the criminal justice system. The woman "confessed to stealing a shawl because the (police) officer told her that she would not be punished if she confessed," a promise that was not honored. In letters on her behalf the trial judge admitted that he doubted her guilt, the state's attorney acknowl-edged that the jury was "strongly prejudiced against Negroes," and a former employer described her as "an honest girl and a good servant." Despite these three favorable recommendations and the slight value of the shawl she had been accused of stealing, the governor denied her pardon.[15]

Imprisoned African American women shared bonds that strengthened their capacity for resistance. Most were former slaves who had only recently entered the state. They were the youngest cohort of women ever incarcerated: 42 percent were teenagers, in contrast to 16 percent of white women. In the post–Civil War years, these young, recently freed African American women, most sentenced for minor crimes, may have deeply resented their incarcera-tion and may have imported into the prison forms of resistance they had de-veloped under slavery. These skills, combined with their youthful exuberance and intoxication with their newly won freedom, may well have made them a particularly unruly and unmanageable population. More than immigrant or white women, former slave women were skilled in strategies of resistance and rebellion, including subterfuge, sassiness, dissembling, malingering, feigning sickness, and otherwise defying authority. Half were sentenced with two or three "accomplices," suggesting that after the war groups of young African American migrants came under intense surveillance and suspicion. Once they were incarcerated, the support of others inside the prison—both friends and family members—may have further emboldened these young women in their defiance of prison authorities. Indeed, when prison officials accused them of being in "constant communication" with men, these men may very well have been their husbands, lovers, fathers, or brothers.[16]

By the mid-1870s conditions finally began to stabilize at Joliet. In 1867 the state legislature abolished the infamous lease system and took control of the institution; two years later the second large cell house was completed, significantly reducing male overcrowding; and the General Assembly authorized the construction of a second state penitentiary in southern Illinois, which would further ease overcrowding. In 1870 the prison chaplain reported that the state's first "good-time" law, which allowed prisoners to earn one month off every year of their sentences for good behavior, had become "the most reliable agent to the preservation of good order." This sentiment was commonly repeated by wardens and penitentiary commissioners throughout the 1870s. Yet despite these claims, prison staff routinely relied upon extreme and ingenious forms of corporal punishment. In 1873 a male inmate's death after a "cold bath" treatment unleashed a storm of criticism that culminated in the dismissal of warden and commissioners alike.[17]

This scandal led to the appointment of a new warden, Major Robert Wilson McClaughry, who became a national leader in the prison reform movement that emerged after the Civil War. In 1870 the first National Prison Congress had been held in Cincinnati. At the congress's annual meetings, wardens, reformers, and academics developed and disseminated the ideas of the "new penology." The roots of this progressive penology can be traced to one of the major convention addresses, given by famed warden Zebulon Brockway, the founding father of the male reformatory prison. In his talk Brockway spelled out his "Ideal for a True Prison System of a State." He proposed a finely graded system of "correctional" and reformatory institutions, including district houses of correction, juvenile reform schools, and reformatories for young men and young women; central state classification centers where prisoners would be examined and "incorrigibles" identified and detained for life; precise systems for marking and grading inmate conduct; and indeterminate sentences.[18]

Major McClaughry became a leading advocate of the new penology. At Joliet he succeeded in establishing an authoritarian yet effective regime that incorporated a reward system as an incentive for good behavior. He opened a library and prison school, allowed special entertainment and recreation periods on major holidays, and boasted of having eliminated all forms of corporal punishment other than solitary confinement. Although such innovations applied only to male convicts, the overall quality of care prisoners received improved significantly in terms that were discernible by most prisoners, both male and female. After the abolition of the lease system in 1867 the state assumed full fiscal responsibility for the maintenance of the institution, including provision of the inmates' food, clothing, medical care, and other essential goods. Whereas corruption and graft were rampant at many prisons during this era, with wardens siphoning off state funds intended for the inmates' food or for institutional repairs, McClaughry earned a reputation as an honest, able, fair, and humane administrator. More important, he oversaw the development of a highly profitable model factory prison. Private manufacturers set up shop within the penitentiary, contracting with the state for the inmates' labor. In return for cooperation and hard work, male prisoners could earn additional good-time credits that would shorten their sentences, as well as a growing array of privileges. As a result, McClaughry was able to combine "a concern for work discipline with the maintenance of high inmate morale." Under his fourteen-year rule, Joliet was widely portrayed as a "model penitentiary."[19]

Despite this, neither McClaughry's new programs nor his philosophy offered any innovations for the care or rehabilitation of women offenders, who benefited only indirectly from his "model" regime. McClaughry shared many of the negative views of female convicts expressed by his predecessors. In one pardon request for a pregnant woman he explained that as "no facilities are provided for such cases" it would be necessary to "supply a nurse for the occasion, as the female convicts cannot be employed or trusted." When a pardon was not immediately forthcoming, McClaughry wrote a second letter, this time adding that the woman evidenced a "higher moral character" than the average female prisoner and was "altogether undeserving to be any longer kept here." The governor consented and the woman was released. Yet this was an exceptional appeal. Other than in cases of pregnancy or grave sickness, McClaughry never endorsed women's pardon petitions.[20]

· · ·

From 1870 to 1896 female convicts at Joliet were imprisoned on the fourth floor of the main administration building that made up one of the prison's outer walls; it was otherwise known as the Warden's House. This space consisted of several windowless dormitory-style sleeping rooms housing twelve to fifteen cots each; a sewing room, laundry room, and dining room; and four isolated "punishment cells" located in the corner towers. Throughout this twenty-six year period the women were literally locked away, denied all outdoor recreation privileges other than a once-a-year "stroll" in the prison yard on the Fourth of July.

By the mid-1870s, Warden McClaughry was particularly pleased with the management of the female department. He lavishly praised a new matron, reporting that "it is due to that department to say, that under the excellent management of its efficient Matron, Mrs. J. E. Judson, the earnings of each prisoner have averaged as much as those of the male department, and the prison is a model of neatness and order." In 1876 the commissioners similarly commended the female department for being a "model of neatness and good order," noting that the women's labor was a "benefit to the prison equal to that derived from the labor of the male convicts." In the following biennial report, both warden and commissioners offered equally profuse praise. From these limited references it is clear that the success of the female department was measured only by the amount of profit that could be extracted from the women's labor, by the cleanliness of their quarters, and by the effectiveness of the discipline maintained by the matron.[21]

This unprecedented and extravagant praise suggests that the discipline of the female convicts remained somewhat problematic prior to Matron Judson's tenure. In 1876 the commissioners reported that Matron Judson's success in the management of her female charges "is attested by all . . . and also by the large amount of labor exacted from and performed by her most un-willing subjects." Expressing popular sentiment, the commissioners con-cluded that "female convicts in a penitentiary are universally regarded as the most degraded of their sex, if not of humanity. To control and discipline them is no easy task, and requires constant care and attention." In 1878, however, the commissioners adopted a more sympathetic tone. Voicing con-cern over the highly restricted routine in the women's fourth-story quarters, they recommended that the female department be moved to a first-floor lo-cation "as soon as possible," so that "these unfortunate women should at least have the opportunity one or more times during the year of stepping on the earth, on which they now look from their windows fifty feet in the air."[22]

The commissioners' more sympathetic tone may have been influenced by their wives, the only other women who would have had any contact with the female convicts. At Illinois's biennial Conference of Charities and Cor-rections, a woman identified only as Mrs. John Beveridge, wife of a peniten-tiary commissioner, expressed her concern that "while the men are led from their cells twice a day across the yard and get a little taste of sunlight . . . the women never go from theirs in a month." She further pointed out that while male convicts worked "in trades in which they are interested," the women were employed "doing the rough work for the men" (referring to the wash-ing and mending of male convicts' clothing). Beveridge concluded, "I think there is nothing very reformatory or interesting in that."[23]

These concerns were ignored. In 1878 Matron Judson resigned. The job of matron was demanding and staff turnover remained high; at least three ma-trons came and went over the next decade. After 1878 the female convicts again disappeared from the biennial reports. Perhaps they continued to be "profitably employed" and "competently managed," and thus no longer posed any problem to or attracted the interest of male officials. As long as the women remained isolated and safely locked away, they could exert no "pernicious influence" on the rest of the prison. They reappear in the records only in the 1890s, when officials could no longer ignore the mounting over-crowding and deteriorating sanitary conditions in the women's quarters.

The only contemporary source that offers a glimpse into daily life inside the Joliet penitentiary comes from the writings and photographs of Sidney W. Wetmore, Joliet record clerk and official prison photographer. Wetmore's writ-ings need to be interpreted with caution. He was a dedicated prison official who wrote to entertain. Wetmore extolled the wonders of the nation's "most perfect penal colony" and later made his living touring the country, lecturing and presenting his slide show to curious audiences. Wetmore admitted that he had almost no interaction with the female prisoners. Even as a high-level prison employee, he needed special permission to gain entry into their locked quarters. This sequestering did not happen in many other penitentiaries. It suggests a high level of vigilance over the female convicts and a genuine con-cern for securely isolating them from easy contact with male staff.[24]

Wetmore believed that the women's lot was better than that of the men. He held that, "the severity of prison discipline of women is not to be com-pared with that prescribed for men. They are not confined in cells, they are not given hard work and they are under the care of matrons who treat them kindly." Yet he admitted that while their work may not have been as "hard"— that is, it may not have required the same brute physical effort as labor in the men's rock quarry—it was equally deadly in its monotony. Moreover, whereas men could be assigned to one of several dozen workshops that provided opportunities for some outdoor exercise and daily movement within the large prison compound, the female convicts were limited to sewing, knitting, and other types of needlework in the close, confining quarters of their fourth-story apartment (see photograph, p. 82).[25]

In a chapter titled "Purloiners in Petticoats," Wetmore described the women at work in their sewing room:

> The women sit facing these windows all day long, their chairs are in an even row, and they have great piles of stockings in their laps. With darning needles and raveled wool they mend and repair heel and toe, it is terribly monotonous work, a dreary routine, a truly penitential task. The women keep their eyes bent on their work, and if the outside scenes remind them of the freedom they have lost, they do not show it in their repressed and stolid faces.[26]

The biennial reports confirm that approximately half of the women were employed in contract knitting, which helps to account for the rigid discipline and strict regime of silence. Theirs was no idle or leisurely "mending," but piecework from which prison officials fully expected to reap a substantial profit. The female convicts also performed valuable domestic chores, including washing and ironing officers' uniforms and sewing and mending male convicts' clothing.

Like late nineteenth-century reformers nationally, Wetmore portrayed female convicts in a surprisingly sympathetic manner. Throughout he emphasizes their essential femininity; gone are the images of wild, undisciplined, and depraved beings of an earlier era. Instead, Wetmore depicted female convicts as poor, forlorn creatures whose overriding concern was with maintaining an acceptable feminine appearance and whose greatest suffering was derived from the loss of quintessential feminine apparel. He told how one woman succeeded in maintaining a glossy head of hair by skimming the fat from her soup and using it for hair oil, while another, equally creative, managed to achieve a rouge color on her cheeks by rubbing them with the bright red dye from her yarn. He concluded that "not even a prison can curb a woman's vanity nor deprive her of the use of those little arts that contribute to personal adornment." Using a little "feminine ingenuity," even female convicts could find ways of adorning themselves. Corsets were permissible and reputedly highly prized by "those who desire to preserve a small waist beneath the rather baggy outlines of their gingham dresses." Bustles, however, were strictly prohibited. Wetmore claimed, somewhat fancifully, that "loss of liberty and loss of bustle seem to be equal trials" for female convicts.[27]

Despite his generally sympathetic tone, Wetmore could not resist pandering to the public's lurid fascination with female criminality. Adopting an approach that would become standard among journalists and outside observers of women's prisons down to the present day, Wetmore delighted in contrasting a woman's demure and undistinguished appearance with the purportedly heinous nature of her crimes. "Taken as a class," he remarked, "the [female] convicts are a respectable looking set of women. It is almost impossible to believe them guilty of the hideous crimes they are expiating in prison." Indeed, it was this very contradiction that both confounded and titillated his audiences. By the end of the century some observers were finding it increasingly difficult to reconcile the very ordinary appearance of female convicts with the popular image of depraved female criminality. Whereas previously female felons had been universally regarded as degraded creatures capable of any monstrosity, their criminality now appeared increasingly problematic. In contrast, prison visitors had no difficulty perceiving male convicts as dangerous and vicious brutes who were capable of any and every type of monstrosity.[28]

Wetmore used this new narrative construction several times in his 1892 book, *Behind the Bars at Joliet: A Peep at a Prison, Its History, and Its Mysteries.* He began with the case of Mollie Mott, graciously describing her as "a trim-looking person" whose downcast eyes "give her a meek expression." Wetmore was unable to detect any indication from her outward features "which might provide a telltale sign to her hardened nature." A third-time offender, Mollie Mott's seemingly demure and very ordinary appearance confounded Wetmore. He could not reconcile it with her "thirst for a policeman's blood": the vicious murder for which she had been convicted. Wetmore then narrated the case of an elderly Swiss woman whose first countenance "excites pity." Her equally undistinguished appearance concealed the even more monstrous nature of her crime: she had cruelly and mercilessly abused her own child. Together with her husband she had been convicted of beating and burning her son and finally leaving him outside in the winter to freeze to death. The child was now a helpless cripple with both feet amputated. Beyond the horror of this crime, which contravened Victorian notions of women's maternal nature, Wetmore was perturbed by the fact that "the woman who could do such a fiendish thing looks not unlike other women, and she is said to show many traits of tender heartedness among her sister convicts."[29]

To the extent that criminal women were indistinguishable from others, the core of Victorian gender taxonomies was thrown into question. Indeed, Cesare Lombroso's theory of criminal anthropology was reassuring precisely because it held that criminal women could be readily identified by their physiognomy: their depraved natures were inscribed in their masculine physical traits, darker and coarser features, overabundance of hair, protruding foreheads, and assorted skull abnormalities. Such telltale markers were comforting to Victorian-era observers who regarded men and women as both physically and psychologically distinct.

Wetmore was far less confounded by the equally depraved acts of male prisoners; even their most evil deeds were perceived as well within the boundaries of normal masculinity. Wetmore delighted in recounting their exploits: their cunning, guile, and greed; reckless escape attempts; acts of sabotage and arson; and assaults on staff and other inmates. Wetmore readily acknowledged that male prisoners were one's ordinary neighbors, ranging from the "clerk at the counter" to the "field-hand from the plough . . . cobbler from his shop . . . doctor from his patient . . . and even the pastor from his church." Whether the inmate's crime was cold-blooded murder, brutal rape, or crippling assault, Wetmore presented men's misdeeds in a matter-of-fact tone. None of their offenses was portrayed as transgressing the limits of ordinary male behavior.[30]

In the end, however, Wetmore sought to reassure his nervous yet titillated readers. He acknowledged that few female convicts were convicted of such depraved or heinous acts. In reality, the majority were ordinary "sneak-thieves and shop-lifters." Many suffered from ill-health while others were "slaves to the liquor or opium habit." Suggesting that for such ill or addicted women a prison sentence offered a positive respite—a nourishing diet, ample rest, and adequate medical care—Wetmore offered his audiences a highly favorable and comforting assessment of women's conditions of incarceration.[31]

• • •

Despite Wetmore's sympathetic portrayal, no Illinois official championed the rehabilitation of female convicts. The lack of any reform impulse was especially obvious at Illinois's third penitentiary, established at Chester, fifty miles southwest of St. Louis, in 1878. Only sixty-nine women were ever sentenced to the prison at Chester (now Menard Correctional Center), where they averaged three to five women amidst roughly five hundred men. As at Joliet, the original architectural plans for the Chester penitentiary called for a separate "female department," which was to be located inside the male prison yard and "surrounded by a high stone wall." For unknown reasons this women's department was never constructed. Instead, female convicts were housed in a cellar under one of the workhouses. Despite these inadequate conditions, the commissioners were pleased to report that the women were productively employed "in making up clothing for the convicts." They noted that "their services are worth from a dollar to a dollar and a half per day" and concluded, "we find them very valuable."[32]

In 1882, in an unusual move, Chester's penitentiary commissioners called for the construction of an entirely separate female prison, asserting that "there is neither wisdom, economy, nor humanity in keeping female prisoners cooped up in the attic of one and basement of the other prison for male convicts of the State." They boldly asserted that the "practice of keeping male and female prisoners in the same prison . . . is one that the better thought of the day universally condemns." Perhaps influenced by the experiment taking place in the neighboring state of Indiana (where the first independent, female-staffed women's prison was established in 1873), they recommended that such a female prison be entirely autonomous and "managed and governed by a board of philanthropic Christian ladies." Despite this humanitarian rationale, the commissioners were even more concerned that the new institution be financially self-supporting. Recommending that it be constructed near a large city "where the inmates could be profitably employed on some of the lighter work connected with the manufacturing, such as binding shoes, making paper boxes, or similar work," they took pains to assure the General Assembly that the prison "need be but of very small expense to the State, if not, indeed, self-sustaining." Thus, the Chester commissioners' recommendation for an entirely separate and autonomous female prison, while seemingly bold and progressive, was based equally upon practical and financial rationales.[33]

The state legislature ignored their radical proposal; the commissioners never again referred to it. Instead, in 1884 they quietly transferred Chester's female convicts from their basement quarters inside the prison compound to the outer "Warden's House." They also and hired a matron. Commending her "efficient management," they again singled out the female convicts' profitability for special praise. The warden calculated that "with the aid of two knitting-machines" the women had "furnished the men with 4,846 pairs of socks," had made "underclothes, coats and pants" for the officers, and had "done all the laundry work for the warden's house." "All of which," he concluded, "if computed in dollars and cents would show how valuable this department is to the institution." As at Joliet, the profitability of the female labor was the state's primary concern. In contrast to their many lofty pronouncements regarding the reformation of male convicts, prison officials never voiced any further interest in women's rehabilitation. Nor did they develop any guidelines for the female inmates' care, treatment, or protection.[34]

Official's acknowledgment of the profitability and productivity of female convict labor is intriguing. In his 1880 national prison survey Enoch C. Wines reported that the commissioners at Joliet made "the rather uncommon statement that the earnings of the women are fully equal to that of the same number of men." Both contemporaries and current historians have considered female prison labor less profitable than male. Yet whether contracted to private parties or employed in the maintenance of the institution, women's work may have been more valuable than generally recognized. The domestic tasks that female convicts performed—cooking for officers, sewing, mending, laundry, and housekeeping—provided essential services and freed male prisoners for more remunerative contract labor.[35]

In 1887 the Illinois General Assembly passed a resolution directing Chester's commissioners to transfer all female convicts to Joliet "in order to save expense and secure economy in management." However, this order was not carried out. Two years later the General Assembly passed a second act, this time supplying a two thousand dollar appropriation. Again, economy and expediency were the only rationales given. Neither the warden nor any other penitentiary officials commented publicly upon the removal of the women from Chester to Joliet in late 1889.[36]

During the 1880s the average number of women prisoners incarcerated at Joliet had increased to forty, twice the daily population of the 1870s. The transfer of all female prisoners from Chester, coupled with an increase in average sentence length (from 1.2 years in the 1860s to 2.2 years in the 1890s) further contributed to this rising daily population and, as a result, to deteriorating living conditions. After 1895 the number of women sentenced to prison annually nearly doubled. In 1896 a *Chicago Tribune* reporter painted a portrait of the women's quarters at Joliet that was much bleaker than Wetmore's earlier portrayals:

> For several years between sixty and seventy women have been crowded into a few small rooms on the top floor of the Warden's House. . . . Sanitary conditions in the rooms are bad. In the dormitories twenty-five cots are crowded into a space originally intended for twelve or fifteen. There are no windows in the cells, which are dark and poorly ventilated. The work rooms are small. Laundry and dining-room are the same. One small room, not removed from the rest, has served as a hospital. These conditions have menaced the health of both the inmates and the officers and made the administration of discipline difficult.[37]

After 1890 prison officials continually reminded their readers that the construction of a separate female prison had been "recommended continually by Commissioners and Wardens for years." In 1894 the newly appointed Warden Allen maintained that it was "unfair, unjust and inhuman to confine the large number of female convicts . . . in the space provided for them." Like Warden McClaughry before him, Warden Allen offered extravagant praise for the new chief matron, Maria S. Madden. Officials' criteria for the successful management of female convicts remained the same: neatness, order, discipline, and profit. Warden Allen reported that "laboring under the greatest difficulties, [the matrons] have maintained a high order of discipline among the convicts, have accomplished the work expected of them, and have been successful in making an earning for the department by looping stockings." The women's quarters were, he concluded, the "cleanest, neatest place . . . surely than in any great penal institution."[38]

In 1895 Warden Allen began the practice of allowing the women out for a walk in the prison yard every Sunday and arranged special services for them in the prison chapel. The warden's act was spurred by the intercession of a Mrs. Wiens, a Chicago woman who had befriended one female convict. Admitting that this weekly walk "lacked much of being sufficient," Allen concluded that "it was the only way open to me in which to partially relieve their unpleasant situation." Disregarding the "cat calls and hooting from the eagerly-watching male prisoners," the women greatly appreciated this new opportunity. In an exuberant letter prisoner Maggie Tiller revealed the significance of this modest improvement: "My dearest friend," she wrote Mrs. Wiens, "You don't know how much you did for us. . . . you and you alone saved more than one life in the old prison. If you had not asked [the warden] for us to go in the yard on Sundays, more than one [woman] would of [*sic*] been dead with consumption."[39]

Finally, in July 1895 the state legislature heeded the warden's pleas and voted an appropriation of $75,000 for "the construction of a suitable building and walls around the same for the use of female convicts." The only official rationale ever offered for a separate unit was a statement by the commissioners: "The new Women's Prison is, in effect, a separate establishment, erected in order that the male and female convicts should be kept entirely separate and apart." Nationally, Nicole Hahn Rafter contends, the tendency of custodial women's prisons to "detach themselves from the central prisons where they originated" was simply a "by-product of administrative considerations, not a result of a desire to reform."[40]

• • •

During the late nineteenth and early twentieth centuries Illinois stood at the center of national reform movements, yet none championed the plight of the state's female felons. As in most states, the motive for a separate women's unit came not from reformers but from male prison administrators. Throughout the nineteenth century pecuniary rather than philosophical motives dominated the state's prison policy. In the antebellum period the warden of the penitentiary was the lessor of the convict's labor; in the post–Civil War era, when the state managed the penitentiaries, the prisoner's labor was leased out to private contractors. In both systems profit was the overriding motive, and the quality of the care and treatment received by prisoners, both male and female, suffered accordingly.

Near the end of the century prison officials began championing innovative programs for male prisoners, resulting in the establishment of a special unit, the Hospital for the Criminally Insane at Chester in 1887 and a young men's reformatory at Pontiac in 1891. However, no prison officials campaigned for a reformatory-style women's institution. Similarly, no nineteenth-century religious, charitable, or women's groups expressed more than a passing interest in Joliet's female population. Instead, Chicago's women's clubs, the most active in the state, engaged in a broad range of criminal justice projects much closer to home than Joliet, fifty miles away. During the 1890s women reformers focused their energies on settlement house work; the establishment of the nation's first juvenile court; campaigns for the hiring of female police officers; agitation against the "white slave trade," which allegedly trapped unsuspecting young women in lives of prostitution; and the improvement of the deplorable conditions that affected literally tens of thousands of women who were detained or incarcerated annually in Chicago's notorious police stations, county jail, and house of correction.

Although newspaper accounts regularly trumpeted stories of fallen and falling women, convicted women were forgotten as soon as they entered the penitentiary. As historian Anne M. Butler observes, upon their conviction women prisoners immediately "disappeared from society's stage." Their value was only as a "cautionary tale": a warning of the dire consequences women faced when they dared to challenge the boundaries of respectable femininity. Once a woman fell, few came forward to advocate on her behalf. Yet despite the odds against them, a handful of female convicts did succeed in their Herculean efforts to make their voices heard, rouse community support, and have their cases reopened. The next chapter examines women's pardon petitions and explores the ambivalence that some judges, prosecutors, and community members expressed after their incarceration.[41]

CHAPTER FOUR

"FOR GOD SAKE YOUR HONOR LET ME OUT OF HERE"

Nineteenth-Century Pardon Petitions

On March 8, 1868, twenty-five-year-old, Irish-born Mary Kelly wrote Governor Oglesby: "You told me when you were here that you would take one year off my crime . . . and that promise has cheered me through the long weary hours that have passed since then." However, that pledge had been made many months before. Convicted of an eighteen-dollar robbery, Kelly had been incarcerated for slightly over two years. She was now anxious to know when the governor planned to fulfill his promise.

Kelly's impassioned letter reveals the significance of pardons in prisoners' lives. Like Mary Brennan four years earlier, Kelly crafted an emotional appeal emphasizing her aloneness ("I have no friends or relatives in this part of the country"), maternal obligations ("My poor little boy is without a parent's care"), and utter despair ("Many a weary night I have spent . . . since I come here") in an attempt to evoke a sympathetic response. Her efforts were to no avail. Three months later Kelly sent a second letter. Penitentiary Commissioner John Reid also wrote on her behalf, requesting that Kelly be pardoned as a "personal favor." He explained that she "was never naturally a bad or mischievous woman" unless, he acknowledged honestly, "under the influence of Whiskey which was all that brought her here." Kelly was that rare "exemplary female convict" whom both Warden McClaughry and the commissioner's wife had offered to employ in their own homes. The governor pardoned Kelly a week later, after she had served three years of her four-year sentence.[1]

Reconstructing the experience of women prisoners in the nineteenth century requires piecing together the fragmentary evidence contained in governors' executive clemency files. Governors and, after 1896, parole boards offered no written explanations for their decisions. Instead, letters were simply stamped "approved" or "denied." Between 1840 and 1860 nearly all pardon requests were authored by the prison warden. Most consisted of a perfunctory letter seeking an early release due to pregnancy, poor health, age, or emotional disturbance. However, between 1860 and 1900 roughly one-third of the files included a letter from the woman herself.

This chapter begins with an analysis of how women represented themselves, their crimes, and their experiences of incarceration, then examines official and community responses to their pardon petitions. The more complete clemency files also included letters from prison wardens, matrons, and commissioners; statements from the local judge, state's attorney, and jurors who had originally convicted the women; and letters and petitions from defense attorneys, family, and neighbors. These sources disclose the contested nature of women's crimes, as well as the ambivalent responses of prison staff, local officials, and townspeople to women's incarceration. Official and community reactions could be volatile and contradictory. Many times the very officials who had convicted or sentenced a woman later endorsed her efforts to secure a pardon, pointing to "mitigating circumstances," "reasonable grounds for doubt," or the simple fact that her children were "desperately in need of a mother's care." These nineteenth-century pardon petitions further expose the many inequities and popular prejudices that confronted women, particularly poor, working class, minority, and immigrant women, in their encounters with the criminal justice system.

• • •

Nineteenth-century women's pardon letters were neither carefully crafted nor coolly reasoned: most were hastily written and highly emotional, almost hysterical, in tone. Mary Brennan's fervent plea, "For God sake your honor, let me out of here," while more impassioned than most, fully captured this style. Louise McNeil's earnest entreaty to a penitentiary commissioner "to the love of god . . . use your influence for me," suggests an equally desperate plea. Although two-fifths (41%) of women offered claims of "mitigating circumstances" in relation to their offense, rarely did they provide any type of reasoned or systematic legal defense. Other than in cases of murder, most said almost nothing about the details of their crime, trial, or conviction. Only a handful attempted to convince the governor of their actual innocence. Nor did many women profess that prison had reformed them or made them into better people. Fewer still expressed deep remorse. A handful, like Mary Brennan, duly proclaimed that if released they would never err again, but such pronouncements often appear as afterthoughts.[2]

Even though their sentences were short by modern standards, averaging less than two years, most women vehemently asserted that they had already "served far more than sufficient time" and had "suffered enough" for their crimes. Essie Stewart's letter represents one such appeal. Having served what she described as "four years at hard labor, not loosing [sic] a day only when sickness compelled me," Stewart concluded her letter on a note common to many: "The remaining time which I have to serve is almost immaterial to the great state of Illinois, and to you Honorable gentlemen of the State Board of Pardons; but to me it is of great importance and incalculable value."[3]

Wardens' and matrons' affirmations of good conduct were essential to securing a pardon. Indeed, on many pardon letters the governor penciled "wait for warden's certificate" (i.e., recommendation). Not all female convicts received official endorsement. In 1868 one warden declared that Mary Cassidy's conduct "has just been good enough to avoid punishment, but not such as to induce me to recommend her as a better woman than when she came in or as likely to lead a better life when released. In brief," he concluded, "she is not a proper subject for executive clemency." Likewise, when Kitty Brine sought a pardon in 1875, the matron advised against it, claiming that Brine had "not been a good convict" and revealing that she was "an *old offender*" who had served a previous sentence at Sing Sing in New York. Instead, this matron took the liberty of suggesting that the governor pardon three other women, explaining that, "I have three good true *hard working* faithful girls that have served the State for years— *one over seven*—now to pardon one like Kitty and leave them who are more worthy creates a dissatisfaction that is hard to overcome." The governor took the matron's advice and denied Brine's pardon request.[4]

Governors greatly appreciated prison officials' careful weighing of who was truly deserving. In 1888 Governor Oglesby wrote that he had taken the recommendation of the prison matron and pardoned an elderly woman and her middle-aged daughter who had served five years of their fourteen-year sentences for infanticide. He noted that "the Matron of the penitentiary . . . has been exceedingly careful and prudent in making recommendations for pardon" and explained that in this exceptional case the matron had vigorously supported the two inmates' efforts "because she feels that all has been accomplished that can possibly be by any further punishment." Matron Ives, who had urged Rosetta Callahan and Matilda Hitchcock's pardon for several years, testified that they were "both very ignorant" and argued that it was only from their delay in reporting the infant's death "that the supposition grew [among neighbors] that the child was born alive and was immediately destroyed." The neighbors, who had originally initiated prosecution, had themselves recently presented a petition on the women's behalf. Now contending that there was "reasonable and well-grounded doubt as to the guilt of said convicts," they also pointed out that the older woman was in frail health and that her daughter's remaining "half orphan" children were "in a very destitute condition."[5]

Although the trial judge was convinced of Callahan's and Hitchcock's guilt and protested their release, both Matron Ives and Governor Oglesby were willing to overlook or reinterpret evidence that hinted at their culpability. Claiming that the two women would "go out far better women than when they came in," Governor Oglesby simply asserted, "it is likely that the child was not born alive." This case was unusual because both the governor and the prison matron took pains to convince themselves of the women's innocence. Most petitioners said little about a prisoner's guilt or innocence. Instead, they appealed to practical issues as their primary concern.[6]

In a half dozen other cases, matrons took the initiative in securing the release of the few women they categorized as clearly deserving. In 1872 a matron wrote a second letter to Governor John M. Palmer after an earlier pardon petition had failed. Explaining that she would be resigning within a few weeks, Matron Katie Grace begged the governor to reconsider another infanticide case: "Could I before that time place in Mary's hand a *pardon* it would indeed be a *pleasure*. I sincerely desire and earnestly ask your honor to grant—believing that she has suffered so long and repents *so* truly her crime." Governor Palmer acquiesced. Matrons expressed an unusual sympathy for women convicted of infanticide, perhaps because of the severity of the women's sentences (Mary Weber had already served seven years of her twenty-five-year sentence) and the capricious nature of such prosecutions (discussed more fully in chapter 6). Yet glowing endorsements from prison officials were rare. The evidence suggests that nineteenth-century matrons, like most wardens, regarded the majority of the female convicts as morally depraved and beyond redemption.[7]

During the second half of the nineteenth century the percentage of prisoners released early by gubernatorial pardons dropped rapidly, falling from nearly one-half (47%) of all female convicts at Alton in the 1850s to 23 percent at Joliet in the 1860s and 15 percent in the 1870s. After that time women's pardon rates stabilized around a mere 5 percent through the 1930s (see table 1). Similarly, men's pardon rates declined from 24 percent in the 1850s to 6 percent after 1872. Nationally prison reformers were vehemently opposed to the widespread use of pardons, claiming that they were granted in a capricious, arbitrary, and often corrupt manner. In place of pardons, officials such as Warden McClaughry advocated a rationalized and standardized system of "good-time" credits.

The Illinois General Assembly passed the state's first "good-time law" in 1863. It was later revised and expanded several times. During their first year, prisoners could earn one month off their sentence for good behavior. Thereafter, good-time credits increased exponentially: during their second year prisoners could accrue two months off, followed by three months in their third year, up to a maximum of six months off for every year served after six years. Long-term prisoners, who may have otherwise become the most disruptive, now had the most to lose by being openly defiant. Good conduct reduced a twenty-year sentence to twelve years. This new system applied equally to male and female convicts. Still, the dramatic decline in women's pardon rates may have also signified a hardening of attitudes toward female offenders.[8]

• • •

Despite the increasing rarity of pardons, the hope of receiving one continued to shape the dreams and everyday actions of female convicts. Pardon requests were a legitimate means by which women could challenge their incarceration and contest their status as criminalized women. A successful pardon petition necessitated the redefinition of a woman's moral character; such

Table 1

PERCENT PARDONED AND AVERAGE TIME SERVED
BY FEMALE FELONS IN ILLINOIS, 1850–1960

	Percent Pardoned	Average Sentence	Percent serving over		Longest Sentence
			5 yrs.	8 yrs.	
1850s	47	0.9 yrs.	0	0	3 yrs.
1860s	23	1.2	4	0	7
1870s	15	1.6	8	1	16
1880s	5	2.0	11	1	11
1890s	4	2.2	13	4	13
1900s	5	2.3	18	7	11
1910s[a]	17	1.8	8	3	11
1920s[b]	4	3.8	35	16	24
1930s	2	4.4	33	20	27
1940s[c]	2	3.4	20	12	n.a.
1950s[d]	1	3.2	23	15	n.a.

Source: Alton, Chester, and Joliet Convict Registers and Dwight inmate jackets, Illinois State Archives. Felonies only.

[a] During World War I many prisoners were granted an unspecified "special discharge."

[b] After 1920 the Illinois parole board became one of the most restrictive in the country. From 1930 to 1970 prisoners in Illinois served among the longest sentences in the nation.

[c] Illinois's sentencing laws were radically revised in 1944. Judges, rather than parole board members, gained control over setting sentence lengths. Average sentences for nearly all offenses (but not murder) declined. See chapter 11.

[d] Due to the large percentage of cases missing in the late 1950s, includes 1950–55 only.

petitions indicated that women were well aware of the power of gender stereotypes and sought to turn them to their advantage. In one exemplary case, a Chicago judge wrote the governor that he had misjudged a woman's character. Originally he had been convinced that she was a "professional thief," and he had given her the maximum six-year sentence for larceny. However, her petition persuaded him that she was a woman of virtuous character who had stolen only out of desperation and the need to support her young children. Instead of being construed as a "professional thief," she now evoked sympathy as a "desperate" mother. The governor granted her pardon.[9]

Proof of a woman's upstanding "moral character" was essential for convincing governors and, after 1896, parole board members to grant a pardon. Supporters frequently claimed that an inmate was "a woman who prior to this trouble bore a very good reputation" or was "always known as a virtuous woman before this crime." One representative petition signed by several dozen townspeople maintained that Louise Jackson "was always a poor hard working woman, and had always borne a first class reputation as a good and virtuous wife, and her one ambition was to furnish a good home for herself and her husband." Recasting Jackson as a dutiful wife and homemaker, the petitioners claimed that the husband whom she had confessed to killing had "abused and mistreated her for a long time" and had "flaunt[ed] his immorality before her." In other cases petitioners cited the good character of a woman's family or husband. Prosecuting officials themselves recommended Almira Humphry's release after verifying that "her family connections are highly respectable and she has always born a good character until charged with this offense." Such appeals to "respectable" family connections biased the pardon process in favor of native-born and nonimmigrant women who had well-established connections with influential local citizens.[10]

Jennie Rose's case illustrates how a woman's moral character and community standing could undergo several transformations during the course of her arrest, trial, and incarceration. Rose, a twenty-three-year-old "mulatto" woman accused of killing her husband in 1866, had initially succeeded in rousing sympathy and strong community support. Despite her mixed racial heritage, several of the town's "best citizens" donated money for her bail and later her defense. As Judge Sanders reported, "the populus [sic] was all in her favor." The first time her case went before the judge it ended in a mistrial even though Judge Sanders was himself firmly convinced that she "ought to have been acquitted." Unfortunately, before her second trial began, Rose "became involved in some other little trouble . . . that resulted in giving offense to some influential individuals here who . . . commenced manufacturing public sentiment against her." Their efforts succeeded; Rose was thrown back in jail and her volunteer attorney abandoned her. She began her second trial with a new judge, a court-appointed lawyer who had "no time to prepare for her defense," and "a very strong populus prejudiced against her." Rose was convicted and received a twenty-year sentence. According to Judge Sanders, the second trial judge refused to allow evidence showing that her husband was "cruel and barbarous in the extreme." He was alleged to have "beaten her and knocked her with such violence that it caused her to have an abortion [i.e., miscarriage]" the evening before his death.

Governor Richard J. Oglesby refused to pardon Rose, who had served only a few months in prison. Two years later, however, local passions had cooled and the "populus" was again in her favor. The state's attorney himself now testified that "nearly all of the people of Cairo favor her release." A petition signed by numerous local officials and leading townspeople portrayed Rose as a morally upright young woman and characterized her deceased husband as a "brutal desperado . . . universally regarded as a dangerous man, capable of almost every crime." The petitioners now concluded that "the punishment she has thus far suffered is . . . ample punishment for her crime." Rose was soon pardoned.[11]

As Rose's case reveals, both community and official support could be fickle. Governors usually weighed the opinions and interpretations of local authorities, not local citizens, most heavily in their decision making. After five years the case of Mary McWilliams remained highly contested. In 1892 the twenty-two-year-old McWilliams was sentenced to seven years for "assault to kill" in a failed attempt to poison her husband. Many friends of her prominent family wrote on her behalf, claiming that "at the time of the plea of guilty we understood the sentiment of the people . . . was against her, but since that time the entire community are in sympathy with her, and believe that a gross injustice has been done." However, the state's attorney countered that such assertions, advanced by "a few obscure citizens," were "entirely false." Adamantly convinced that McWilliams had conspired with her lover in a "cold blooded and premeditated attempt" to kill her husband, he concluded that "no good citizen of our country who knows anything of the facts are asking for her release." The state's attorney also pointed out that McWilliams had already received a more lenient sentence than she deserved. Although Judge Mathews had sentenced her male accomplice to fourteen years, "he kindly took into consideration that the petitioner was a female" and gave her half that time. Judge Mathews himself refused to endorse her petition for clemency; in his eyes McWilliams's reputation had been forever tainted by her adulterous relationship. Despite letters from dozens of local citizens favoring her pardon, Governor John P. Altgeld accepted the judge's and state's attorney's hostile verdict and refused to grant an early release.[12]

Despite her family's prominence, Mary McWilliams failed to convince local authorities that she was a wronged woman of previous "chaste repute." In only one case were officials willing to endorse a pardon or commutation (sentence reduction) for a woman of alleged "low moral character." In 1897 Chicago Judge Abner Smith wrote supporting Essie Stewart's petition for a commutation, despite the fact that he had sentenced her to life in prison only the year before. The judge explained: "She was drunk when she shot Lulu Watson and it seemed to be the drunkenness of a reckless woman rather than anything else." At the time, however, her act was construed by the press and court as cold-blooded murder because she had fired five shots at close range. Stewart was convicted of first-degree murder rather than manslaughter. As in Jennie Rose's case, less than a year later officials revised their interpretation: two judges, the state's attorney, and the court clerk all signed a petition averring that the shooting death was entirely accidental and that Stewart had "had no malice in her heart." Judge Smith admitted that her life sentence was "a little too severe" and now supported a commutation to eight or ten years. He concluded with the highly atypical reflection, "She did not appear to be a moral person but perhaps this is in no sense a reason why she should not receive the same treatment so far as her punishment is concerned, as would be imposed upon other persons whose moral character was better." In an equally unusual move, the parole board agreed to commute Stewart's sentence to eight years, rationalizing their decision with the argument that "it appears that the parties involved were both ignorant, dissolute, colored women."[13]

In this rare instance, Stewart benefited from the fact that African American women were held to lower standards of morality. Despite her reputedly amoral character, Stewart was one of only three African American woman convicted of murder who succeeded in winning a pardon or commutation before 1930, in contrast to 10 percent of white women convicted of the same crime. Regardless of the mitigating circumstances of their offenses, African American women uniformly failed in their efforts to refashion their image into that of respectable women. Popularly defined as outside the domain of proper femininity, African American women were denied the benefits of official chivalry.[14]

Some prison officials frankly admitted the role that race played in determining whether a woman received a prison sentence or, after her incarceration, a pardon. In 1869 Commissioner John Reid penned a letter to the governor on behalf of Sally Bentley of Southern Illinois, who had been sentenced for manslaughter. Reid contended that "only for her color she never would have been here." Reid's wife also wrote, offering to employ Bentley in her own home and promising that she could be pardoned "with the fullest confidence that in the future she will live a better life." Even though Bentley's file contained a petition signed by the mayor, sheriff, treasurer, clerk, several aldermen, and other prominent townspeople who claimed that Bentley was not a "malicious woman" but had fired only in a fit of passion, Governor Palmer refused to grant a pardon.[15]

Similarly, Louise McNeil, a twenty-five-year-old "mulatto" woman from Peoria, was denied a pardon despite strong letters of support. Like Bentley, she had served over half of her fourteen-year sentence for murder. In 1875 she wrote to a former warden imploring him to "use your influence on my behalf." Although she had less than two years of her sentence left, she begged, "Please Mr. Edwards, I scarce heed [sic] tell you how much more I could appreciate that time were I at liberty after being so long deprived of that presious [sic] boon." She would not make such an appeal "if did I not feel my constitution breaking up and my health giving way." The former warden obliged, writing the governor that he knew McNeil to be a "first class convict." He added that as warden he had been "fully impressed with the opinion that colored people usually had to contend with the 'presumption of guilt' instead of the contrary—especially was this so from Egypt [southern Illinois]." Convinced that "many colored persons came under long sentences where 'our people' may have been 'let off,'" Edwards also offered to employ McNeil in his own home. Despite this glowing endorsement, McNeil's pardon was denied.[16]

Nineteenth-century pardon petitions reveal judges' and prosecuting attorneys' ambivalence over sentencing women to the penitentiary. After their conviction, some female convicts were able to convince previously unsympathetic officials of either the "mitigating circumstances" of their cases or their worthiness for an early release. Often one wonders why these women were even sentenced to prison in the first place. If local state's attorneys or judges were so easily persuaded to write on the inmates' behalf, why had they prosecuted, convicted, and sentenced them to begin with?

In some cases officials felt legally compelled to convict, despite their personal preferences or their doubts as to a woman's guilt. Several state's attorneys contended that a grand jury had initiated the indictment, which they were then obliged to pursue. In other cases juries convicted a woman because she had clearly committed the offense, but the jurors themselves felt that mitigating circumstances should have spared her a penitentiary sentence. For example, immediately after Mary Cosgriff's 1868 murder trial, the jurors all signed a petition asserting that they had "felt bound to convict" because several witnesses had testified to having seen Cosgriff shoot her lover in the back in public. Nevertheless, the jurors "earnestly recommend[ed] her pardon" in view of the fact that "the person killed had on a previous occasion cruelly beaten her."[17]

Likewise, following Lydia Ann Starks's 1865 larceny trial, local authorities reported that "immediately after the sentence was passed a petition asking for her pardon was circulated" and signed by the "entire bar present at trial"— judge, prosecutor, and "a large number of the grand jurors and a majority of the best and most influential citizens." Petitioners noted that Starks had "been a peaceable and quiet woman" who had "borne a fair name among her neighbors." Even though they had convicted and sentenced her only the day before, they now portrayed her crime as insignificant: "the amount of property proved to have been taken was small—two pairs of shoes of barely sufficient value to make the offense grand larceny." Perhaps officials had only intended to make a temporary example of her. Or, as in several other cases, perhaps the fact that "she has now an infant at the breast of four months of age" persuaded local authorities to minimize the seriousness of her offense. Whatever their reasons, the governor found their petition persuasive. The twenty-three-year-old Starks was pardoned after only three weeks in prison.[18]

In other cases pardons provided a means of rectifying mistakes made through hasty judgments or lack of information. Local prosecutors and judges, faced with predominantly poor, foreign-born, and minority women, most of whom were recent migrants to the state, initially spent little time sorting out the complexities of individual cases. Officials who rushed to convict under the glare of inflamed passions and community pressure, or simply because caseloads were heavy, sometimes later admitted that there were "reasonable grounds for doubt" as to a woman's guilt. In cases where "community sentiment" was originally "excited against a woman," memories often faded, tempers cooled, and doubts increased as the years passed. Sometimes officials later acknowledged that a poor woman had lacked counsel, competent legal representation, or an understanding of the law.

Even when there were no doubts as to a woman's guilt, authorities and community members were occasionally persuaded by a prisoner's appeal that the "time already served" was punishment enough and agreed that the woman had "suffered sufficiently for her crime." In one larceny case petitioners even claimed, "we think the punishment greater than the crime." Another state's attorney, writing that recently revealed "facts" had convinced him that a defendant was "unjustly convicted," admitted that even if she were guilty, he and the trial judge agreed that "the punishment has been quite sufficient for the offense."[19]

In most pardon cases local officials remained convinced of a woman's guilt, but they now downplayed the seriousness of her offense or the value of the goods stolen. Occasionally they even maligned the character of witnesses or victims who had testified against her. Such denigrations provided a convenient rationale to justify a pardon for far more pragmatic reasons. The image of a woman "needed at home" offered the most compelling reason for a pardon. Local authorities, fully cognizant of the costs born by the county when children became wards of the state, were reluctant to sentence women with children to the penitentiary. When they did, they often quickly regretted their decision. Their second thoughts stemmed not from any abstract Victorian belief about the sanctity of motherhood, but from their belated recognition of the utter desperation that prisoners' unattended children often faced.

• • •

In 1896 Illinois established its first Board of Pardons and Paroles, which immediately enacted far more restrictive clemency guidelines. Only in the most serious cases, typically of murder or manslaughter, were prisoners allowed to submit pardon petitions. After 1896, two-thirds of requests included a direct statement from the woman herself. These typed letters lost all traces of desperation, hysterical overtones, and impassioned pleadings for mercy. Instead, female convicts carefully conceived and crafted their letters under the direction of attorneys, resulting in more standardized, formalized, and legalistic appeals. Precisely because most petitioners now had "corpses to explain," female convicts and their lawyers increasingly emphasized legal justifications, mitigating circumstances, and alternative interpretations of the facts.[20]

Women who killed their spouses continued to present themselves as the long-suffering victims of their husbands' abuse, alcoholism, or marital infidelities, thereby reframing their image as victims rather than victimizers. Because many had not murdered in the heat of passion, however, they often found it difficult to justify their seemingly premeditated and cold-blooded acts. Lena Schreiner was one of the lucky few who succeeded. In 1888, after a night of beatings, the nineteen-year-old Schreiner poured a can of kerosene over her husband, whom she had found lying in a drunken stupor in the walkway outside their apartment building. She then lit a match and set fire to him. For a week she denied all knowledge of the event, but she eventually pleaded guilty and was sentenced to ten years for manslaughter. Unable to claim that she had acted in self-defense or immediate fear for her life, Schreiner vowed in her pardon petition that she hadn't "meant to kill him, but to both scare and hurt him so he would be a good man." Emphasizing her own status as victim and long-suffering wife (although she had been married barely a year), she contended that she had "done everything in my power to make a good man of him," all to no avail. Her husband drank away the family's earnings, forced her to "sew for our daily bread," and beat both her and her elderly mother to such an extent that "neighbors frequently had to intervene." Her neighbors testified to the abuse, and the judge himself wrote, "It is certain her husband was a brutal worthless fellow and had acted so infamously towards her, her children and mother, as to justify a *heroic* remedy."[21]

Like many women who killed, Schreiner blamed her act on a momentary lapse of sanity, concluding, "Even now I cannot think but what I was crazy when I committed the deed." The state's attorney and prison matron wrote letters on her behalf, as did many of her neighbors. The governor granted her pardon, conveniently ignoring several inconsistencies in her account. In court Schreiner had freely admitted to drinking "half a dozen pails of beer" that evening, but in her pardon petition she took great pains to establish that she had been a virtuous, obedient, and duly submissive wife. Claiming that she had vehemently protested her husband's drinking, she averred that she had joined him that night only after he repeatedly threatened her with a beating if she refused. Schreiner also did not mention the prosecutor's claim that she had been motivated in part by a thousand-dollar life insurance policy that had recently been transferred into her name. While the true character of Schreiner's act remains unknowable, her appeal exemplifies how successful pardon petitioners sought to recast their seemingly "barbarous" and "terrible" deeds, representing themselves as exemplary wives and mothers in order to win sympathy for their plight.[22]

The crime of poisoning, which necessarily involved premeditation, required the greatest imagination to justify and defend, but even in these cases white women occasionally succeeded in their appeals. In one of the most publicized cases of the 1890s, Mamie Starr, a twenty-year-old servant girl, poisoned an entire family by adding to their dinner Rough on Rat, a substance frequently cited in cases of poisoning. The two children survived, but their parents died. Starr's case astonished the public because she had no relationship to her victims; the poisoning occurred on the day she was hired as a maid. Hence her actions appeared to have no rational motive. Nor could her deed readily be incorporated into any popular narrative, whether that of jealous lover; seduced, abandoned, and betrayed maiden; or abused and long-suffering wife. At her trial Starr never denied her actions. Her only defense was that of temporary insanity. She was convicted of first-degree murder. Still, one juror claimed that rather than reflecting a total lack of sympathy, the divided jury had given Starr a life sentence in order to "better her chances for official clemency" in the future.[23]

After Starr's sentencing a group of prominent women rallied to her defense. Accepting her claims that she had recently run away to Chicago to escape an abusive husband, they championed Starr as the helpless and hapless victim of an "unhappy early life, early marriage, ill usage, continued and repeated cruelties, and neglect." A stranger in distress, she had found herself in Chicago with no friends and with "a child to care for with no means of support." Arguing that such a tragic life history caused her to temporarily become insane, they maintained that she should not be held legally accountable for her actions. Despite the lack of a coherent and convincing narrative, Starr's supporters succeeded in persuading the governor that her conviction was unwarranted and that if she was released she would "not be a menace to the public." Starr was freed after less than a year in prison.[24]

In contrast, Kate Williamson, an African American prisoner who had been similarly convicted of murder by poisoning and also sentenced to life, failed to secure a pardon even after many years in prison. Williamson's remarkable confession letter represents one of the most elaborate efforts by a female prisoner to craft a coherent pardon tale defined by the strictures of Victorian morality. In her letter, which was transcribed by her lawyer and written in the third person, Williamson admitted that she had been "keeping company with one Henry Miller, who made great professions of love, thereby securing her confidence and love in return." Miller had pledged to marry her, and the happy couple had set a wedding date. Casting herself within the confines of respectable womanhood, Williamson explained that only "on the strength of his [marriage] promises" and "in a moment of weakness" she "yielded to him . . . and for sometime afterwards . . . was to said Miller all that the word wife implies." Although Williamson acknowledged her status as a "fallen woman," she professed to have maintained her sense of modesty and virtue. Upon discovering that she was pregnant, she had begged her fiancé "to marry her and in a measure cover up the disgrace he had brought upon her." However, he "kept putting her off" until finally, "without any cause," he had abandoned her entirely.[25]

Using the melodramatic language of Victorian seduction narratives, Williamson presented herself as the aggrieved, dishonored, and injured party. She explained how "deserted in her then [pregnant] condition and burning under her great disappointment produced by his deception, unfaithfulness and treachery," she "conceived the idea of taking Miller's life." Unfortunately, her attempt to poison her lover by mixing Rough on Rat into his coffee failed miserably. "It so happened" that Jerry Thompson, another boarder at her lover's lodging house, "got home sometime before Miller that morning," drank two cups of the poisoned coffee and died that night. Her lover, coming home unexpectedly late, drank only half a cup and survived. The death of an innocent person, her "diabolical" use of poison, and her "color" all inflamed community outrage, and explain, in part, why Williamson received a life sentence. Five years later, however, passions had cooled. Many community members were now willing to forgive Williamson, testifying to her "industry" and upstanding character "till she got into this trouble."

Williamson professed ample remorse for the "unfortunate" turn of events (far more than had the taciturn Mamie Starr) and admitted that she was fully "guilty of criminal negligence in taking the course she did to get rid of Miller." However, her efforts, like those of most African American women prisoners, to present herself as virtuous, deserving, and upstanding proved unsuccessful. Even though both the warden and chief matron verified that despite her "shattered health" she was "the best girl in the prison and a splendid worker where she is able," the governor denied her pardon. Williamson refused to give up. Five years later she wrote a second appeal to a new governor, this time fully supported by a new chief matron, Maria S. Madden. Liberal governor John Altgeld was persuaded by the numerous petitions he received from local townspeople that Williamson's sentence had been unduly harsh. Concluding that "from all that I can learn had she been a white woman, she would have been given hardly ten or fifteen years," Altgeld commuted her life sentence to twenty years. A model prisoner, Williamson was eventually released after twelve, the longest sentence of any woman committed during the 1880s.[26]

• • •

Kate Williamson's melodramatic confession, carefully crafted to appeal to Victorian-era conventions of proper womanhood, is illuminating in its exceptionality. Most nineteenth-century female convicts submitted far briefer appeals and offered few moral or legal defenses. Instead, they justified their requests in pragmatic terms, describing their motherless children, wifeless husbands, advanced age, failing health, and good conduct in prison, and portraying the virtuous lives they previously had led. Most women begged for pardons as an act of mercy. Women's supporters endorsed their pardons for equally pragmatic reasons. Questions of guilt bore little weight. For some supporters a woman's youth or the fact that she had "hitherto" exhibited "good character" or was now portrayed as a "poor ignorant country girl" aroused sympathies that they had not previously harbored. For others, the needs of unattended children spoke most persuasively. In some cases evidence that had previously convinced a judge or twelve-man jury, and often a defendant's community as well, that the woman was guilty "beyond a reasonable doubt" was reinterpreted over time. Mitigating circumstances, previously ignored, were raised and reconsidered. For a successful outcome, the endorsement of local judges, state's attorneys, prison wardens, and matrons was critical.

At the time of their arrest, many women failed to realize that they faced a possible prison sentence, and with good reason: of the estimated four to five hundred women convicted annually of felonies in late-nineteenth-century Illinois, barely twenty were sentenced to the penitentiary each year. Nor were the crimes of these imprisoned women necessarily the most heinous or infamous: in the nineteenth century three-quarters were convicted of larceny. As some women's supporters explained: "the finding of the jury was a matter of surprise to many," or "everyone thought the prisoner would be acquitted, or, if convicted, would not see the inside of the Penitentiary." Only after their incarceration did these women succeed in mobilizing their supporters. Yet such favorable shifts in community sentiment were not automatically forthcoming. Female prisoners, who had failed to elicit judicial sympathy during their initial arrest, trial, and sentencing stages, engaged in concerted campaigns to win community and official support for their pardon petitions. Other than in cases of pregnancy or infirmity, those most likely to succeed were native-born and literate white women. These were the favored few who could author their own letters and marshal the resources of "respectable" family, friends, and neighbors to lobby local and state officials.[27]

Through the pardon process a small minority of female convicts succeeded in forcing a redefinition of their crimes and generating a more positive appraisal of their character. Their petitions further expose the many extrajudicial and extralegal factors that influenced arrest, prosecution, conviction, and sentencing. The next three chapters explore the highly selective and discriminatory process by which cases were (and are) filtered through the criminal justice system. Only the most marginalized, disadvantaged, and allegedly disreputable women failed to escape its net.

PART II

THE SOCIAL CONSTRUCTION
OF CRIME AND CRIMINALITY

CHAPTER FIVE

"AN ACT BECOMES A CRIME ACCORDING TO THE COMMUNITY IN WHICH IT IS COMMITTED"

The Social Construction of a Criminal Act

On November 25, 1896, sixty-six heavily guarded female convicts were escorted across the street to the new Joliet Women's Prison. Three years later prisoner Maggie Tiller voiced mixed emotions over their new home. She began a letter to Mrs. Wiens, her benefactress, on a cheerful note, reporting, "We are having such lovely weather for the last three days. I can look out of my window and see the beautiful trees and bright green grass, and the odor is something grand from the grass." Yet even though she expressed genuine appreciation for the women's new yard space and their daily outdoor recreation periods, Tiller concluded in a plaintive tone: "I don't know of anything more to write, only lots of work and plenty of sickness here now. The girls all seem to be out of order in some way or nother [sic]. I guess they all want liberty more than any thing else."[1]

Maggie Tiller had already endured nearly five years in prison. By the end of the century a growing population of "long-term" women transformed the prison world. Due to their longer sentences, women convicted of serious crimes tended to pile up in the daily prison population. Thus, even though only 15 percent of women admitted during the 1890s had been convicted of murder or manslaughter, women imprisoned for those crimes constituted one-third (35%) of the daily prison population. Most faced many years behind bars, averaging 4.9 years for white women and 7.7 for African American. This was the inmate world Tiller confronted on her arrival in 1895. Described in the press as a charming, young, articulate, and educated "mulatto actress" with many admirers, Tiller's case attracted unusual media coverage. Indeed, it became a lightning rod for concerns about the many injustices that confronted African American women within Chicago's turn-of-the-century criminal justice system.

Before continuing our examination of the place of female convicts within the penitentiary, it is necessary to explore the complex legal and judicial processes by which an event is constructed as a criminal act and an individual becomes defined and prosecuted as a "criminal." Every potential offense can result in a multiplicity of outcomes other than state prosecution or a penitentiary sentence. Analysis of the events that took place long before a woman ever arrived at the gates of the penitentiary reveals the essential roles that discretion, discrimination, and selective prosecution play in the legal system.

Criminal cases are filtered through a lengthy judicial process in which large numbers of cases are eliminated at each stage. At the first stage, police can fail to make an arrest or can choose to file misdemeanor rather than felony charges. Even after a formal arrest occurs, state's attorneys can decide not to prosecute, grand juries can fail to indict, witnesses can refuse to testify, and jurors can acquit. Judges can dismiss a case at any stage from the preliminary hearing to trial. Consistent with national patterns, in the 1920s (the first decade for which there exist statewide statistical data) Illinois's justice officials decided not to pursue prosecution in approximately two-thirds of felony arrests. Of the one-third of cases that they chose to prosecute, only one-quarter (24%) reached a verdict in trial court. Nearly three-quarters of prosecutions (71%) were eliminated at earlier points in what criminologists label the "criminal justice funnel."[2]

Minor cases were not the only ones to be dropped. In Cook County, where Chicago is located, 83 percent of prosecutions for serious assault, 80 percent for homicide and rape, 77 percent for larceny, 66 percent for forgery, and 63 percent of prosecutions for robbery were dismissed and the suspects freed. Of course, not all arrests were valid; nor were all those initially prosecuted guilty. However, given that state's attorneys only initiated formal prosecution when the evidence was fairly strong to begin with, the large proportion of cases that were dismissed exposes the enormous discretion legal authorities wielded in selecting which cases and which defendants they were most committed to pursuing.[3]

This chapter examines the many legal and extralegal variables that influenced, and continue to influence, decisions made by police, prosecutors, judges, juries, and coroners. Each stage in the legal process—from arrest, bail hearing, and preliminary hearing to grand jury indictment, trial, and sentencing—is closely analyzed. The goal is to uncover the many points at which discretion, discrimination, and bias entered the system. Attrition through the criminal justice funnel was neither a passive nor a proportionate process. Legal authorities actively chose to prosecute certain crimes and certain "criminals," while dismissing similar charges against many other defendants. The profile of cases that ended in conviction does not simply constitute a representative sample of the original pool of arrestees. Especially when we expand the starting point of our analysis to police decision making that takes place long before a case reaches the courthouse door, it becomes clear that discrimination was and is inherent in the system.

• • •

Any discussion of women's criminality must include an analysis of how variables such as race, ethnicity, class, age, marital status, and nativity interacted to construct differences in reporting, arrest, prosecution, conviction, and sentencing rates for different groups of women. Victims, neighbors, police, prosecutors, judges, and juries were motivated by many factors, legal and extralegal, in their decisions to press charges and to arrest, prosecute, and convict. The system seemed capricious and arbitrary to those caught in its jaws. In many cases, neither the seriousness of the offense nor the degree of social harm bore any direct relationship to whether an arrest was made, charges filed, an individual prosecuted, or a prison sentence handed down. Community sentiment often played a critical role in determining whether an event was construed as a crime that warranted prosecution and official state sanction.

Maggie Tiller's case clearly illustrates Danielle Laberge's contention that "the combination of sex, race, and social class create specific groups who vary in their capacity to elude penal treatment . . . or neutralize its negative effects." Tiller maintained throughout her trial and twelve years of imprisonment that the victim, Charles Miller, had attacked her first and that his shooting was entirely accidental. She had gone to his apartment to retrieve a trunk containing all of her belongings, which another woman had taken from her. During a heated argument Miller purportedly pulled out his pistol and fired twice. Tiller attempted to wrestle the gun away from him, and in the ensuing scuffle it discharged, inflicting a fatal wound. No one denied that Tiller immediately went to the police and voluntarily led them back to the scene. Miller died shortly afterward, and even though on his deathbed he refused to name her as his killer, Tiller was arrested.[4]

The coroner's jury could have easily exonerated Tiller, accepting her claim of self defense and classifying the death as justifiable homicide. There were no eye witnesses to testify against her, and Tiller had voluntarily turned herself in. Legally, the Cook County coroner's office was empowered to evaluate only the specific cause of death. In reality, it also decided whether suspicious deaths should be attributed to natural causes, accident, self defense, or homicide. Coroner's juries were composed of ordinary citizens trained in neither medicine nor the law. Their views fully reflected community norms, sensibilities, and racial and gender biases. Between 1900 and 1930 Cook County coroner's juries exonerated between thirty and seventy citizens a year in shooting-, stabbing-, and assault-related deaths. Many of these deaths were far more suspicious than Miller's.

Newspaper headlines regularly trumpeted the exoneration of white women, even under the most dubious or questionable of circumstances. For example, under the headline "Mother of Six Exonerated in Mate's Slaying," the *Chicago Tribune* reported that Pauline Drummond had admitted to shooting and killing her husband while he was sleeping. The coroner's jury accepted her improbable story that she "grabbed the shotgun on impulse and it went off accidentally," and the case was dismissed. A "score of women neighbors" applauded when the verdict was read. Drummond enjoyed a sterling reputation and her long history of domestic abuse was well-known. In contrast, newspapers rarely heralded the exoneration or acquittal of African American women in similar circumstances.[5]

If a woman was not cleared by the coroner's office, the state's attorney could choose not to prosecute, the grand jury could fail to indict, or the trial jury could acquit. Yet none of these actors were willing to offer the same degree of leniency or judicial chivalry to Tiller that they routinely extended to more privileged women. Like the majority of imprisoned African American women, Tiller was disadvantaged in many ways. An orphan and recent migrant to the state, she was unmarried and childless. Her self-proclaimed occupation as an actress threw her moral character into question. Despite these liabilities, the African American community rallied to her support. Clergy collected money for her defense, maintaining that a white woman who fired and killed a male attacker under similar circumstances would never have been arrested, much less convicted of first-degree murder. Two lawyers, one white and one black, volunteered for her legal defense.[6]

Meanwhile, Tiller's case aroused controversy among Chicago's established African American citizens. This small group had achieved a precarious social acceptance that was threatened by the large-scale migration of African Americans from the South in the 1890s. Chicago's white citizens responded to the new migrants by hardening racial lines. The city witnessed ever-increasing segregation in housing, employment, and public space. County Commissioner Theodore W. Jones, a leading African American politician, publicly opposed Reverend J. M. Townsend's efforts to raise money for Tiller's defense. Characterizing Tiller as a "depraved woman" and "disreputable creature," Jones claimed that "colored people who are charged with crime in Chicago can always receive a fair trial." Although his words were widely reported in the white press, his was a minority view within the African American community. Discrimination and segregation intensified within the legal system in the 1890s. Chicago judges sentenced three times as many African American women to the penitentiary as during the previous thirty years, while sentencing three times fewer white women.[7]

At Tiller's preliminary hearing Judge R. W. Clifford promised that he would not hand down a life sentence if she pleaded guilty. When a lawyer informed her that the sentence might still be fifteen years or more, Tiller reportedly replied, "Why that is worse than death." Boldly rejecting the judge's offer, Tiller demanded a jury trial, gambling that her youth, acknowledged beauty, lack of culpability, and perhaps her theatrical skills as well, would enable her to convince the all-white, all-male jury to acquit. In the end the jury rejected her claims of self-defense. Tiller was convicted of first-degree murder, achieving the dubious distinction of being the first woman ever sentenced to death in Cook County. The African American press responded with outrage. Judge Clifford eventually agreed to commute Tiller's death sentence to a still-weighty twenty years imprisonment in exchange for a guilty plea. He averred disingenuously that "the defendant appeals to me more strongly than if she were a white woman; more strongly than if she were a rich woman; her poverty, her dependence, her color, all appeal to this court."[8]

The judge's words offered little lasting consolation. Tiller watched nearly two hundred women come and go before her release. Like many long-term inmates, she was reluctant to form close relationships with these "short-term" women, whose constant arrivals and departures disrupted both prison routines and the inmates' social world. Alluding to her sense of separation, Tiller wrote after four years in prison, "I say to some of the girls that are here, when they get to warring and crying about their time, I say oh you simple woman. To make yourself so unhappy when you can go out in one year's time. Just look at me, I have 20 years and have not but *one* friend in the world."[9]

• • •

Maggie Tiller's case, which could easily have been dismissed long before it ever entered the courtroom, illustrates the tremendous discretion that is exercised at each step in the legal process. From 1890 to 1930 the number of women found guilty of felonies in Illinois increased from approximately 330 to 1,200 annually. However, from 1880 to 1925 the number of women sentenced to prison remained remarkably steady at approximately one hundred per five-year period (or twenty annually). The only exception occurred during the unprecedented 1895–1899 peak in commitments that immediately followed the opening of Joliet Women's Prison (see graph 1). This miniscule number—twenty female prison commitments annually from the entire state—raises complex questions about the relationship, or lack of relationship, between rates of imprisonment and rates of real criminality. Throughout this study I argue that the number of women sentenced to prison bore no direct relationship to the absolute number of crimes women committed.[10]

The degree of police and other state surveillance in a community has a significant impact on the number of arrests and thus on officially constructed crime rates. Garry L. Rolison argues that patriarchy "predisposes certain women to become objects of discipline." These "certain women" are much more likely to be lower class, poor, minority women living in high-density urban communities already perceived as "bad places" and already under the extensive surveillance of police, criminal justice, and other public agencies such as those devoted to welfare, housing, or child protection. Following Foucault, Rolison contends that "surveillance is the cornerstone of disciplinary power. Surveillance gives to agents of social control the ability to develop a file on individuals and later punish those individuals for specific transgressions." Accepting the claims of critical criminologists that the commission of crime is dispersed throughout all classes and social groups, Rolison concludes that "the intense surveillance of some groups allows agents of social control the capability of exercising discipline over these individuals."[11]

Police decision making, one of the most hotly debated topics in criminology, is often the most significant, yet least visible, point at which discretion enters into the criminal justice process. When approaching the scene of an alleged crime, police must agree that a crime has occurred, and they must find it worthwhile enough to initiate an investigation and seek an arrest. This critical decision-making process remains completely hidden: no record is made of potential arrests. Several factors influence how police respond to a possible crime. The first involves the legal seriousness of the event. Even here, however, great discretion exists. Donald Black's classic study found that police routinely dismissed between 26 and 42 percent of "potential" felonies reported to them, a process officially referred to as "unfounding." Second, police decision making is significantly affected by the class, race, and gender of both the complainant and the alleged offender. Police are more likely to arrest in situations where the complainants are white and middle-class, especially if the suspects are poor or of a minority group.[12]

The massive 1922 report by the Chicago Commission on Race Relations, *The Negro in Chicago: A Study of Race Relations and a Race Riot,* graphically details the discrimination African Americans faced throughout the criminal justice system. The authors begin by noting that "testimony is practically unanimous that Negroes are much more liable to arrest than whites, since police officers share in the general public opinion that Negroes 'are more criminal than whites.'" Police arrested African Americans more frequently and with weaker evidence, believing that "there is little risk of trouble in arresting Negroes, while greater care must be exercised in arresting whites." African Americans, less than 4 percent of the city's population, made up 21 percent of all male and female felony arrestees in 1920 and 30 percent of all women arrestees in 1930.[13]

Unlike white suspects, African Americans were automatically brought to the city's central bureau of investigation upon their arrest. There they were photographed and fingerprinted on the racist pretext that it was "harder to identify them." Yet in the end African Americans were only 11.5 percent of suspects officially charged, testimony to the fact that they were frequently arrested on much weaker evidence than were whites. As one informant explained, it was safer for a policeman to "pick up and mug" (i.e., photograph) a black than a white person as there was "less fear of an unpleasant 'comeback.'" Thus, African Americans were routinely arrested and detained on the least suspicion, and this brief detention automatically led to the creation of an official police dossier. Once arrested, they were booked on more serious charges than their white counterparts. They also were more likely to be convicted, more likely to receive a penitentiary sentence rather than jail or probation, and less likely to receive early parole. Upon their release from prison, African Americans came under increased police surveillance and harassment and thus found it harder to "make good."[14]

Chicago police statistics, which were reported by both gender and race/ethnicity for the years 1913 to 1930, reflect these contradictory forces. Although African American women were arrested in vastly disproportionate numbers, for nonviolent property crimes they were slightly *less* likely to be found guilty than native-born white women (29% versus 34% in the 1910s and 39% versus 44% in the 1920s). These ratios suggest that African American women were often arrested on weaker evidence that could not hold up in court. However, for violent crimes African American women were two to four times *more* likely than white women to be convicted. African American women, 4.1 percent of the city's population in 1920, represented 36 percent of robbery arrestees and 48 percent of women found guilty; 31 percent of assault arrestees and 65 percent of those convicted; 31 percent of murder arrestees and 78 percent of those found guilty; and 27 percent of manslaughter arrestees and 100 percent of those convicted. These numbers are so astonishing that they challenge any presumed relationship between conviction rates and rates of real criminality.[15]

Similarly, European-born, immigrant women were also somewhat *more* likely to be convicted in Chicago courts than were native-born white women: 42 percent versus 34 percent in the 1910s, a gap that narrowed to a three-point difference in the 1920s. However, despite their higher conviction rates, after 1890 immigrant women were *not* overrepresented in the state's female prison population. Thus, even though immigrant women were more likely to be found guilty than native-born white women (a result of discrimination and their greater poverty, lack of English-language skills, and unfamiliarity with the American legal system), judges did not disproportionately sentence them to the penitentiary. The only exceptions involved immigrant women convicted of murder or manslaughter by abortion (which will be discussed in chapter 6). Meanwhile, African American women, averaging barely 2.5 percent of the state's population, represented 42 percent of females sentenced to prison between 1890 and 1930.[16]

Although present-day police wield enormous discretionary power, they must operate within a "legal culture" that stresses procedural rights and provides some constraints over their individual decision making. Yet this has only become true fairly recently. Well into the twentieth century police were free to detain suspects indefinitely, prevent arrestees from contacting a lawyer, and find evidence and extract confessions using whatever means they saw necessary. They were "the law." Police violence was routine and unexceptional.

A brief overview of the history of policing in Chicago, the state's largest metropolis, offers a revealing illustration of this unfettered police power. The police force was organized in 1855, but new police recruits received no formal training. Instead, a new officer simply became apprenticed to a veteran officer and learned on the job. It was not until the 1920s that a regularized one-month training school was instituted, and half of its curriculum consisted of military drills and weapons practice. Historian Mark H. Haller argues, "not only were policemen untrained in law, but they operated within a criminal justice system that generally placed little emphasis upon legal procedure."[17]

Until 1906 most arrestees were tried before local justices of the peace, who themselves rarely possessed any legal education. Law enforcement was an integral part of Chicago's machine politics. Most police officers, judges, and justices of the peace acquired their jobs through patronage appointments that were rewards for party loyalty. In 1906 reformers succeeded in dismantling the justice-of-the-peace system and replacing it with a centralized municipal court. Yet even under the new system judgeships were handed out according to party affiliation. Mass processing of suspects continued, and most defendants lacked defense lawyers. In 1929 the authors of the *Illinois Crime Survey* offered a scathing critique of Chicago's entire municipal-court system.[18]

The issues of selective policing and selective prosecution are central to understanding how the criminal justice system responded historically to the legal transgressions of different classes of women. In 1915 Anne Hinrichsen, who would play an important role at Joliet Women's Prison in the 1920s, conducted the first statewide study of police and criminal justice procedures using data from thirteen of Illinois's largest cities. In her one-hundred-page report, Hinrichsen railed against the arbitrary and discretionary nature of local law enforcement. She argued that identical actions might constitute "a recognized custom in one community and a felony in another." Her conclusions were supported by both exhaustive statistical summaries and colorful anecdotes. In one rural community, "A man may commit half a dozen robberies . . . and find himself enriched and . . . [granted] immunity from prosecution." In a neighboring county a man "impelled by hunger" might "help himself to a chicken from a farmer's hen roost and a few weeks later find himself in the state prison."[19]

Likewise, Hinrichsen maintained that "In one city a woman may commit murder without serious consequences. . . . In another she may receive the jewelry or money which her husband or sweetheart has stolen and she will be sent to the state prison." The view that in many counties women could literally get away with murder, as well as with many other crimes, was well-supported by the evidence. Between 1890 and 1930, one-quarter (25%) of Illinois counties failed to sentence a single woman to the penitentiary, while another quarter (24%) sentenced only one woman. Hinrichsen reported this with little exaggeration:

> No two counties have the same standards of crime or of law enforcement. An act becomes a crime according to the community in which it is committed. . . . In one county a violation of the law will be ignored . . . while in an adjoining county a violation of the same law under identical circumstances will result in a penitentiary sentence.[20]

Rural and southern Illinois counties sent a disproportionate number of their convicted felons, including many first-time and minor offenders, to the state penitentiary, whereas the more urban northern counties relied on fines, probation, and sentences to local jails. Although community sentiment played an important role, structural and economic factors were equally significant. When southern Illinois judges sentenced minor felony offenders to the state penitentiary, the expense of imprisonment was borne by the state, rather than the county. Although all counties had their own jails, most were small and terribly maintained. Almost none provided separate accommodations for female prisoners. Rural probation services were also inadequate. In contrast, Chicago's House of Correction included a spacious, well-equipped three-story women's building designed to house 198 female prisoners, and the Cook County jail had a thirty-bed women's wing. In 1915, when the daily population of Joliet Women's Prison was less than fifty, the Chicago House of Correction housed two hundred women; 1,300 passed through the institution every year, representing 11 percent of total commitments. As a result, judges in southern Illinois sentenced women to the state prison for minor offenses that in Chicago would have incurred only probation or, at most, a brief sentence to the House of Correction. Chicago's court system accounted for roughly 90 percent of women's felony convictions in Illinois but only 45 percent of women's commitments to Joliet Women's Prison.[21]

• • •

Hinrichsen's 1915 study was one of the first of its kind both locally and nationally. Beginning in the 1920s legal reformers undertook comprehensive surveys of local criminal justice agencies. Conducted in over forty cities and states, these crime surveys yielded results that shocked both scholars and the public by revealing the large-scale attrition of cases throughout the system. In all states and localities most of those arrested were released or never charged. Most prosecutions were dropped or resulted in a plea bargain and conviction on a lesser charge. Only a tiny fraction of the guilty were ever sentenced to prison, and many of those were subsequently released early on parole. The massive eleven-hundred-page *Illinois Crime Survey,* published in 1929, falls completely within this Progressive Era paradigm. Investigators used official court records to determine what happened to each of 16,812 felony cases that entered the courts in twenty of Illinois's 101 counties over a two-year period. Of these original cases, only one-quarter (24%) ever came to a verdict; three-quarters (71%) were completely dismissed at earlier points.[22]

Yet even these high dismissal rates disguise the fact that the number of eliminated cases was at least two to three times greater. Chicago police reports from 1926 and 1927 listed 33,335 felony arrests. However, only 12,500 prosecutions were initiated in all of Cook County during those two years. Because nearly two-thirds of cases never made it into the court docket, their disappearance escaped official scrutiny. Some arrestees spent a few days in jail before police released them without pressing charges. Others were innocent bystanders rounded up in police dragnets or were victims of false accusation. Some were guilty but were released because officials lacked sufficient evidence or interest in pressing charges. These unprosecuted arrests and the many complaints police received but never pursued represent the unknown figure in crime statistics.[23]

Once a state's attorney initiated prosecution, the preliminary hearing was the next stage at which cases were eliminated. At this hearing the judge decides whether there is sufficient evidence to warrant prosecution. In Illinois nearly two-thirds (62%) of cases that made it into the courts were dismissed at this critical yet often overlooked step. Two-fifths of cases were dismissed for "want of prosecution": the original complainants—alleged victims—did not show up in court, or if they did, it was difficult to get them to "stick to their stories." Victims were more likely to exhibit reservations about testifying if they perceived the suspect as an otherwise respectable or deserving woman, the hapless victim of poverty or of circumstances beyond her control. The second most frequently cited reason for dismissal, "lack of evidence," seems to be based on objective legal factors, but it could equally result from the police officers' or prosecutor's lack of commitment to pursuing a particular case. Nor were only minor felonies dismissed at the preliminary hearing. Statewide two-fifths (41%) of all homicide, rape, and assault charges, along with half (53%) of all larceny cases were terminated at this point.[24]

Another one-sixth (17%) of terminated cases were dismissed by the grand jury. Grand juries are composed of ordinary citizens who, like the judge in a preliminary hearing, are empowered to decide whether an indictment should be filed and prosecution continued. Grand juries provided no written explanation of their decisions; dismissed cases were simply listed as "not billed." Like those of coroner's juries, their decisions fully reflect popular prejudices and community standards. For example, the *Illinois Crime Survey* reported that in Cook County grand juries exonerated 45 percent of white women charged with murder but only 9 percent of African American women.[25]

The remaining 21 percent of all dismissals occurred after formal court proceedings had begun. Of these one-third (34%) were "stricken with leave to reinstate" by the state's attorney. This resulted in an unofficial form of probation over which the state's attorney exercised total discretion. As long as the defendant maintained good behavior, charges remained suspended. Such a decision strongly favored middle-class defendants and those with otherwise favorable reputations.

In the end, nearly three-quarters (71%) of felony cases were dismissed as they wound their way through the legal system. It is highly significant that of the remaining defendants, nearly all (84%) were found guilty. Theirs were the cases in which officials were determined to prosecute. Not only was the evidence strong, but the defendants garnered no official sympathy.

The authors of the *Illinois Crime Survey* did not analyze the extent to which defendants' gender, race, ethnicity, or social class correlated with the likelihood that their cases would be dropped. Defining the problem as one of "inefficiency," progressive reformers remained blind to the influence of prejudice and discrimination. Instead, the survey's authors identified only purely legal factors that correlated with a favorable verdict: competence of legal representation, release on bail, and whether the defendant pleaded guilty.

Most Illinois counties (although not Cook County), provided court-appointed attorneys for indigent defendants. However, most were overburdened, underpaid, and inexperienced. Defendants with assigned counsel were one-third more likely to be found guilty than those with private attorneys in urban areas (64% versus 47%), and three-quarters more likely to be found guilty in rural counties (79% versus 45%). Female convicts frequently complained that they lacked competent legal representation. In a representative pardon petition, Louise Jackson's attorney explained that at her trial in 1912 "she was without means to pay for a defense or any investigation, that a young lawyer, admitted to the Bar less than one year, volunteered to defend her, and that owing to his inexperience he probably did not furnish her the best advice."[26]

Indigent defendants with assigned counsel were enormously disadvantaged. A competent and committed lawyer is often able to have a case dismissed either at the preliminary hearing or by the grand jury. Because court-appointed attorneys were provided only at the trial stage, uncounseled defendants were forced to represent themselves during the early stages of processing. Unaware of their legal rights and equally ignorant of the law, they often provided testimony or evidence that was later used against them. During the pretrial stage, attorneys were also instrumental in convincing judges to grant bail, which only one-third of defendants received. Defendants released on bail were significantly more likely to have their cases eliminated before trial (71% of defendants granted bail versus 53% denied). Of defendants going to trial, only 29 percent of those granted bail were found guilty versus 46 percent of those denied.

Of course, judges were more likely to offer bail when the evidence against a defendant was weak to begin with. However, release on bail significantly increased defendants' ability to prepare their defense, uncover evidence, locate friendly witnesses, and hence be found not guilty. By its very nature, the bail system favored middle-class defendants. When deciding whether to grant bail, judges took into account an individual's economic and social status, steadiness of employment, length of residence within the state, family and marital relationships, and community and religious ties. Bail was rarely offered African American defendants. When it was, only those who could afford to pay (or who could find a bail bondsman who would underwrite their release) could take advantage of it.[27]

Finally, the *Illinois Crime Survey* revealed that when it came to sentencing, defendants who pleaded guilty were treated far more leniently: 42 percent received probation compared to 14 percent of those who pleaded not guilty to comparable offenses but were later convicted. Such leniency was even extended to defendants who initially proclaimed their innocence but later changed their plea. Judges perceived defendants who admitted their guilt or quickly agreed to plea-bargain as more contrite, cooperative, and deserving of a lesser punishment. Because a guilty plea saved the state the time and expense of a trial or other lengthy legal process, strong pressure was placed on defendants to plead guilty, and those who did not "cooperate" were far more likely to receive a prison sentence. Hence, it is not surprising that between 1890 and 1930 two-thirds (66%) of women committed to the penitentiary in Illinois maintained their innocence, like Maggie Tiller, and refused to cooperate by agreeing to a plea bargain.[28]

Not surprisingly, even though imprisoned African American women were more likely to plead guilty than white female convicts (averaging 40% versus 28%), their cooperation was rarely rewarded. Indeed, their pleas were often coerced. In 1929 parole board members questioned Loretta Perkins, a young African American woman, as to why she had "voluntarily" pleaded guilty to manslaughter, "when she now claimed that her husband's killing was entirely accidental." Perkins explained that she had been represented by an inexperienced attorney and had faced a particularly hostile judge who issued the following threat: "You want a jury trial and get the electric chair, or plead guilty and get no less than one nor more than fourteen." Perkins dared not resist. Once she was incarcerated, the parole board rejected her claim of self-defense and required her to serve the maximum 8.3 years. As this example intimates, by pleading guilty women sacrificed their future ability to convince parole board members of their innocence. They also forfeited the right to legally appeal their cases.[29]

In cases of murder and manslaughter, African American women were doubly disadvantaged. They were nearly three times as likely as white defendants to plead guilty (50% versus 18%). Some reported that they feared being tried before an all-white jury. One judge admitted that "a jury will convict a colored man with less hesitation than a white man on the same kind of evidence." Evelyn Forester's attorney was convinced that she had killed her drunken husband in self-defense. However, despite her "good reputation" and lack of prior criminal record, he advised her to plead guilty to murder rather than risk a death sentence in a jury trial. He explained that as "there had recently been four convictions for murder in [the] county . . . all defendants being colored people, there was a strong feeling for sentence to death." The state's attorney, fueling community anger, characterized the killing as "deliberate and vicious." Forester served nine years.[30]

Thus, instead of being rewarded with a more lenient punishment for their cooperation, African American women were summarily sentenced to the penitentiary. Poverty, prejudice, and coercion all contributed to this outcome. African American women were less able to afford private attorneys, who rarely advised their clients to plead guilty. Maggie Tiller was defended by two volunteer lawyers who disagreed publicly over legal strategy. Fearing the death penalty, her white lawyer beseeched her to plead guilty, whereas her African American lawyer (whom the press described as "young and inexperienced") gathered evidence and affidavits in an unsuccessful effort to present a strong legal defense. Tiller rejected her white lawyer's advice and demanded a jury trial; she was initially sentenced to death, although this extreme sentence was later commuted to twenty years.

In other instances, poor women—both black and white—contended that they had not understood their legal rights or the court proceedings. When asked why she had pleaded guilty to manslaughter in a woman's death that resulted from an abortion (which she later denied having performed), midwife Olivia Jones responded, "Because I didn't know the law; I was so green it wasn't even funny." Some women protested that they had been advised by prosecutors that they could avoid a prison sentence by admitting their guilt, a pledge that was not always honored by the judge. In 1937 one state's attorney explained that his predecessor had promised Paula Putnam probation if she pleaded guilty to chicken stealing, then had rescinded the offer. Characterizing such conduct as "unfair treatment," the new state's attorney strongly recommended Putnam's parole, although he was "still against parole of any kind for [her husband], as he is the one who led her into this trouble." More often women were misled by both judges and prosecutors. Some were promised that if they pleaded guilty they would only have to serve the one-year minimum sentence rather than the maximum. However, parole board members rarely honored such promises, viewing them as illegal challenges to their decision-making authority.[31]

• • •

Critical, nonpositivist criminologists view both crime and criminality as socially constructed categories and are deeply skeptical of the extent to which officially recorded measures of crime reflect objective "real rates" of offending. Contending that it is far more accurate to speak of "criminalized" rather than "criminal" women, Danielle Laberge argues that "there are many official criminalities: the suspected, the prosecuted and the sentenced criminalities." Critical criminologists focus their analysis on the process by which some acts are construed as crimes and some individuals defined as criminal while others escape arrest, prosecution, and punishment.[32]

In contrast, liberal or positivist criminologists treat crime as an objective social fact and assume that a direct relationship exists between reported rates of crime, such as the number arrested or imprisoned, and "real crime" or "real criminality." As Piers Beirne and James Messerschmidt explain, "In the early nineteenth century, when official crime data were first systematically recorded, 'positivist' criminologists . . . believed that crime could be observed directly by using the procedures of the natural sciences. In this view, crime—like rocks, plants, and insects—exists in a natural state quite independently of the concepts and the theories of the criminologist." Rejecting this paradigm, critical criminologists argue that criminality is not a characteristic that adheres in individuals but is the outcome of a complex social process.[33]

The evidence presented in this chapter thoroughly challenges the tenets of liberal, positivist criminology. As Maggie Tiller's case clearly demonstrates, whether an act was prosecuted as a crime depended as much upon the status and character of the accused, the prejudices of local authorities, and the community norms of the county in which it occurred, as on the nature of the deed itself. Even murder, presumably the least ambiguous offense, is a highly subjective category. Each year in Chicago dozens of women were involved in fights, altercations, and scuffles with husbands, boyfriends, lovers, and acquaintances in which men died. The causes were varied: a fall, blow to the head, thrown object, knife or gunshot wound. Few cases were extraordinary. Most women, including nearly all white women, were exonerated or acquitted, their claims of self-defense or temporary insanity readily accepted no matter how improbable or unconvincing. Between 1913 and 1925 not a single white woman was found guilty of manslaughter in Chicago (out of forty-three prosecutions). Similarly, only 2.4 percent of white female murder defendants were convicted (5 out of 208 women tried), compared to nearly 20 percent of African American women (18 out of 92).[34]

Although she had gone to the police and voluntarily turned herself in, Maggie Tiller's act was construed and prosecuted as cold-blooded murder. While her supporters alleged that "had the aforesaid Maggie Tiller money and friends to have aided her . . . we are sure that it [the trial] would have terminated very differently," her more powerful and influential detractors successfully characterized her as "depraved and disreputable." The press concurred, transforming the newly arrived, twenty-year-old Tiller into a wanton woman, a conniving actress who had hunted her victim through the streets of Chicago. The all-white jury that found her guilty and handed her a death sentence may have intended to send a powerful message: young African American women who actively defended themselves—whether on the streets or in the courtroom—could expect only the harshest treatment. As the data presented in the next chapter demonstrate in more detail, gender offered almost no protection to African American women, especially those charged with violent crimes.[35]

On December 18, 1899, after exactly five years in prison, Maggie Tiller penned a plaintive letter to Governor John R. Tanner: "I plead to you honorably [sic] sir as only a poor friendless girl can plead. . . . Will you in the name of Jesus act upon my case. Kind sir I can not do more, I have repented of all my transgressions and shortcomings." Echoing the sentiments of many nineteenth-century prisoners and facing the prospect of another New Year's Day behind bars, she concluded: "Oh may god in his tender mercy touch your heart and let me through your kindness be a free girl for the 20th century." Despite the endorsement of a prominent white woman, Governor Tanner refused to grant a pardon and also rejected Tiller's alternative request for a second commutation.[36]

One year later Tiller wrote an equally impassioned letter to the parole board, which flatly rejected her request for a pardon, contending that Judge Clifford's previous commutation of her death sentence to twenty years in prison provided "sufficient leniency." In contrast to their response to the pardon petitions authored by the more fortunate—and predominantly white—women discussed in the last chapter, no legal authorities expressed second thoughts over Tiller's incarceration. Neither Judge Clifford, nor the state's attorney (who took credit for winning her death sentence), nor any of the jurors or court officials involved in her trial endorsed her appeal. Despite her despair, Tiller remained a model prisoner. Earning all possible good-time credits, she was released after twelve years.[37]

Alton Penitentiary, 1835–58. The only surviving photo of Illinois's first penitentiary shows the prison as it was being demolished. Initially female convicts were incarcerated in a cellar under the "Warden's House." In 1843 they were transferred into this male cellhouse. In 1852 a six-cell women's building was constructed in the center of the prison yard. (Courtesy of the *Alton Telegraph*)

Women Prisoners Sewing, Joliet c. 1890. The women, seated in rows, passed their days employed in contract knitting and sewing under a strict regime of silence. Their fourth-story quarters consisted of several windowless, dormitory sleeping rooms; sewing, laundry, and dining rooms; and four isolated punishment cells. Throughout this period female prisoners were literally locked away, denied all outdoor recreation privileges other than a once-a-year "stroll" in the prison yard on the Fourth of July. (Joliet Prison Collection, G1987.0129.3.14. Courtesy of the Chicago Historical Society)

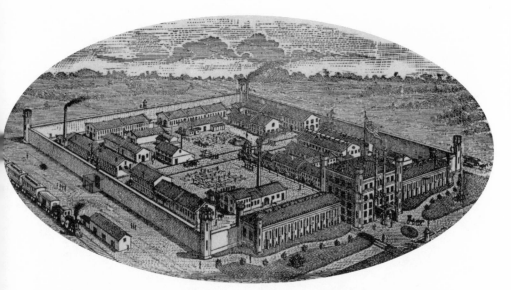

Joliet Penitentiary, 1859–1896. A two-story building containing one hundred cells was originally designed for the female convicts at Joliet. The unit, located behind the main administration building (the structure with flag), adjoined the chapel, hospital, and dining hall. However, because in the 1860s there were never more than thirty women incarcerated at any one time, the female convicts were transferred to the fourth floor of the administration building, where they were housed between 1870 and 1896. (Courtesy of the Illinois State Historical Library)

Joliet Women's Prison, 1896–1933. Architecturally the one-hundred-cell women's prison was an exact miniature replica of the male prison, which stood across the street. The cell house extends to the back. The chief matron and her assistant lived on the second floor of the center section. Note the surrounding twenty-foot-high stone wall and securely barred windows. (Courtesy of the Illinois State Historical Library)

Female Prisoners in Cell House Corridor (Joliet), c. 1915. Even though African American women averaged only 2.4 percent of the state's female population between 1890 and 1930, they represented two-thirds of the daily population at Joliet. Illinois's racial patterns reflected national trends. In 1923 African American women were 65 percent of female convicts incarcerated in state penitentiaries, yet only 12 percent of those sentenced to the nation's new reformatories. (Joliet Prison Collection, G1987.0129.3.17. Courtesy of the Chicago Historical Society)

Chief Matron Grace Fuller, 1914–22. A former college dean and national leader in the domestic science movement, Fuller was part of a new generation of college-educated women who went into "prison work" during the Progressive Era. At Joliet, Fuller inaugurated classes in cooking, sewing, laundry work, and gardening, along with a basic school program. Unlike many other female prison administrators, Fuller never lost her faith in the possibility of reforming female offenders. (Courtesy of the University Archives, Eastern Michigan University)

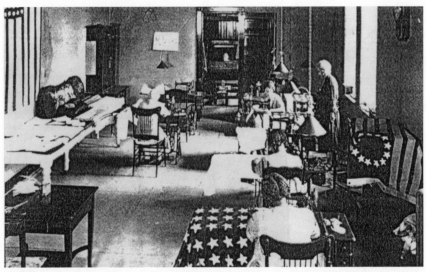

Women Prisoners Sewing Flags (Joliet), 1927. Many prison reformers viewed the teaching of domestic skills and appropriate gender-role behaviors as essential to women's rehabilitation. During World War I a "flag industry" was begun. This program continued at the Illinois State Reformatory for Women at Dwight into the 1960s. Even in the 1990s sewing remained the major prison industry at Dwight Correctional Center. (*Institution Quarterly* 28 [July–September 1927])

"Typical Cottage," Illinois State Reformatory for Women (Dwight), 1931. Each of the eight original cottages contained fourteen rooms designed for single-cell occupancy; a spacious, well-equipped kitchen; formal dining room; living room; and sun porch, all impeccably furnished. Until 1963 cottage warders worked twenty-four-hour shifts. Typically older, widowed women, warders lived in the cottages with their charges. (Illinois Department of Public Welfare, *Dedication of Oakdale* [Springfield, 1931])

"Typical Dining Room," Illinois State Reformatory for Women (Dwight), 1931. Although extremely attractive, the intimate dining rooms enabled cottage warders to closely monitor prisoners' behavior and conversations. Women were graded daily on attitude, work, and citizenship. In 1967 a central, cafeteria-style dining hall replaced the individual cottage kitchens and dining rooms, which were converted into dormitories. (Illinois Department of Public Welfare, *Dedication of Oakdale* [Springfield, 1931])

Administration Building, Illinois State Reformatory for Women at Dwight, 1931.
Throughout the 1920s Illinois clubwomen campaigned for a reformatory-style
women's prison. To all outward appearances, the new reformatory fulfilled its supporters' deepest hopes. Located eighty miles southwest of Chicago, the institution consisted of a central administration building in an attractive, Tudor-style design; sewing
factory; hospital with nursery; multi-purpose building serving as school, chapel, and
assembly hall; and eight large, stone "cottages" on a 160-acre setting. (Illinois Department of Public Welfare, *Dedication of Oakdale* [Springfield, 1931])

"All Girls Learn to Cook," Dwight 1953. In order to ensure prisoners' anonymity, all publicity photographs were taken from behind so inmates' faces would not be visible. Despite the placid appearance of this staged photo, the 1950s was a troubled decade. In 1950 Superintendent Doris Whitney instituted a short-lived program of classes in home economics, which cottage warders vociferously opposed because of the extra workload they created. (*The Welfare Bulletin*, March/April 1953)

CHAPTER SIX

"LURED TRAVELING SALESMAN TO HER ROOM"

The Character of Women's Crimes, 1890–1960

n 1902 the appropriately named Grace Wilder (Joliet #7786c) was committed to Joliet Women's Prison on an indeterminate one-to-ten year sentence. Wilder, a twenty-two-year-old housekeeper, had earned an unsavory reputation in her rural county. Despite her youth, she had already served two jail sentences for drunkenness and one term at the Geneva girls' reformatory. Unlike most incarcerated domestic servants, who were sentenced for stealing from their employers, Wilder had been convicted of the youthful act of "joy riding": she "hired a rig and drove off with it to another town," where she abandoned it. Arrested, charged with larceny, and convicted, she had been released under a suspended sentence "subject to good behavior." Instead of learning a lesson, the high-spirited Wilder continued to flout social norms. Only recently married, she "commenced living in an open state of adultery" shortly after her conviction. The local state's attorney reinstated the larceny charge. This time the judge sentenced the unrepentant Wilder to Joliet.[1]

Wilder's case illustrates how violating social conventions could result in a prison term. If Wilder had settled down, returned to her husband, and lived an otherwise respectable life, her youthful transgression would have been forgiven and forgotten. However, her semi-free status under a suspended sentence meant that any further violations of conventional norms could result in her sentence being reinstated. Local authorities exercised complete discretion over whether to impose or revoke such sentences, and a woman's degree of infamy weighed heavily in their decision making. The Joliet prison clerk characterized Wilder's "disposition" as "not vicious, but drinks and carouses." He described her associates as "of the lowest sort" and rated her "general reputation" as an unqualified "bad." Wilder lived up to her poor reputation, losing several months of good time for unspecified offenses. Denied parole after completing her one-year minimum, Wilder was forced to serve an unusually long three years. A month after her release, she broke parole and disappeared, at which point she also disappeared from the historical record.

. . .

The story of Wilder's "larceny" of a rig and buggy, read together with the brief notes recorded in the convict register, offers a glimpse into the context and meaning of women's offenses. Such portrayals reveal how complicated and varied the circumstances behind a woman's charge could be. As in Wilder's case, offense categories reveal little about the character or social context of women's deeds. What exactly constituted larceny, robbery, burglary, con game, assault to kill, manslaughter, or even murder? How serious were these acts and how much physical, economic, and social harm did these women cause? What distinguished their crimes from the dozens or hundreds of similar acts committed by women who never received a penitentiary sentence? Focusing on the 1890–1960 period, this chapter offers a portrait of the types of crimes for which women were policed, prosecuted, and imprisoned.[2]

Perhaps the most notable variable in conviction patterns is the role of race. Ethnicity had little discernible impact: native-born white women and European-born immigrant women were incarcerated for similar offenses. However, as table 2 reveals, African American women were grossly overrepresented in most violent crime categories and underrepresented in others. African American women, whose proportion of the state's population tripled from a bare 1.5 to 4.3 percent between 1890 and 1930, were sentenced for 77 percent of all serious assaults by women, 70 percent of robberies, 65 percent of manslaughter deaths, and 52 percent of murders. For murder and manslaughter their proportions increased further between 1930 and 1955. In contrast, African American women were almost never prosecuted for monetary crimes such as forgery and embezzlement, which they were rarely afforded an opportunity to commit. Likewise, they were rarely incarcerated for sex-related crimes, including infanticide, child abandonment, incest, accessory to rape, manslaughter by abortion, and "harboring a minor for the purpose of prostitution." Authorities expressed little interest in prosecuting when the victims were African American infants, children, or women.[3]

This chapter analyzes each category of crime, beginning with the most common property offenses (larceny, robbery, and burglary) and proceeding to the least common, sex-related, crimes (infanticide, murder by abortion, bigamy, and harboring). Such specifically "women's" crimes challenge androcentric definitions of crime and punishment. Although infanticide, abortion,

Table 2

TOTAL FELONY OFFENSES OF WOMEN BY RACE AND CRIME, 1890–1929 AND 1930–1955

Offense	1890–1929 Total	%	Percentage White	Black	1930–1955 Total	%	Percentage White	Black
PROPERTY								
Larceny	315	34	56	44	216	23	69	31
Burglary	67	7	63	37	57	6	75	25
VIOLENT								
Murder	104	11	48	52	95	10	40	60
Manslaughter	102	11	35	65	150	16	28	72
Robbery	96	10	30	70	86	9	55	45
Assault to Kill	35	4	23	77	30	3	37	63
Manslaughter by Abortion	9	<1	100	0	21	2	90	10
Infanticide	6	<1	67	33	3	<1	100	0
MONETARY								
Forgery	42	4	93	7	74	8	96	4
Con Game	26	3	85	15	77	8	66	34
Embezzlement	0	—	—	—	18	2	94	6
Counterfeiting	8	<1	100	0	0	—	—	0
OTHER								
Harboring Minor	54	6	87	13	1	<1	100	0
Bigamy	22	2	86	14	5	1	100	0
Perjury	15	2	80	20	7	1	86	14
Accessory to Rape	11	1	100	0	10	1	80	20
Arson	8	<1	62	38	9	1	89	11
Narcotics	0	—	—	—	10	1	0	100
Child Abandon	0	—	—	—	10	1	100	0
Miscellaneous	25				46			
TOTAL:	945				925			

Source: Joliet convict registers and Dwight inmate jackets, Illinois State Archives. Felonies only. The 1890–1929 periodization corresponds with the existence of the Joliet Women's Prison. After 1930 numbers increased and offense patterns changed dramatically with the opening of 254-bed Illinois State Reformatory for Women at Dwight.

and prostitution were widespread practices, women were only prosecuted for these actions in the most extraordinary circumstances. In one of the few comprehensive historical studies of female criminality, *Sex and Secrets: Crimes Involving Australian Women since 1880*, Judith A. Allen argues that "women who killed their babies were the largest group of people who killed in nineteenth-century Australia." Yet only in the most blatant cases—such as when a neighbor witnessed a frantic woman abandoning an illegitimate child in a well, outhouse, or haystack; instances where a woman aroused community suspicion by attempting to conceal a pregnancy; or when two women deliberately and consciously colluded in an infant's death—were authorities willing to arrest, prosecute, and convict.[4]

Allen argues that there exists no adequate historiographical context in which to frame a study of "crimes involving women." Contending that "illicit practices that are not policed, or under-policed, or erratically policed, are at least as historically significant as those criminalities which are most policed," Allen critiques the few general "histories of crime" that are embedded within a positivist framework and that focus exclusively on official crime rates and officially defined criminality. She argues that the criminalization of such practices as infanticide, abortion, harboring, incest, and prostitution was aimed not at "wholesale suppression," but rather at selective policing. The handful of women who were prosecuted served as a visible warning to all women.[5]

LARCENY

Although larceny declined steadily from 87 percent of all crimes in the 1860s to 19 percent in the 1950s, it always represented the largest offense category. Larceny carried an indeterminate sentence of "one-to-ten" years, but the average woman served less than two years until the 1920s. Under the indeterminate sentence, it was the state's parole board that decided when a prisoner was eligible for release. She could be paroled at any time after serving the one-year minimum, although she could not be incarcerated longer than the ten-year maximum.

Shoplifting was the most common form of larceny. In 1898 a prison clerk characterized Minnie Waller as the "Notorious 'Sneak Thief' of Chicago." A record of repeated offenses, rather than the value of the goods stolen, often weighed most heavily against women accused of larceny. Not surprisingly, African American women were sentenced for stealing significantly smaller amounts than white women: goods valued at $46 versus $142 during the period from 1895 to 1911 (the only period when prison clerks dutifully recorded the value of stolen items in the convict registers). Despite the lesser value of the items they stole, black women served longer average sentences (by more than three months) than white women.[6]

Mabel Taylor was one habitual shoplifter whose repeated petty acts confounded local authorities. She had served four terms at the Chicago bridewell in her teenage years, before a judge finally sentenced her to the penitentiary for the theft of a single blouse in 1921. Taylor served an unusually long four years before her release, only to be returned one year later as a parole violator. She had resumed shoplifting after losing her waitressing job (for refusing her employer's request that she "entertain male customers in the back room") and was subsequently arrested for stealing a clock valued at twenty-six dollars. The prison psychiatrist concluded that although she "conducted herself well" in prison, "only prolonged institutional custodial care will prevent further criminal activity." Calls for the permanent institutionalization of habitual shoplifters and petty offenders were repeated by prison psychiatrists throughout the 1920s and 1930s. Three years later the parole board decided to release Taylor, acknowledging that "the crimes are of a petty nature, never receiving articles of very much value. This clock being the most expensive item."[7]

Even during the 1920 to 1950 time period, women continued to be sentenced for stealing small sums or shoplifting a few items of clothing. At the same time, others exhibited lengthy police records or had stolen far larger amounts. In 1931 Sandra Peters, a housekeeper for an elderly wealthy man, "used her influence over him" to persuade him to deposit all of his cash, securities, and valuable jewelry in a safe deposit box she had rented. Soon afterward she disappeared along with $50,000 of his life's savings.[8]

As this last example intimates, many incarcerated women were domestic servants convicted of stealing money, jewelry, and items of clothing from their employers. Often it was the employer's word against the employee's. In the case of Mahalia Lewis, a middle-aged black housekeeper "accused of stealing $34 from a pocketbook," the prison clerk noted that she was "convicted on only circumstantial evidence." Domestic thefts and burglaries were routinely attributed to servants who lived at the residence of their employers and therefore could be easily apprehended. The fact that employers fully prosecuted cases against their employees hints at the strained nature of their relationships. These tensions were exacerbated by ethnic and racial differences. Most domestic servants convicted of theft were sentenced for stealing amounts valued at less than $100, although a few stole far higher sums or used their employment as a cover for professional theft. In 1899 Inga Nelson was convicted of "thirteen cases for theft committed as a domestic from employers" and in 1905 Blanche Benboy was convicted after she allegedly "stole $317 from old lady employer."[9]

ROBBERY

From 1890 through 1950 female robbers represented roughly 10 percent of all committed women, a figure that remained remarkably consistent across the decades. By definition, robbery involves the direct threat or use of violence against a victim. Hence, it was regarded as a more serious crime than larceny and carried a sentence of "one-to-fourteen" years. The legal line between robbery and larceny was never entirely clear. In many cases officially prosecuted as larceny, the prison clerk stated that the woman had "robbed" someone of a certain amount. A woman's race, rather than the character of her actions, most often determined whether she was prosecuted for larceny or robbery. White women were far more likely to be charged with the lesser crime, even when they stole directly from a person. Only in the 1920s did judges begin sentencing large numbers of white women for robbery.

Despite the fact that robbery is classified as a violent crime, before 1920 there was rarely any indication that a woman had resorted to violence or even to threats of violence. One-fifth of robbery convictions were for no more than pickpocketing. In 1904, Rosa Kling, a mulatto servant with several previous jail sentences, served a year for "$40 pickpocket from a male." Bessie Small served two full years after she "robbed a man of two pocketbooks" valued at two dollars each, and Mamie Hyatt served two years for pickpocketing five dollars from a white man.[10]

Officials frequently categorized female robbers as prostitutes. In two-fifths (41%) of robbery cases, the woman was accused of robbing a man whom she had "lured" or "enticed" into her room. In 1899 Pearl McLaughlin was convicted of the "larceny of $17" after she "decoyed a man into her room." Similarly, Pauline Smiley "relieved one D. of $20 while he was paying her a visit." The clerk noted that she was "an abandoned woman of whom we know nothing until this offense." Many other robberies occurred while the victim was drinking. Laura Williams "stole $90 from a drunken man in the rear of a saloon." Occasionally women robbed in pairs. In 1898 Maggie Young and Mollie Steel, who were described as "depraved and licentious," were "convicted of robbing an old soldier." According to the prison clerk, they had been "in numerous affairs of this sort before, but have escaped by skillful lying, and on account of the character of their victims." The shady character of women's victims occasionally drew such negative comments. After dutifully noting that Mary Sommers had "robbed an old man of $87 dollars," the clerk added that "she was a prostitute but I don't think he was much better as a citizen." In many prostitution-related robberies, white male victims failed to appear in court, due to their "reluctance of admitting that they were in a colored sporting house." Proceedings in such cases were routinely dismissed.[11]

In unusual instances robberies netted women significant sums of money and valuables, and this may explain why their victims risked social opprobrium by bringing charges against them. In 1905 May Allen was reported to have "lured traveling salesman to her room where she robbed him of $500 after he became intoxicated." The clerk reported: "heretofore had given police considerable trouble but never convicted." Similarly, Mamie Ray and two other women "enticed John H. to a house of ill fame and robbed him of a bag of coins of value of $500 and a gold nugget of value of $500." In the majority of cases, however, the amounts stolen were significantly lower. Despite a few exceptional instances, the mean value of the goods stolen in robberies was $40, less than half the value stolen in larceny cases. Female robbers were prosecuted less because of the value of the goods they stole than because of the perceived threat that their actions posed to patriarchal privileges. African American prostitutes who robbed from their clients, "loose" women who stole from their lovers, and cunning vagrants who pickpocketed unsuspecting males threatened both gender and racial hierarchies. In these circumstances, the moral character of their victims became irrelevant.[12]

Women continued to be convicted of "robbing" or pickpocketing such trifling sums in the 1920s and 30s. However, in those years force was more likely to be involved. Women, often acting with male or female accomplices, were frequently said to have "strong armed" men—threatened them with knives, razors, guns, or physical assault. In 1928 Hattie Johnson asked a man whether he "cared to have a good time," then led him toward her apartment and robbed him of $140 at knife point. When he resisted, Johnson's male partner appeared and assaulted him. On five previous occasions Johnson had been fined or sentenced to the Chicago House of Corrections for similar deeds. In 1937 Ginny Southers severely beat a woman and robbed her of three diamond rings and a fur coat. The state's attorney described Southers as a "dangerous woman; one of the cleverest criminals the authorities of this County have ever had to deal with." Although she and her husband had been arrested several times previously, authorities had "never been able to convict her."[13]

The cases of Hattie Johnson and Ginny Southers, both white women, illustrate a trend appearing in the 1920s: authorities increasingly portrayed women as the masterminds behind male gangs. Fears of newly liberated and enfranchised women translated into predictions that women would assume leadership roles in serious criminal activities. In 1929 the Illinois Banker's Association protested Rebecca Gordon's parole, explaining that "While it is true that she did not go into the bank, yet she helped plan this robbery, furnished the automobile, got her share of the money and aided in the escape of the men who actually committed the crime." Portraying Gordon as capable of any monstrosity, the association concluded: "This woman's reputation is very bad and we feel that as soon as she is released from prison she will not stop at committing murder if necessary to commit other crimes which she is sure to perpetrate." The local banker's association also passed a resolution condemning Gordon's release. The parole board bowed to the association's preferences and forced her to serve seven years.[14]

As this example suggests, the parole board treated female robbers with increasing severity even if they took "no actual part in the holdup" or had only served as decoys or look-outs. In the 1920s the board doubled the average time served for robbery, from less than two years to 4.1 years for white women and 5.2 years for African American women. This increase in time served bore no correlation to the seriousness of women's acts. After 1930, however, female robbers were more likely to rely on weapons to silence or coerce their victims. No female robbers were convicted of "armed robbery" during the 1920s, but one-quarter (25%) were so convicted in the 1930s and nearly half (45%) in the 1940s.

BURGLARY

From 1890 to 1950 female burglars averaged 5 percent of all women committed to the penitentiary. The line between burglary and larceny was also often dependent on the social characteristics of the offender. Some domestic servants were charged with burglary for stealing money or items from their employer's house, even though their thefts did not involve forced entry.

Although female burglars stole goods that were valued even lower than those stolen by women convicted of either larceny or robbery ($25 on average for burglary, in contrast to $75 for larceny and $40 for robbery during the 1895–1911 period), burglary carried the most severe sentence: "one-to-twenty" years. Burglary was perceived as a greater threat than shoplifting or even robbery because it involved breaking and entering and was therefore a more extreme violation of private property.[15]

As in cases of larceny and robbery, African American women received severe punishments for minor offenses. In 1895 Annie Jackson, "in conspiracy with her paramour," was convicted of stealing "articles of apparel and eatibles [sic] mostly" from a local store and was sentenced to a year. Even the charge of attempted burglary could send a black woman to the penitentiary. In 1899 Annie Smith was caught in the act of burglarizing a house while the owner was away. Although the clerk noted that "she was not known as a criminal before and comes of respectable parentage," she received a penitentiary sentence. Perhaps resenting her incarceration, the twenty-two-year-old Smith became an unruly inmate. During her first year she lost two months of good time for "refusing to work, insolence and disobedience" and was subsequently denied parole. She died after three years in prison.[16]

African American women with prior criminal records faced the harshest treatment of all in burglary cases, perhaps because they had violated the homes of white people. In 1911 Flora Childs, an illiterate, thirty-year-old black woman who had served a previous sentence at the Missouri State Penitentiary, "entered a dwelling house through back window" and stole some clothing and a piece of bacon. She was imprisoned for two years for this offense. Likewise, in 1930 forty-three-year-old Hattie Walker, described as a "mentally defective, happy-go-lucky negress," who had already served three prior prison sentences for pickpocketing in neighboring states, served over four years for stealing a five-dollar purse hanging on the back door of a house.[17]

ASSAULT TO KILL

Assaults that resulted in serious injuries could be prosecuted as "assault to kill," "assault to murder," or "attempted murder." From 1890 to 1950 assaults represented 4 to 5 percent of all commitments. As for robbery, women sentenced for assault were overwhelmingly African American (77%). The average sentence was 2.5 years, only seven months less than the average sentence for manslaughter. Indeed, many women convicted of manslaughter served shorter sentences than women who had only injured their victims, a discrepancy that may have engendered resentment among inmates.[18]

Unfortunately, the prison clerk provided few details in cases of assault. Most often women were convicted of attacking other women. Between 1896 and 1904 Jessie Davis "slashed another woman in the face with a razor," Laura Gardner "threatened and tried to kill a woman over a man with a knife," and Lizzie Briton "shot at a woman in the hip at a dance after a quarrel." Female victims may have been more likely than male to prosecute other women. Conversely, women's assaults against females may have been taken more seriously than their assaults on men, who were assumed to be more capable of defending themselves. The few exceptions include incidents in which either a police officer was attacked or the male victim was permanently disabled. Women who committed assault appear to have been more outspoken, aggressive, and disruptive than the typical female convict. They were three times more likely to be punished and four times more likely to be transferred to the nearby Kankakee insane asylum.[19]

MONETARY CRIMES

Monetary crimes such as forgery, "confidence games," and embezzlement increased steadily from 4 percent of all offenses in the 1890s to 20 percent in the 1950s. Female forgers were typically women who out of economic hardship sought to pass bad checks to local merchants and banks. The charge of "con game" typically involved the procurement of another's money or property through deceptive practices or "false pretenses." Stella Dixon, claiming to be a spiritualist, "represented to an Emily J. that treasure buried on her property would be unearthed on payment of $35." After receiving the payment, Dixon attempted to flee the city but was arrested at the train depot. Forgery and con games were overwhelmingly committed by white women (93% and 85% respectively). After 1930 a few white women (four to eight per decade) were sentenced for embezzlement of amounts ranging from $5,000 to $30,000. All were accountants or bookkeepers who embezzled from their employers. A similar number were convicted of committing forgery to acquire comparably large amounts. However, even amidst the Great Depression, and well into the 1950s, women continued to be sentenced for forging checks for small amounts to pay for groceries or other necessary items.[20]

HARBORING A MINOR FOR THE PURPOSES OF PROSTITUTION

Before the opening of the Illinois State Reformatory for Women at Dwight in 1930, no women was ever sentenced to prison in Illinois for such misdemeanor "morals offenses" as prostitution, adultery, or fornication. Prostitutes were routinely fined and repeatedly committed to local jails and houses of correction, but were never sentenced to the state penitentiary no matter how extensive their arrest records. Similarly, managing or "keeping" a "house of ill fame" was also only a misdemeanor offense. Although two to three hundred "keepers" were arrested annually in Chicago alone, even the most notorious brothel owners were shielded from incarceration. Thus, even though both prostitution and keeping were criminalized activities, their classification as misdemeanors rather than felonies implicitly condoned males' pursuit of commercial sex.

Prostitution was not wholly unregulated or unpoliced. In 1887 the Illinois General Assembly passed the first law designed to combat, or at least to regulate, the widely feared "white slave trade." Tales of young and ignorant but otherwise virtuous country girls deceived into lives of prostitution haunted the popular imagination at the end of the nineteenth century. Under the 1887 law a keeper who permitted "any unmarried female under the age of eighteen to live, board, stop, or room" in the establishment could be sentenced to a one-to-five-year penitentiary sentence. Revealingly, the original law applied only to the harboring of girls of "chaste life and conversation," although this limitation was removed two years later. Similarly, Illinois's 1899 "Seduction Law" applied only to sexual intercourse with unmarried females under the age of eighteen who were "of previous chaste character." Thus, men who sought sex with underage prostitutes could not be penalized. Moreover, because the new crime was only classified as a misdemeanor, men who "seduced" previously chaste young women could receive little more than a fine or a short-term jail commitment.[21]

Both laws were rarely enforced. On average, only one woman a year was sentenced to prison for harboring a minor for the purposes of prostitution (5% of total commitments). Convicted women were overwhelmingly white (89%), as it was literally the "white slave trade" that aroused public outrage and indignation. Women convicted of harboring were the oldest offenders, excepting abortionists; their average age was thirty-eight years. The evidence suggests that they were regarded as particularly notorious, incorrigible, and "hardened" women. In 1933 a probation officer protested the parole of fifty-seven-year-old Ella Wagenar, describing her as an "old police character." Wagenar had been "arrested numerous times for using narcotics," was known as "a shop-lifter and a prostitute all her life," and was responsible for "ruin[ing] the life of many a young girl from the age of fourteen on up." Several white women were convicted of harboring their own young daughters, a gross violation of socially sanctioned maternal behavior. Lina Plank served two years for "keeping her two female children (aged 11 and 13) in a house of prostitution and using them as common prostitutes."[22]

INFANTICIDE

References to both infanticide and abortion appeared among Illinois's earliest laws. The state's 1827 revised law code included several new crimes. A woman who "concealed the death of a bastard child" risked a one-year jail sentence while anyone "inducing a woman with child to miscarry" faced a three-year sentence and fine up to a $1,000. Such acts, however, were virtually never prosecuted. Only a dozen women were ever committed to the penitentiary for infanticide, and then only between 1872 and 1906. A child's untimely death could easily be concealed, and coroners often supported a mother's protestations that the infant had simply died in its sleep or through an accident brought on by her exhausted state. Coroners seemed unable to acknowledge that women might deliberately kill their own children; historian Roger Lane contends that they frequently failed to find infanticide "in even the most glaring of incidences."[23]

Only the most marginal or socially outcast women were ever prosecuted for infanticide, and then only in the most egregious of circumstances. Prison clerks frequently characterized such women as "feeble-minded" and "very ignorant" or as "poor unsophisticated country girls." Anna Smith, described as "weak but not vicious," served four years for drowning her illegitimate infant in a pail of water. Most women convicted of infanticide were unmarried.

Their single status may have inflamed neighbors' suspicions and influenced officials' decisions to intervene with legal action. In half of infanticide cases women were convicted in pairs, suggesting that judges and juries were less likely to accept a child's death as accidental if two women appeared to have colluded. In 1882 Rosetta Callahan and her elderly mother each received a fourteen-year murder sentence in the death of the daughter's infant. On average, women served 6.2 years for infanticide, a sentence second only to murder in severity. Male parole board members appear to have regarded murdering mothers with horror. In contrast, prison matrons expressed considerable sympathy, but their pardon campaigns succeeded only after the women had completed many years in prison.[24]

Only two African American women were ever imprisoned for infanticide. The untimely death of African American infants failed to rouse official concern. In Chicago nearly all officially identified infanticides involved white babies. Similarly, African American women were rarely identified as victims in abortion-related deaths, and their abortionists were never prosecuted, even in instances of extreme negligence.

Infanticide was far more common among women of all races than this tiny number of convictions suggests. Beginning in the 1860s accounts of the discovery of dead and abandoned infants appeared regularly in the newspapers. After 1897 the Chicago Department of Health reported a conservative average of five infanticide deaths annually, and Chicago police data offered far higher estimates. The 1929 *Illinois Crime Survey* reported that in the two previous years alone, forty-eight white infants were found dead in Chicago. The coroner's jury officially attributed all of their deaths to infanticide. Yet charges were brought in only one of these cases; all others were simply listed as "unsolved." Even in situations involving unmarried women, the coroner's jury and the Illinois Crime Commission found it impossible to believe that white women were capable of killing their own newborn babies. Instead, they suggested that the responsibility for the infants' deaths must lie elsewhere:

> It is certain that in every one of the infanticide cases the mother of the child could not have been in physical condition to commit the murder herself, and most of these cases may properly be ascribed to persons who for one reason or another were interested in disposing of the bodies of illegitimate children.[25]

In 1930 the Illinois General Assembly reclassified infanticide as a misdemeanor. Over the next three decades ten women, all white, served one-year sentences for the offense.

BIGAMY

Women were rarely sentenced for bigamy (2.3% of total commitments), and of these 86 percent were white. It seems that African American women were not held to the same marital norms. White women were prosecuted for bigamy only in the most unusual circumstances, such as when a first wife pressed charges or the local community was deeply offended by a woman's actions. In 1899 Emma Hicks, a white woman, raised community ire after she "left her husband a white man and without any pretense of divorce married a negro." Similarly, in 1931 Lodemma Mae Atkins had attracted "numerous complaints" in her new community for her "improper conduct" and unspecified "immoral habits." When it was discovered that she had married her second husband without divorcing her first, the state's attorney promptly brought charges.[26]

As this example suggests, "morals" offenses such as bigamy provided a pretext for incarcerating women suspected of other crimes. In 1938, the sheriff and state's attorney both protested Ermeline Unger's parole, explaining that she possessed a "very bad reputation." Unger had cohabited with her third husband for several years before marrying him. She was suspected of two arsons for which she had collected insurance, as well as of hiring two men to kill her third husband, who was heavily insured and had died under mysterious circumstances. Although "local authorities" and "most of the neighbors" were convinced she had murdered him, "it was impossible to get any direct evidence." However, after officials discovered that she had never legally divorced her second husband, Unger was convicted of bigamy. Unfortunately bigamy was not punished very harshly: these women served an average of only 1.1 years.[27]

MANSLAUGHTER BY ABORTION

Although abortion was illegal, Illinois's 1867 law code exempted abortions performed for "*bona fide* medical or surgical purposes" that were never clearly specified. Despite abortion's criminalization, abortionists were rarely sanctioned; nor was any woman ever imprisoned for receiving an abortion. However, between 1890 and 1940 nine women, five of whom listed their occupation as midwife or nurse, were committed for performing a "criminal operation in which a woman died," otherwise known as "manslaughter by abortion." Prosecutions increased in the 1940s, with another nine women sentenced.

As with infanticide, far more women died from abortions than this tiny number suggests. Beginning in the 1880s trials of accused abortionists, both male and female, appeared regularly in the newspapers. In 1888 a month-long *Chicago Times* investigative series offered an in-depth study of the commercial abortion underground, revealing hundreds of practitioners.[28] Chicago police statistics from the 1890s listed an average of eight arrests annually in abortion-related deaths; that number increased to thirty-seven in the 1920s. There was a far larger number of cases in which a woman died but no arrest was made. Between 1901 and 1919, the Cook County coroner's office investigated over sixty abortion-related deaths annually and sent twelve suspects a year to the grand jury. Yet grand jurors rarely indicted. Even when they did, prosecution almost never resulted in conviction. The *Illinois Crime Survey* reported that fifty-eight women died of "undetermined abortion" in Chicago in 1926 and 1927. Nearly all (93%) of these cases were solved and the abortionist identified, but prosecution was begun in only nine cases. Yet even in these, the charges were quickly dropped. The authors reasoned that because the deceased women had voluntarily submitted themselves to the operation:

> some of the sting of criminality is thereby removed from the act; moreover, the practice appears to be so wide-spread among certain classes of persons who desire to be relieved of the physical suffering and the responsibilities of childbirth, that it is difficult to attach the same degree of culpability to the act of abortion that is associated with the act of shooting or stabbing another.[29]

The public condoned the practice of abortion, which was widespread at the turn of the century, and expressed sympathy for pregnant women who sought abortions. Despite its criminalization, no woman in Illinois was ever prosecuted for procuring, or receiving, an abortion. However, when an abortion resulted in a woman becoming seriously ill and she had to go to a hospital for medical care, state law required doctors to pressure her to name her abortionist in a "Dying Declaration." Yet even in cases in which a woman died, Chicago prosecutors, recognizing the futility of attempting to convict midwives, nurses, and physicians for the crime of manslaughter by abortion, rarely pressed charges. Instead, as in harboring and infanticide, prosecution was aimed at regulation rather than complete suppression. Abortionists were found guilty of manslaughter only in situations of extreme negligence, when they were characterized as "butchers" and believed to be responsible for the deaths of several women through poorly performed or botched operations.

For example, Austrian-born midwife Carla Sahovey had been arrested on six different counts of manslaughter by abortion; all charges but the last were dismissed. The sixth charge was "stricken with leave to reinstate." When another woman later brought charges after a botched operation for which she had to be hospitalized, the state reinstated the sixth manslaughter indictment. Describing Sahovey as an "unattractive appearing woman who speaks quite broken English," the state's attorney protested her parole on the basis of her "long record for abortion and murder by abortion." Yet she served only three years. Like Sahovey, most convicted abortionists were foreign-born women. The sentences they received were relatively light. Although the average time served for infanticide was 6.2 years and for manslaughter 3.1 years, the average woman convicted of manslaughter by abortion served only 1.7 years.[30]

Although few abortionists were ever convicted, the seemingly unsuccessful police investigations served a punitive purpose. In *When Abortion Was a Crime*, Leslie J. Reagan argues that, "Our understanding of what punishment is needs to be refined and redefined, particularly in cases of women who violate sexual norms, to include more subtle methods of disciplining individuals." Lurid newspaper accounts of botched or fatal abortions warned women that they risked not only death but public exposure of their sexual transgressions. Although most women who sought illegal abortions were married and middle-class, police and the press selectively focused on young, unmarried, poor, and working-class women. If their abortions were discovered, women faced humiliating interrogations about their sexual lives by police, physicians, and hospital staff. These interrogations often involved their lovers, families, and friends. For most women, however, the health risks, emotional trauma, and financial costs of an abortion were experienced as punishment enough.[31]

MURDER AND MANSLAUGHTER

The percentage of female convicts who were committed for murder and manslaughter combined rose from 5 percent in the 1870s, to 15 percent in the 1890s, and to 33 percent in the 1920s and 1930s, then declined slightly to 25 percent through 1950. Critical criminologist Ian Taylor warns that "the widespread view of homicide as a highly 'factual' offense, thought to be evidenced by the existence of a corpse" is enormously deceptive. As the discussion in the last chapter demonstrated, whether a suspicious death was attributed to an accident or to natural causes or was classified as justifiable or felonious homicide involved a complicated calculus of many factors. After completing her 1915 investigation Anne Hinrichsen concluded, "The state's reputation for legal leniency is founded on the fact that in certain communities a woman can not be convicted of murder." What she should have said was that native-born, white women were virtually never convicted.[32]

Chicago police data lend vivid support to Hinrichsen's claim. Between 1913 and 1925 in Chicago, the only years for which complete data are available, 92 African American women were arrested on charges of murder, and eighteen (20%) were found guilty. During the same period, 208 white women were arrested, but only five (2.4%) were found guilty; all of them were foreign born. It is possible that black women were nearly ten times as likely as white women to be guilty (20% versus 2.4%), but not plausible. And the conviction rates for murder do not fit the general pattern of women's convictions. For most crimes, white women in Chicago were *more likely* to be found guilty than black women (45% versus 35%), suggesting that police arrested African American women on weaker evidence. In the end gender offered no protection for black women charged with murder, whereas for white women race and gender privileges combined to dramatically increase the odds that they would acquitted. Whereas white women were significantly *less* likely than white men to be convicted of murder (2.4% versus 14%), conviction rates for black women and black men were almost identical (20% versus 24%) in Chicago.[33]

White women were prosecuted and convicted of murder or manslaughter only when their actions appeared exceptionally cold-blooded and their social status was particularly marginal. Inmate files from the 1920s and 1930s provide vivid support for this conclusion. Nearly all examples of white women convicted of murder involved particularly brutal deeds or killings motivated by financial gain. Five white women, several with male lovers, murdered their husbands to gain the proceeds of their insurance policies. Likewise, three were convicted of murdering children in order to benefit from their life insurance policies. Tillie Klimek received a ninety-nine year sentence for poisoning her twelve-year-old daughter with arsenic.

Ruby Tate was convicted of poisoning her husband with arsenic so she could marry her lover. Essie Malinsky killed her married lover's wife with arsenic and was "suspected of previous like crimes" in the death of her second husband. In the most notorious murder case of the 1930s, Evelyn Smith and Blanche Dunkel were given 180 and 75 years respectively for strangling the latter's son-in-law, dismembering his body, and dumping the pieces in an Indiana swamp.[34]

Jamella Reynolds, an African American woman incarcerated during the 1960s, recalled: "The few white women who were there were in for such horrible stuff. We [African American prisoners] were always amazed by what crimes they had committed. One put a baby in a roasting pan and cooked it in the oven. Another shot her daughter while she was sleeping." In contrast, African American woman convicted of murder between 1920 and 1963 had typically killed husbands or lovers in the heat of passion. That is, the deaths had occurred during the course of drunken arguments, physical fights, or momentary explosions of rage or jealousy, often after years of abuse. Although the women inflicted wounds that ultimately proved fatal, few of these attacks were calculated or premeditated. Almost none of their victims were children, and hardly any of the murders were motivated by financial gain.

Chicago prosecutors openly admitted that it was "almost impossible to convict a [white] woman for killing her husband," especially when the woman was "attractive, young, and wealthy." In 1935 *Chicago Tribune* journalists conducted an investigation of all women convicted of murder in Cook County in the previous thirty years. They used photos to illustrate their conclusion, offered with a noticeable lack of either outrage or surprise, that "the few who were sentenced to prison were either old, unattractive, or both." One state's attorney acknowledged that verdicts were "inversely proportional to the charm of the woman defendant. . . . The homelier the woman, the more severe the penalty." An earlier newspaper examination had resulted in similar conclusions. Such extrajudicial variables were both widely acknowledged and publicly endorsed as legitimate factors in the decision making of all-white and all-male juries (women in Illinois did not win the right to serve on juries until 1939). The only white women found guilty of murder in Chicago were described by the press as: "not a beauty," "well over the slope of both beauty and age," "more than forty, sarcastic and bad looking," or exhibiting "unpleasant, erratic, and repellent" behavior. Ethnic stereotypes abounded. A "squat, dumpy Polish woman" and an "ignorant, stupid, Italian peasant" both received the death penalty, although their convictions were later overturned. The Italian woman had offended jury members with her "distorted figure, chewed off fingernails and inarticulate grunts."[35]

Despite the greater brutality involved in the killings they committed, white women were much more likely to be pardoned. Between 1860 and 1960 African American women virtually always served longer prison terms than white women for nearly every offense category: larceny, robbery, assault to kill, burglary, arson, and confidence game (see table 3, where some

Table 3

AVERAGE YEARS SERVED FOR MAJOR CRIMES, BY RACE, 1860–1960

	1860–89		1890s		1900s		1910s		1920s		1930s		1940s a		1950s	
	W	B	W	B	W	B	W	B	W	B	W	B	W	B	W	B
Larceny	1.2	1.3	1.3	1.7	1.9	2.1	1.2	1.6	2.2	2.9	3.0	3.1	2.5	3.0	2.9	2.1
Robbery	—b	—	1.6	1.8	1.0	1.6	1.1	1.9	4.1	5.2	3.8	5.0	3.0	2.5	2.9	3.3
Assault to Kill	—	—	2.4	1.7	1.7	2.5	—	2.3	—	4.2	4.7	5.3	2.8	4.0	—	4.8
Manslaughter	2.5	3.6	2.0	2.4	2.8	2.4	2.2	1.3	4.6	4.6	5.0	5.8	4.0	4.6	3.1	2.2
Murder	4.8	7.5	4.9	7.7	6.4	6.0	4.0	6.8	8.1	9.3	10.5	8.7	10.6	9.5	10.0c	9.6

Source: Joliet convict registers and Dwight inmate jackets, 1931–1957. Average time served is based on all women who *entered* the penitentiary during a particular decade. Averages do not include extra time women might have served as parole violators. Average sentences for the 1950s were calculated on the basis of the years 1950 to 1957 only. An estimated 20% of women committed to prison in 1958 and 1959 were not released until after 1963, the last date for which Dwight prisoner files have been preserved. Thus, their release dates were unknown and their time served could not be calculated.

a Illinois's sentencing laws were radically revised in 1944. Instead of open-ended indeterminate sentences, judges could select sentences such as "1 to 3 years" or even "1 to 1.5 years." As a result, judges, rather than parole board members, gained far more control over the length of time a prisoner was required to serve. Because judges tended to select lower ranges, compared to the 1920s and 1930s, average sentences for all offenses except murder declined after the mid-1940s.

b There were not enough cases in these offense categories to allow for a decade-by-decade analysis by race.

c Because files for women released after 1963 are missing, 1950s figures for murder sentences include a +10% adjustment.

of these offenses are shown). This pattern occurred despite the fact that in property crimes African American women stole items valued less than those stolen by white women. In contrast, average time served for murder and manslaughter showed no such consistent patterns. During the nineteenth century African American women served substantially longer prison terms for both offenses: 7.6 years for black women convicted of murder versus 4.8 years for white and 3.0 years versus 2.2 years for manslaughter. However, between 1900 and 1960 *white* women averaged slightly longer sentences for murder during four of the six decades (1900s, 1930s, 1940s, and 1950s) and slightly longer sentences for manslaughter during three decades (1900s, 1910s, and 1950s).[36]

Experts offer several theories to explain these contradictory patterns. As we have seen, white women typically committed more brutal killings than black women convicted of either murder or manslaughter, and this may account for the greater length of their sentences after 1900. Victim devaluation theory offers another explanation. According to this theory, legal authorities value the lives of white victims more highly than those of black victims and thus punish their killers more harshly. Because white women's murder victims were overwhelmingly white, they would thus be punished more severely (with longer sentences) than women whose victims were black.

But neither of these explanations helps us to understand why black women served significantly longer sentences for murder and manslaughter during the nineteenth century or during certain decades of the twentieth century. Racial biases appear to have exerted contradictory pressures. Although outright racism may account for the longer average sentences black women served for most crimes during most decades, after 1900 murder and manslaughter defied this general trend. At the same time, frequent turnover and changes in the membership of the state's parole board, which determined release dates after 1895, may account for some of the seeming inconsistencies in patterns relating to average time served for murder and manslaughter after 1900.[37]

DRUG OFFENSES

During the early 1950s federal officials fanned public fears of an upsurge in addiction, especially among teenagers. Drugs were portrayed as a new social menace that threatened the Cold War–era ideals of middle-class American life. Federal Bureau of Narcotics director Harry Anslinger, who served from 1930 to 1962 as the nation's first drug czar, linked drug addiction to the communist threat, accusing "Red China" of seeking to destroy Western society by smuggling heroin. In 1951 Congress passed the Boggs Act, which established a two-year mandatory minimum prison sentence for first-time violators of federal drug-trafficking laws and a five-year minimum for second-time offenders. In 1954 President Eisenhower called for a new war on drugs and appointed a special commission that recommended even more severe sentences. Two years later Congress passed the Narcotic Control Act of 1956, doubling maximum penalties for first-time possession. Illinois was at the forefront of this crusade. In 1954 the Illinois General Assembly passed a revised Narcotics Control Act, which redefined both drug possession and drug trafficking as felony offenses.[38]

Between 1930 and 1950 white women represented 81 percent of those sentenced on misdemeanor drug charges to one-year terms to the Illinois State Reformatory for Women. During its first decades, judges viewed the new institution as a benign treatment facility where drug-addicted, white women would receive medical care. These white, misdemeanor, drug offenders came from more middle-class backgrounds than the average female prisoner. Many had begun their drug use inadvertently: one-third (35%) claimed they had become addicted after having been prescribed drugs by a physician, while another 19 percent had turned to drugs to relieve illness or fatigue. Despite the fact that half (54%) had used morphine and one-third (30%) heroin as their primary drug, they were not perceived as "hard core" or "unsalvageable" addicts. In contrast, during the 1950s and 1960s African American women constituted 94 percent of felony drug commitments. Even though three-quarters were sentenced for possession, as opposed to selling or trafficking, they served an average of 2.5 years. Between 1955 and 1965, this new (and greatly maligned) population constituted one-third of women sentenced to prison in Illinois. Their experiences will be explored in more detail in chapter 10.[39]

• • •

In *Punish and Critique: Towards a Feminist Analysis of Penality,* Adrian Howe argues that most feminist criminologists and historians have succeeded only in "adding women in" and have failed to challenge the tenets of liberal positivism. "Studies of women's imprisonment," she contends, "continue to connect changing patterns within the women's prison system to changing patterns of women's lawbreaking. . . . [They] have not succeeded in fulfilling Foucault's injunction to 'release the question of punishment from the question of crime.'" In these last two chapters I have attempted such a release.[40]

Historically the number of women sentenced to prison in Illinois has borne no relationship to the amount of crime women have committed. Few female offenders were arrested, prosecuted, or convicted. Only the most marginalized or disadvantaged were ever sentenced to prison. In this final section I analyze patterns of incarceration for the two major offense categories, property crimes and violent crimes. At first glance, female criminality appears to show several distinctive trends (see graph 2). Commitments for property crimes fell steadily from 86 percent of female prison commitments in the 1850s and 1860s to one-half (50%) in the 1890s, and to 31 percent in the 1940s. The proportion of female convicts who were committed for violent offenses (robbery, assault to kill, murder, and manslaughter combined) quadrupled from 11 percent in the 1860s to 45 percent in the 1950s. The central question is whether these shifting proportions reflect real changes in the nature or character of female criminality. Were women engaging in more violent crimes after 1890, or did these changing proportions reflect shifting patterns of prosecution? The evidence supports the latter explanation.[41]

Although an increasing proportion of commitments were for violent

GRAPH 2

Women Committed, by Type of Criminal Offense, 1850–1950

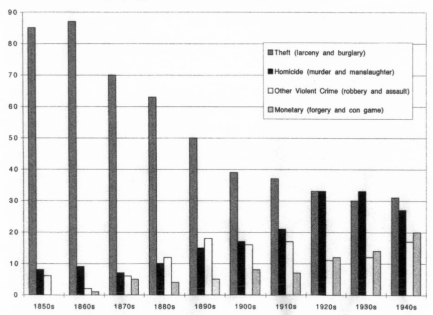

Source: Alton, Chester, and Joliet convict registers; Dwight inmate jackets.

crimes, when the category of "violent crime" is subdivided according to type of crime and race of the offender, no consistent pattern emerges. For the most part, numbers did not increase until the 1890s, when the new Women's Prison opened at Joliet. Then, even though the state's population doubled between 1890 and 1950, the total number of women sentenced for assault and robbery showed no increase until the 1940s. Indeed, for assault white women's numbers remained absolutely stable, averaging two per decade. Similarly, white women's robbery commitments did not increase until the 1920s, and black women's declined after 1900. Numbers for murder and manslaughter increased, but they too remained stable for decades at a time.

More important, the tiny number of women incarcerated per decade for each offense further challenges the positivist assumption that a direct relationship exists between female prison commitments and real rates of offending. Judith A. Allen's concepts of the underpolicing, selective policing, and nonpolicing of different types of potentially criminal activities offers a useful theoretical paradigm. An equal number of nineteenth-century as twentieth-century women may have engaged in murderous assault and other violent and lethal acts, but authorities rarely found them guilty. Even when they did, they hardly ever sentenced the perpetrators to prison.[42]

These observations suggest that the shifting proportions of women committed for particular categories of crime, rather than mirroring shifting

Table 4

NUMBER OF WOMEN COMMITTED FOR CRIMES OF VIOLENCE,
BY RACE, 1850–1950

	Assault to Kill		Robbery		Murder		Manslaughter[a]	
	Black	White	Black	White	Black	White	Black	White
1850s	0	1	0	1	0	2	0	2
1860s	1	0	0	2	2	1	6	5
1870s	1	2	1	1	0	0	3	1
1880s	2	4	3	5	3	1	4	8
1890s	9	3	27	3	14	10	8	7
1900s	4	3	18	2	10	8	11	6
1910s	8	1	15	6	9	9	18	7
1920s	7	1	7	14	21	19	29	14
1930s	5	3	17	18	23	26	47	20
1940s	12	8	11	30	20	11[b]	43	28[c]

Source: Compiled from the Alton and Joliet convict registers and Dwight inmate jackets, Illinois State Archives.

Note: Numbers include only those cases for which race could be ascertained. Data from Chester penitentiary were omitted since Chester's convict registers indicated neither race, nationality, nor a physical description (skin, hair, and eye color). After 1895, race was always clearly designated in the Joliet convict registers. Statistics for the nineteenth century are not significantly affected by missing data. For each decade's crime categories, at most only one case involved a woman of unknown racial background. The following represent the only exceptions: five women of unknown racial background were commited for manslaughter in the 1860s and four were committed for murder in the 1890s.

[a] Includes women convicted of infanticide and manslaughter by abortion.

[b] The number of women committed for murder in the 1940s may be underestimated by 10–15%. Dwight inmate jackets for women released after 1963 have not been preserved. Thus, a woman committed for murder in 1949 who was released after 15 years (in 1964) would be omitted from my calculations. However, even assuming a 15% error rate, the absolute number of women committed for murder showed no consistent increase from 1920 to 1950.

[c] 1940s manslaughter cases include 8 white women convicted of manslaughter by abortion in contrast to four in the 1930s and one or two in each earlier decade.

patterns of female offending, reflected the changing role and social-control functions of the penitentiary. Instead of assuming that female violence increased after 1890, this analysis suggests that is was African American women who were increasingly prosecuted and incarcerated for violent offenses. Even during the 1930 to 1955 period, when the number of white women sentenced for violent crimes doubled, African American women still accounted for 72 percent of all commitments for manslaughter, 63 percent of commitments for assault, 60 percent for murder, and 45 percent for robbery. Meanwhile, their percentage of the state's female population increased from 4.4 to 8.9 percent. Such extreme racial disparities seriously undermine the belief that women's rates of incarceration corresponded with their real rates of offending.[43]

• • •

"Violent crime" is a socially constructed category. Whether an event was legally defined as the violent crime of robbery or the nonviolent crime of larceny was highly dependent upon the race of the offender. African American women who stole from a person were far more likely than white women to be charged with the more serious crime of robbery. Even for the most "factitious" of crimes, murder and manslaughter, a wide range of variables influenced whether a particular killing was defined as a criminal act. White women's murderous deeds were constructed as crimes only in particularly egregious situations in which the offender was an unattractive, older, or immigrant woman who poisoned her husband or children for the sake of financial gain; killed a spouse in order to marry a lover; or mutilated the body of her victim. In these atypical scenarios, the woman was perceived not just as a murderess, but as a monster. Yet in other cases of equally calculated and cold-blooded killings, those in which attractive, young, upper-class white women killed husbands or lovers for similar reasons, juries acquitted with little hesitation.

In contrast, juries routinely prosecuted and convicted African American women of murder and manslaughter under far less egregious circumstances. In 1935 fifteen-year-old Susie Lattimore, a young African American girl, stabbed another teenager in a fight in a bar where both had been drinking. The girl died several days later. Despite the unpremeditated nature of the killing, the state's attorney chose to charge Lattimore with first-degree murder and to prosecute her in adult court. Lattimore was summarily convicted and sentenced to thirteen years at Dwight women's prison. Despite public outcry by some reform organizations, including the highly respected Juvenile Protective Association, the Illinois Supreme Court upheld the murder conviction. Lattimore's prosecution in adult court became a landmark case in the turbulent history of the Cook County Juvenile Court. Although she was eligible for parole after eight years, the parole board denied Lattimore's release three times. Despite her youth, she was forced to serve her full sentence.[44]

"WHORES AND THIEVES
OF THE WORST KIND"

A Collective Profile of Female Prisoners,
1890–1960

I n 1941 Anne Hinrichsen reflected that in her years of contact
with Joliet Women's Prison, "I saw not more than eight or ten women of definite criminal type." These few "intelligent, cold blooded, scheming women"
included the "abortionists, the panderers, some of the confidence game
workers, two or three cold blooded murderesses" and "one young and very
silly 'gun moll' [armed robber]." Overall, Hinrichsen contended, female convicts were simply "stupid, friendless, penniless creatures, victims of circumstances rather than their own criminality." She argued:

> An appallingly large number of women had been drab creatures of the street and
> the low class disorderly resorts, arrested many times, fined, held in jails, sent back
> to their usual environments and occupations, arrested again, taken through the
> courts, until finally the exasperated officials were able to find them guilty, techni-
> cally, of a legal felony, and sent them to prison because they were public nuisances.[1]

These were the women whom police chose to arrest, prosecutors selected
to prosecute, juries decided to convict, and judges sentenced to the penitentiary. Many, she said, did not understand why they were imprisoned, confid-

ing in her that "'I only did what all the other people I know did. If you do what everybody else does what's so wrong about it, except that we weren't smart enough to get money and influential friends?'"[2]

Taking Hinrichsen's anecdotal evidence as its starting point, this chapter offers a collective portrait of female prisoners, examining such variables as class, race, ethnicity, nativity, age, marital status, motherhood, education, occupation, and age of leaving home. Table 5 summarizes the results of this collective profile. To supplement and provide a larger context for the limited historical sources, I occasionally draw upon findings from more current studies in criminology. Feminist theories help to illuminate the many ways in which certain groups of women have been and continue to be discriminated against in their dealings with the criminal justice system.

Since the 1930s, social scientists have sought to analyze the degree to which the legal process is affected by the social characteristics of offenders. The vast majority of these "disposition" studies have dealt with the effects of race and class on the treatment of male defendants. A far smaller body of research compares the treatment of male and female offenders. Mainstream criminologists traditionally have held that women received preferential, more lenient treatment by the criminal justice system. During the 1970s feminist criminologists began challenging this "chivalry" or "paternalism" hypothesis. Moheb Ghali and Meda Chesney-Lind point out that many early studies failed to use comparable populations or introduce adequate controls. For example, they did not take into account differences in prior criminal record or in the severity of the offense. When such controls are introduced, Ghali and Chesney-Lind contend, "much of the advantage enjoyed by women tended to dissipate" and, in the end, "virtually identical percentages of men and women received penitentiary sentences."[3]

Other researchers continue to accept the chivalry hypothesis, but only with significant qualifications. Joanne Belknap points out that chivalrous treatment is highly discriminatory; that is, it is only extended to "certain kinds of females, according to their race, class, age, sexual orientation, demeanor, and adherence to 'proper' gender roles." A number of recent studies, although not all, suggest that African American, poor, and younger women are treated more harshly by criminal justice authorities. The studies "confirm that being married, caring for dependent children, and being a homemaker increases a woman's chance of chivalrous sanctioning." Thus, to the extent that chivalry exists, it is primarily extended to middle-class white women and then only when they conform to traditional gender stereotypes.[4]

In some situations female offenders are treated more harshly than comparable male offenders. Some researchers have uncovered evidence to support a powerful "evil-woman effect." They argue that women accused of more "manly" crimes, particularly violent crimes, are sanctioned even more harshly than men, as well as more severely than women charged with more traditional offenses. Ilene Nagel and John Hagan contend that "female defendants will be sanctioned not only for their offenses, but also for their inappropriate sex role behavior." They posit that the theory of the evil-woman effect is not the opposite of the chivalry theory, but its corollary.

Table 5

COMPOSITE PROFILE OF FEMALE FELONS, BY RACE, 1860–1889, 1890–1929, AND 1930–1950

	1860–1889		1890–1929		1930–1950	
	White	Black	White	Black	White	Black
Total Number	348	75	524	397	449	258
Total Percentage[a]	82%	18%	57%	43%	64%	36%
Foreign-Born	55%	0	19%[b]	2%[c]	9%	0
Born in Illinois	13%	24%	43%	20%	58%	16%
MARITAL STATUS						
Married	56%	49%	64%	42%	50%	48%
Widowed	4	3	11	15	12	16
Divorced or Separated	1	1	12	10	27	17
Never Married	39	47	13	33	11	19
MATERNAL STATUS						
No Children	49%	70%	43%	60%	47%	59%
Average # of Children	2.4	1.8	2.1	1.2	2.4	1.6
4 or more Children	19%	n.a.	17%	3%	18%	7%
FAMILY BACKGROUND						
No Parents Living	45%	40%	32%	37%	34%	37%
Both Parents Living	28	31	32	22	33	29
Mother Living Only	16	25	22	30	20	20
Father Living Only	11	4	14	11	13	14
Left Home by Age16	56%	60%	45%	50%	39%	47%
Left Home by Age 18	86	89	68	75	67	71
EDUCATION						
None/Very Limited	18%	34%	13%	23%	5%	11%
3rd–8th Grade	72	66	73	71	52	59
Some High School	0	0	11	4	38	26
Some College or Business/Trade School	0	0	3	2	5	4

Table 5, cont.

	1860–1889		1890–1929		1930–1950	
	White	Black	White	Black	White	Black
OCCUPATION						
Domestic Service	62%	73%	52%	69%	21%	38%
Seamstress/Dressmaker	11	1	6	3	2	4
Cook/Laundress	4	5	4	12	4	10
Sales/Waitress	1	3	6	3	14	10
Factory	0	1	3	1	12	11
Office/Clerk/Secretary	0	0	7	0	13	3
Nurse/Midwife/Doctor	4	2	5	1	3	1
AGE						
Average Age	30.0	22.2	30.8	26.3	31.9	30.0
19 or under	16%	37%	14%	16%	12%	9%
20–29	42	55	41	61	39	46
30–39	25	5	28	19	25	28
40–49	11	3	13	3	17	12
50+	5	0	5	2	8	4

Source: Joliet convict registers and Dwight inmate jackets, Illinois State Archives. (Chester registers do not include race.) Does not include misdemeanor cases from Dwight.

Note: Periodization roughly corresponds with the existance of different women's units and institutions. Complete data is not available after 1950, because only some inmate jackets were preserved (see appendix A). All data is self-reported. Professional staff at the Dwight reformatory made a concerted effort to verify women's marital status, education, vocational background, and other information, but they did not always succeed. Nor were staff members' corrections necessarily made on the outside of the inmates' jackets.

[a] Calculated on the basis of only those cases for which race was given or could be determined (see Table 7).

[b] National origin of foreign-born white women: 35% Germany, 17%, Eastern Europe, 13% Canada, 8% England, 7% Scandinavia, 7% Ireland, and 13% other western European nations.

[c] National origin of foreign-born African-American women: 86% Canadian, 14% Caribbean.

Favored groups of women receive chivalrous treatment in certain situations as long as they commit less serious crimes and exhibit "appropriate" gender role behaviors. When defendants fail to adhere to traditional expectations, "the woman is moved into the evil woman category and preferential treatment ceases."[5]

The debate over whether women currently receive or have historically received chivalrous or preferential treatment within the criminal justice system remains unresolved. The findings of this study clearly support the theory of selective chivalry. Those whose cases crowded the court dockets and who filled the jails and prisons were overwhelmingly poor, minority, and otherwise marginalized women, many of whom failed to adhere to traditional standards of proper femininity. Because the women were already branded as immoral, disreputable, and deviant, judges experienced fewer ideological contradictions over sentencing them to prison.

Class, Employment, and Education

Regardless of their race or ethnicity, virtually all female convicts were poor or working-class. Half gave their occupation as housekeeper, domestic servant, or maid. Although their employment options expanded during the 1940s and 1950s, most female convicts continued to exhibit a history of unskilled labor: during those decades 22 percent gave domestic work, 20 percent factory work, 18 percent waitressing, and 4 percent cooking as their occupation. Only 10 percent responded "wife," "housewife," or "none." Likewise, although the educational background of female convicts improved over time, their level still fell substantially below that of the state's general female population. Even as late as 1950, one-half (51%) of female convicts had gone no further than eighth grade.[6]

Class stereotypes exacerbated the harsh treatment poor women received. Anne Worrall concludes:

> Respectable, middle-class wives and mothers are assumed to be so sensitive that they will be reformed by a minimum of punishment (or no punishment at all). Working-class women are perceived to be tougher (more like men) and therefore need to be treated more harshly if any impression is to be made on them, on the grounds that punishment is the only thing "people like that" understand.[7]

Working-class women are further disadvantaged by both their lack of financial resources (to hire a competent lawyer) and by the fact that their employment outside the home violates traditional gender norms. Recent research suggests that working women receive harsher sanctions than do homemakers, perhaps because authorities do not regard them as primary caretakers or good mothers.[8]

Ethnicity

In 1913 Anna Ostroska, a recent Polish immigrant, was convicted of a murder in which she played, at most, a negligible role. Characterized as an "immoral woman," Ostroska had freely engaged in the "elicit [sic] selling of intoxicants." During a drunken argument for which she had supplied the liquor, a boarder in her house shot and killed another man. Witnesses provided conflicting testimony. Some claimed that Ostroska had encouraged the shooting, yelling "Shoot him!" Others testified that she had shouted just the opposite: "Don't shoot him!" Despite the contradictory evidence, a jury convicted her of first-degree murder and sentenced her to fourteen years in prison. In a pardon petition presented four years later the prosecuting attorney condemned this sentence as "entirely unjust." Noting that "public feeling [had been] very high at that time," he explained that "the applicant is an uneducated, illiterate woman, of peasant stock. She had only been in this

Table 6

PERCENT FOREIGN-BORN: COMPARISON OF ILLINOIS STATE
POPULATION, MALE FELONS, AND FEMALE FELONS, 1850–1970

	State Population	White Prisoners		White Female Prisoners			
	Foreign-born Male & Female	Foreign-born Male	Female	% Irish	% German	% Western European	% Eastern European
1850s	15	45	74	55	0	19	0
1860s	19	29	63	47	6	10	0
1870s	20	24	52	31	7	4	0
1880s	24	20	45	8	19	17	1
1890s	24	18	26	2	9	14	1
1900s	20	15	21	2	9	9	1
1910s	20	17	19	3	8	2	6
1920s	19	8	12	0	1	9	2
1930s	14	2	10	0	2	1	5
1940s	11	2	8	0	1	2	3
1950s	8	n.a.	2	0	0	2	0
1960s	6	n.a.	0	0	0	0	0

Note: The proportion of foreign-born females in the state population was typically 1% less than that of males. Foreign-born percentage for the state's general population represents an average from the census data for the decade. Thus, the figure of 15% foreign-born in the 1850s was derived by averaging the percentages from 1850 and 1860.

Source: Alton and Joliet convict tegisters and the Dwight inmate jackets (felony only). Data on male prisoners from 1850 to 1920 are combined averages derived from tables in the published biennial reports of Alton, Joliet, Chester, and Pontiac penitentiaries. Data for 1920–1942 compiled from the Illinois Department of Public Welfare, *Annual Report of the Statistician.* Percentage of foreign-born in the state population calculated from *U.S. Census Reports,* 1850–1970.

country a short time; was not familiar with its laws or civilization." Recognizing the injustice, the governor promptly commuted her sentence.[9]

After class, race and ethnicity continue to be among the most potent predictors of an individual's treatment within the criminal justice system. As table 6 indicates, for most of the nineteenth century, foreign-born women were vastly overrepresented among female prisoners. During the 1890s, however, their percentage fell, reaching virtual parity with the percentage of foreign-born women in the state's general population. The most dramatic decline occurred among Irish women. This decline coincided with the unprecedented rise of the Irish in Chicago's social and political life. As early as the 1860s, the Irish held one-quarter of all public and political jobs, including one-third of Chicago police officer positions. Although the Irish faced lingering nativist prejudices throughout the late nineteenth century, they suffered far less discrimination within the criminal justice system.

Germans were the only other European ethnic group to be greatly overrepresented; the brief peak in their numbers in the 1880s (at 19% of white women) corresponded with their large-scale migration into Illinois. Skilled and highly literate, the Germans quickly achieved relative economic success. Despite popular prejudices and fears, Eastern European women never made up a disproportionate share of the female convict population; their proportion peaked at only 6 percent during the 1910s. Thus, the ethnic prejudices reflected in Ostraska's case represented an exception to the norm. After 1920 female prisoners were less likely to be foreign born than women in the state's general population. This may be attributed, in part, to the aging of the immigrant population. Restrictive new laws curtailed immigration after 1921, and few Europeans arrived during the Great Depression and World War II. More important, as members of European ethnic groups assimilated into and were increasingly embraced by American society, they were less likely to suffer institutionalized discrimination in their interactions with the criminal justice system.

Race

As the proportion of foreign-born women declined, the proportion of African American women increased, doubling from 17 percent in the 1880s to 42 percent in the 1890s, although their percentage of the state's female population remained constant at 1.5 percent (table 7). Definitions of proper femininity have always been intimately connected with constructions of race. Almost by definition, African American women were not regarded as "proper Victorian ladies." When not romanticized as the devoted "Black Mammy," African American women were widely portrayed as more violent, aggressive, dominating, promiscuous, and immoral than their white counterparts. Under the influence of such racist ideology, African American women were easily made to fit the popular image of female criminals as more masculine than "normal" females. Joanne Belknap posits that "crime-processing decisions are often based on stereotypes that Anglo women are more feminine, fragile, and deserving of protection than women of color." At the same time, criminologist Diane K. Lewis points out, African American women often adopt gender role behaviors "which contradict acceptable feminine behavior, as defined by the dominant society."[10]

Illinois's racial patterns reflected both regional and national trends. In 1880, 29 percent of the female convicts in Midwestern prisons were African American. By the time of the 1904 prison census their percentage had increased to nearly one-half (48%). It then fell to 22 percent by 1923. This decline, however, is deceptive. It reflected the rise of the women's reformatory prison, which was designed for young, predominantly white, misdemeanor offenders, rather than a decrease in the absolute number of black women in state prisons. In 1923 African American women continued to represent two-thirds (65%) of the population of the nation's state penitentiaries, whereas they were only 12 percent of those incarcerated in the new women's reformatories.[11]

Similar to national statistics, after 1920 African American women's percentage of the female prison population in Illinois fell slightly and stabi-

Table 7

PERCENT AFRICAN AMERICAN: COMPARISON OF ILLINOIS STATE
POPULATION, FEMALE FELONS, AND MALE FELONS, 1850–1970

	Population		Prisoners	
	Illinois	Chicago	Female	Male
1850s	0.6%	1.0%	2%	2%
1860s	0.4	1.1	15	7
1870s	1.1	1.2	12	10
1880s	1.5	1.2	17	12
1890s	1.5	1.6	42	17
1900s	1.8	2.0	48	20
1910s	2.4	3.1	44	21
1920s	3.6	5.5	36	20
1930s	4.6	7.6	36	19
1940s	6.2	8.7	36	32
1950s	8.9	13.8	66	42
1960s	11.6	16.0	70	46

Note: Before 1895 the convict registers did not provide a space for race. Instead, "negress," "colored," or "mulatto" was typically designated under "complexion," a category that did not appear at all on the Chester registers. The percentage of cases in which race was omitted or could not be determined is as follows: 1850s, 19%; 1860s, 14%; 1870s, 25%; 1880s, 33%; 1890s, 7%; 1900s, 0%. Thus, the percentage of African-American female felons is most likely underestimated for the nineteenth century. After 1895 the convict registers included a space designated "color," which was always completed.

Source: Data on female felons compiled from the Alton and Joliet convict registers for 1850 to 1930; Dwight inmate jackets for 1930 to 1963; and annual statistical reports (unpublished) for 1963 to 1970. Chester cases were omitted because race was not indicated. Data on male prisoners is from the published biennial reports of Alton, Joliet, Chester, and Pontiac penitentiaries and annual reports of the DPW and DPS. Percentages of African Americans in the Illinois population are decade averages calculated from U.S. Census Reports, 1850–1970. Statistics for Chicago from 1850 to 1930 are from Allen H. Spear, Black Chicago: The Making of a Negro Ghetto, 1890–1920 (Chicago, University of Chicago Press, 1967). Chicago statistics for 1930 to 1970 are my calculations from U.S. Census Reports.

lized at 36 percent through 1954. This decline reflected an increasing number of white female convicts, rather than a decrease in the absolute number of black women's commitments, which remained unchanged. With the emergence of "liberated woman" in the 1920s, Illinois judges more readily sentenced white women to prison even when they had only served as accomplices or accessories. Chicago judge Marcus Kavanaugh blamed "women's liberation" and women's increasingly aggressive "entry into the wider world" for "continually enlarge[ing] the number of women criminals." Like many, Judge Kavanaugh believed that women's right to vote, won in 1920, had dangerously eroded traditional gender roles, distinctions, and privileges. At the same time the 1930 opening of the "gender appropriate" Illinois State Reformatory for Women, which could house roughly 250 women, encouraged and facilitated the greater incarceration of white women. Indeed, white women made up 85 percent of the nearly one thousand women committed for misdemeanors during the 1930s.[12]

White women were being sentenced to the penitentiary in growing numbers at a time when the public was becoming ever more fascinated with female criminality. During the decade of Prohibition newspapers entertained the public with sensational accounts of a purportedly modern breed of female offender. The woman bootlegger, "gun moll" (armed robber), forger, and murderess provided new images of dangerous, calculating, and cold-blooded female criminality. In the popular imagination this exotic new creature played an increasingly dominant role in the criminal underworld. She was no longer simply a low-level shoplifter, a "sneak thief," a check forger, or a woman who passively received stolen goods procured by a conniving boyfriend or husband. Instead, female criminals were portrayed in the news accounts of the 1920s and 1930s as full participants in male gangs and as cold-blooded and remorseless leaders who carried their own weapons, drove getaway cars in major felonies, and used their fatal attractions to lure innocent and unsuspecting men who were then robbed, assaulted, and occasionally even murdered. These new images tapped societal fears generated by the advent of women's voting rights, a loosening of traditional sexual mores, and the rise of the "liberated woman."[13]

In the 1920s, for the first time since Maggie Tiller's conviction in 1895, Illinois judges began sentencing women to death. Five of the six so sentenced were white women. The first five were spared through a retrial or a highly publicized last-minute commutation. However, in 1938 Governor Henry Horner "overcame his scruples" and allowed Marie Porter's execution to proceed. Porter, a white woman, had induced her lover to kill her brother on his wedding day to prevent his insurance from going to his new wife. Even the judge who imposed Porter's death sentence expected that "her life would be spared," given Governor Horner's previous commutations as well as public uneasiness over executing women. On the eve of her death, Porter remained equally confident, yet this time Horner failed to intervene. The newspapers had breathlessly followed the many delays, temporary stays, and ultimate last-minute reprieves of the three women sentenced to death in 1935, 1936, and 1937, speculating on when the state would execute its first woman, but most recoiled after Marie Porter's execution was actually carried out. Despite several horrific murder cases over the next few years, no other woman in Illinois was sentenced to death until the 1980s.[14]

Nativity

Even though the prison population's patterns of race and ethnicity shifted dramatically over time, incarcerated women were always far more likely to have been born outside of Illinois than women in the state's general population. Women's pardon petitions are replete with references describing them as strangers in a strange land. Newcomers faced both greater police surveillance and less community tolerance for possible legal transgressions. Because of their transient status and because they could not easily be traced through local family ties or community connections, newcomers were arrested on the least signs of suspicion. Police feared that if they waited to gather evidence, they risked losing such suspects. Officials were also more willing to deal informally with offenses committed by local women. When local women were convicted, officials were more likely to offer them probation.

Minority women who were recent migrants to the state were especially vulnerable. In 1922 the Chicago Commission on Race Relations reported, "Being unknown to the police, there is concerning them [African Americans] naturally a greater suspicion than would attach to the white [person] who had lived for a greater length of time in the same district." Between 1890 and 1950, 80 percent of African American women incarcerated in Illinois prisons, in contrast to roughly one-half of their white counterparts, had been born out of state. They were thus doubly burdened, facing a pariah status as both suspect outsiders and racial outcasts.[15]

Marital Status

The degree to which female prisoners conformed to accepted ideals of proper womanhood can be partially assessed by examining their status as wives and mothers. Recent studies suggest that courts are less likely to sentence women "who are in stable marriages and who have relatively 'normal' lifestyles." Unmarried women, detached from male authority, occupy a suspect status. Imprisoned women were far more likely to be single—unmarried, separated, divorced, or widowed—than women of comparable age in the state's general population. In 1890 over one-half of white female convicts reported that they were married, but their marriage rate was twenty percentage points lower than that of women of comparable age in the state population. African American female inmates, who were younger on average, were even less likely to report being married.[16]

Yet these self-reported answers must be viewed with caution. Women often responded that they were married even though evidence hints that their marital ties were weak or non-existent. When asked to provide a reference, only 16 percent gave their husband's name (most gave their mother's or a sister's). Five percent admitted that they did not know if their husband was still alive or answered that he was living in another state or country, making their claims to married status tenuous. Another 3 to 5 percent had husbands who were in prison or jail. In addition, many of the women's "marriages" were common-law relationships that did not meet middle-class standards of respectability and that were denigrated by local officials and parole board members. Although board members begrudgingly acknowledged that common-law marriages were "quite common among the colored people in Chicago and other places," they often lectured white women on the immorality of such relationships and sought assurances that they would legally marry in the future. Any hints of adulterous relationships seriously prejudiced police, prosecutors, judges, and juries against female offenders.

In other significant ways the marital patterns of incarcerated women differed from those of their nonincarcerated peers. Between 1890 and 1930 female prisoners were over ten times more likely to be separated or divorced (averaging 11%) and four times more likely to be widowed (averaging 13%) than were women of comparable age in the state's general population. Lacking the traditional male provider, separated, divorced, and widowed women all bore the burden of financially supporting themselves and their children. Their greater economic hardship may have tempted some into prostitution, theft, check forgery, and other crimes. However, the fact that separated and divorced women were more disproportionately incarcerated than widowed women suggests that social, rather than purely economic, factors played a critical role. Widowed women may have received more community support in their economic distress, while divorced and separated women faced greater social ostracism and opprobrium. Thus, widows who committed crimes out of financial need may have been treated more leniently by criminal justice authorities because widowhood did not defy conventionality to the same degree that separation or divorce did. These disparities increased over time. During the 1930–1970 period the percentage of incarcerated women who were widows remained stable while that of women who were divorced and separated tripled. Overall divorced and separated women averaged one-quarter (24%) of female felons and one-third (31%) of misdemeanants, far beyond their proportion in the state's general female population.

Motherhood, Family Ties, and Age

Many women who were convicted failed to fulfill their designated social roles as mothers. Slightly less than half reported that they had children, and those who had children averaged only one or two. Illinois judges, fully cognizant of the cost counties bore when they were left to care for dependent children, showed great reluctance in sentencing women with large families. Indeed, until the 1980s children were considered a valid mitigating factor in sentencing decisions. One state's attorney offered this revealing explanation of his decision to prosecute a white woman for minor check forging: "She had no children living and no one dependent upon her." As this statement suggests, dependents could also provide an excuse for economically motivated crimes.[17]

In their pardon letters one-fifth of female petitioners appealed to maternal responsibilities, as did many of their supporters. Yet this plea was rarely effective by itself. On average, from 1860 to 1930 white women with children served only slightly shorter sentences than those without for many crimes (although not all). Nevertheless, these differences typically translated into only one to three months. There was no such difference between African American women who did have children and those who did not. Thus, even though motherhood influenced whether a local prosecutor chose to prosecute or a judge chose to sentence a woman to the penitentiary in the first place, appeals to maternal responsibilities and maternal emotions carried little weight in the calculations of governors and parole board members, who may have regarded the petitioners' criminality as "prima facie evidence of their inadequacy as mothers."[18]

Just as their marital ties were weak or nonexistent, female convicts had few family connections or resources to draw upon in their dealings with the local criminal justice system. Nearly one-half (47%) had left home before the age of sixteen and 71 percent had left by the age of eighteen (table 5). Many may have been orphaned. At the time of their incarceration, one-third reported no living parents and another third claimed only one parent, almost twice as likely to be a mother as a father (23% versus 13%). Their widowed mothers may have been unable to support them economically. At the same time, their lack of a father meant that they were bereft of a patriarchal figure who might have been able to intervene more successfully, forcefully, or knowledgeably in a situation of trouble with the law.

Disproportionately orphaned, unmarried, and childless, convicted white women were further disadvantaged by their relatively advanced ages. Few offenders were youthful. Between 1860 and 1950 white women's average age remained remarkably stable at 30–32 years. Before 1930 imprisoned African American women were, on average, significantly younger. Although this corresponded with the younger age distribution of adult black women in Illinois's general population, it also reflected the fact that the justice system treated young, white women with greater deference and leniency, shielding them from incarceration until they reached "middle age" and had earned well-established reputations as immoral or improper women. After 1930, the ages of white and African American women prisoners equalized at roughly thirty-one years. Indeed, judges were slightly more likely to sentence white teenage girls than black teenage girls to the Illinois State Reformatory for Women during the 1930s and 1940s, suggesting that initially they viewed the new institution as a benign, treatment-oriented setting appropriate for young white women in need of moral guidance and rehabilitation.[19]

Respectability, Reputation, Prior Criminal Record, and Associates

Assessments of a women's respectability, reputation, and moral character were central in determining how authorities handled female lawbreakers at every stage of the criminal justice process. From 1890 to 1930 nearly one-fifth (18.5%) of female convicts possessed previous criminal records. The majority had spent time in local jails or houses of correction, often on such misdemeanor charges as public drunkenness, disorderly conduct, prostitution, or petit larceny. Roughly 6.5 percent had served previous penitentiary sentences, either in Illinois or in another state. After 1930 the proportion of imprisoned women with at least one prior arrest nearly tripled, from 23 percent in the 1920s to 60 percent in the 1940s.

The lack of an official prior record could be misleading. Local officials frequently referred to female convicts as "known police characters" even if they had previously escaped formal arrest, prosecution, or conviction. Indeed, sometimes it was a woman's poor reputation, rather than any real evidence, that convicted her. According to one local sheriff Gertrude Vilmar had been a "petty offender for a number of years" and had been "implicated in various affairs [although] there was never enough evidence for conviction." The state's attorney admitted "there was a real question of her actual part in the present theft. . . . The feeling was that she was probably innocent of this particular thing but that she really deserved her sentence because of all her other activities." Similarly, a state's attorney reported in 1929 that Margaret Williams "has caused the police of Peoria endless trouble and has been arrested at least twenty-five times,"

Table 8

FEMALE PRISONERS: PRIOR COMMITMENTS AND PERCENT WITH
HUSBAND OR ACCOMPLICES IN PRISON, 1880–1930

	Prior Commitments by Type of Institution			Associates in Prison	
	Prison	Jail	Juvenile	Husband	Accomplices
1880s	9.1	7	0	n.a.	23%
1890s	6.6	17	0	8%	29
1900s	8.7	22	1	7	26
1910s	6.7	19	2	3	28
1920s	3.9	16	4	3	27

Source: Joliet convict registers, Illinois State Archives. Comparable statistics are not available after 1930. Note: These statistics can easily be challenged. Local officials may have been unaware of all prior arrests and convictions, especially for migrant or immigrant women.

although always for misdemeanor offenses. He admitted that her latest conviction for assault represented "the first time we have been successfully able to prosecute her on a penitentiary offense." Likewise, in 1931 a parole board chairman admonished Leona Andrews, who was sentenced in southern Illinois for chicken stealing: "Down there they say you have been a source of trouble to them for about fifteen years, always getting into difficulty."[20]

Female convicts' poor reputations were further compromised by those of their families, husbands, and friends. According to one state's attorney, Violet Marks's family had been "a thorn in the side of law-enforcing officials" for the past twenty years. Two of her sisters were prostitutes and her brothers were repeatedly in and out of jail. Marks left her first husband without divorcing him and became the common-law wife of another man, a situation that the parole board found "particularly reprehensible" given that she was a white woman. No one found grounds for leniency after Marks fractured her common-law husband's skull with a ketchup bottle during a drunken argument. The unsavory reputations of women's associates further incriminated female offenders in the eyes of local authorities. In 1896 one prison clerk bluntly characterized a female prisoner and her accomplices as "whores and thieves of the worst kind." One-quarter of female convicts were sentenced with an accomplice. Police, prosecutors, judges, and juries expressed less sympathy for women who acted in concert with others; such partnerships suggested more calculated, organized, or ongoing criminal activity. One might also speculate whether lesbians, particularly those who fit popular stereotypes of "manly" women, were also more vulnerable to being sentenced to prison.[21]

Any hints of interracial relationships further compromised the reputation of a white woman, and the race of women's accomplices and victims was routinely noted. Mattie Philips's associates were denigrated as "low negroes and white trash." In 1899 Nancy Blakney and another white woman "robbed a man of $30 while he was drunk." The prison clerk characterized her "general reputation" as "bad as could be" because she "has had one or two negro babies." In 1947 a prison psychiatrist noted that Mary Krienert "had many affairs with colored men." Similarly, a prison sociologist explained that Verdna Germaine, convicted of several minor check forgeries in 1956, was "considered in her community as being a bad woman and a thief and crook. . . . She stepped out on all her husbands and mistreated her child." Even more damning, he noted, "she has been known to associate with colored people."[22]

• • •

Despite the fanfare that surrounded the opening of Joliet Women's Prison in 1896, relatively few women were ever incarcerated there. As graph 1 disclosed, the number of women sentenced to prison rarely exceeded twenty annually (or one hundred per five-year period). Indeed, between 1880 and 1925 the number of female commitments remained remarkably stable despite a doubling of the state population. However, twice during the nineteenth century these numbers rose dramatically (1860–1869 and 1895–1899), but each peak was followed by an equally sharp decline. The 1860s increase coincided with the opening of the one-hundred-cell women's building at Joliet, which replaced the six female cells at Alton. The second crest coincided with the establishment of the separate Joliet Women's Prison, indicating that judges were more disposed to sentence women when they believed that adequate quarters existed for them. The rapid declines after both periods suggest that state officials quickly became disillusioned, viewing the new facilities as inadequate or inappropriate for all but the most hardened or vicious of women.

Indeed, even at its height in 1899, Joliet Women's Prison was not more than three-quarters full. African American inmates, popularly regarded as the most vicious and most depraved, represented two-thirds of the daily population. After 1900 Joliet's female population averaged only fifty, half of the Women's Prison's one-hundred-bed capacity. Not until 1928 did the facility first reach capacity. In contrast, male prisons were virtually always filled to overcrowding within a few years of their opening, regardless of how many new prisons a state constructed.

Nicole Hahn Rafter uncovered a similar pattern in her study of female imprisonment in New York state. By the early 1900s New York had established three women's reformatories and one state prison. While the reformatories were quickly overcrowded, the New York State Prison for Women at Auburn, like Joliet Women's Prison, was rarely more than half full. Rafter surmises that New York judges "felt Auburn was an unsuitable place of commitment for all but the most hardened women." She hypothesizes that

> Judges avoided sending women to this institution. When they did sentence prisoners to Auburn, they apparently made their decision partly on the basis of characteristics associated with the stereotype of the female offender as hard and masculine. This is a stereotype that Auburn women might well have seemed to fulfill: serious offenders with long sentences, they were relatively mature and often either foreign-born or non-white. They were, in short, women who probably seemed incapable of resocialization to meet middle-class standards of womanliness.[23]

Such "middle-class standards of womanliness" similarly governed the selection of women sentenced in Illinois. Despite the opening of the separate Joliet Women's Prison in 1896, its ongoing association with the male penitentiary, along with its traditional, custodial architectural design, meant that state officials continued to view a sentence to this new facility as an inappropriate punishment for most women.

• • •

The next chapter returns to the chronological narrative, exploring daily life at Joliet Women's Prison between 1896 and 1919 within the context of shifting social constructions of female criminality. As these last three chapters have made clear, discretion and discrimination play critical roles in processing individuals through the various levels of the criminal justice system. For every woman who was sentenced to prison for a theft, robbery, assault, burglary, murder, or other transgression, at least another dozen, if not another hundred, women committed identical acts under similar circumstances, but they were not prosecuted for their actions, or if they were, they did not receive a penitentiary sentence. In and of themselves, few crimes were heinous enough to demand state intervention or necessitate a penal response. Women—and men—in Illinois often did get away with murder, and they got away with larceny, robbery, forgery, assault, and many other crimes—but the state needed to punish *some* women (and a larger number of men) and hold them accountable for their actions. These few female convicts provided an example that women were neither completely above the law nor completely beyond the power of the state to punish.

Not every woman was as equally vulnerable to becoming such a living example of the rule of law. Those whom officials selected for prosecution and punishment were typically the most socially and economically marginal. The majority were unskilled and poorly educated working-class women. Before 1930 most worked as maids or servants. They were disproportionately drawn from the ranks of minority, immigrant, and migrant women, and few evidenced long-standing community ties or deep familial roots. Fewer than a third had been born in Illinois.

In other significant ways incarcerated women failed to conform to conventional notions of proper femininity. They were ten times more likely to be divorced or separated than women in the state's general population. Fewer than half reported that they had children. Many were already branded as immoral and disreputable women. One-fifth had served prior jail or prison sentences. As one parole board chairman stated in reference to a minor offender who "did not make a very favorable impression" upon the board, "Her life has been an improper one." This moralistic assessment encapsulated the attitudes of authorities toward most female offenders. Whatever the nature of their legal transgressions, it was others' estimates of their character, and particularly their sexual reputation and community standing, that often determined their fate within the criminal justice system.[24]

PART III

DOING TIME AT JOLIET WOMEN'S PRISON,

1896–1933

CHAPTER EIGHT

"DEFECTIVE DEGENERATES" VERSUS "THESE POOR UNFORTUNATES"

Managing Female Felons and Delinquent Girls, 1896–1919

On Saturday, November 21, 1896, the doors of Joliet Women's Prison were thrown open to the public in a "grand house warming." A local reporter observed, "A great deal of praise was heard for the bright and cheerful aspect of the whole building. . . . Even the cells, with their clean, white walls illumined with a bright incandescent light, the comfortable little cot and the tiny dresser, looked inviting." Extra trolleys were on hand so that thousands of townspeople could tour the facility. A *Chicago Tribune* reporter concluded that the new female prison "represents the most healthful and the most humane method yet devised for the detention of criminal women" and characterized the institution as "the best appointed women's prison in America." Given the deplorable conditions most female convicts endured at the turn of the century, this claim may represent only a slight exaggeration.[1]

Despite all the media coverage devoted to the prison's opening, the press paid almost no attention to the female convicts themselves. Economy rather than reformation was the sole focus of the public's concern. Journalists stressed only the magnificence of the building, lavishly praising the warden for his "ingenuity and business sagacity" in constructing "such a massive structure within the appropriation and time given him." Nor were there signs of a rehabilitative or reformatory ideology. Notwithstanding the fact that Chicago stood at the center of most national reform movements during the late nineteenth century, no organizations—religious, charitable, or women's—came forward to champion the plight of the state's female felons. As in most states, male wardens, not outside reformers, had led the campaign for a separate women's unit.[2]

This chapter traces the history of Joliet Women's Prison from its founding in 1896 to its transformation into an independent facility in 1919. During this quarter century the prison was managed as a subunit of the men's penitentiary, with the male warden in charge of both divisions. Housing over one hundred women at its height in the late 1920s, Joliet Women's Prison was one of the nation's largest women's penal institutions, clearly typifying the model of a custodial prison. Unlike the women's reformatory prisons, which were constructed according to a cottage-style architectural design intended to foster family-type relationships and instill in women a desire for a home of their own, Joliet Women's Prison resembled a typical fortress-style men's penitentiary.

Through World War I most of the nation's female convicts did their time in custodial units either within or attached to state penitentiaries for males. Despite their heavily fortified and immutable appearance, custodial women's prisons were far from monolithic or static. Beginning in 1914 at Joliet, a new generation of college-educated professional women began introducing reformatory methods based on an ideology of domesticity and proper femininity. New superintendents expressed far more positive attitudes toward their charges than had their nineteenth-century counterparts. At the same time, there emerged in Illinois a rabid eugenics discourse that branded female offenders as "defective degenerates" whose irrepressible tendencies toward criminality and immorality were inscribed in their very genes. Vocally denouncing their charges as incorrigible, officials at the nearby Illinois State Training School for Delinquent and Dependent Girls at Geneva, the state's female reform school, repeatedly warned the public that such girls represented a grave social menace. Staff at Geneva openly advocated forced sterilization and permanent institutionalization to prevent their charges from becoming "the feeble-minded mothers of a very undesirable grade of population."[3]

Given the paucity of other sources, a comparison of the attitudes of Joliet and Geneva officials will be used to illuminate conditions at the Joliet Women's Prison during the early nineteenth century. Such a comparison also exposes the complex and contradictory nature of social attitudes toward female criminality. Neither professional nor popular ideology was ever monolithic. Even as some observers pointed to evidence of a dormant feminine sensibility that was only in need of a gentle awakening, others expressed horror, attributing the behaviors of incarcerated women and girls to their reputedly immutable and defective biology.

· · ·

From 1899 to 1913, Joliet penitentiary was governed by Warden Everett J. Murphy, a "typical, old-fashioned prison disciplinarian" who ruled with an "iron hand." Under his leadership Joliet developed a reputation as one of the toughest prisons in the United States. Women prisoners were governed by the same rules as the men; female matrons had no authority to develop their own programs. Although Murphy instituted some reforms by 1910, he "continued to be known as a reactionary." Progressive reformers campaigned vigorously for his removal.[4]

Upon entering, few female convicts would have considered Joliet Women's Prison inviting. Located directly across the street from the men's penitentiary, the women's unit was a miniature replica of its male parent institution. Constructed of the same massive blocks of yellow limestone, its facade, with its rounded turrets, small barred windows, and ornate trim, resembled a medieval castle. The women's cell house was an imposing, two-hundred-foot-long, three-story unit extending out from the central administration building in a *T* formation. The central area housed the business office, visiting room, rudimentary hospital, and staff dining room, along with living quarters for the chief matron and her assistant matrons, who also lived at the institution. Like its male counterpart, the entire structure was enclosed by an enormous stone wall twenty-eight feet high and six feet thick (see photograph, p. 83).

Large and imposing, the prison, with its heavily barred windows, steel doors, high wall, and fortress-style architecture, offered prisoners a constant reminder of their status. Although matrons took pains to refer to the women's cell block as a dormitory, security was the overriding concern. Cell windows were securely barred, and as one reporter noted, throughout the building "every stairway . . . is carefully shut off by iron gratings so that escape is practically impossible." Referring to her first impression, one female convict told the parole board, "I quit [my criminal career] when I saw this place." True to her vow, and despite several previous arrests for forgery, this woman never returned to prison. Also included in the original design were special punishment cells where recalcitrant female prisoners, like disruptive men, could be handcuffed to the bars and forced to stand for twelve-hour intervals.[5]

Despite the women's unit's foreboding appearance, throughout its first two decades its physical and sanitary conditions received nothing but praise, while the men's institution was vocally condemned. Between 1892 and 1905 nearly five hundred male inmates died at Joliet, two-thirds from tuberculosis. The penitentiary's own commissioners declared it "a violation of health to keep men there." Although the General Assembly appropriated funds for a third state penitentiary in 1908, Stateville, located only two miles from the Joliet penitentiary, did not officially open until 1925. Thus, male prisoners at Joliet experienced little improvement in their physical living conditions for several decades. And after Stateville opened, it was quickly filled to capacity. The "Old Prison" at Joliet continued in use.[6]

In comparison, Joliet Women's Prison appeared a model of comfort, health, and sanitation. The women's cells were twice as large as the men's, and each was provided with its own sink and toilet, amenities not installed in the men's cells until the 1950s. Moreover, unlike the men's "internal" cells, the women's one hundred cells, fifty to a floor, were located along the outer walls of their cell house. As a result, each had its own window, individual exhaust fan, hot-air duct, and electric light. And because the population of the women's unit averaged only fifty prisoners, every woman had her own cell.

Regardless of these many advantages, life in the new women's prison remained harsh and austere. The female convicts worked nine-hour days, six days a week. As Maggie Tiller wrote a friend in 1899, "I don't know of anything more to write, only lots of work and plenty of sickness here now." Half the women were assigned to heavy industrial labor in a "modern" steam laundry that took up the entire first floor of their cell house. Commercial laundry work was among the most arduous and exhausting of the industrial occupations open to women at the turn of the century. Laundresses stood all day operating mangles, huge machines with revolving heated cylinders, or starching tables with large ironing machines that spewed out jets of hot gas. The noise, heat, and odors penetrated the entire building and were a constant source of complaint. In the 1920s superintendents claimed that the female prisoners washed and ironed 500,000 pieces of laundry per month, nearly all for the male convicts. In the prison's official bookkeeping the women's laundry work was calculated as an exchange for the electricity, heat, and water that the women's unit received "free" from the men's penitentiary. The female convicts' labor was also contracted for the weaving of rattan-cane-chair seats, a tiresome and exacting job.[7]

"You know that one day in the penitentiary is like a month" one woman wrote wistfully in 1907. The only programs or special activities were religious. On Sundays the women now enjoyed regular services in their own "chapel room," after which they were locked in their cells for the entire day in order to afford matrons their day off. Once a month the local Will County Women's Christian Temperance Union (WCTU) conducted special services. The WCTU was the only women's group to express sustained interest in the plight of female felons. In 1906 the prison chaplain noted that the "Christian Temperance women have been interested in this work for about 30 years, and they always send some Christmas remembrance to the women in the prison."[8]

As the penitentiary commissioners had fully intended, the women now lived "entirely separate and apart" from the male convicts. Never again did officials complain about the "pernicious influence" of female prisoners on male inmate discipline. Yet even as many women delighted in the spaciousness and privacy afforded by their new facility and the protection it provided from sexual harassment and abuse, others regretted that they now had few opportunities for communication with their male counterparts, some of whom were their husbands, boyfriends, and accomplices. Nevertheless, hurried communiqués could still be passed through male trustees who transported the laundry, performed repair work, maintained the grounds, and continued to deliver all food and water from the men's prison.

Kate Richards O'Hare, a socialist antiwar activist incarcerated at the women's unit of the Missouri State Penitentiary in 1919, described the severe punishments that female prisoners risked in order to relay messages to their incarcerated husbands and boyfriends. With a note of condescension she explained that "communication between the inmates of the men's and women's departments is more frightfully and fiendishly punished here than any other thing, yet . . . both men and women will run risks that make my blood run cold, to send their tragically pathetic little love notes over the walls." Likewise, illicit communication between male and female prisoners was never entirely cut off at Joliet. In 1926 one visitor observed a woman confined to her cell as punishment for "flirting with the men in the hospital 'on the other side'" despite the fact that "two stone walls and a thoroughfare intervene."[9]

. . .

For an unprecedented twenty-six years, from 1888 to 1914, the venerable Maria S. Madden, unmarried sister-in-law to the previous warden, Robert Wilson McClaughry, held the position of chief matron. The first and only published account of life at the women's prison during this era comes from an interview with Madden on the eve of her retirement. Claiming that the institution was "more like a boarding school than a prison," the elderly Madden downplayed its obviously penal character. She was pleased to note that "in every room one will see the *woman's touch* in the shape of decorations of various kinds." Speaking sympathetically of the women under her care, Madden concluded with an appeal to their friends and family to "help me in my work of reformation" by "writing letters and visiting [the prisoner] regularly during her years of sorrow." No evidence exists to indicate how the female convicts viewed Madden or her elderly, all-white staff. The "neatness and good order" for which Madden was praised in the 1890s appears to have been maintained under a light hand. Of the nearly five hundred women committed during her tenure, fewer than two dozen (4.4%) ever suffered an official loss of good time.[10]

Little more can be gleaned about life at the women's prison during its first two decades. No separate biennial reports were published; nor did officials ever author specific statements of program, policy, or philosophy. However, in their few public interviews chief matrons Maria Madden (1888–1914) and Grace Fuller (1914–1921) and superintendent Elinor Rulien (1921–1929) all adopted a benevolent rhetoric, repeatedly characterizing their charges as "these poor unfortunates." Each was convinced that female convicts could be reformed through a regime of domesticity and proper moral guidance.

This belief stands in marked contrast to the eugenics discourse that was widespread among other Illinois reformers and prison administrators. In each of her biennial reports, Ophelia L. Amigh, founder of the Illinois State Training School for Delinquent and Dependent Girls at Geneva, and its superintendent from 1895 to 1911, offered rabid comments about the purportedly incorrigible and perverted nature of her young charges. In 1902 the elderly Amigh warned, "No one can realize what a great danger threatens us. . . . If only these delinquent and degenerate classes could be kept under proper surveillance during their entire lives." Fearing that the state would be bankrupted from the cost of "keeping the breath of life in a class of people who are simply consumers and not producers, except as far as production of a very undesirable grade of population is concerned," she proposed a law enabling authorities to "place and keep under supervision during the childbearing age all feeble-minded girls of this and every other school of this kind."[11]

Notwithstanding the Geneva inmates' youth and the minor nature of their offenses, in 1914 Geneva physician Dr. Olga Bridgman despaired that "work with these girls has often been deeply discouraging." Most were "already old offenders before coming to the school." Like Amigh, Bridgman railed, "the moral and mental defects which these girls show are being considered more and more as permanent and incurable." Concealing a punitive approach within a rhetoric of treatment and care, she concluded:

> These girls are not criminals whom a sentence in a reformatory and a little training will reform. . . . What they need is protective and friendly detention in some institution other than a reformatory for a period far longer than the gravity of their offenses would warrant, where they can be properly supervised and their anti-social tendencies be held permanently in abeyance.[12]

In a 1918 article revealingly titled "Plea for an Early Commitment to Correctional Institutions of Delinquent Children," Dr. Esther Stone, another Geneva staff physician, expressed even more pessimistic views, arguing that sixteen "is far beyond an age when any institution can hope to correct habits and ideas formed" for so many years." Stone was deeply disturbed by nearly all aspects of the girls' behaviors. Outside investigators were equally appalled by the girls' open defiance of sexual and moral norms and were outraged by their refusal to exhibit any sorrow or remorse for their actions. Dr. Stone concluded that the only solution was to "cull out these defectives from the rest of society at a very early age" and "prohibit procreation." Only in this way "will defectives eventually be eliminated, to a great extent, from the population."[13]

Bridgman, Stone, and others championed eugenics as "the hope of modern civilization." Convinced that human behaviors such as criminality, promiscuity, immorality, alcoholism, and insanity were biologically determined and racially based, eugenicists sought to improve the hereditary qualities of human populations through selective breeding and the sterilization of groups they deemed biologically inferior or otherwise unfit. Historian Frank Dikotter argues that "eugenics was a fundamental aspect of some of the most important cultural and social movements of the twentieth century." Eugenics was not a set of fringe beliefs advocated by a few extremists; rather, it was "widely seen to be a morally acceptable and scientifically viable way of improving human heredity." Its tenets were espoused by intellectuals and social reformers "from one end of the political spectrum to the other." Eugenicists depicted female offenders as sexually promiscuous breeders of future generations of delinquents and imbeciles, elevating such women to the status of "social menace." As Nicole Hahn Rafter has observed, "The old imagery of the bad woman thus underwent considerable modification and embellishment in the Social Darwinist family studies. They showed her promiscuity to be a matter far more serious than mere personal immorality: the loose woman became a prolific breeder of harlots and a criminal type in her own right."[14]

At first glance it may appear paradoxical that staff at Geneva branded the young girls committed there as beyond salvation, whereas Joliet's chief matrons portrayed older female felons committed for more serious offenses as redeemable. The contradiction can be explained, in part, by the differing pressures placed upon staff at the two institutions. As Nicole Hahn Rafter has perceptively argued, it was administrators at the nation's fledgling reformatories, both women's and girls', not at the traditional custodial penitentiaries, who "took the lead in detecting degenerates." Rafter observes that "rehabilitative institutions are keenly aware of their failures, whereas merely punitive or custodial institutions have no reason to distinguish between reformable and incorrigible inmates." Reformatory superintendents "unable to admit institutional failure . . . pinned the blame on unruly inmates." With far higher expectations of success, as well as a far greater need to justify and prove the value of their highly touted disciplinary and rehabilitative regimes, reformatory personnel quickly turned to a mixture of genetic, biological, and psychological explanations to account for their charges' seeming failures to conform.[15]

By the 1910s the nation's leading female reformatory advocates were already expressing negative assessments of the rehabilitative potential of the women under their care. Their views were widely publicized in Illinois. Voicing sentiments identical to those of Ophelia Amigh, Dr. Katherine Bement Davis, superintendent of the model New York State Reformatory for Women at Bedford Hills, argued in a speech before Chicago's women's groups, "Personally I believe that every woman criminal is a mental defective. Girls do not 'go wrong,' do not steal or commit murder for the pleasure of it. Find the reason back of the sin . . . and in nine cases out of ten you will find it the outgrowth of a mind diseased." Whereas in her earlier writings Davis had stressed the environmental and social causes of such "diseased minds," by the 1910s she emphasized their biological and hereditary roots.[16]

Study after study purported to reveal that criminal women were genetically and mentally inferior. Mabel Ruth Fernald, Mary Hayes, and Almena Dawley concluded in their influential 1920 work, *A Study of Women Delinquents in New York State*, that half of incarcerated women had "defective strains": they were carriers of genes for such social ills as criminality, alcoholism, feeble-mindedness, insanity, neuroticism, sexual irregularities, and other forms of degeneracy. The magazine of the Illinois State Board of Charities, *Institution Quarterly*, regularly promoted the findings of local and national research that emphasized feeble-mindedness and other forms of mental and physical degeneracy as the major cause of criminality. The publication's authors expressed little faith in the capacity of offenders, whether juvenile or adult, male or female, to reform. Into the 1920s and 1930s, *Welfare Magazine*, a successor journal published by the Illinois Department of Public Welfare (DPW), contained frequent articles advocating compulsory sterilization and the "permanent segregation" of criminals as well as of the mentally and physically handicapped. Conveniently construing women's and girls' resistance to reformatory regimes as indicative of a constitutional incapacity to reform, administrators and reformers rarely questioned their own concepts of rehabilitation, morality, or proper femininity, or their understanding of the economic, social, or cultural constraints that affected their charges' lives and constricted opportunities after their release.[17]

Given this widely reported and accepted eugenics discourse, the fact that none of the female matrons or superintendents at Joliet Women's Prison ever offered similarly rabid denunciations is revealing. Indeed, their silence on this topic, coupled with their frequent characterization of female prisoners as "these poor unfortunates," suggests that they harbored more positive assessments. While it is possible that their benign rhetoric cloaked far harsher or even brutal practices, no accusations of abuse, excessive discipline, or corporal punishment were ever raised against staff at Joliet Women's Prison, whereas Geneva superintendent Ophelia Amigh weathered several scandals and was finally forced to resign. A 1911 investigation by the State Board of Administration revealed that Geneva staff frequently flogged the girls with heavy rawhide whips "well-laid on, in such a way as to constitute unnecessary, excessive and cruel punishment." Although Amigh claimed that corporal punishment was justified in light of the girls' intractable, unrepentant, and depraved natures, the board condemned such whippings as "unnecessary, excessive and cruel punishment." Nevertheless, Amigh's views, if not her methods, remained deeply entrenched. Through the mid-1920s Geneva superintendents and staff continued to write disparagingly about the possibility of reforming wayward girls.[18]

. . .

In another paradoxical contrast, at the same time that eugenics ideology was gaining in popularity, a new generation of male prison officials in Illinois expressed high hopes for the reformation of their male charges. They offered a range of creative proposals for the rehabilitation of male offenders, including minimum-security prison farms, institutions for male misdemeanants, cottage and dormitory living units, public works programs, and unwalled "farm colonies." In 1913 progressive Edward F. Dunne was elected governor of Illinois. He immediately acted to fulfill his promises of prison reform by appointing Edmund M. Allen warden at Joliet, replacing the conservative Murphy. Allen, a champion of progressive penology, immediately inaugurated dramatic changes at the institution.[19]

Male prisoners occupied the main focus of Warden Allen's ambitious reform agenda, but Allen did not completely neglect the female convicts. In 1913 he hired a nurse to provide full-time medical care and classes in nutrition and hygiene. On May 1, 1914 the indomitable matron Maria S. Madden, then aged seventy-three, resigned, two weeks before her death. Two other long-term employees, both "far advanced in years," also retired. Frances Cowley, the young nurse, was elevated to acting matron. Throughout her brief tenure, Cowley voiced highly sympathetic attitudes, characterizing female convicts as victims more than victimizers. Concluding that "men, more than anything else, cause women to be imprisoned in penal institutions," Cowley blamed men for "ensnaring women in their evil deeds and deserting them unprotected" and "turning state's evidence to clear themselves." Although this discourse likened offending women to children who had no agency of their own, it acknowledged women's many social and legal disadvantages. Moreover, unlike eugenics proponents, Cowley attributed women's criminality solely to environmental and social factors.[20]

Despite Cowley's progressive attitudes, she was not appointed chief matron. Instead, on August 18, 1914 Warden Allen announced that he was selecting educator Grace Fuller, a "lifelong friend of both warden and Mrs. Allen," as Joliet's new head matron (see photograph, p. 85). The local press hailed Fuller as "one of the three best known domestic science instructors in the United States." For the previous nine years she had held the positions of dean of women and head of the household arts department at the Michigan State Normal College, where she was extremely popular. Yearbook students lauded her as "genial," "wise," and "efficient."[21]

Grace Fuller's acceptance of the position reflected her genuine commitment to prison reform, entailing as it did a two-thirds reduction from her previous salary. Fuller represented a new generation of college-educated professional women who began entering "prison work" after the turn of the century. Unlike earlier generations of widowed or unmarried matrons who were typically relatives of wardens or other prison officials, these women viewed prison work as a calling and themselves as part of a nationwide movement for moral uplift and social reform. Most were attracted to the new reformatory women's prisons. However, Fuller came to Joliet with the expectation of introducing a reformatory regime based on domesticity, vocational education, and "wholesome" physical training. As one reporter noted, "Her earnestness is too apparent to be denied." Only two days after her arrival Fuller laid out an ambitious domestic science program that included classes in sewing, baking, dressmaking, and "first class laundry work." Her goal was to "make each of the women self-supporting when she leaves." Fuller claimed that her primary goal was to "make our work educational"—unlike the previous job assignments at the women's prison. Henceforth, profitability to the institution would be a "secondary consideration."[22]

Fuller immediately installed eight sets of kitchen cabinets and eight miniature gas stoves in the space that had served as the women's cane-seat factory. Under the headline "Convicts to Cooks: Matron to Instruct," the *Joliet Evening Herald* described her first cooking class. Fuller quizzed the eight carefully selected students, all dressed in maid's outfits, on scientific kitchen measurement: "How many teaspoons in a tablespoon? Tablespoons in a standard cup? Cups of butter to the pound? Cups of flour?" Fuller failed to recognize that few convicts could look forward to a middle-class home of their own. Nor did she realize that most female prisoners viewed domestic work as the most demanding, demeaning, and least desirable occupation open to them.[23]

Despite her very middle-class perceptions, Fuller initiated a number of tangible improvements. Stressing the importance of "wholesome exercise," she increased outdoor recreation from twice a week to two hours daily and began a three-acre garden. Gardening was a popular work assignment, and the vegetables that were grown and later canned greatly improved the women's diet. Fuller also expanded the inmate-taught literacy program that Cowley had begun. In 1920 she persuaded Episcopalian "parish workers" to offer grade-school-level classes two evenings a week. It was the first real education program in the unit's history. The local Episcopalian church also donated 450 books to start a library.[24]

Notwithstanding her generally sympathetic attitudes, Fuller's views toward her African American charges must have been patronizing at best. Although she never made overt references to race in her official reports, Fuller's racial attitudes are unmistakably revealed in a children's book she wrote shortly after leaving Joliet. In *Too-Loo Byrd: The Story of a Little Negro Waif,* Fuller created an appallingly condescending tale about an orphaned African American boy. The story's underlying theme is the problem of finding servants who were "good," i.e., docile, subservient, and efficient. Fuller portrays all of her African American characters as fawning, ignorant, and self-deprecating, totally devoted to serving white people. One can only speculate about the extent to which these racist attitudes informed her domestic science classes and her interactions with the African American women under her care.[25]

After six years in office Fuller firmly retained her commitment to domestic science. In 1920 she reported, "We plan to have every woman made competent in each branch of work carried on in the institution, sewing, cooking, serving, washing, ironing, and housework." There is no evidence, however, that Fuller or the superintendents who followed her maintained her formal program of domestic science classes, which may have imposed too much of a burden given the superintendents' many responsibilities and limited personnel. Despite her enthusiasm and ambitious reform agenda, Fuller also failed in another of her major goals. In 1914 she had boldly declared, "I come to Joliet to fulfill a life wish. For twenty years I have wanted to go into this work. I expect the backing of every woman in the state." Claiming that Chicago women reformers such as Jane Addams, Ellen Flagg Young, and Bertha McCormick were all "patronesses of the movement," Fuller contended that she would have the advice "of prominent students in sociology both in Chicago and New York." As it turned out, Fuller never succeeded in involving Chicago's women leaders, reformers, or criminologists in her work. She may have simply lacked the time to develop these connections. Joliet was forty miles from Chicago. With the outbreak of World War I, Joliet's poor reputation, and a large number of worthy causes and pressing social problems closer to home, female reformers never offered the support, volunteer services, or outreach Fuller had optimistically envisioned.[26]

Yet even as they remained oblivious to the needs of the female convicts at Joliet, Chicago's women's groups spent the decade of the 1910s lobbying for a wide variety of criminal justice reforms that affected far larger groups of female offenders. They monitored and provided services for the thousands of women convicted of prostitution in Chicago's new Morals Court (established in 1913), crusaded against the white slave trade, campaigned for female police matrons and a women's central house of detention, raised funds for new buildings at the Geneva girl's reformatory, agitated for the establishment of "farm colonies" for "feeble-minded" and delinquent women and girls, and lobbied for an ill-conceived state "sanitarium" where female misdemeanants could be incarcerated and "treated." This last project sowed the seeds for a statewide campaign for a woman's reformatory in the 1920s. All of these efforts provided Chicago club women invaluable firsthand experience with the city's police stations, courts, and jails, generating the knowledge, skills, and ideology that would inform their decade-long reformatory campaign.

• • •

Between 1915 and 1919 Joliet Women's Prison all but disappeared from the historical record, events there subsumed in the turmoil at the institution during the World War I years. In an incident that has never been satisfactorily explained, two years after Warden Allen's appointment his wife was murdered by a prisoner. Allen resigned shortly thereafter and his penal experiments were abruptly halted. Two interim wardens were appointed who were unable to maintain order. The war caused acute shortages of personnel and scarcity of food and supplies at all state institutions. In June 1917 the first major riot broke out in the Joliet penitentiary's history. There is no indication of any disturbances at the women's unit. Although the riot coincided with a series of prison uprisings that swept the nation during World War I, the press quickly pinned the blame on the unprecedented freedoms granted under Allen's administration. More perceptive observers noted that the riot reflected widespread prisoner dissatisfaction with the arbitrary and corrupt policies of the parole board. In 1917 the conservative Warden Everett J. Murphy was brought back to Joliet to reestablish control; he remained there until his death in 1922. Murphy immediately shut down the prison newspaper, restricted all outside communication, and adopted a closed-door policy toward the press.[27]

On July 1, 1917, a month after the riot, control of the state's penal, reformatory, and charitable institutions was centralized under the newly established Illinois Department of Public Welfare. In assessing the department's new acquisitions, DPW director Charles Thorne concluded that the women's prison was "a failure, being lost in the larger [men's] unit." He recommended that the state establish a new institution that would combine the characteristics of a woman's prison and a woman's reformatory. Such an institution "could handle the forty women now in the prison and the larger number who could properly be sent to a reformatory but not to a prison." Thus, despite Grace Fuller's ambitious reform agenda, state officials continued to perceive Joliet Women's Prison as an inappropriate placement for all but the most hardened female offenders. The DPW's first step was simply to rescue the women's prison from its administrative subordination. On July 1, 1919, the unit was renamed the Illinois Women's Prison and declared an autonomous institution, fully independent of the male penitentiary.[28]

Fuller served under the new title of superintendent until 1921, when she was summarily dismissed after the election of a new Republican governor. While patronage and party politics played the greatest role in her dismissal, five escapes also undermined public confidence in her abilities. On June 28, 1920, three women absconded in the first escape in the institution's history. Fuller scoffed at the press's theory that the escape was a carefully planned event involving ties to the Chicago underworld. Admitting that "perhaps we were a little careless because we never dreamed of anyone escaping from the woman's prison," she refused to condemn or disparage the escapees. She stated impatiently to one reporter: "It isn't news. . . . Who cares to read about these poor unfortunate girls? They aren't just exactly 'right' you know, or they wouldn't be here. Of course they have the cunning that such individuals have, but they are good girls and will make good citizens some day." Thus, even an incident that brought public scrutiny and embarrassment could not shake Fuller's warm tone or her fervent belief in the basic goodness of "these poor unfortunate girls."[29]

Authorities tracked down and returned two of the women within days, but the infamous Hazel Burmeister, called the "Chicago Underworld Queen," was not returned for five years despite a nationwide search. In 1921 two more women escaped, neither of whom was ever apprehended. The first was Cleo Hurtzman, whom the press dubbed the "Blond Tigress" or "Blonde Lure" for her role in enticing "over a score of men into the hands of a gang of men who robbed and beat them." Hurtzman and Burmeister exemplified the new image of calculating, cold-blooded, and uncontrollable female criminality that emerged during the 1920s. Three weeks later Pearl Jones, a young African American woman and a far less glamorous figure, also escaped. She was never apprehended either, but because she was a low-level pickpocket and petit larcenist, her escape generated less lurid coverage and fascination. Again Fuller candidly acknowledged the lack of security at the institution. Three months later, she was dismissed.[30]

• • •

Most of the recent historiography on women's prisons has focused on the predominantly Progressive Era women's reformatory prison. Despite the significance of the reformatory, it is important to emphasize that it was never fully representative of women's experiences of imprisonment. Through World War I the majority of female convicts did their time in traditional, custodial units either within or attached to their state's male penitentiaries. As late as 1927 California erected a traditional, one-hundred-cell women's unit directly outside the walls of San Quentin. Other states also continued to construct custodial units. Even in states that built reformatories, some women continued to be housed in their previous quarters within the male state penitentiaries. In 1933 thirty-four states still housed male and female convicts within the same prison. Reformers continued their vigorous but unsuccessful campaigns to remove women from male penitentiaries.[31]

Joliet Women's Prison clearly fit the model of a custodial women's prison, mirroring the male penitentiary in its architecture, management, and disciplinary regimes. Nonetheless, it provided a gendered space within the penitentiary where a new generation of female matrons attempted to develop rehabilitative programs based on an ideology of domesticity and proper femininity. Grace Fuller, brought to Joliet with much fanfare in 1914, maintained a humanistic philosophy throughout her tenure and continued her commitment to and belief in a reformatory approach. Fuller weathered whatever difficulties she may have encountered in her transition from dean of women at Michigan's Normal College to chief matron of a women's prison without losing her vision, her faith in the rehabilitative powers of domestic training, or her belief in the women's essential goodness.

During the same era, 1895 to 1921, superintendents and staff at the Illinois State Training School for Delinquent and Dependent Girls at Geneva embraced eugenic solutions, openly campaigning for compulsory sterilization and the permanent institutionalization of delinquent girls, whom they freely characterized as incorrigible, degenerate, and depraved. While the personalities of individual staff members influenced their reactions to and assessments of the women and girls under their care, the differing expectations that the public held for their institutions—reformatory versus custodial—generated competing and contradictory pressures. The public, the press, reformers, and state officials expected that the expensive and highly touted reformatories, with their younger and presumably more salvable populations, would and could succeed. In contrast, they continued to dismiss the more hardened female felons committed to male state penitentiaries as unworthy or incapable of reformation.

Yet ideological constructions of female criminality were never monolithic. Even as some reformers proposed eugenic solutions, others advocated regimes based on domesticity, convinced that a "homelike" environment could revive female offenders' feminine and maternal natures. Illinois offers an ironic twist on these national debates. Ophelia Amigh, superintendent of the girls' reformatory, did not believe reformation was possible. She and her staff embraced eugenics doctrines when the girls under their care refused to conform to their ideas of reformation. Grace Fuller, in charge of the state's custodial women's prison, implemented reformatory-style programs that she never stopped believing in.

At the same time, sharp differences of opinion often existed among institutional staff and between staff and inmates. At Joliet Women's Prison in the 1920s a handful of vocal matrons spoke out against Superintendent Elinor Rulien's (1921–1929) leniency and purported lack of discipline, pointing to reports of widespread intoxication and homosexuality among the inmates. In contrast, the female convicts portrayed Rulien as a compassionate, understanding, and forgiving administrator. The next chapter analyzes these conflicting sources to assess conditions at the Women's Prison in the 1920s, when the institution encountered its first public controversy.

CHAPTER NINE

"THE ROTTENEST HOLE IN THE WHOLE PRISON SYSTEM OF ILLINOIS"

Joliet Women's Prison in the 1920s

In 1887 Sarah M. Victor, who had been incarcerated at the Ohio State Penitentiary for nearly twenty years, commented on the significance of elections in prisoners' lives. "Those knowing nothing of prison life may wonder that election times should have any interest to the convict," she wrote, "but there are, probably, none, not even the candidates themselves, who feel greater anxiety over a change of administration in state matters than do those in prison bondage." A new governor "means a new warden and, usually, an almost complete change throughout."[1]

The Illinois prison system was no different from that of Ohio. By the 1920s Illinois's prisons were fully entrenched in the state's spoils system of political party patronage. Despite the passage of civil service legislation in 1911, guards and higher-level staff were regularly replaced following each gubernatorial election or change of warden. Thus, on September 20, 1921, after the election of a new Republican governor, Superintendent Grace Fuller was summarily dismissed. She was succeeded by a Joliet woman, C. Elinor Rulien, who served for eight years until she was similarly removed.

Elinor Rulien's administration from 1921 to 1929 left a highly contested legacy in the historical record. Although Sarah Victor observed that prisoners "are usually too wise to make their preferences known," Rulien's dismissal in 1929 evoked a strong statement of inmate support. Indeed, the very day her termination was announced, the women prisoners rioted in protest. It was the first sign of organized resistance in the history of the Women's Prison. Two weeks later the *Joliet Evening Herald-News* printed a lengthy farewell message signed by all 116 inmates. Presented by Virginia Foster, it began:

> We, the inmates of this division, offer you this momento [*sic*] as a token of our earnest regret at the hand fate has dealt us in removing you from our midst. . . . We wish to say that in losing you, we feel that we will have lost an interested friend, as well as a good, considerate official. Briefly, you have been a "good fellow" and a "square shooter." And we feel that . . . no one can do more for us than you have done. To us, you have been kindness personified.

Highlighting the inmates own frequent lapses in good behavior, as well as openly expressing their appreciation for Rulien's kindness, mercy, and fair judgment, Foster continued:

> We realize that many of us haven't always been what we should have been, and a few of us have been just impossible, and yet you, with your keen knowledge of human nature and fair judgment, have always shown us consideration, dealing with us mercifully when many times we deserved drastic punishment. Like a mother you forgave us time after time, seeing good even in the worst of us. Can we, in the face of such facts, feel otherwise than regret at your leaving? In many ways you have bettered conditions for us, always making our interest your own.[2]

Virginia Foster, the main author and instigator of this farewell letter, was greatly in need of the merciful treatment and continual forgiveness for which she praised Rulien. A young African American woman with a lengthy record of prior thefts, Foster was in repeated difficulty at Joliet for "fighting, refusing to obey orders and in other ways resisting disciplinary officers." By the time she read her farewell address, Foster had been demoted in grade several times. Indeed, she had only just concluded a term in solitary confinement for her participation in the recent "riot." The role of this highly troubled and troublesome prisoner in presenting the farewell speech suggests the genuinely high esteem in which prisoners placed Rulien.[3]

The public's assessment was far less positive. In 1926 a grand jury accused Rulien of gross mismanagement, corruption, and lack of discipline. Citing matrons' allegations concerning widespread homosexuality, drinking, and smoking among the female convicts, the grand jury blasted Rulien for her overly tolerant and permissive administration and concluded with calls for her immediate dismissal. Rulien weathered the 1926 investigation, but three years later she was fired. Her successor proved to be a far stricter disciplinarian. Meanwhile, a coalition of Illinois women's groups campaigned throughout the 1920s for an entirely new institution for female offenders.

To assess the validity of the grand jury's accusations this chapter weighs the accomplishments and failures of Rulien's administration; examines the tensions between matrons and their college-educated, professional supervisors;

and explores how allegations of inmate homosexuality prejudiced public perceptions. The last half of this chapter chronicles the events leading to the founding of the Illinois State Reformatory for Women at Dwight in 1930 and the closing of Joliet Women's Prison in June 1933. The chapter concludes with a brief comparison of the two institutions.

The 1920s were a pivotal era in female corrections in Illinois. The difficulties Superintendent Rulien confronted at Joliet Women's Prison foreshadowed those that would plague female superintendents over the next fifty years. Tensions over how to confront inmate homosexuality, conflicts between treatment and custodial staff, the problem of unqualified patronage appointees, and the increasing difficulty of maintaining discipline were recurring themes in the history of the Illinois State Reformatory for Women from 1930 to 1972.

• • •

Like Grace Fuller, Elinor Rulien was part of a new college-educated generation of professional women. An 1896 graduate of the University of Minnesota, Rulien was a high school principal before moving to Joliet in 1905 as the bride of a prominent doctor. Seven years later her husband died, leaving her with two children to support. The Women's Republican Club of Will County campaigned for her appointment, citing her role as "an active welfare worker and a prominent club woman." As superintendent, Rulien expressed the same concern with rehabilitative goals and the same faith in domestic ideology as had Grace Fuller. Reiterating the mantra, "reform rather than punishment is our aim," Rulien embraced a rehabilitative ideology rooted in domestic training. In every annual report she proclaimed: "Our first aim is to make good housewives and home-makers."[4]

By the 1920s, confidence in the rehabilitative powers of domestic regimes, championed by the nation's first generation of female reformatory advocates, had waned considerably. Although in Illinois this faith remained strong through the 1930s, high recidivism and parole violation rates presented a growing ideological and practical challenge. Rulien had reason to be concerned. The percentage of women who broke their parole had declined from 30 percent of all releases in the 1890s to 15 percent in the 1910s, but during the 1920s violation rates increased to 25 percent. While other female administrators responded with derogatory denunciations of their charges, often concluding that such women were constitutionally incapable of reform, Rulien maintained a compassionate tone in all her official pronouncements. Sensitive to the prejudices paroled convicts confronted, Rulien pointed out that "public opinion is not kind to a woman who has made a mistake and been convicted." Even women who were model prisoners "easily become lonely and discouraged."[5]

The experiences of paroled women bore out Rulien's argument. Many blamed the stigma of being an ex-convict for their return. Delores Sanders served one year with a perfect conduct record, but was returned as a parole violator less than six months after her release. She had been overwhelmed by the prejudices she confronted in her small town:

I went straight as long as I could but you know when you have a stepfather and you are told that you are an ex-convict, what's the use of trying to make good in a place like that? I am going to be perfectly frank with you. I don't really know why I did it [wrote bad checks], only from having so many slurs at me. . . . I went down in the country where everybody knew me. I was a fool but I have no excuse to make. It is all my fault.

Sanders concluded that she would rather be in prison than "go back as an ex-convict where everybody has known me since I was a young girl." Similarly, Harriet Westman, who was returned to prison after nine months for stealing a purse, also complained of the taunts she had received as an ex-convict. She explained to the parole board:

If I had a good job, I wouldn't mind it [parole]. But if you go home to your brother's and they treat you like that and keep saying "penitentiary," would you like that? If they did you like they done me and every time you get around people have them keep saying, "penitentiary"? You don't know how it is, Mr. Jones. . . . It's awful hard.

When Chairman Jones failed to offer any reassurances, Westman responded sarcastically, "Oh, I expect they will give me the electric chair when you get through talking."[6]

Women returned as parole violators found only modest changes at Joliet. The regime at the Women's Prison in the 1920s resembled that of the previous two decades. Each woman was expected to labor nine hours a day at one of five job assignments: laundry, sewing, institutional cooking, housekeeping, or gardening. Despite her best intentions, Rulien admitted that "the work done is for the most part routine household duties." The laundry continued to be the main industry, employing half of the women. Although Rulien could not lessen the odious nature of laundry work, she built upon several programs initiated by Grace Fuller. She introduced monthly motion pictures, installed a radio and speakers in the cell house, and doubled the size of the women's library to 1,000 volumes. She enlarged the vegetable garden and built a large chicken coop where two hundred chickens supplied fresh eggs. Sensitive to the lack of recreational opportunities, Rulien repeatedly called for the appointment of an "occupational therapy" staff person to plan a "proper program" of physical education. In 1928 a new director of prisons heeded her pleas and hired a full-time "Recreation Matron." Rulien also sought improvements in medical treatment, although she failed in her persistent efforts to secure a full-time nurse.[7]

Convinced that "ignorance" rather than heredity was a major cause of crime and delinquency, Rulien expanded the limited education program begun by Fuller, which consisted of two evening classes a week in basic literacy. In 1924 Catholic nuns began offering shorthand and bookkeeping for the "more advanced women." In every report Rulien repeated her "great hope" that a formal school program would be established in the near future. In August 1929, the month before Rulien's dismissal, a full-time college-educated teacher was finally hired. Three classrooms were constructed, annexed to the women's cell house. Two years later, on the eve of the institution's closing, half of the inmates were enrolled in compulsory half-day elementary classes. Yet Rulien can not be given full credit for this last improvement. The establishment of the women's school coincided with the reorganization and expansion of educational and recreational programs in all Illinois prisons. The extent to which these new programs reflected state authorities' genuine concern for the plight of female convicts is debatable. Between 1925 and 1930 the daily population of the Women's Prison nearly tripled, from 47 to 130, only half of whom could be gainfully employed. Nationwide prison officials increasingly turned to educational, vocational, and recreational programs to supplement labor as a central disciplinary tool and to occupy the time of otherwise idle inmates, both male and female.[8]

Throughout the 1920s as she labored to enhance the work, recreational, educational, and medical circumstances of her charges, Rulien also sought to improve their living conditions. She and her chief assistant matron lived at the Women's Prison and experienced firsthand the inadequate heating, poor plumbing, and general disrepair. The prison's location near a steel mill district, where factories spewed out huge quantities of soot and pollution, and next to the prison rock quarry, where frequent dynamite blasts scattered dust and debris, further contributed to the constant need for maintenance. Due to shortages of money and personnel, few repairs were made during the World War I years. During the 1920s Rulien regularly reported on various painting, cleaning, repair, and replastering projects.

Rulien's annual reports chronicled these many accomplishments, but omitted any reference to the chief controversy surrounding her administration. In May 1926 the entire Joliet-Stateville penitentiary system came under a grand jury investigation after an assistant warden was murdered and eight male prisoners escaped. Over a two-week period the grand jury called 110 witnesses, including the governor and ranking prison and Department of Public Welfare (DPW) officials. The grand jury's final report sharply criticized reform-minded warden John L. Whitman for his liberal policies, which were blamed for eighty-three escapes over the previous three years. Similar to several matrons at the Women's Prison, male guards complained bitterly that Whitman "failed to give them proper support to maintain discipline." The Women's Prison was not an initial focus of this investigation, but as Superintendent Rulien and several of her matrons were called to testify, bitter differences and divisions were exposed among the female staff in the course of the hearings. Concluding that "the same lack of discipline and cooperation exists in this institution as was found at the men's prison," the jury accused Rulien of gross mismanagement and demanded her resignation.[9]

The charges leveled against both Whitman and Rulien were hardly disinterested, impartial, or informed by expert knowledge. Grand jury investigations, conducted by ordinary citizens who have no special expertise, are notoriously unreliable. The 1926 inquiry fully reflected the prejudices regarding prison administration held by Joliet's citizens, many of whom were relatives, friends, or neighbors of prison guards. The grand jury's principal charges involved Rulien's purported lack of discipline and her condoning of female prisoners' "immoral" activities, including alcohol consumption, smoking, and "sex perversion." Citing "evidence given by the employees," the grand jury reported that in the previous month widespread intoxication among the women had resulted in "the discovery of fourteen gallons of fermented liquor made from fruits and juices which had been pilfered from the kitchen." Smoking was also purported to be a "common practice," although it was "strictly against the rules." (Male convicts had always been allowed to smoke and were even given a weekly tobacco ration.)

These sensational charges underscored a long-standing division at the prison between college-educated administrators, such as Rulien, and the patronage appointees under their supervision. The matrons' dissatisfaction emerged, in part, from the nature of their jobs. Matrons shared little of the prestige, power, or pay enjoyed by their supervisors. They were required to compel inmates to work; to monitor every detail of their daily lives; to subdue unruly, unbalanced, or hostile women; to censor inmates' language, mail, and visits; and to endure occasional threats, taunts, insubordination, and vulgar comments. On a day-to-day basis, prisoners were far more likely to vent their frustrations and hostilities on matrons than on higher-level staff. Whereas both Grace Fuller and Elinor Rulien repeatedly characterized the majority of female convicts as capable of becoming "good citizens some day," their assistant matrons expressed attitudes that were less generous and sympathetic.

Prison matrons were often equally reviled by their superiors. In the context of scientific, reform-oriented, progressive penology, matrons represented a throwback to an earlier era. After touring Joliet Women's Prison in 1926, Florence Monahan, nationally acclaimed superintendent of Minnesota's model State Reformatory for Women, observed: "In these old prisons the type of women secured for matrons are generally very ordinary and low grade. If politics enter into the appointments, they are apt to be the mothers, aunts, or sisters of the ward heelers [machine politicians]." Indeed, Monahan concluded, "Many times they are no higher type than the women in their charge."[10]

In 1931 Monahan became superintendent of the Illinois State Training School for Girls at Geneva. There she experienced firsthand the "ruthless game of playing chess with employees" that took place when the Democrats won the governorship in 1932 after sixteen years out of office. Political sponsors sent her a variety of "odd characters." These included "a lame woman who couldn't move around but sat and rocked all day," another who "was so afraid of the inmates she locked herself in her room," and a third who, fearing syphilis, "wrapped a handkerchief around her hand whenever she picked up articles touched by the girls." Although several new matrons proved to be "better than those they replaced," in the end it was all a gamble. Monahan resigned in despair only two years later. It is likely that superintendent Elinor Rulien had similar stories of equally "odd characters" whom she was forced to hire and was equally "powerless to dismiss."[11]

The grand jurors, rejecting Rulien's explanations regarding the incompetence of many matrons, concurred with the matrons' views. Calling for Rulien's immediate resignation, they demanded the appointment of a new superintendent "who would be able to gain the confidence and support of the employees, and restore order and discipline among the inmates." Another outside investigator, University of Chicago doctoral student Wiley B. Sanders, wholeheartedly agreed with one grand juror who "declared that the Women's Prison was the rottenest hole in the whole prison system of Illinois." However, Sanders admitted that both he and the grand jury had gained most of their information from three matrons "openly unfriendly" to the superintendent. Although he "saw no reason to doubt the truthfulness of their statements," both he and the grand jury ignored the views of nine other matrons, who were never called to testify.[12]

. . .

By far the most inflammatory accusation that the matrons hurled against Elinor Rulien involved the female convicts' allegedly flagrant homosexuality and Rulien's purportedly tolerant response. Horrified, the grand jurors reported:

> There was a wealth of evidence . . . to show that immoral practices between women inmates have become so common and open that it stands out as the most revolting and disgusting feature of this investigation. Proper precautions apparently were not taken to prevent those inmates who were so inclined from committing acts of immorality and perversion and to punish these offenders.[13]

Although the jurors admitted that homosexuality was equally rampant at the men's prison, along with gambling, insubordination, drinking, and sexual intercourse with female visitors, these abuses did not generate the same degree of outrage or horror as the allegations of Rulien's toleration of same-sex relationships at the women's unit. Since the turn of the century researchers had described homosexuality as a common practice in female prisons. For the public at large, lesbianism increasingly came to symbolize female prisoners' complete moral corruption and perverseness.[14]

The three hostile matrons claimed that Rulien was fully aware of and responsible for this situation but "merely reprimanded the guilty parties when they were caught" and failed to demote them in grade, which would have resulted in loss of privileges and, more importantly, good time. Rulien's purported leniency contrasted with the practices of staff at the Illinois State Training School for Girls, who shared these matrons' outrage. In 1918 Geneva physician Esther H. Stone recoiled in revulsion from girls' openly homosexual behaviors: "They form attachments for each other, sending love notes, messages, trinkets, etc., indulge in hugs and caresses, try to get into bed with each other. Nauseating love scenes, amounting to actual perversions, are common."[15]

The more abundant reports from the Illinois State Training School for Girls help illuminate the meaning of homosexuality within female inmate subcultures. Defiantly rejecting the staff's definitions of such conduct as "perverse," the "girls" spoke candidly to outside investigators about their sexual experimentation. Their accounts emphasized romance and heterosexual role-playing and challenged traditional gender roles and sexual identities. As one sixteen-year-old "sex delinquent" explained, "When I go to the cottage after I see a good movie I try to practice love-making on my girl sweetheart. We do all sorts of stuff. We act like William Haynes and Ramon Navarro and Joan Crawford, Anita Page, Janet Gaynor." In the 1920s and 1930s the term love-making encompassed a wide range of activities, from flirting and teasing to kissing and petting. Within girls' and women's institutions romantic same-sex relationships carried a variety of meanings and were expressed in many ways. Unfortunately, we know little about what same-sex relationships meant to the women at Joliet. The atmosphere of a girls' reform school and a women's prison may differ to a significant extent; the age, background, and heterosexual experiences of the adult population may create a different meaning for and experience of same-sex relationships within a women's prison. However, some of the women at Joliet had served earlier sentences at Geneva, and it is likely that important aspects of their experiences were similar.[16]

One sixteen-year-old girl was well aware that society regarded such behavior as perverse. Yet her fears failed to alter either her feelings or her behavior. "Movies here worry me," she explained, "for you haven't got one to make love to you. The girl next to you is all, and if you were to give her a kiss, put your arm around her, pinch her, or something, you wouldn't be counted decent." Even such relatively innocent activities were severely punished. If discovered, "we would be here three years or more before our papers would be passed to go out or 'put in punishment' for months." Yet despite her fears, she proclaimed, "If I can't kiss, make love, I don't want to live. Movies here get me all aroused, make me crave for love, romance, fine clothes, money, gay parties with plenty of drinking."[17]

Such romantic desires had to be either repressed or redirected: "All we can do here," the sixteen-year-old concluded, "is take some Negro girl behind the screen at the Chapel or somewhere else. Kiss them for all we are worth. That is all the thrill we get." Several other girls also connected forbidden sexuality with forbidden interracial relationships. Indeed, for many, sexual and racial taboos were intertwined. To staff, same-sex activities that crossed racial lines were especially threatening, as they increased the possibility of inmate resistance. At Geneva, the black and white girls were expressly forbidden to "mingle closely with each other." Occasionally they conspired together and openly flaunted this prohibition. Like many observers, staff physician Esther Stone singled out for special condemnation liaisons that crossed the color line. Staff employed popular stereotypes depicting African American women as the masculine "aggressors." Yet the white girls' own accounts reveal that they were fully active agents.[18]

Even as Geneva staff publicly denounced the lesbian activities of their charges, other female prison administrators, like Elinor Rulien, chose to ignore, deny, or tacitly tolerate such practices. Following the 1926 grand jury investigation, however, Joliet's prison psychiatrists increasingly included overt references to homosexuality in their reports. Their occasional comment that a prisoner "denies perverted sex activities," suggests that prison psychiatrists were beginning to openly question women about suspected lesbianism. Bertha Finnegan, the superintendent who succeeded Rulien, regularly disciplined prisoners for their indiscretions. In 1930 Virginia Foster, the rebellious inmate-author of Rulien's farewell speech, lost thirty days of good time for allegedly "sending a note of a homo-sexual character to Jane L., one of the most degenerate women in the Women's Prison." That same year Joanna Debroshky "had her privileges taken from her once for being too intimate with a girl, [but] otherwise has never been punished." Whereas Rulien had ignored such conduct, Finnegan forwarded these punishment reports to the parole board, which used them as a rationale for denying parole. Nonetheless, surveillance was sporadic and tacit acceptance remained the norm through the 1930s. After World War II, however, same-sex relationships came under far greater scrutiny at women's prisons across the nation. This scrutiny culminated in a veritable witch hunt at Dwight in the 1950s (discussed in chapters 13 and 14).[19]

• • •

Rulien weathered the 1926 investigation even though several senior male prison officials, including Warden Whitman, were immediately fired. The *Joliet Evening Herald-News* reported that at the time "strong pressure had been brought to bear upon Governor Emmerson by many local leaders to retain Mrs. Rulien." To defend herself against future attack, Rulien dutifully stressed her adherence to Joliet's "Progressive Merit System" in all of her subsequent annual reports. The system, inaugurated in 1920 by reform-minded Warden Whitman, divided prisoners into five grades: A, B, C, D, and E. Entering prisoners were assigned to grade "C" and worked their way up. Whereas previously prisoners had enjoyed an automatic right to a parole hearing after serving their minimum sentence, they were now required to have spent three months in grade A prior to their hearing. Good-time credits were also tied to grade level. Grade A prisoners earned ten days per month off of their sentence, while those in grade E forfeited ten days. In practice discipline remained flexible. Under Rulien, as under chief matrons Fuller and Madden before her, demotions in grade and loss of good time were used only as a last resort.[20]

Rulien's "leniency" may have represented, in part, an accommodation to rising inmate unrest. During the 1920s the parole board doubled time served for all categories of crimes and also returned twice as many parole violators to prison. Stricter release policies and longer sentences generated bitter opposition from male prisoners, contributing to the turmoil in 1926 as well as another major riot in 1931. In the 1920s a full 35 percent of female convicts were incarcerated for five years or more, in striking contrast to only 8 percent during the previous decade. As sentences lengthened the prisoner subculture deepened. Long-term women confronted the task of creating a bearable and meaningful existence, of transforming their environment into a home that could sustain them for many years. Some became more committed to establishing relationships with their fellow prisoners than to currying favor with prison officials.[21]

Although an unequivocal assessment of Rulien's administration remains elusive, such an objective evaluation was irrelevant to her demise. Despite "strong pressure" by many local leaders for her retention, Rulien was fired on September 12, 1929, following another gubernatorial election. The "riot" by the inmates on the day Rulien's dismissal was announced, along with their impassioned farewell letter, suggest that they genuinely appreciated her administration. In their eyes, Rulien's laxness in enforcing prison discipline was the result of a kind, forgiving, merciful, and fair temperament that they would sorely miss as her successor quickly sought to tighten discipline and remove customary privileges.

Bertha Finnegan, an active political supporter of the new governor who was credited with "bringing out the Will County Republican women's vote," was rewarded with the superintendency. Finnegan's was openly acknowledged to be a purely patronage-motivated political appointment. Unlike Fuller and Rulien, Finnegan lacked both a college education and a reform vision. On her first day in office the dour-faced former court reporter declared that she would "insist on discipline at all times" and would "rigorously enforce all prison rules." Her tone represented a sharp departure from Rulien's in her first statement to the press. Rather than emphasizing discipline, Rulien had expressed her fervent belief that "the principal points of good administration are justice, efficiency, and kindness. With those one can accomplish wonders."[22]

Over the next year, women were punished for minor offenses that previously had not been officially recorded. The comments of one prisoner provide a glimpse into the nature of prison discipline under Finnegan. Audrey Williams had served a term at a girl's school in Indianapolis followed by sentences at women's prisons in Ohio and Kentucky. She escaped three times from the Ohio reformatory and was twice accused of stealing money and clothing from matrons there. Yet despite her rebellious background, Williams proved a model prisoner at Joliet. She bragged to one parole board member, "I haven't a mark or solitary or nothing since I have been in here," and concluded, "If all the prisons I was in was like this I wouldn't be in here now, because they are so very strict here." More tellingly, in 1930, the summer after Finnegan took office, a second inmate riot broke out. The women's anger was sparked by Finnegan's revocation of traditional privileges, including their right to receive food packages from friends and family. Participants were severely punished. Finnegan also opposed the traditional practice of pardoning pregnant women. In 1931 she proudly reported that two women were returned to Joliet to complete their sentences after giving birth at a local hospital.[23]

Although Finnegan was a stricter disciplinarian than either Rulien or Fuller, by 1930 institutional control may have become more difficult to maintain. The prison population had more than doubled from a daily average of forty women between 1900 and 1926 to an average of eighty-five in 1929. The year after Finnegan took office it climbed to 120, resulting in double-celling for the first time in the prison's history. Finnegan, totally inexperienced in prison administration, had taken over at a time when the institution was undergoing rapid changes.

THE CAMPAIGN FOR A STATE WOMEN'S REFORMATORY

Even as the number of women's prison commitments in Illinois began to increase after 1925, it remained far below the national average. It was this "failure to convict" and concomitant "failure to provide disciplinary treatment and care" that most agitated Illinois's women reformers. Led by the newly established League of Women Voters, club women pursued their vision of a women's reformatory throughout the decade, despite opposition from state legislators, governors, and even the director of the DPW. The League, committed to nonpartisan electoral and lobbying efforts, offered a timely vehicle for mobilizing the coordinated statewide crusade for a new women's prison that local women's groups had been unprepared to undertake. As a new organization with no established agenda, the League could devote its full resources to this campaign.[24]

League members and their affiliates never expressed any interest in the rehabilitation of Joliet's female felons. Instead, they focused exclusively on the "care and treatment" of female misdemeanants, the young women who had been appearing by the thousands before the Chicago Morals Court on repeated charges of immorality, prostitution, disorderly conduct, and petit larceny. The widely heralded Morals Court, founded in 1913, had quickly proven a dismal failure. Instead of being provided with privacy, specialized services, treatment, and care, convicted women were simply fined and released, only to appear in court again weeks or months later on the same charges. Compared to other major cities, Chicago was arresting far more women, mostly on prostitution and morality-related charges, but was convicting and committing far fewer.[25]

Reformatory advocates were convinced that with "modern" and "scientific" methods of diagnosis, classification, and individualized treatment, one third of female delinquents could be "cured." In contrast to earlier generations of female prison reformers, Illinois's club women rejected the language of sisterhood, domesticity, and moral uplift in favor of a "scientific" approach to studying, classifying, and—when deemed possible—correcting the moral, intellectual, educational, and vocational defects exhibited by female offenders.[26]

In the eyes of the club women, the "essential defect" of Joliet Women's Prison was that it "failed to provide for modern-day standards of individualized treatment" that "recognized women offenders as individuals with potentialities for good or evil, with aptitudes which intelligent direction might turn into skills, with desires which could be developed into regeneration." Instead, "regimentation was the rule." According to Anne Hinrichsen, Joliet Women's Prison "might have been a medieval fortress or an ancient castle." For all prisoners, "there was one form of existence . . . and to that form they must be adapted. The half-witted girl, the hardened panderers . . . the cheap prostitute from the street, the psycho-paths, the neurotics, the sick, the well were forced into the same mould [sic]."[27]

Although Illinois club women employed a rhetoric stressing that wayward and misdemeanant women were deserving of specialized "care and treatment," they held equally punitive views. Most women convicted of misdemeanors possessed long records of minor offenses, most commonly prostitution, vagrancy, disorderly conduct, and public drunkenness. Many had already proven resistant to and even openly hostile toward the voluntary social services offered by women's groups in Chicago courts during the 1910s. In a typical campaign article, Charlotte S. Butler, a prominent reformatory-movement leader, described these women as "anti-social members of the community who are unwilling or unable to conform to the laws governing our state." Why, she asked, should taxpayers shoulder the cost of repeated arrests and court appearances for "individuals who are mentally incapable of or morally averse to adjustment"? Butler proposed that instead of giving female misdemeanants short jail sentences, officials should undertake careful scientific study and psychiatric classification in order to

> discover where the cause of maladjustment lies—whether or not these cases are psychopathic or the result of environment—in short, whether or not the expense to the taxpayer might not be materially reduced by the classification of such individuals before trial and by providing suitable institutions to which they may be committed for custodial care or for rehabilitation.[28]

In other words, if psychiatric diagnosis suggested that an offender could not be reformed, Butler advocated permanent institutionalization, what she called "custodial care."

In 1919 club women won passage of a law authorizing the establishment of a vaguely defined "state sanitarium for women," but the state legislature subsequently refused to fund it. Over the next several years, reformatory advocates made sporadic efforts to revive the act. In 1925 Mary McDowell, Commissioner of Public Welfare for the City of Chicago, called a meeting of various women's groups to form a Joint Committee on the Care and Training of Women Offenders. The committee brought together representatives of the League of Women Voters, Chicago women's clubs, and social service agencies. Spearheaded by Jessie Binford, executive director of the Juvenile Protective Association, the committee adopted two objectives: the first was the establishment of a Central House of Detention for women arrested in Chicago and the second was the establishment of a "farm colony" for female misdemeanants.[29]

Committee members immediately set upon a full agenda of work. Within a week they had sent questionnaires to all counties requesting information on the number of women arrested annually, the charges against them, final court dispositions, and any other statistics available on the arrestees' "physical condition, nationality, education, and occupation." That fall they sponsored a highly successful one-day conference. Dr. Mary Harris, recently appointed superintendent of the federal women's reformatory at Alderson, West Virginia, proved an inspirational keynote speaker. Women's clubs from around the state pledged to join the campaign for a woman's reformatory. During the winter of 1926, committee members visited reformatories in other states. That same year the Chicago City Council approved plans for a Central House of Detention for Women, which was never subsequently funded or constructed. Having seemingly accomplished one goal, the Joint Committee on the Care and Training of Women Offenders turned its full energies to campaigning for a woman's reformatory, renaming itself the Committee for a State Reformatory for Women.[30]

Despite the changes initiated by Fuller and Rulien, Joliet Women's Prison was still viewed as a penitentiary, not a reformatory. Anne Hinrichsen, the DPW's information officer and a frequent visitor to the prison, conceded that significant improvements had been made in the 1920s, but argued that they did not transform Joliet's essentially custodial character. Drawing a sharp distinction between a prison and a reformatory, Hinrichsen unabashedly declared: "The institution had been too long a prison. The prison psychology was as definitely a part of the prison as the medieval architecture." The matrons, "though kindly, were prison minded civil service employees." Even though Hinrichsen was quick to note that "there was no physical cruelty nor corporal punishment; there was no strait jacket or straps," she asserted that "there was only the deadly round of duties, each woman a piece of the mechanism by which floors were scrubbed, dishes washed, thousands of male prisoners' uniforms washed and ironed. An early supper, an hour in the assembly room, and then a small, cold cell, a hard bed, lights out." The only ideal embodied in Joliet's traditional architecture and daily routine was "impregnable incarceration as a punishment for evil-doing."[31]

Superintendent Elinor Rulien had actively encouraged local religious and women's groups to volunteer at Joliet, but like Grace Fuller before her she had failed to gain the support of Illinois's women's clubs and female reformers. During the grand jury's 1926 investigation the Committee for a State Reformatory failed to rally to Rulien's defense. Instead, members seized the opportunity to press their case for an entirely new women's institution. At the time rumors abounded that the entire Joliet penitentiary would be closed once Stateville, the state's newest male prison, was fully functioning. The rumors later proved false. Focusing on the increased costs of running the Women's Prison in light of the anticipated closing of the men's unit, committee members wrote Governor Small: "It will neither be practical nor economical to continue using this [Women's Prison] building when the men prisoners are all moved. . . . New provisions will have to be made." Then, flexing their newly won political muscle, they declared, "The women of this state do not wish their Women's Prison in connection with the men's prison. Now is the time when this State Prison is to be given up to make a new provision altogether for the women prisoners."[32]

Motivated by pragmatic economic and political concerns to sell their ideas to male politicians who had hitherto expressed little interest, in their earliest proposals advocates offered a "combination plan" of penitentiary and reformatory. Club women continued to express ambivalence toward the female felons at Joliet. Most did not see them as proper or potential subjects of reformation, and their proposals assumed that the Joliet women would be kept physically separate from the more reformable misdemeanant population.

In 1927 reformatory lobbyists succeeded in convincing the state legislature to appropriate $300,000 for the construction authorized under the original 1919 Sanitarium Act. Governor Small remained unsupportive and refused to release the funding. More pressure was applied. In the fall of 1928 and spring of 1929 Republican party activists Emma T. Mason and Charlotte S. Butler spent four months in Springfield lobbying legislators. Fall elections brought a new Republican governor into office, Louis Emmerson, who was committed to a large-scale expansion of the state's social welfare institutions. With the backing of the new governor and Rodney Brandon, his new DPW director, women lobbyists finally succeeded in winning passage of an entirely new bill for a state reformatory for women. This time the act included an unprecedented $1.1 million appropriation. Construction was begun in early 1930 and the first inmates were admitted to the new facility that November.[33]

• • •

On March 14, 1931, four months after the reformatory opened, male prisoners at Joliet commenced a week of rioting. This outbreak coincided with the nation's second wave of prison riots. With 135 inmates under her charge, Superintendent Finnegan feared a similar uprising among the women and requested a supply of "tear gas bombs." Although the female prisoners remained calm, four days later the men at Stateville began a larger and more serious rebellion, which the Illinois National Guard was needed to subdue. The riots were sparked by the fatal shooting of three inmates during an escape attempt. However, as in 1917, many later testified that the riots were due "to the parole board and the parole board only." Male prisoners complained that the parole board was "'stacking up too much time,' . . . and that made for a spirit of unrest and dissatisfaction." Two chaplains testified that board members exhibited blatant favoritism and preferential treatment. Charges of corruption also abounded. The men's discontent was further fueled by Joliet's antiquated physical plant, severe overcrowding, lack of educational and recreational opportunities, harsh system of discipline, and inadequate medical facilities. After national surveys in both 1926 and 1929, penal reformers Austin MacCormick and Paul Garrett had condemned conditions at Joliet as "far below modern institutional standards," concluding that the Illinois prison system "needed to be reorganized perhaps more than in any other large state."[34]

The uprisings at Joliet and Stateville dealt a deathblow to the Women's Prison. Six months after the riots, DPW Superintendent of Prisons Frank D. Whipp announced that the women's three-story administration building would be converted into a desperately needed hospital for male prisoners while their cell house could comfortably house two hundred men. After October 1, 1931, all female convicts, both felons and misdemeanants, were sentenced directly to the Illinois State Reformatory for Women at Dwight.

To all outward appearances the new reformatory fulfilled its supporters' deepest hopes. Located eighty miles southwest of Chicago, the institution consisted of a central administration building in an attractive, Tudor-style design; an "industrial" sewing factory; a hospital with nursery quarters (where mothers could keep their infants up to one year of age); a multipurpose building that served as school, chapel, assembly hall, and recreation building (christened Jane Addams Hall); and eight large, stone "cottages" on 160 acres. Each cottage had fourteen single rooms; a spacious, well-equipped kitchen; formal dining room; living room; and sun porch, all impeccably furnished (see photographs, pp. 86–88). A full-time elementary-school teacher and a physician, psychologist, and social worker served a daily population averaging 240 women. Helen H. Hazard, superintendent from 1930 to 1953, was a former high school principal with a master's degree in social work from Columbia University. A native of Illinois, she was an experienced reformatory administrator, having served as acting superintendent at the Connecticut State Farm for Women from 1923 to 1926 and assistant superintendent at the federal women's reformatory at Alderson from 1928 to 1929.

Anticipating the final closing of Joliet Women's Prison, Hazard demanded an appropriation for a specially designed maximum security unit. This thirty-six-cell building, completed in May of 1933, exactly mirrored the traditional penal design of the Women's Prison at Joliet. On June 30, 1933, the Joliet Women's Prison was officially closed and all female prisoners were transferred to the fledgling reformatory. Staff expressed apprehension over their institution's ability to absorb such a large population of "hardened felons." As Hazard explained, "The women from the state prison had been impregnated with prison practices and prison traditions. A change was necessary in their attitude."[35]

Despite these fears, the Joliet women were transferred without incident. In fact, as long-term prisoners, they often proved more docile than the women committed for misdemeanors. One matron's daily report expressed a common complaint, "Since Lillian's time is so short she seems to not care about observing rules and regulations." Because misdemeanants were automatically released after six months, the fear of the parole board did not constrain their behavior. Meanwhile, the constant turnover created by the presence of hundreds of "short-term" women acted as a destabilizing factor during the institution's first decade. Hazard and her supporters campaigned vigorously for a change in the state's sentencing laws so misdemeanants could also be incarcerated under an indeterminate sentence, such as "one-to-three" years. When lawyers pointed out that the Illinois General Assembly was unlikely to pass such a measure because it eradicated entirely the legal distinction between misdemeanors and felonies, they abandoned this vision. Instead, Hazard lobbied for a doubling of misdemeanor sentences from six to twelve months. This measure passed in 1935.[36]

The opening of the Dwight reformatory represented a qualitative increase in the state's ability to police, penalize, and punish women's legal, moral, and sexual transgressions. Whereas 343 women were sentenced for felonies during the 1930s, nearly one thousand were incarcerated for misdemeanors. Previously women could only be sentenced to short jail stays (a few months at most) for such crimes. Many moral and sexual offenses had never before been penalized. Prostitution, adultery, fornication, and vagrancy (which often referred to soliciting) together totaled over one-third (36%) of misdemeanor commitments after 1930. Even after the reformatory movement disappeared nationally, hundreds of women in Illinois continued to be imprisoned for misdemeanors, which represented three-quarters of all female commitments in the 1930s (993 women) and two-thirds in the 1940s (738). Only in the 1950s did the proportion of misdemeanants fall to less than half (38%) of total commitments, and this group was not entirely eliminated from the female prison population until the 1980s.[37]

This new level of policing represented a greater change for the white women than for the African American. Although white women were 64 percent of the 347 women committed for felonies during the 1930s, they were

85 percent of the nearly one-thousand women committed for misdemeanors. These numbers suggest that judges were more inclined to sentence white women to a reformatory-style penal institution than to the former Joliet Women's Prison, especially if they could commit them on lesser, misdemeanor, charges. Even during the period from 1955 to 1970, when white women represented only 30 percent of felony commitments, they continued to make up 80 percent of women committed for misdemeanors. In contrast, police, prosecutors, and judges expressed far less interest in the moral transgressions of African American women, who were only 4 percent of the women sentenced for adultery and fornication, 8 percent of those incarcerated for prostitution, and 13 percent of women imprisoned for public drunkenness. Automatically excluded from bourgeois definitions of proper womanhood, black women were never perceived as ideal subjects for the reformatory's program of moral rehabilitation.

Sophie Danzer, convicted of forging a check for twenty-eight dollars at a local grocery store, seemed to embody reformers' ideal of a young, white first offender. The judge advised the parole board in 1932: "This is a proper case for parole—if the girl's home life had not been so bad I would have granted probation." Yet Danzer proved far from docile. She twice attempted to escape and was suspected of a lesbian involvement. The board refused her release. The next year the judge, unaware of her poor conduct, wrote, "It would have been a proper case for probation under ordinary circumstances. I sentenced this girl to Dwight for her own good." Danzer was finally released two years later.[38]

As Danzer's case suggests, few misdemeanants were the docile young "girls" envisioned by the reformatory's founders. Averaging 30.6 years (exactly the same as felons), many were repeat offenders whom local authorities perceived as public nuisances. Indeed, misdemeanants often represented an even more marginalized and disadvantaged population than female felons. During the 1930s over half (51%) had prior arrests and 33 percent had served time in local jails or houses of correction. Roughly one-third had histories of alcoholism and one-fifth were drug addicts committed for misdemeanor narcotics violations. Few had strong family or community ties. Only 30 percent were married: 40 percent were separated or divorced, compared to 12 percent of felons. Sixty percent were childless, compared to 48 percent of felons. Most (86%) were unemployed at the time of their arrest. In contrast to felony offenders, misdemeanants were disproportionately sentenced from rural areas that offered few social services or alternative institutions for troubled or troublesome women. Ten percent were sentenced to Dwight for a second or third term. Yet despite their often overwhelming poverty and their otherwise disadvantaged status, few perceived the reformatory as either a genuine home or a benevolent, treatment-oriented institution.

Reformatory advocates failed to recognize the extraordinarily repressive and oppressive nature of the institution they had so ardently championed and lovingly designed. Instead of a wide array of individualized treatment services, security and custodial concerns dominated institutional life. Over the decades rules and regulations grew increasingly restrictive. The small, "intimate" cottage setting allowed for an unprecedented level of surveillance and control. Rules governed every aspect of women's lives, dictating how they must fold and wear their clothes, sit at the dining room table, and style their hair. Few inmates believed that they were in anything other than a prison. Indeed, in all their confiscated notes and censored letters, prisoners regularly referred to Dwight as a "prison" or "penitentiary."

· · ·

Even as Illinois club women campaigned throughout the 1920s for a new, reformatory-style women's penal institution, the evidence suggests that Joliet Women's Prison was ably and humanely managed by Superintendent Elinor Rulien. Rulien continued to advocate a regime of domestic science, education, regular work, outdoor exercise, and gardening as adequate rehabilitative tools for even the most "hardened" female offenders. Throughout the decade she strove, often in vain, to improve educational, recreational, medical, and physical conditions at the prison, consistently referring to the women under her care as "these poor unfortunates." However, several of Rulien's assistant matrons were outraged by her purported failure to adequately discipline inmates, particularly those who engaged in openly lesbian conduct. Similar conflicts between patronage-appointed custodial staff and reform-minded superintendents continued over the next four decades.

Although Grace Fuller and Elinor Rulien publicly expressed only sympathy for their charges, prison psychiatrists and parole board members voiced far less faith in the possibility of women's reformation. Psychiatric reports and parole board transcripts reveal that these officials were not at all satisfied with the past, current, or predicted future behaviors of female convicts. Concluding with the standard phrase "success upon parole is doubtful," prison mental health officers lambasted female offenders for having led "improper" lives and frequently called for their permanent institutionalization. The following two chapters interrupt the chronological narrative in order to explore the blatantly moralistic, racist, classist, and sexist nature of both psychiatric classification and parole board decision making from the 1920s to the 1960s.

PART IV

FINDING A CURE

Psychiatrists, Sociologists, and the Parole Board,

1917–1963

CHAPTER TEN

"WE SEEM TO BE DEALING WITH A PSYCHOPATHIC PERSONALITY"

Psychiatric Constructions of Female Criminality

In 1928 Dr. Walter B. Martin, Joliet's first mental health officer (prison psychiatrist), reported that twenty-three-year-old Lucille Gary admitted to having shot her lover's wife after the woman came to her house one morning and attacked her. Witnesses had testified that the other woman had wielded a meat cleaver first, and Gary had been convicted of manslaughter rather than murder. Aside from this brief summary, Dr. Martin expressed no interest in Gary's offense in his one-page "Case Report of the Mental Health Officer," the evaluation that he wrote for the parole board. Instead, prison psychiatrists focused their assessments on female convict's adherence (or lack thereof) to middle-class standards of morality. Gary was unmarried, had no children, and was suffering from syphilis. Dr. Martin surmised that even though she "denie[d] being a commercial prostitute, occasionally men friends have supported her when she was out of work." He recommended against parole, concluding, "The woman is first of all a borderline defective. She is a casual prostitute and 'kept woman' of low moral standards and unindustrious habits. She will probably return to her old habits of living when released." Accepting his recommendation, the parole board voted to deny parole.[1]

Four years later Gary was scheduled for her next parole hearing, which necessitated another mental health report. Dr. Roy G. Barrick, Joliet's second mental health officer, reiterated his predecessor's accusation that Gary was a "loose woman given to prostitution." Disregarding her five years of perfect conduct in the institution, he too characterized Gary as an "inadequate personality" and "borderline defective." However, he recommended release, perhaps because Gary had already served the average time for manslaughter. The board acknowledged the mental health officer's favorable recommendation, but again refused parole.

Instead, board member Frank Cannon expressed outrage that Gary had "stolen" another woman's husband, with whom she had been "living in open adultery." Gary responded that her lover had been separated from his wife for many months and reiterated that the woman had come to her house early one morning and attacked her. Cannon shot back, "Our story is that that woman tried to get her husband back, and when she went to your place at 7:00 you filled her full of lead." Even though official reports all verified that Gary had fired a single shot, and only after the woman had attacked her, Cannon abruptly ended the interview. He observed that if Gary had committed her crime in Texas, where she was from, "You wouldn't be here today. No, you would have been strung up by the neck until you were dead. . . . That is all I have got to say." While Cannon's approving reference to the death penalty was extreme, it fully reflected board members' attitudes toward women who transgressed the norms of proper female behavior.[2]

At Gary's third parole hearing in 1937, board chairman W. C. Jones offered a final lecture, warning Gary against her "former practice of taking some woman's husband away from her." Gary assured him, "That's ten years ago, Mr. Jones, and I don't have any desire to do those things now." Gary was forced to serve ten years, twice the average sentence for manslaughter, before she was finally released.[3]

This chapter analyzes the evolution of both psychiatric discourse and the role of clinical staff (psychiatrists, psychologists, sociologists, and social workers) in Illinois women's prisons from the 1920s to the 1960s. French philosopher Michel Foucault has argued that with the creation of the penitentiary in the early nineteenth century, punishment shifted from disciplining the body to "treating" the psyche, that is, "punishment that acts in depth on the heart, the thoughts, the inclinations." Foucault places the emerging disciplines of psychiatry and psychology at the heart of the modern "carceral society." He contends that it was now necessary to *know* the criminal, "his reasons, his motives, his inner will, his tendencies, his instincts." However, it was not until the twentieth century that prison authorities developed either the resources or the rhetorical commitment to such sophisticated and intrusive disciplinary techniques.[4]

Progressive Era penal reformers in Illinois uncritically championed the introduction of psychiatrists, psychologists, and social workers into the prison system as a means of gathering knowledge about prisoners and individualizing treatment. In 1920 the Department of Public Welfare (DPW) established the position of mental health officer within each prison, a position that was filled by a full-time psychiatrist. The mental health officer, who served over three thousand inmates at the combined Joliet-Stateville complex, provided little counseling and offered few genuinely therapeutic services. Instead, his primary responsibility was to examine all prisoners before their parole hearings and make recommendations as to their "probability of success" if released. Few talented or ambitious professionals could be attracted to poorly paid prison positions, and psychiatric data collection and knowledge construction remained fragmentary and incomplete. Meanwhile, prisoners' resistance to treatment, along with conflicts among clinical, custodial, and administrative staff, further undermined efforts to utilize psychiatric knowledge as an effective therapeutic or disciplinary tool.[5]

As Lucille Gary's case exposes, the supposedly modern and scientific criteria that psychiatrists used in diagnosing female criminality were highly gendered and heavily laden with moralistic evaluations. Clinical staff, rarely the most skilled members of their profession, expended little effort in probing the complex causes of women's behavior. Psychiatrists classified most female prisoners as mentally inferior and as having severe psychological abnormalities; they were most commonly diagnosed as exhibiting psychopathic, inadequate, or unstable personalities. Both psychiatric assessments and parole board decision making (examined in the next chapter) invoked the construct of the "morally inadequate" woman. Authorities felt little compunction over incarcerating, and hence incapacitating, women for lengthy periods on the basis not only of the seriousness of their legal offenses, but also of their sexual histories and former lifestyles.

Earlier chapters examined how official and community perceptions of a woman's moral character affected which female transgressors officials selected for prosecution and which convicted women judges subsequently sentenced to the penitentiary. Women who adhered to conventional standards of proper femininity were less likely to be prosecuted, convicted, and punished with a prison sentence than those who violated traditional norms. This chapter extends that analysis by exploring how assessments of a woman's moral character remained central to her treatment long after her incarceration began. In nearly every "Mental Health Officer's Report" from the 1920s through the 1960s prison psychiatrists questioned women on the nature of their sexual histories and moral reputations. Even in cases of murder or manslaughter, such as that of Lucille Gary, mental health officers and parole board members weighed women's sexual transgressions as heavily as their legal offenses in their decision making.

• • •

Classification and individualization lay at the heart of progressive penology. Progressive Era penal reformers repeatedly condemned prison regimes, both male and female, for their failure to individualize treatment. They argued that prisoners must no longer be treated en masse, marched in lockstep, or subjected to an absolute discipline. After the centralization of prisons under the DPW in 1917, a new generation of academically trained and treatment-oriented professional administrators sought to introduce the methods of progressive penology into the prison system. Illinois was the first state to establish a Division of the Criminologist within the DPW. Under Anne Hinrichsen's prompting, the state criminologist agreed to initiate data collection at Joliet

Women's Prison in 1918. The data-collection process involved personal interviews, mental testing, medical examinations, and home visitations.[6]

Despite this early beginning, the DPW staff were unable to continue their ambitious classification program owing to limited resources and personnel, a material factor that Foucault's abstract theorizing overlooks. No other complete case studies were made of women prisoners until the opening of the Illinois State Reformatory for Women in 1930. During the 1920s psychiatric classification was cursory at best. The mental health officer's examination was little more than a hurried ten-to-fifteen-minute interview. In 1920 State Criminologist Dr. Herman M. Adler described the difficulties in winning prisoners' trust: "Prisoners are naturally suspicious. This work depends for its success . . . upon their cooperation. If they believe that this work is intended to demonstrate that they are all feebleminded or insane, such cooperation cannot be obtained." Some mental health officers frankly acknowledged the coercive nature of their positions, although others continued to proclaim their ability to develop a "friendly rapport" with prisoners. In a 1925 article Dr. Adler and Dr. John Larson admitted that the mental health officer was regarded by most prisoners "as a representative of the Division of Pardons and Paroles," which, in fact, he was. Warning that verbal interview techniques could not be trusted, Adler and Larson blithely described their "promising" experiments with lie-detector tests as one technique for "sorting truthful statements from evasions and falsifications."[7]

Over the next decades prisoners repeatedly voiced fears of, and resistance to, the role of prison psychiatrists. Fully comprehending that the mental health officer's primary responsibility was to write a recommendation for the parole board, female convicts warned new women not to reveal anything of significance to the "bug doctor." Unlike other professional personnel, such as teachers, chaplains, and nurses, the mental health officer was a virtual stranger to the prison and the prisoner. At Joliet he had no regular contact with inmates and rarely observed them in their daily interactions. Despite this, parole board members weighed the mental health officer's recommendation heavily in their decision making. In the world of the prison, psychiatric diagnosis and intelligence testing became powerful tools against which prisoners had little resort.

As prisoners suspected, mental health officers classified most women as psychologically abnormal and mentally defective. Intelligence testing remained a central component of classification through the 1970s and provided seemingly scientific and objective confirmation of prisoners' defects. Such tests were also used to refute women's educational claims, thereby challenging the veracity of all their statements. In Priscilla Heckner's case the mental health officer reported: "She claims to have been graduated from the eighth grade. . . . Mental tests, however, indicate a mental age of only ten years. It appears, therefore, that this claim, like many others made by the woman, is untruthful." Neither psychiatrists nor prisoners entered the interview situation in a spirit of trust or mutuality. Women knew that they had to offer as advantageous an interpretation of their actions as possible, while mental health officers were poised to challenge their claims.[8]

In addition to denigrating female convicts' truthfulness and intelligence, mental health officers exposed women's sexual pasts to official scrutiny and condemnation. Nearly every Mental Health Officer Report focused on its subject's sexuality, as the following comments reveal: "She admits going with boys and having coitus with them." "She admits she became promiscuous sexually and learned to drink at a young age." "She admits she was pregnant at the time of her second marriage." "She denies prostitution but is rather vague about her life experiences between her two marriages." "She denies drinking but admits promiscuous sexual relations with boys and admits that she has had two illegitimate children." Through the 1960s the same "admits" and "denies" appeared regularly, indicating that female prisoners continued to be gauged by the same moral yardstick.[9]

This preoccupation with women's sexuality was fully consistent with dominant sociological and psychological discourses that placed sexual maladjustment and sexual deviance at the center of explanations of female criminality. As we have seen, under the influence of Social Darwinist and eugenics theories, women's heterosexual deviance took on unprecedented significance during the first decades of the century. In their massive and highly influential 1934 study, *Five Hundred Delinquent Women,* Sheldon and Eleanor Glueck claimed that "the major problem in [their] delinquency and criminality . . . is their lack of control of their sexual impulses." The Gluecks concluded that 86 percent of the women displayed "bad sex habits," which, in their eyes, included everything from occasional prostitution to premarital sex to living with a man out-of-wedlock.[10]

The Glueck's study served as the reigning text on female criminality for the next four decades. After a flurry of academic investigations of female delinquency from 1900 to 1920, researchers lost nearly all interest in women offenders. With the discrediting of eugenics ideology, liberalizing attitudes toward female sexuality, and the emergence of medical treatments for venereal disease, the menacing specter of both the prostitute and the depraved, degenerate, diseased, and profligate criminal woman constructed by Progressive Era moral reformers receded. Yet even as criminologists after 1930 increasingly turned to sociological and ecological explanations in their analyses of male criminality, those who researched female offenders continued to draw upon psychological and biological explanations. Allison Morris observes, "Criminal activity by men . . . is more likely to be viewed as normal, explicable, or rational." In contrast, when women commit the same offenses, it is believed that "they do so for pathological or irrational reasons." Until challenged by a new generation of feminist scholars in the 1970s and 1980s, mainstream criminologists routinely acknowledged economic causes in their explanations of men's offending, but conflated women's criminality with sexual deviance and attributed female law breaking to inadequate psychosexual adjustment or female biology.[11]

In Illinois, mental health officers and parole board members concurred that past promiscuity and improper sexual relationships were critical factors to consider when assessing the nature, quality, and extent of a woman's criminality, as well as the likelihood of her success upon parole. In 1932 Dr. Roy

Barrick classified Helen Williams, a young white woman committed for receiving stolen property, as "emotionally unstable, a mental defective and a casual prostitute." He repeated this diagnosis the following year. Although Barrick admitted that Williams's prison record was "very satisfactory," he concluded that her chances of succeeding on parole were highly problematic, not because of any predicted future criminal activity, but on the basis of her possible future relationships with young men. "Unfortunately," he wrote, "we fear that she will not be able to resist the temptation to go out with boys, drink with them and have heterosexual experiences. Obviously, the type of supervision will have to be very strict in order to avoid further trouble."[12]

Conversely, mental health officers occasionally offered a favorable assessment based on a woman's lack of promiscuity. Thirty-seven-year-old Cora Harden was committed for manslaughter; she had been convicted of killing her husband with a bird gun after he struck her with a stove poker. In contrast to his harsh response to Lucille Gary's shooting of her lover's wife that same year, Dr. Martin's reaction was highly sympathetic. He classified Harden as exhibiting "no gross personality defect" (a rare diagnosis) and of "high average" intelligence (equally atypical). Persuaded that "she shows every evidence of having been really afraid of him," Dr. Martin portrayed Harden as an utterly conventional and duly submissive wife. Highly impressed by the fact that "unlike many of her companions at the Women's Prison she does not seem to have been promiscuous in her sex relations," he concluded that "in her own way she was 'true to her husband.'" Martin closed with a rare positive recommendation. The board, however, refused to grant her release. Although board members were initially sympathetic, they became hostile upon discovering that the husband to which Harden was so devoted was "part colored" and that she herself was "part Indian" rather than "white" as indicated in her file.[13]

In comparison, mental health reports on male inmates almost never offered assessments of men's moral character. Mental health officers made no attempt to assess whether a man was a good husband or provider, lived with a woman out-of-wedlock, had divorced or abandoned a wife, had fathered illegitimate children, was sexually promiscuous, or drank. Instead, they probed in greater detail the nature of men's crimes; their prior criminal histories; their educational and employment backgrounds; their future work plans; and their parole sponsors. Mental health officers rarely suggested that male prisoners be permanently institutionalized. Rather, they recommended "extra-mural activity as soon as possible" for all but the most recalcitrant. Even when men refused to cooperate and told "unconvincing stories" claiming their innocence, mental health officers routinely recommended parole. Neither they nor parole board members weighed men's rule infractions very heavily. Instead, they appeared to accept one or two punishments per year as a normal male response to incarceration. In contrast, a single violation of prison regulations could haunt a female convict throughout her entire prison career.

Mental health officers also regularly acknowledged men's economic motives, especially in cases of larceny and even armed robbery. The following remarks were typical: "This man tells a frank story of being out of work and of stealing chickens in order to live," or "it would seem criminality resulted from an immediate economic pressure." A man who had been caught burglarizing a grocery store professed that he needed to feed his starving family. One board member responded sympathetically: "If his story is true, it is not an abnormal reaction and he should be given some consideration." This last comment—"it is not an abnormal reaction"—unmistakably conveys the attitude of mental health officers and parole board members toward male, but not female, burglars, forgers, and thieves.[14]

Even for men with lengthy criminal records, mental health officers ordinarily proposed steady employment as a sufficient corrective to keep them out of future trouble. Only in rare instances did they dismiss men's economic motives and substitute psychological ones. In a typical case, one mental health officer gave a glowing recommendation to a thirty-five-year-old armed robber who was a repeat offender. Although the inmate had served five previous prison and jail sentences dating back to his youth, the mental health officer optimistically concluded: "We think that this inmate is potentially capable of good adjustment in spite of his criminal record provided, of course, he is fortunate to secure steady employment and has other stabilizing influences." "Steady employment" and "stabilizing influences" were major factors for any ex-convict's parole success; however, mental health officers rarely offered women the benefit of the doubt.[15]

Many women convicted of "con game" and "fraud" had forged checks for relatively small amounts, often at local grocery stores, but mental health officers gave little weight to such women's economic pressures. Harriet Kavanaugh, a young white woman serving a "one-to-ten" year sentence for engaging in a "con game" admitted to having written as many as twenty checks when she was unemployed. In 1931 Dr. Barrick diagnosed her as an "inadequate personality with dull normal intelligence." He concluded: "She denies drinking but admits promiscuous sexual relations. . . . She will have to have close supervision and steady employment when released or she will be apt to resort to issuing checks again." Although he acknowledged that "steady employment" was required, Dr. Barrick was as concerned with Kavanaugh's sexual relations as with her check-writing. He added: "She will probably continue her promiscuous sex practices under any circumstances." Sharing his reservations, the board denied her parole. Nor were these isolated examples. As state criminologist from 1942 to 1961, Dr. Barrick freely promoted such narrow-minded and traditionally chauvinist views.[16]

Before their incarceration, most female prisoners had lived precarious lives, struggling at the margins of economic survival. Receiving occasional gifts or money from male friends with whom they sometimes exchanged sexual favors was an important survival strategy. However, mental health officers weighed their morality, rather than the economic factors that contributed to their limited choices, most heavily against them. Anna Hemmings, a twenty-seven-year-old African American woman born in Louisiana, was committed for an eighty-dollar robbery. She had married at age fourteen, given birth to two children, separated from her husband, and then migrated to Chicago where, the mental health officer reported, she had "supported herself at common labor and hustled for a living trying to take care of her children." ("Hustling" was prostitution.) Dr. Barrick acknowledged that "her attitude toward imprisonment is obedient and she is profiting by disciplinary treatment." Due to her previously immoral lifestyle, however, he forecast that "success upon parole is doubtful" and predicted that "she will return to her former anti-social habits of living when released." Again the parole board concurred.[17]

Likewise, prison psychiatrists and parole board members rarely commented upon the economic factors that led many women to remain in relationships with abusive men. In 1947 thirty-eight-year-old Nola Mae Owens shot and killed her common-law husband after he had repeatedly threatened to kill her. Trying to flee their house, she grabbed his gun when he blocked her way and fired with the intent to scare him. The bullet's wound proved fatal. Owens had no criminal history and had never before been in trouble with the law. The judge, accepting her version of events, gave her a one-to-five year sentence for manslaughter.

Owens explained to the mental health officer that she had lived with this man for two years; originally she had appreciated the fact that he "provided well for her," but he had then begun drinking heavily. She "thought repeatedly of leaving him but she had no means of living so she postponed it again and again." For fifteen years previously Owens had struggled to raise two children on her own, working as a maid after she had left her first husband, who was also an abusive alcoholic. However, because her obesity and a back injury eventually prevented her from doing heavy work, she was no longer capable of supporting herself. Dr. Ulrich Ledien did not find Owens's explanations persuasive. His evaluation reveals the distrust and suspicion that permeated mental health officers' relationships with their "patients," as well as the middle-class standards of morality against which they judged female convicts. Dr. Ledien offered the following sweeping judgment:

> She is not a mental defective but makes a rather dull impression . . . . The fact that she avoided any previous conflict with the law speaks in her favor. However, it should be checked if she actually worked so courageously to rear her 2 children on her own and was so even-tempered as she tries to make believe. The picture she gives of herself does not explain her crime. That she continued her common-law relationship with the deceased who was 26 years her senior, chiefly because she did not have any means to support herself, betrays a lack of willpower and low moral standards.[18]

Board members agreed with this assessment and refused to parole Owens.

Ledien's statement, "the picture she gives of herself does not explain her crime," tellingly reveals his inability to comprehend the economic or psychological forces that circumscribed the lives of poor women and influenced their choices. Instead, Ledien attributed Owens's actions (or rather, her failure to act) to an innate moral and psychological defect, explicitly defined as a "lack of willpower" and "low moral standards." Mental health officers frequently accused women of failing to take full responsibility for their actions.

The following year Dr. Buch, another mental health officer, noted that Owens stated "that she knows that she did wrong but feels there was no other recourse to be taken at that time. She states that it never would have happened had this man let her out of the house, and tends to blame him." Dr. Buch concluded that Owens was "unduly shifting the blame."[19]

Unable to formulate cogent sociological, economic, or environmental explanations for female criminality, mental health officers relied heavily upon the construct of the "psychopathic personality." This diagnosis was useful precisely because of its vagueness. It encompassed an elastic and indeterminate set of character defects that psychiatrists themselves had difficulty agreeing upon. The essence of the diagnosis was that psychopathic individuals exhibited to an extreme degree traits that were well within the bounds of normality, which is precisely what made psychopathology so difficult to both describe and detect. State Criminologist Dr. Herman Adler offered the following definition:

> By psychopathic personality we mean an individual in which there exists a definite and positive trend towards a variety of behavior difficulties. . . . Under this heading is included the vagrant, hobo, profligate, liar, swindler, eccentric or contentious individuals, chronic litigant, the violent, short-tempered person who impulsively commits serious crimes, and a long list of other similar difficulties. These cases are not feebleminded; on the contrary, they may have a high degree of intelligence. They are not insane or epileptic, but they deviate none the less from the healthy, normal type so far as to represent a definite problem of mental pathology.[20]

The label "psychopathic" served to absolve institutional staff of any responsibility for the failure of their programs to reform prisoners. As several of these examples intimate, even a perfect conduct record and a positive attitude toward imprisonment could not outweigh an immoral past. This contradiction created a serious dilemma for progressive ideology. On the one hand, prison conduct was supposed to be a major factor in assessing the degree to which a convict had been reformed. On the other hand, staff were well aware that many repeat offenders had perfect institutional records. In seeming despair, the mental health officers embraced the concept of psychopathy, advocating permanent institutionalization or preventative detention for repeat offenders.

Likewise, the dominant discourse on "feeble-mindedness" that emerged during the Progressive Era must also be interpreted as a response to the failure of institutional administrators to engender compliance, achieve rehabilitation, or instill a version of proper femininity in their charges. Like Geneva superintendent Ophelia Amigh, prison and reformatory officials both locally and nationally expressed their frustration over girls and women who "appeared physically normal" but who failed to conform to middle-class standards of femininity and sexual restraint. Psychiatrists commonly diagnosed these women as both psychopathic and feeble-minded. In the eyes of officials, the behavior of resistant, unrepentant, and unreformable women (and girls) could be accounted for only by proposing a psychological and intellectual defect that was not apparent to the unschooled eye.

Most studies of deviant women, including prisoners, prostitutes, and sexually delinquent girls, reached the same conclusion: the majority were feebleminded and hence constitutionally incapable of reform. After analyzing the records of five hundred women paroled in the 1920s from the Massachusetts Reformatory for Women, considered by many a model institution, Sheldon and Eleanor Glueck openly characterized female offenders as a "sorry lot." They concluded that even while incarcerated only one-half had conducted themselves "satisfactorily": 30 percent violated minor regulations, and 20 percent were frequent or major-rule violators. Five years after their release, one-half (55%) remained "delinquent." Admitting that only a "small proportion . . . may be deemed to have ceased their misconduct quite directly through the efforts of the institution," the Gluecks concluded that it was the women, rather than the institution, who were at fault: *"The women are themselves on the whole a sorry lot."* Many were "burdened with feeblemindedness, psychopathic personality, and marked emotional instability." The task confronting the reformatories was enormous: *"This swarm of defective, diseased, antisocial misfits, then, comprises the human material which a reformatory and a parole system are required by society to transform into wholesome, decent, law-abiding citizens."* The authors concluded with a rhetorical question: "Is it not a miracle that a proportion of them were actually rehabilitated?"[21]

Helen H. Hazard, the very competent and committed superintendent of the Dwight reformatory from 1930 to 1953, ultimately reached the same conclusion. In 1936 she wrote: "Perhaps the time will come when we will recognize that some, at least, of the women committed here are incapable of making adequate social adjustments." Although society assumed that such women "could have behaved differently had they wanted to," after seventeen years of employment at three "model" women's reformatories, Hazard had begun to question this faith.[22]

Hazard's growing pessimism contrasted with her earlier optimism, shared by the reformatory's founders, that deviant women could be "reclaimed through modern reformatory techniques." Harriet Comstock, a major campaigner for the Illinois women's reformatory, had argued that unlike at Joliet, at modern "correctional" institutions women were "committed not to be punished, not just to scrub floors and wash clothes . . . but to be diagnosed by physicians of the body, mind, and spirit, all of whom . . . try to work out together a beneficent regime which will eventually affect a cure." Comstock acknowledged that the "first prescription" might not always succeed. However, she claimed that the new reformatories provided a variety of medical, psychological, social service, and educational specialists dedicated to thoroughly studying each individual offender in order to ascertain "the contributing cause that prevented a normal adjustment to society." These reformatories became "at once a laboratory and a school." Twentieth-century reformatory advocates preferred the language of medicine and psychiatry to that of religion or moral reformation. As another advocate explained in 1942, "Correctional treatment, like medical treatment, must be individually prescribed according to the needs and potentialities of the offender. It is useless, and oftimes as dangerous, to apply the same kind of treatment to all offenders . . . as it would be to prescribe the same medicine to all sick people."[23]

Advocates sought to implement this ambitious program at Dwight. During the 1930s every new prisoner spent one month in the "classification" or "intake" cottage. There she underwent a battery of medical, psychological, intelligence, educational, and achievement tests. A social worker wrote up a thorough "social history" consisting of an extraordinarily detailed, single-spaced, two-to-four-page report covering all aspects of women's lives from childhood illnesses to family, work, school, and marital histories. The social worker was responsible for verifying all information and sent questionnaires to prisoners' families, friends, relatives, schools, and former employees. Neither family members nor friends could correspond or visit until they had completed the questionnaires, and sometimes not until they were investigated by a social worker or parole agent. Information was also secured from local police, state's attorneys, probation officers, and any social service or charitable agencies that had been involved with either the woman or her family.

On the basis of their initial classification, inmates were to be placed in the most appropriate school, work, and housing assignments. Dwight's classification committee met biweekly. All staff, including cottage warders, job supervisors, and teachers, submitted regular written reports on each prisoner, who was called before the classification committee every three months for a progress review. Hazard repeatedly described these classification meetings as the "very heart of the individual program which the reformatory endeavors to carry out." Yet by 1940 the frequency of prisoners' classification reviews had been reduced to once every six months due to the burdens they placed on staff as well as their limited utility.

In practice, classification proved both less thorough and less useful than the institution's founders had envisioned. The reformatory was supposed to have a full-time female doctor and psychiatric social worker in addition to a part-time psychiatrist and psychologist whose sole responsibility was to administer intelligence tests. However, it proved difficult to attract qualified professionals to the small farming town of Dwight. Salaries were low. Although room and board were provided at the institution, staff housing was inadequate and few professionals relished the opportunity of living on the grounds with the inmates. Moreover, due to the entrenched patronage system, there was no guaranteed tenure in office. Consequently, a full "classification team" consisting of a psychiatrist, psychologist, social worker, and medical doctor was in place for only a few years in the mid 1930s. Although State Criminologist Paul L. Schroeder proudly claimed in 1940 that "this service was believed to be the best of its kind in any women's correctional institution in the country," personnel shortages during World War II completely undermined the classification program, which was not reestablished until 1955.[24]

Even during the mid 1930s, when a full classification team existed and Dwight was, in fact, one of the nation's best-equipped and most fully staffed women's reformatories, professionals had little time to offer individualized counseling or other therapeutic services. Although Hazard claimed that "an endeavor is made to give the girl some insight into her difficulty," most of the mental health officer's time was devoted to writing reports. Hazard claimed that prisoners quickly came to regard the psychiatrist as a friend, from whom they voluntarily sought advice and counsel. However, the mental health officers' own notes indicate that many women continued to view prison psychiatrists, psychologists, and social workers with suspicion, resenting the fact that staff interpreted inmate resistance as a sign of psychological disturbance. In 1945 Dr. Ledien reported that one woman who was being punished in isolation had refused his interview, snapping: "You are here to find out if I am feeble-minded, and in which state of insanity I am." The psychiatrist offered some "reassuring words" only to receive the curt response, "You are for the state, that is all that counts." The following year Ledien duly noted that another prisoner, equally antagonistic, had declared: "I do not know why I have to see the psychiatrist every time I am in punishment. I am not nuts." Nor was there any pretense that psychiatric sessions were confidential. Prisoners were well-aware that any information they revealed would be shared with other staff and could be included in the evaluations mental health officers wrote for the parole board.[25]

Prison psychiatrists also failed to provide custodial staff with effective aid in dealing with troubled or troublesome prisoners. Even though inmates enjoyed a wider range of educational, vocational, and recreational programs at Dwight than at Joliet, in practice "individualization" meant little more than transferring an unruly or dissatisfied inmate from one housing, work, or school assignment to another. In 1941 a cottage warder (a staff member who lived in and supervised one of Dwight's cottage living units) sought advice on how she should handle Eva Majeski, an "agitator in the cottage" who "likes to stir up arguments and keep them going." Characterizing her as a bitter woman and a chronic complainer, the warder asserted that Majeski was a "constant source of irritation" who "encouraged dissatisfactions and disagreements between other girls." The "girls" themselves had campaigned for Majeski's transfer to another cottage. Convicted of poisoning her lover's wife with arsenic and "suspected of previous like crimes," Majeski and her lover had aroused community suspicion by marrying shortly after his wife's untimely death. Now aged fifty-nine, the garrulous Majeski had completed fifteen years of her life sentence.

Psychiatrist Dora Fishback interviewed Majeski, but could offer no concrete help. Fishback readily perceived Majeski's irritating nature: "We are dealing with an egocentric person who has made a poor adjustment at Joliet and has continued to adjust poorly at Dwight. During the interview she was putting her best face forward but examiner can readily see that she might be a very irritating factor among a group of women." Acknowledging that Majeski would "probably . . . cause difficulty wherever she goes," she concluded that the warder had little choice but to put up with her. Abdicating her role as purveyor of psychiatric expertise, Dr. Fishback passed the problem over to Superintendent Hazard: "It is left to the discrimination of the administrative staff as to whether there is some other place where she could fit in better . . .

or whether she would get into even more difficulty if transferred from the present cottage."[26]

Yet even such limited interventions were often difficult to arrange. A woman's housing placement was based on her security classification: maximum, medium, or minimum. Because the eight cottages were racially segregated until 1960, after classification there were usually only one or two cottages to which an inmate could be appropriately assigned. Moreover, even the so-called "minimum security" cottages offered few extra privileges. For reasons of security and staff convenience, daily routines were equally restricted regardless of the prisoner's security classification. The first real honor cottages were not established until the 1980s.

Although revealing, Majeski's case was highly atypical: it was rare for cottage warders to seek the advice of the reformatory's mental health officer. Conflict between the psychiatric and custodial attitudes deeply divided staff at Dwight. Psychiatric labels gave warders little guidance in how to handle the numerous day-to-day problems they confronted. Warders were responsible for managing and disciplining twenty to thirty adult women twenty-four hours a day, six days a week. To the extent that they could treat all women the same, their tasks were eased. Special diets, treatment, or individualized routines generated resentment and disrupted security, adding to the staff's workload. Warders made clear their displeasure, as well as the more punitive attitudes they harbored toward female offenders.

Superintendent Helen Hazard was deeply concerned by the warders' poor qualifications and their lack of "professional" attitudes—in other words, their lack of commitment to a philosophy of rehabilitation. Like Elinor Rulien at Joliet in the 1920s, Hazard had little choice but to accept the patronage appointees local politicians sent to her. Most cottage warders were older widowed white women from small farming towns who coveted the room and board that came with their modest salaries. The only qualification was a high school degree. As Hazard stated flatly in 1940, "The majority of workers have no training whatever for their tasks here." Many warders also shared the general public's view that prisons should punish; they believed that when the institution offered rehabilitation programs, special classes in art or music, and other "frills" it was doing little more than "coddling criminals."[27]

In 1936 Hazard first openly admitted that "the problem of obtaining qualified personnel continues to be the most important and difficult problem." In 1938, observing that the cottage warders form the "backbone of an institution of this type," Hazard argued that "if any advancement is to be made in solving the problem of delinquency and criminality, it must come from enlightened and informed personnel." Convinced that most female prisoners harbored "deep-rooted emotional problems," she explained that "it would be impossible to furnish even so small an institution as this an adequate psychiatric staff." To address this need, Hazard initiated a monthly lecture series conducted by the prison psychiatrist in an effort to "assist the staff in securing a more professional and educated attitude." Yet conflicts continued. In 1939 Hazard reported cryptically that the psychiatrist's lecture program "presented certain difficulties." She conceded, "In an institution of this type it is somewhat difficult to reconcile the differences between the psychiatric attitude and conventional attitude of the public toward the problem of punishment." Nevertheless, Hazard remained committed to bridging the divide, repeating her conviction that it was "imperative that both the custodial and department staff have a psychiatric approach" to their work. She continued the lectures until the institution lost its psychiatric staff during World War II.[28]

While Hazard sought to educate cottage staff in modern theories of psychology and instill in them a commitment to rehabilitative goals, she pleaded for greater psychiatric services. Like most criminologists she pathologized female offending and ignored economic, environmental, and social causes and solutions. In 1938, concerned that the reformatory had been without a psychiatrist for over a year, Hazard warned: "Because practically all of the women have deep-seated emotional conflicts, the institution believes it is only able to help them meet their problems through the assistance of psychiatry. Unless expert service is obtained in this line, the institution believes it is only marking time, largely providing custodial care instead of arriving at anything which resembles a permanent solution." She concluded that "the only hope for an enlightened penology . . . lies in the field of mental hygiene and psychiatry" and appealed to the DPW to provide the full range of resources that the reformatory's founders had envisioned.[29]

By the 1940s, however, Hazard's faith in psychiatric intervention had waned considerably. During World War II the institution was plagued by acute staff shortages. Departing from her earlier optimistic emphasis on rehabilitation, Hazard focused on more pressing day-to-day physical and managerial concerns. The 1940s was a troubled decade. Staff shortages, racial tensions, and radical changes in the state's sentencing laws and parole board policies generated a period of turmoil characterized by more open and vocal inmate unrest. In 1949 Hazard resigned in despair.

Personnel shortages were exacerbated by the fact that from 1941 to 1954 the women's reformatory remained under the supervision of the DPW while all other state penal institutions were placed under the jurisdiction of the newly created Department of Public Safety (DPS). Although Dwight may have benefited from its continuing association with the state's welfare bureaucracy rather than its penal bureaucracy, it lost its access to the clinical staff employed by the Division of the Criminologist. Between 1942 and 1954 the DPW either failed to fund or was unable to fill nearly all psychiatrist, psychologist, and social worker positions at Dwight. In 1950 Doris Whitney, a new superintendent, attempted to reestablish the 1930s classification program. However, the new psychiatric social worker she hired left soon after Whitney was dismissed. The social worker was disillusioned by the open hostility cottage warders displayed toward clinical staff and by the failure of Whitney's brief reform administration.

Another superintendent resigned the following year, and in 1954 Dwight was transferred to the DPS, which reestablished a rudimentary classification program and staffed it with part-time male professionals borrowed from the men's penitentiary at nearby Pontiac. Meanwhile, the DPS abolished the position of mental health officer, replacing prison psychiatrists with much lower-paid sociologists. This move reflected national trends. Despite the hopes of Progressive Era reformers, by the 1950s barely a dozen states employed full-time prison psychiatrists. In 1956 the DPS assigned its first full-time sociologist to Dwight. Bernard Robinson, the institution's first African American professional employee, was popular among African American prisoners, who frequently requested meetings with him to discuss their grievances. However, in his official reports Robinson expressed little sympathy or empathy toward the women he evaluated.[30]

The only qualification for the position of prison sociologist was a bachelor's degree in sociology or social work. Although several sociologists continued on to advanced degrees and prominent positions, at the time they were young, straight out of college, and inexperienced. Most had never taken a single course in criminology. Revealing little psychological sophistication, one novice sociologist characterized an inmate as "somewhat weird" and another as a "lone-wolf, seclusive [sic] type of individual."[31] In an amusing but fairly typical report, another simply threw up his hands in despair:

> This examiner fails to see how Norma Jean can possibly cope . . . with even the smallest problems in free society. She is an almost constant source of upheaval and disturbance among the inmates. . . . She is so volcanic, so unpredictable, so impetuous and so dangerous to others at times that this examiner can't see how on God's good, green earth she can live anywhere other than in a rigorously controlled environment. Her prognosis for rehabilitation . . . is extremely unfavorable.[32]

Several former sociologists acknowledged the difficulty of their position. Lois Green (1964–1977), hired at Dwight shortly after her college graduation, reported that she "didn't have a clue as to what I was doing when I went in. It was a real learning curve the first few years. If inmates didn't tell you what to do you were sunk." After a month at Joliet learning diagnostic procedures, she simply "followed another sociologist around [Dwight] for a week." Her secretary showed her how to write the parole prediction (mental health officer) reports, which Green described as "operating off of clichés." Likewise, she referred to the admissions classification reports as an "exercise in futility, but everyone thought it had to be done." Green's frustration mounted: "We gained tremendous knowledge about individuals but nobody was acting on it. I had to verify the social history meticulously. We acquired a very clear picture of the individual but there were very little in the way of programs to meet their needs." Nathan Kantrowitz, a young sociologist at Stateville (1957–1963), was more blunt: "Nobody gave a damn about what we did." Lacking Green's secretarial support, he was "entirely trained by inmate clerks." The "canned" parole prediction reports were "mostly crap." Using the same words as Green, he concluded, "it was an exercise in futility, but as long as you have a parole board they have to make a decision and they need some inputs."[33]

As they engaged in these self-proclaimed "exercises in futility," prison sociologists introduced a new diagnostic vocabulary: fundamentally delinquent, chronic offender, criminal orientation, psychosexual maladjustment, lack of motivational goals, disorganized life, product of a broken home, and (Robinson's favorite) "lifestyle characteristic of Negroes of the lower socioeconomic class." Yet little had changed. Similar to earlier generations of mental health officers, sociologists drew upon a narrow repertoire of constructs in almost every assessment. Indeed, they repeated the same derogatory diagnoses verbatim in many different women's reports. Whereas in the 1920s and 1930s mental health officers typically concluded with the stock phrase, "Success upon parole is doubtful," in the 1960s they ended their reports with the more awkward and jargon-laden construction: "Her prognosis is doubtful, suggesting that the inmate has limited capacity to adjust to the free community, and may fail on parole unless circumstances are favorable and supervision is close."

Sociologists rarely defined what constituted "favorable conditions" or offered specific treatment plans. Nor did they address women's needs for well-paying jobs, housing, child care, counseling, drug treatment, education, physical safety, and medical care upon their release. Instead, they implicitly acknowledged the limits of state intervention: prisoners would return to the same environments and same problems they had left. Instead of challenging either the reformatory or the state to provide genuine support and treatment services, they, like earlier generations of prison administrators, blamed the women themselves for their failures.

Such "doubtful" or "extremely unfavorable" prognoses were increasingly common. Prison sociologists in the 1950s and 1960s were even less likely to offer positive parole predictions than their predecessors. When it came to estimating the probability of parole success, sociologists offered an unqualified "favorable" prognosis in only 4 percent of women's cases and 3 percent of men's, although in their admissions reports they classified as "improvable" twice as many female prisoners as male prisoners (22% of women versus 10% of men). In comparison, statistics from 1937 to 1942 reveal that earlier generations of mental health officers had classified 41 percent of prisoners as "improvable." Indeed, in his 1942 report State Statistician Howard Hill optimistically seized upon this finding, commenting that these statistics "suggest a more hopeful picture of the rehabilitative possibilities of prisoners than is found in the usual pessimistic reports on recidivism."[34]

By the 1950s official optimism had entirely evaporated. Clinical staff no longer maintained the pretense that their admissions classification reports might provide clues for an individualized treatment program. One 1959 diagnosis was typical: "This is an advanced and chronic offender. She gives no evidence whatsoever of intent to change. She remains tough, cynical, worldly-wise and braggadocio. It appears that she is quite unchangeable and definitely equipped with deeply entrenched criminal habits and patterns of action." Racial biases, exacerbated by the fact that African American women constituted nearly three-quarters (70%) of new prisoners after 1955, fueled this decline in optimism.[35]

This pessimism was most pronounced in the case of drug addicts. After 1954, when both drug possession and drug trafficking became felonies in Illinois, drug offenders represented one-third of female commitments. Ninety-four percent of them were African American. Prison sociologists rarely concluded that such prisoners might be reformed. Carol Rawlings recalled bit-terly: "In the 1950s a drug-addicted prostitute was seen as the worst criminal element on the street, especially if she was black." Although one might argue that sociologists' pessimism was justified given the tenacious nature of drug addiction, the possibility of drug treatment was never mentioned. Rawlings eventually kicked her drug habit and later returned to Dwight as part of a prison ministry program. Yet despite the fact that at least half of female pris-oners had histories of drug abuse, no drug treatment programs were offered until the 1980s. An Alcoholics Anonymous group was begun in 1958, but it operated sporadically after that.[36]

Instead, clinical staff continued to focus on women's sexual morality, in-cluding promiscuity, illegitimate childbearing, and common-law marriage. As Bernard Robinson observed in a typical case: "This woman has never made an adequate personal social adjustment and there is nothing to indicate that she has the capacity to secede [sic] from her pattern of immoral sexual behavior." In the case of an African American drug addict whose only previous arrests had been for prostitution, Robinson reported: "Her personal social-sexual ad-justment has been unstable. She has practiced prostitution for more than ten years." Reiterating his earlier claim that "her criminal orientation is consider-able, Robinson concluded: "*Her pattern of living is immoral, inadequate, and delinquent.* There is no evidence that any fundamental change of significance has taken place in her general orientation to society." Although he acknowl-edged that she had "used narcotics for only a six-month period" two years previously, Robinson concluded emphatically: "*She is fundamentally a delin-quent person,* and there are no indications that she intends to change her mode of behavior in the foreseeable future." Although many of these phrases could have been culled from reports from any decade (with the substitution of "psychopathic" for "fundamentally delinquent"), in the 1950s and 1960s sociologists applied these labels even more uniformly, expressing virtually no hope that the reformatory could rehabilitate wayward women or that the women would succeed after their release.[37]

African American prisoners, who regularly requested interviews with Robinson, seem to have been unaware of his contradictory attitudes. Ex-inmate Carol Rawlings (incarcerated from 1957 to 1963) described Robinson as "the most wonderful black man. He was trustworthy and inmates would tell him confidential stuff." She claimed that he "fought for all inmates" and credited him with "breaking down the [cottage] segregation" in 1960. Office employee Ann Wagner recalled, "He did a lot of counseling and talking with inmates." In 1958 Yvette Emmerson wrote Superintendent Biedermann:

> This is my second letter to you of this nature. I asked to have my name down to see Mr. Robinson almost 3 weeks ago. For some reason most staff here aren't concern [sic] to have just a heart to heart talk with an inmate. I asked three dif-ferent staff members would they try to see if I could get a talk with someone. And still I've had no response. I understand that the population is of enormous number. Mr. Robinson is a very busy man. I also realize that I'm no one special. And I must wait my turn.

Even though many African American prisoners perceived Robinson as an advocate and ally, his written assessments, couched in the era's standard psychological jargon, reveal little warmth or sympathy.[38]

The hostile tone of sociologists' reports and their declining faith in rehabilitation reflected the dominant ideology of leading officials in the DPS and the Division of the Criminologist, as well as the overall atmosphere at the women's institution. After Superintendent Hazard's final resignation in 1953, Dwight superintendents came from backgrounds in law enforcement rather than education or social work. Although Ruth Biedermann (1954–1962) and Margaret Morrissey (1962–1972) verbally endorsed a treatment rhetoric, in practice, security, discipline, custody, and control were their overriding concerns. Both regarded clinical staff with suspicion. Sociologists, hired and supervised by the Division of the Criminologist, were effectively outside their control.

• • •

The founders of the Illinois State Reformatory for Women confidently assumed that scientific classification would result in a specialized treatment program for each prisoner. In actuality, the institution lacked the facilities, resources, and personnel to offer genuinely individualized services. At most, a prisoner could be shuffled from one limited housing, work, or school placement to another. By 1940 the vaunted four-person classification team of full-time psychiatrist, psychologist, social worker, and resident physician was reduced to a single position filled by a part-time psychiatrist. After 1956 young sociologists with little training beyond undergraduate coursework, became responsible for diagnosing, classifying, and predicting the future behavior of women they barely knew. Although ostensibly trained and supervised by senior staff from the Division of the Criminologist, they were primarily instructed by their secretaries and inmate clerks. The numerous admissions, classification, and pre-parole reports they authored parroted the same jargon and stock evaluations of their predecessors, routinely reducing the complexities of women's lives to prototypical diagnoses.

Echoing Superintendent Helen Hazard's conviction that "practically all of the women have deep-seated emotional conflicts," conventional criminology continued to pathologize women's law-breaking, emphasizing psychological and physiological explanations in contrast to economic or social factors. Although the term *psychopathic* fell out of favor, prison sociologists persisted in labeling nearly all women as psychologically abnormal. In the 1950s they constructed an equally elastic category, "inadequate personality," and diagnosed one-half (56%) of the women with this disorder. In the same period they classified a bare 1 percent as exhibiting "no gross personality defect." Adhering to the dominant criminological discourse, in the 1950s and 1960s sociologists continued to gauge female inmates by their sexual practices as well as by an implicit diagnostic category of moral inadequacy.

The next chapter examines the history of the Illinois parole board and explores the many extralegal variables, including morality, race, reputation, and appearance, that influenced parole board decision making. The mental health officer's evaluation was one of most important factors parole board members weighed in their deliberations. Unlike admissions reports, which provided background information prison staff could draw upon for surveillance, security, and placement purposes throughout a woman's prison career, mental health officers' reports served a single institutional purpose: they were designed to be read at a glance by harried board members whose deliberations typically took only minutes. The unstated intent of the reports was to provide the board with the appearance of objectivity and the pretense of scientific evaluation.

No one noticed or questioned the disjunctions and contradictions that constantly emerged. The accusation that Dr. Ledien leveled against Nola Mae Owens in 1947, that "the picture she gives of herself does not explain her crime," was equally applicable to the shallow portraits rendered by prison psychiatrists and sociologists. Few reports offered any sophisticated analysis of the complexity of human behavior and motivation or of the tangled web of social and economic forces that circumscribed women's lives. Instead, to the authors and readers of the mental health officers' reports, the sources of a woman's criminality required little reflection. Female offending appeared self-explanatory: the fact that a woman had been immoral, had led an intemperate and improper life, was all the explanation that was required.

CHAPTER ELEVEN

"SUCCESS UPON PAROLE IS DOUBTFUL"

Women before the Parole Board

Similar to one-quarter of female convicts released during the 1920s, Anna Booth, a twenty-seven-year-old African American woman convicted of manslaughter, was returned to prison as a parole violator after two years of freedom. At her violation hearing in 1929 Booth explained that shortly after her release she had married a man with whom she had quickly discovered she could not get along. Characterizing him as a "shell-shocked and nervous" World War I veteran, Booth admitted that she had left him without officially divorcing, and had for a short time lived with another man. At this point board member Ward E. Thompson interjected, "Of course, Anna, I would not condone that; that is not right even if you were not on parole." Thompson then explained the hidden subtext of parole: "You know, a parolee must be just a little better than if you were not a parolee?" Booth responded with the usually contrite words, "Yes, sir."

This brief exchange deftly exposes the dilemma that confronted women on parole. They were expected to be "just a little better than" the average woman while facing economic, social, and marital circumstances that were often far more limited or far worse. In defending herself, Booth claimed that her husband had created constant problems. When he "got on his nervous spells" and she tried to leave him, he would "go to the parole agent and tell her all sorts of things on me, things that weren't true." When the parole agent found out that Booth had left her husband to live with another man, the agent threatened to return her as a parole violator unless she promised to break off the relationship. Booth promptly left her new boyfriend. She explained, "I found out it was only going to bring me trouble, and I didn't want to get in trouble. I have done three long years and I know what prison is." Instead of returning to her husband, Booth went to live with her sister.[1]

This chapter examines the gendered nature of parole board decision making, the board's role in disciplining prisoners, and the shifting policies and practices of the Illinois parole board from 1917, when board transcripts were first recorded, to 1963, after which no transcripts have been preserved. During these years the Illinois parole board was among the most restrictive in the country. In addition to doubling sentence lengths for both male and female prisoners, board members denied parole outright to a growing proportion of inmates, from 10 percent in the 1920s to 46 percent in the 1950s, releasing prisoners only after they had served their full sentences.[2]

Legally board members were not supposed to retry prisoners; however, that was essentially what they did, especially under the leadership of board chairman W. C. Jones (1929–1946). Unlike court proceedings, the parole board's hearings were not constrained by legal rules of evidence. Board members routinely grilled women on a wide range of issues irrelevant to their offenses. Similar to mental health officers, board members were as interested in assessing a woman's moral character as they were in ascertaining the severity or nature of her legal transgressions. Even after their release on parole, women were expected to conform to conventional standards of proper femininity. A woman who left her husband, lived with a man out of wedlock, bore an illegitimate child, stayed out late drinking, associated with the wrong friends, acted promiscuously, or became involved in a lesbian relationship risked having her parole revoked and being returned to prison.

Anna Booth's case clearly illustrates both the gendered assumptions of mental health officers' evaluations and the gendered subtext of parole board decision making. For two years after her release Booth turned in her parole reports on time and in person every month, until one month she became ill and was bedridden. At that point Booth's sister called the parole office to leave word that she was unable to report. Booth believed that all was taken care of. She explained to the parole board: "I didn't hear anything else from her [the parole agent] until the police called me out of my bed at my sister's." Earlier that same night her husband had visited, seeking to persuade her to return to him. When Booth refused and told him she had decided to get a divorce, he became enraged and threatened, "You won't get a divorce because I will put you where you can't get a divorce." Booth claimed that he then called her parole officer and lied about her behavior. The agent had her arrested and returned to prison, ostensibly for her failure to report in person that month.[3]

At both Joliet and Dwight, parole hearings were held in an office in the main administration building. The prisoner, seated at a large table, was confronted by the superintendent, one to three board members, and a secretary who transcribed the proceedings. Ward Thompson, the board's main examiner at Booth's hearing, did not challenge or question her version of events. Instead, he quickly switched to another line of questioning, asking whether she drank. Booth admitted that "I do drink some but I don't get drunk or run around on the street and drink." Seemingly impressed by her honesty, he responded, "Now, girl, listen, you are pretty fair here, you are pretty honest, . . . but the question is, how can you get along out on parole?" Booth replied that she had "gotten along fine" on parole, working steadily at the stockyard for the past two years. "If you all would give me a chance," she pleaded, "I will make good, because it was not my intention to break parole. I didn't leave the state and I never intended to, and I never missed reporting. Every report I sent in just as it was due."[4]

Thompson, ignoring her pleas, again interrupted with an entirely new line of questioning, inquiring whether she had ever "run a little sporting house down in Peoria." Booth responded that she had never been in Peoria, and after a brief exchange, Thompson realized that he had confused her case with that of another convict. Perhaps to cover his own mistake, he became intent on finding fault with Booth's character. When she was admitted to prison in 1925, Dr. Walter Martin had diagnosed the twenty-two-year-old Anna Booth as "emotionally unstable," a "pronounced psychopath" and "borderline defective." Alleging that Booth "used alcohol to excess" and was "promiscuous in her sex relations," Martin had concluded that since her admission she "had shown, not less, but more instability." As evidence, he reported that Booth had once been disciplined for "attempting to flirt with Negro visitors coming to see other women" and also for her involvement "in one 'near riot' that resulted in her demotion from A to C grade."[5]

Defending herself at the hearing, Booth attempted to present herself as a proper woman, acceding to the parole board's position that a proper woman was not the kind to flirt with a man. Their extraordinary exchange continued:

Q. Do you think, Anna, you could go out of here and let men alone for a while?
A. Yes sir.
Q. Do you know what they say about you here, that no man can come in here and visit somebody else that you do not flirt with him?
A. I don't know how they could say that. Of course, I had this fellow, but I was not a girl that would flirt around or fool around with somebody else.
Q. They say men come in here to visit other girls and that you flirt with them.
A. No, indeed.
Q. You think that can't be right?
A. No, I never done such a thing as that.
Q. All right.

Booth concluded emphatically, "I never done that in my life. I would not dare to think of anything like that." She promised that she would do anything to avoid another "three long years" in prison. Meanwhile, Thompson continued to question her on her ability to avoid relationships with men:

Q. Do you think you could let men alone now and make a parole?
A. Yes sir, I will do anything to make a parole, because I know what it is to be back here three long years and I have had so much trouble. . . . If you please give me a chance I will make good. I will go back to work.

Q. You have been here an awful short time [on her current parole violation].
A. I will make good.
Q. Well, you will have to do a whole lot better than you have.

The board's implicit definition of doing a "whole lot better" included not just holding steady employment, but also reporting regularly, not engaging in criminal activity, and eschewing common-law or other irregular relationships with men. The board was determined to police women's sexual activity, as Thompson made clear during their final exchange:

Q. Well, you can't go around living with fellows.
A. I won't do that. I was not living with this fellow at the time. [My parole officer] called me into the office and she spoke to me about this . . . and I promised I would not have anything to do with this man again. . . . When you are out you don't want to come back to this place for as little a thing as that, and I swore I would not see this man.

Concluding with a final plea that she be paroled again so she could take care of her son, Booth indicated that she thoroughly grasped the hidden subtext of parole. She understood "how easy it is to come back here. I see now. The least slip you are caught, and I certainly will not ever give you any trouble whatsoever." She now knew that "living with a fellow" out of wedlock was sufficient grounds for parole revocation. Although Booth put up a spirited defense, consistently presenting herself as a responsible worker, dedicated mother, and proper woman whose parole violation was due solely to the interference of an embittered husband, the board rejected Booth's self-presentation and required her to serve four more years in prison for her unintended violation—that of failing one time to report in person.

In 1933 Booth was among the last of the Joliet women to be transferred to Dwight. A new mental health officer, Dr. Edna Longwell deemed her institutional adjustment highly satisfactory. Offering a veiled criticism of the parole board, Dr. Longwell concluded, "it would seem she has not been given a fair opportunity to adjust outside." This time the board voted to release her. In all, Anna Booth served fourteen years under the control of the criminal justice system: seven years in prison and seven on parole. Booth's treatment exemplifies the inordinate control that parole board members wielded over prisoners' lives, both inside and outside the penitentiary.[6]

HISTORY OF THE ILLINOIS PAROLE BOARD

In 1895 the Illinois General Assembly passed one of the nation's earliest indeterminate-sentencing laws and established the state's first parole board. Instead of receiving a fixed sentence—such as one, three, or five years, set by a judge—prisoners were now committed under "undetermined" sentences, such as "one-to-ten" years for larceny. As a result, parole boards rather than judges gained virtually total control over sentence lengths. In theory, the board was to release prisoners only after they could demonstrate their rehabilitation and then was to keep them under surveillance after their release.[7]

Illinois's first parole board, in operation from 1895 to 1917, generated little public controversy until 1917, when it was singled out as one of the causes of that year's massive prison riot at Joliet. Because this board maintained no written transcripts of its hearings, it is impossible to evaluate its policies and practices. However, penitentiary commissioners proudly proclaimed that male prisoners served longer sentences after passage of the 1895 parole law; sentences increased on average by 75 percent, or 1.1 years. In contrast, women's average sentences did not show a consistent increase until the 1920s, suggesting that the state's first parole board failed to apply the same tough standards to female prisoners that they did to males.[8]

In 1917 the Department of Public Welfare (DPW) created a new board structure. The state's second parole board prepared a verbatim transcript of each hearing and a brief summary of their deliberations. These records provide insight into the distinct personalities of different boards. Parole hearings held under Superintendent Will Colvin (1917–1927) were extremely brief and perfunctory. The superintendent and two advisors personally heard all cases, devoting only a few minutes to each. In contrast to Anna Booth's 1929 hearing, the following transcript, representing an entire examination, illustrates the Colvin board's terse approach. The prisoner, Maya Danzer, was a thirty-year-old Hungarian-born woman convicted of larceny.

> Q. You plead guilty of larceny in Cook County, 1 to 10. What was that?
> A. Shop lifting [sic].
> Q. Marshall Field Co? [A major Chicago department store.]
> A. Yes sir.
> Q. Nine suits of underwear and two dresses?
> A. Yes sir.
> Q. What other trouble?
> A. I have been in twice before for shop lifting.
> Q. House of Correction for that?
> A. Yes sir.
> Q. You have been in the House of Correction twice? 5 days and 20 days?
> A. Yes sir.
> Q. What have you decided about it now for the future?
> A. I don't intend to do it any more if I get a chance.
> Q. Parents living?
> A. Yes sir.
> Q. Don't you live at home?
> A. No sir.
> Q. What work have you been doing?
> A. House work.
> Q. We will talk it over and see what we can do.[9]

In this brief interview the board quickly and efficiently gleaned the salient features of Danzer's crime: she was a petty shoplifter with a previous record. On that basis alone they determined she should be punished beyond her one-year minimum. However, her offense was relatively minor, and the following year they voted to release her.

In 1927 Hinton G. Clabaugh, the new superintendent of the DPW's Division of Pardons and Paroles, admitted to a legislative investigating committee that during the previous decade the board had given only two to three minutes for each hearing. As Clabaugh explained, "They could not give much time and get through their work." Despite the superficial character of their hearings, the 1917–1927 board drastically increased women's sentences for all categories of crimes. As table 3 in chapter 6 demonstrates, between 1860 and 1920 the length of women's sentences remained relatively stable, exhibiting only minor and irregular fluctuations. However, in the 1920s the state's second parole board doubled women's average time served for larceny, manslaughter, assault, and murder and tripled the length of robbery sentences. Future boards maintained these longer averages. Indeed, in 1940 the state statistician observed that Illinois prisoners "were serving longer prison terms than those in any other state in the nation," a trend that persisted into the 1960s.[10]

Rumors of corruption and favoritism, apparently well-founded, also plagued the 1917–1927 parole board. At the time of Will County's 1926 grand jury investigation of the Joliet penitentiary, a Chicago grand jury was looking into allegations that the parole board was operating a "pardon mill." Board members were accused of accepting bribes and political favors in exchange for granting parole. The grand juries demanded and won Superintendent Will Colvin's resignation. In 1927 the state legislature again created an entirely new board structure. This time the board would consist of a chairman and nine members, all appointed by the governor. Parole decisions required the vote of six members of the ten-member board. To dispel some of the secrecy and rumor associated with the discredited board, Superintendent Clabaugh opened parole hearings to the public and the press. As Anna Booth's hearing illustrates, after 1927 women's parole examinations became far less perfunctory. Not only did the new ten-member board have more personnel and resources at its disposal, it was philosophically committed to a more rigorous and restrictive release policy. Clabaugh also increased the period of mandatory parole supervision dramatically, from one year to five years. As a result of this policy change, an increased number of women were returned to prison as parole violators.[11]

Whereas Anna Booth blamed her violation on her parole agent, other women pointed to unwarranted police harassment. Dora Kramer, a model prisoner who was described as demonstrating "a very strong effort to adjust herself," was returned on charges of purse snatching fifteen months after her release. Kramer protested that she could have made her parole if she had not returned to Chicago: "There is quite a few officers knew me and they picked me up just on sight. A lot of times I wasn't doing a thing when I would be picked up. I don't know whether you understand it or not, but in Chicago, they pick you up just on your record." The board openly acknowledged this increased surveillance. In a typical case, one board member lectured a woman: "After you have been in prison you are under kind of a cloud and every time anything happens the police are liable to pick you up to take you to the show-up. . . . So you will have to walk pretty straight. You ought to have learned that by this time, haven't you?"[12]

Board members who served between 1927 and 1933 were the most open and unself-conscious about expressing their many racial, ethnic, and religious prejudices. May Peterson's hearing exposes the farcical quality of many of their exchanges. In this 1929 case board members did not initially realize that Peterson was African American. Halfway through her examination board member Thompson interjected, "Colored people mixed up in this?" Peterson responded with some confusion:

A. Sir? Colored people?
Q. Yes. Were there some colored people mixed up in this?
A. Yes, sir. This boy is colored. I am colored.
Q. You are?
A. Yes, sir. Surely, certainly.
Q. There is not much colored blood in you?
A. Well, there is enough to know I am colored.
Q. You would never know it.
A. Know it? Well, I certainly am.
Q. You are down here on the paper [referring to her folder].
A. Well, I came in here colored and I didn't tell them I was anything else.
Q. Let me see your nails. There is very little colored blood in you.

Another board member then interjected, "I think you are a squaw." "Squaw?" Peterson asked, "What is that?" "Indian," he responded. The board turned to another subject, but later, apparently still perplexed, Thompson returned to the issue of Peterson's racial identity: "I can't believe that you are colored. The nails are the best indication of colored people, aren't they?" Thompson then quizzed her on the "exact color" of her husband and daughter. When she answered that both her husbands had been "colored," Thompson replied, "Black?" Peterson responded, "No they were not black, no. Brown skinned." Queried next on her children's color, she answered that her daughter was "more tanner than I am." Finally persuaded that Peterson was indeed a "colored woman," Thompson summarily dismissed her. She was denied parole.[13]

In some instances local officials and parole board members frankly admitted their racism and their assumption that black women exhibited a lower standard of morality. In Annabelle Carruthers's 1929 case a parole board member reported, "Up to the time she got in this trouble she had borne, judging from a Negro standpoint, a very good reputation. She had worked for good people as a maid, worked as an honest, hard working girl." However, she "had many affairs . . . having had two so-called common law husbands." Carruthers was convicted of stabbing and fatally wounding her second husband when he was unarmed. Perplexed as to why the judge had sentenced her for manslaughter rather than murder, the board member reasoned: "It, of course, was nothing more than one of these quarrels that take place between colored people living in an immoral state, and maybe that was the reason she was not indicted for murder."[14]

Reformers, oblivious to the extent to which racial, ethnic, and gender biases infused parole hearings and influenced board decision making, were most distressed that board members remained political appointees who served at the governor's discretion. In September 1929 a new governor, Louis Emmerson, dismissed nearly the entire board. The new board was more diverse—it included an African American lawyer and the first and only woman to serve for the next fifty years—but reformers continued to decry board members' lack of training and professional knowledge. In 1933 another new governor, Henry Horner, dismissed all but one board member. This pattern of patronage appointments persisted over the next four decades: board positions typically served as a sinecure for retired party loyalists with backgrounds in law enforcement. As one 1950s prison sociologist recalled, "They were all a bunch of part-time political hacks with no training in psychology or the social sciences." Aside from the chairman, members were paid for one week's service per month, and for two weeks after 1937. During this time the ten board members visited all four of the state's prisons and heard a total of roughly four hundred cases. They then deliberated in three-man subcommittees and offered recommendations.[15]

W. C. Jones, appointed board chairman in 1929, was the only appointee who maintained his post for more than four years. Jones served under four governors, both Democrat and Republican. Perhaps because he lived only a half hour from the women's reformatory, Jones single-handedly conducted roughly three-quarters of women's hearings from 1932 until his retirement in 1946. In his first statement to the press Jones declared that "paroles will not be easy to obtain. The rules of the parole board . . . will be carried out strictly to the letter." He kept his promise over the next seventeen years.[16]

Jones's hearings were extraordinarily detailed and thorough. A skilled lawyer, he grilled women on every aspect of their offenses, institutional conduct, personal lives, family histories, and future plans. Rarely expressing any empathy, he marshaled trial testimony, police reports, the judge's and state's attorney's statements of fact, and even coroners' reports against inconsistencies in a woman's account. If he was not satisfied or if testimony remained contradictory, Jones drew upon his numerous contacts with local officials to conduct his own investigations, essentially both reprosecuting and retrying prisoners. Viewing such activities as well within his authority, Jones expended more energy than any other board chairman in untangling the legal contradictions, complexities, and uncertainties involved in women's cases. At the same time, he was equally interested in evaluating the degree to which female convicts conformed to conventional standards of respectability. Both moral and legal variables were central in his assessment of women's worthiness for parole.[17]

ASSESSING WOMEN'S WORTHINESS FOR PAROLE

The factors parole boards considered in their decision making remained remarkably consistent over the decades. Although women were carefully interrogated regarding the details of their offenses and prior records, assessment of their moral character remained central to parole decisions. During the 1930s these moral criteria were often explicitly stated. Board member Ward Thompson frequently inquired whether a woman had been "immoral." In 1930 he reported that Dora Eldridge "has the appearance of being a decent sort of young woman." Characterizing her crime as "very petty"—she and her husband had stolen a hog, butchered it, and sold the meat to a local merchant—Thompson dwelled on her respectability. He concluded the session with the following:

> Q. I am trying to get a lone [sic] on you to see what we ought to do. Now, what kind of a girl have you been morally?
> A. I have always been a respectable girl.
> Q. You stand on that, do you?
> A. Yes, sir.
> Q. All right, I don't care to ask you anything else.

Accepting her claims, Thompson recommended Eldridge's parole.[18]

As did mental health officers, board members viewed conformity to conventional marital standards as a key indicator of a woman's respectability. In 1938 Chairman Jones curtly questioned Abigail Cessler about whether she was "going to enter any more common-law relations?" When Cessler responded that she "never intended to do that again," Jones offered a final warning: "You had better not. If you decide you want a home with some man, you better get married, because you must understand you won't have quite the freedom [on parole] that you will have after a Final Discharge some day." Through the 1950s parole board members continued to weigh "immoral" marital or sexual relationships heavily. Dwight sociologists diligently sought to verify the legality of every marriage and divorce. Prisoners had few effective means of refuting suspicions. In 1957 one board member wrote, "Although she says that she was properly married, this examiner believes that [her two marriages] were common law relationships." This suspicion was enough to eliminate her as a candidate for parole.[19]

Similarly, alleged promiscuity, premarital sex, or illegitimate children were potent "black marks" against a woman's moral character. A seemingly uncontrollable sexual drive could brand a woman as deviant and subject her to ongoing supervision by state authorities. In 1931 nineteen-year-old Luella Austin was committed for bigamy. Explaining that she "didn't know anything about the law," she had married for a second time, trusting that her first husband had obtained a legal divorce. The mental health officer reported that she had no previous criminal record and "has reacted well to imprisonment." However, he had reservations about her release, warning that she might "succeed on the outside with careful supervision," but only if "her sexual drive can be controlled." If not, he recommended, she should be committed to "an institution for the feeble-minded."[20]

More damning, the statement of fact signed by the state's attorney and the trial judge reported that Austin was widely regarded as an immoral woman. Not only had she married without divorcing, but she had "consorted with a third man in such a notorious manner as to elicit protests from many good people." The state's attorney had "received numerous complaints about this woman on other charges of adultery and disorderly conduct for about a year before the bigamy charge was discovered." Both he and the judge refused to recommend parole, explaining that Austin "had a bad reputation on other matters" and that they could "say nothing to merit leniency." The board decided that "in view of her conduct"—not institutional conduct, but sexual promiscuity previous to her arrest—she "should *not* be paroled at her minimum." Austin's disregard for the formalities of legal marriage may have been more damning because she was a white woman. Whereas board members acknowledged that common-law relationships were "common among colored people," they were particularly incensed when white women evidenced such "immoral" behavior.[21]

Interracial relationships automatically marked white women as beyond the pale of respectable womanhood. In 1930 board member Thompson bluntly told one woman: "Well, I don't know, Muriel, what else a woman can do besides what you have done and lower herself as a woman, married to a colored man." Similarly, in 1941 Chairman Jones asked Emily Lewis whether she was considering "going back [to] live with that colored man?" Lewis responded that if she was released she planned to live with her mother. Jones replied, "Good. You can never be happy living with a colored man." However, he later noted that according to the parole agent's investigation, Lewis's mother "has a number of colored friends and thinks it is perfectly all right to associate intimately with Negroes." Local gossip revealed that while Lewis's mother was working as a cook at the county home, she "was the only employee who would work and eat with colored people." Chairman Jones fully concurred with the parole agent's conclusion that "the mother's home would not be suitable." The board voted to deny parole.[22]

Like interracial relationships, venereal disease was perceived as another irrefutable indicator of female immorality. As one examiner concluded: "The woman did not make a very favorable impression. Her life has been an improper one. She is suffering from syphilis." The three-member subcommittee "respectfully recommend[ed] she be given the Maximum."[23] After 1926 all women entering prison were routinely tested for venereal disease. Through the mid-1940s the board automatically denied parole as long as an inmate was actively infected. If a woman protested that she would continue treatment if released, the board assumed a paternalistic attitude, attempting to persuade her that it was in her best interest to remain at the institution. The following exchange was typical. Elinor Taylor, a nineteen-year-old serving time for automobile theft, was a model prisoner with no previous arrests. Chairman Thompson began on a sympathetic note:

> I sort of feel that your crime has not been of a very serious nature, but you won't get out of here until you show a negative. . . . You are being taken care of better than you could be on the outside, and if you can't get cured in here you never could get cured outside. . . . This is the place for you until you are well, don't you think so?

When Taylor objected that she could get treatment at home, Thompson cut her off: "Oh, there is no use arguing with me, you won't go home until you get a negative." In contrast, men infected with a venereal disease were rarely singled out for opprobrium. Although officials expressed concern that they receive proper treatment, they could be paroled while infected if they promised to continue medical care on their own.[24]

Similar to mental health officers, parole board members expressed little interest in men's moral, sexual, or marital histories. Of a sample of one hundred male files from the 1930s and 1940s, in only one case was a man queried about whether his marriage was common law or ceremonial. Nor were men ever quizzed regarding the behavior or reputation of their wives, children, mothers, or fathers or questioned about whether they had fathered illegitimate children. Even though board members occasionally commented that "your wife and your children need you," only two men were lectured on their marital responsibilities. Men's drinking habits were similarly ignored unless they had clearly committed their crimes while under the influence of alcohol. Nor were men ever queried about homosexuality within prison. The closest officials came to asking men about their moral character was when they evaluated their employment records. Both mental health officers and parole board members questioned men in depth about their work histories. If a man could prove that he was a "good working man" who had been steadily employed for most of his adult life, this factor was weighed heavily in his favor.[25]

In contrast to their interrogations of men, board members routinely questioned women regarding the reputation, morals, character, and criminal histories of their parents, husbands, children, siblings, and associates. "Any of your people have any difficulty with the law?" was the typical query. In the eyes of board members, such inquiries were eminently rational. Ascertaining a woman's family's status enabled board members to assess more closely the degree of informal social controls the woman would be subjected to upon her release. Authorities recognized that "respectable" families would aid parole agents in keeping watch over paroled convicts. Such families could be relied upon to monitor the parolees' choice of associates and how late they stayed out, notifying the board if they were suspected of drinking or "running around" with men.

Motherhood was rarely a critical factor in parole decision making. Before 1930 women with children served only slightly shorter sentences than those without, and after 1930 the correlation between motherhood and sentence length became even weaker. Although board members routinely inquired about who was taking care of a woman's children during her incarceration, they virtually never raised this issue in their deliberations or case summaries. Some board members may have perceived female convicts as inherently unfit mothers. Equally probable, given that judges rarely sentenced women with large families, board members may simply not have considered motherhood to be a significant variable.

In addition to explicitly weighing moral factors in their decision making, parole board members routinely and unabashedly exposed their stereotypical images of both the "criminal woman" and the woman who "seems out of place in a penal institution." From the 1930s through the 1950s members offered such comments as: "You don't look like a vicious girl or woman." "You don't look like a thief at all." "Well, you are a pretty good looking girl. You are a girl that looks like you come from a fairly decent home and have been fairly well raised." In other instances board members judged a woman's appearance to be unfavorable: "This woman gave the impression of having a rather hard appearance and altogether was a peculiarly unattractive woman." Like mental health officers, board members often resorted to this construct of "hardness" in their evaluations. "The prisoner impresses the interviewer as being somewhat hard," was a typical remark.[26]

Sometimes board members released women who appeared "respectable" even when their cases involved serious offenses. In 1938 a state's attorney wrote that Lucinda Matthews was a "respectable old colored lady" who came from a "very fine colored family." Although a jury had given her ninety-nine years for murder, the state's attorney believed that the standard fourteen-year sentence "would have been ample and proper punishment." He admitted that Matthews had shot her husband in cold blood, but she had done so shortly after learning that he had sexually molested her daughter. Matthews's children testified at her hearing in 1952, and board member Myers commented approvingly, "Well, these children of yours look like they are all right people," a point that he noted several times. Unusually impressed, he concluded that the "inmate creates a most favorable impression. She has all of the appearance of being a very intelligent, clean, rather attractive colored woman. She seems to be rather refined." Matthews was paroled, but only after she had served fourteen years.[27]

Appearances, however, could be deceptive. Women knew they had a set role to play and script to follow. Their release depended in large part on how persuasively they could present themselves as remorseful, repentant, respectable, and reformed. Such attitudes and appearances would not by themselves guarantee parole, but they were almost always necessary ingredients. Geraldine Griffith successfully played on the board's stereotypes when she exploited her status as a white woman and mother of six young children. She entered Joliet pregnant in 1927, convicted of forging $2,500 worth of checks. During her first parole board hearing Ward Thompson declared, "It strikes me you are a sort of motherly appearing woman. What are you mixed up in those checks for?" Griffith responded that her actions were motivated by poverty and her "desperate need" to provide for her children. Seemingly pleased with her responses, Thompson repeated his reaction: "A motherly looking woman like this, down here with a lot of loose women of low character." He then admonished her, "Now listen, Geraldine, this Board, every one, everybody in this room sympathizes with you to a great extent, but I don't know whether you need sympathy or whether you need rough treatment to make you go out and . . . go straight."[28]

In this highly atypical case board members responded sympathetically to the prisoner's maternal status, perhaps because Griffith appeared respectable in every other way. Evidently unable to reconcile the categories of "thief" and "mother," Thompson reiterated: "Her appearance is very much in her favor. She seems to be very much out of place in a woman's penitentiary. . . . She has six small children and has the appearance of an ordinary mother."

Thompson proposed disingenuously that the board could dismiss a vocal letter of protest submitted by the Illinois Bankers' Association because it was dated three years earlier. Characterizing Griffith's as a "very pitiful case," Thompson recommended an immediate parole.

Griffith's freedom proved short-lived: she was returned to prison eighteen months later. A matron who was reading another prisoner's mail had discovered that Griffith had extorted three hundred dollars from the prisoner's mother, claiming that she had inside connections with the parole board and could secure her daughter's early release. At her parole violation hearing Griffith was confronted by the newly appointed chairman W. C. Jones, who summarily dismissed her tearful claim that she had committed her check-writing crimes and confidence game "in order to feed her six little children." She was forced to serve out the two years left of her sentence.[29]

With parole violators the mask of remorse was removed. A woman who had previously pledged her desire to go straight could not offer the same promises a second time. No matter how remorseful or repentant she seemed, the board refused to trust her again. Often a woman only generated further suspicion because she could not clearly articulate why she had violated her parole or because her story appeared improbable according to middle-class standards.

The parole board faced the daunting task of predicting future behavior. Yet the underlying factors upon which they based their predictions typically involved women's past behaviors, which prisoners could neither deny, alter, nor erase. Assessments based on former conduct completely undermined the purpose of the indeterminate sentence, which was supposed to enable officials to reward prisoners for their progress and rehabilitation while incarcerated. Although in the written summaries of their deliberations board members dutifully recorded inmates' participation in the reformatory's educational and vocational programs, they almost never weighed such factors explicitly in their decision making.

MAINTAINING COMPLIANCE AND CONTROL

Parole hearings influenced virtually every aspect of prison life and, along with the threat of loss of good time, served as a major tool in maintaining institutional control. Ex-prisoner Jamella Reynolds recalled,

> The overriding concern was, don't mess up your parole. Everyone knew when your parole hearing was. You were taken out of school six months beforehand. The administration felt that women going before the board were under too much stress to deal with anything else. It was true; it was nerve-wracking.[30]

Although women came before the board only once or twice during their incarceration, they had to carefully weigh their every action against its impact on the board. Inmates were not eligible for a parole hearing unless they had spent their prior three months in "A Grade." In a 1928 letter Adelaide Johnson, who later became a three-time parole violator, explained the significance of this policy in a letter to a friend:

I received my A Grade July 28. Now I am striving to keep my grade. If I get a solitary punishment it will cause me to lose all of those grades. And I shall have to do three months again for each grade lost. So you see what it means to keep in good standing. You are only eligible to meet the board . . . if your standing is good.[31]

For female, but not male, convicts, a single act of misbehavior, such as Anna Booth's "flirting with male visitors," or one demotion in grade could haunt a woman for several years. Chairman Jones took every incident of misconduct seriously. He repeatedly lectured women, "If you can't obey the rules and regulations in here, your chances for obeying the laws on the outside are not good." Upon learning that Millicent Myers had received a demerit for eating a lemon cream pie that she and a group of other inmates had stolen from their cottage kitchen, Jones scathingly challenged her, "I should think you would have enough of stealing on the outside without stealing in here." Similarly, even though staff characterized Delia Bannister's conduct as "excellent," in 1939 Jones queried her on a single demerit. Shortly after entering Dwight, Bannister confessed that she had "given a girl a bar of candy because I didn't know you weren't allowed to give anything to anyone." Jones dismissed this explanation. He may have inferred that staff suspected an illicit relationship.[32]

Any exchange of items between inmates was presumed to imply affection and the possibility of homosexuality. Even unsubstantiated suspicions could provide a pretext for denying parole. In another woman's case summary, Chairman Jones reported: "This prisoner has also figured in some disagreements in her cottage and it is thought that she had sex contact with a colored woman, although complete proof of this is not available." Although the inmate denied this accusation, she admitted "having written notes of wrong character to the colored woman." Homosexuality or any reason for suspicion thereof was perceived as a potent marker of "perverse and unregenerate character."[33]

In addition to denying parole outright, board members could continue women's cases indefinitely, threatening that the least misconduct might result in denial of parole. After 1944, however, the parole board ceased granting continuances. Instead, it simply denied parole outright to over half of women after their first hearing, a policy referred to as "maxing out" or "assigning finals." The practice of assigning finals (or "maximums") at a woman's first (and hence last) parole hearing completely undermined the theory of the indeterminate sentence. The board assessed a woman's rehabilitation after she had served only one year in prison; she would never receive a second opportunity to demonstrate her reformation. Whatever new skills, education, or counseling she received would never be credited to her or weighed in her favor. The board's new policy was particularly disturbing to long-term women. Once denied parole, a woman serving the standard "one-to-fourteen" year sentence for manslaughter knew that she would have to serve exactly 8.3 years (her 14-year maximum less all possible good time credits). This policy contributed substantially to widespread inmate discontent and a breakdown in discipline at Dwight in the late 1940s (discussed in the next chapter).

Board members may have simply lacked the time to rehear cases or continue them indefinitely and had therefore adopted the ill-conceived policy of assigning finals as a matter of expediency. The state's total prisoner population increased 42 percent during the 1930s (from 8,800 to 12,500). Whereas Chairman Jones appeared thoroughly familiar with individual women's cases, other board members, who served far shorter tenures, clearly lacked his knowledge, tenacity, and zeal. The practice of assigning finals at a prisoner's first parole hearing may also have reflected mounting skepticism over the reformatory's capacity to rehabilitate women.

The board's increasingly draconian release policies also represented a reaction to the intense criticism it received from Chicago newspapers throughout the 1930s. In 1938 the *Chicago Tribune* launched a concerted campaign against parole. Newspaper reports inflamed public fears that a disproportionate amount of crime was committed by men on parole and fueled popular sentiment that paroled prisoners escaped their just punishment. Board members regularly admonished male prisoners: "Every time you fellows come back after we let you out we get a black eye in the newspapers about the Parole Board being too soft." Although public anxieties focused on male parole violators, women were equally affected by the board's toughening stance.[34]

Bessie Barker's case exposes many of the contradictions engendered by the board's practice of "assigning finals" after a woman's first parole hearing. In 1942 Barker, a thirty-five-year-old white woman, claimed that the state's attorney had pledged "she would go out in a year" if she voluntarily pleaded guilty to manslaughter, which carried a possible one-to-fourteen-year sentence. Despite his alleged promise, one year later the state's attorney wrote the board that Barker had been "connected with a lot of crime in our County" and "bears a very bad reputation." He recommended that she "be held until she has proven to be reformed."[35]

Chairman Jones, concerned about contradictory testimony presented by witnesses in court, launched his own investigation. In his view the evidence "indicate[d] perhaps there was premeditation"; the killing may not have been accidental. The board denied parole and gave Barker a "finals" or "Max X." Shortly thereafter, Barker escaped, only to be apprehended within a few hours. At a special hearing following her failed escape attempt, Jones brusquely cut short Barker's protestations that she had not had a fair trial. He contended: "We can't retry cases. We are not permitted to." This claim was patently false, particularly in light of his own extrajudicial investigation. Barker responded indignantly:

A. But you don't have to give me the Maximum "X."
Q. Your case seemed to warrant it. You were involved in a case where a man died.
A. Other folks have too, and it wasn't no fault of mine he died.
Q. Yes, other people have, and some of them serve much longer and some people are electrocuted.

A. I was absolutely trying to protect myself. He was trying to take my life—
   [Again Jones cut off her explanation.]

Q. As I say, we can't retry cases.

Jones warned Barker against another escape.

Q. I wondered if you had the impression that because you received a Maxi
   mum "X," eight years and three months, that you could do as you
   please, engage in misconduct, with the thought there wouldn't be any
   further penalty?

A. No, I don't exactly think of it that way.

Q. If you escape again we can take all your Statutory Good Time away and you
   will serve all of your fourteen years. . . . You girls must not get the im
   pression that you can do as you please, such as escaping, where you
   have a Maximum "X," without any penalty.

At this point Superintendent Hazard interjected, "I think she made the mistake of listening to a girl who had only a flat [misdemeanor] sentence and therefore had nothing to lose." Jones curtly reminded Barker, "Girls with flat sentences of one year are in a little different position than you other women." The
parole board had no authority over misdemeanants. Regardless of their conduct,
they were automatically released after twelve months. Baker remained defiant. "I
don't know; sometimes I get disgusted and would do anything." When Jones
countered that "you are the only one to pay the penalty for it afterwards," Barker
offered a final bitter rebuttal: "They say the first hundred years is the hardest!"[36]

CONFLICTS AMONG THE PAROLE BOARD,
JUDGES, AND PROSECUTING ATTORNEYS

Throughout his tenure from 1929 to 1946, Chairman W. C. Jones expressed
the least concern of any chairman for the opinions and recommendations of
local court authorities. Trial judges and state's attorneys occasionally promised
defendants that they would be paroled at their one-year minimum if they
pleaded guilty. Sometimes such pledges were part of the informal plea bargaining agreement. However, judges possessed no legal authority to make such
promises, and because parole board members viewed these pledges as a direct
challenge to their authority, they felt no obligation to honor them. This conflict had always existed, but it was exacerbated by Chairman Jones's dictatorial
stance. Although Jones sometimes acknowledged that the parole board was
not legally empowered to "retry" a woman, that is exactly what he did.

The case of Sylvia Sunderland, a twenty-two-year-old African American
woman convicted of manslaughter in her husband's fatal stabbing in 1938,
illustrates the tensions that frequently emerged between local authorities
and the parole board. Jones began Sunderland's hearing in his typical fash-
ion, brusquely interrogating her on a wide range of topics. He asked her age,
her marital history, how many children she had, where she went to school,
the age at which she had quit school, why and when she moved to Illinois,

what her former jobs had been, the date on which she married, her husband's occupation and employer, how often she "frequented taverns," whether any other members of her family had ever been "in trouble with the law," and what the character of her parole sponsor was ("what kind of a woman is she morally?"). Next Jones interrogated Sunderland about the crime scene: the layout of the room, what the knife looked like, where she got it, how she was holding it, how exactly her husband had grabbed her, how close she was when she struck him, and their respective heights and weights—all standard features of his interrogations.

The state's attorney and judge had both recommended an early parole, noting that Sunderland had never before been charged with a crime and that her family were "eminently respectable colored folks." A parole agent reported that her parents' home was "the neatest, cleanest, and in the best taste of any colored home she ever had occasion to visit" and that "the mother amazed her with her refined conversation." Staff reports verified that Sunderland's institutional adjustment was excellent.

Chairman Jones, however, was unconvinced. Sunderland had admitted to frequenting dances and taverns without her husband. Although she claimed her husband had given her permission, Jones clearly felt that his jealousy—the source of their many confrontations, including the fight that resulted in his death—was justified. Moreover, Jones disputed Sunderland's contention that her husband had attacked her first and that she had stabbed him inadvertently as they struggled over a knife. On the basis of the coroner's report and his own questioning, he concluded that "if he [her husband] were behind her (as she claimed) it would have been practically impossible for him to have been stabbed accidentally." Jones speculated that the judge and state's attorney had allowed Sunderland to plead guilty to manslaughter only because there were no eyewitnesses who could testify against her. In his opinion, "Her story does not ring true. . . . While there may have been some provocation for her act, in all human probability she stabbed him with a butcher knife, not accidentally, but willfully." Jones's interpretation outweighed both the trial judge's and the prosecuting attorney's recommendations for leniency. The board refused Sunderland's parole.[37]

In even more fundamental ways the parole board's stance came into conflict with the practical and time-honored realities of judicial processing. Usually when an accused person "voluntarily" pleaded guilty, she pleaded guilty to a lesser offense than the one for which she would have been tried if her case had gone to trial. For example, state's attorneys (who determined the specific charges) routinely reduced armed robbery to simple robbery or even larceny. Once the accused was sentenced under a lesser charge, the question then arose as to whether the parole board should consider the reduced charge or the actual circumstances of the crime when it made its decision. Under Chairman Jones the board routinely based its conclusions upon its own interpretation of the prisoner's crime; it essentially retried the woman. This practice was particularly critical in cases of manslaughter and murder, where the legal line between the crimes was very fine yet the resulting disparities in sentence length were the greatest.

The legal community was itself sharply divided over the appropriate role of the parole board. In 1943 state legislators heeded the voice of the powerful Illinois Association of State's Attorneys, to which many legislators belonged, and passed the Ward-Rennick Bill. Legislators who voted for the bill criticized the parole board's past policies. The new law empowered judges to give any sentence they chose within the traditional minimum and maximum limits. Thus, in larceny cases a judge could now hand down far narrower sentences, such as "2-to-5" years, "1-to-2" years, or even "1-to-1.5" years. Under the Ward-Rennick law judges gained greater control over sentencing. Because they tended to select both lower and narrower ranges, average sentences for nearly all offenses (murder was an exception) declined from the 1930s to the 1940s. The decline in sentence lengths averaged 32 percent for African American women and 23 percent for white women. The reduction in sentence length was especially marked for manslaughter cases, in which the parole board had previously exercised the greatest discretion (see table 3). These lower averages persisted into the 1950s, with some random fluctuations. Still, in the 1960s Illinois's prisoners continued to serve among the longest sentences in the country.[38]

New parole board members acquiesced to their more limited role. After Chairman Jones resigned in 1946, the board never again conducted extrajudicial investigations into individual cases. Although some board members continued to interrogate women closely on the details of their crimes, most took pains to assure them that they were not "trying the case." In 1946 examiner Michael Gross cut off one prisoner's claims of innocence with the response, "Well, mind you, I don't intend to pass on the entire controversy myself, because I don't know any more about it than just what I read here [in the prisoner's file]." In 1956 another board member offered a similar denial: "Of course, I am not trying the case." As a consequence, hearings held during the 1950s tended to be more perfunctory than those held in earlier decades.[39]

Nevertheless, it was humanly impossible for board members to avoid reaching their own conclusions regarding the mitigating and aggravating factors involved in prisoners' legal cases. One way of dealing with this contradiction was to abrogate entirely any responsibility for individual decision making. Thus, the board responded to the 1943 Ward-Rennick law by doubling the number of cases to which it simply assigned finals, denying parole outright, from one-third (31%) of parole applications in the 1930s to two-thirds (66%) in the 1940s. Board members contended that because judges generally handed down sentences with a narrow range, such as two-to-four years, it made little difference whether a woman was paroled at the end of her two-year minimum or was forced to serve her maximum, 3.3 years in this case with good time. Board members regularly concluded: "In view of the fact that she will shortly be discharged" the examiner "recommends that parole be denied and she be held to her maximum."[40]

Thus, despite the 1943 law, the parole board still exercised wide discretion, operating without any judicial or legal oversight. Throughout the 1950s women continued to report that judges or state's attorneys had promised they would only have to serve their minimum sentence if they pleaded guilty. In 1955 Olivia Johnson claimed to have received several assurances: "Three times I asked, 'Are you positive . . . that I will get out in eleven months?'" The judge gave his word and she agreed to plead guilty. The parole board forced her to serve nearly seven years.[41]

In 1957 Margaret O'Connor wrote a bitter letter after she was denied parole:

> I'm angry, I'll admit it—I can't smile and say "it doesn't matter" cause it does. Now is the time that I'm needed at home more than any other due to my mother's mental illness and my children. . . . All I needed was a chance and I was denied. . . . I'm still sort of dazed. . . . I have never hated anyone in my life till now and I am completely filled with hatred. If I didn't have a family the denial would have only hurt my feelings cause I'm capable of shouldering any punishment due me. The situation is different though—I have a wonderful family and they are being hurt . . . Judge Salter sentenced me [for two-to-ten years] with the understanding that I would be given consideration at the end of two years. Why don't they respect his wishes—why should those men take it upon themselves to deny me the opportunity to be with my family?? I've seen girls make parole and come right back [as violators] and be paroled again. Why can't I have my chance?

O'Connor concluded with a sentiment expressed by many women: "How easy 'doing time' would be if I didn't have a family. My thoughts are always at home, so you can easily understand the mental agony that I have to endure."[42]

GENDER AND THE CONTRADICTIONS OF PAROLE DECISION MAKING

Parole boards across the country faced a common dilemma, and in the end most resorted to similar strategies. In 1931 the Wickersham Commission conducted one of the only national investigations of parole board procedures. The commission asked, "How are prisoners actually selected for parole in the American states today?" Its report concluded that "the simplest thing, of course, is to release nobody or everybody." The commission named Illinois as one of the minority of states that "pursued the policy of refusing nearly all applications for parole," in contrast to other states that "released everybody at the earliest possible moment." Despite their practice of wholesale issuing of parole denials, Illinois board members claimed that they carefully weighed the individual factors in every case. Indeed, one member wrote a one-to-four-page summary of the board's deliberations after each hearing. However, most of these summaries are incoherent, a random recitation of negative and positive factors. More often than not, they fail to illuminate why a particular decision was reached in a particular case.[43]

Staff reports and recommendations were equally contradictory. Although board members sometimes reported that "the professionals are all for her," it was far more common for them to conclude that the professionals—the prison psychiatrists, social workers, psychologists, and sociologists—were "on the fence" or disagreed. Reports from the staff were even more difficult to weigh. Many times a single observer offered an inconsistent or incoherent evaluation. This 1948 pre-parole report on Leticia Mullin was typical: "The cottage warder has reported her as emotional, flighty, a religious fanatic, a good and conscientious worker, co-operative when in control of herself, and that she has shown improvement in her adjustment with the girls." The mental health officer then summarized the equally contradictory reports from Mullin's work supervisors:

> In Domestic Arts her effort and behavior were good and she showed great improvement in her sewing ability. In the Administration Building she was sullen and uncooperative. In Power Sewing she was slow and indolent. In the Shirt Factory she was a good worker, her citizenship was good, but she was not dependable. On the Lawn she did fairly well. In the Visiting Room she did quite well, but was emotional and became upset over trivials. In Handicraft she was a fair worker, did not like to be told what to do, and was restless.[44]

How were parole board members supposed to weigh such disparate and discrepant testimony within the five to ten minutes they took to deliberate upon an individual case? The hurried and often incoherent nature of their summary reports suggest little in the way of thoughtful deliberation or informed decision making. Was the parole hearing nothing but a sham? Yes and no. Occasionally, blatant miscarriages of justice were corrected. However, in most cases the likelihood of parole being granted strikes the outside observer—as well as prisoners at the time—as a matter of little more than chance. Illinois parole board members never articulated their criteria or the competing factors they weighed in their decision making. Other than race, no clearly measurable variable shows consistent correlation with length of time served. Some first offenders were paroled early, but many others were held to their maximum, sometimes in direct defiance of judges' and state's attorneys requests for leniency. Likewise, although board members were usually favorably impressed by women who "appeared respectable" and displayed an unblemished moral background, not all such women were granted parole.[45]

The Wickersham Committee, sorely tried and tested, concluded that parole was indeed a lottery—a lottery heavily influenced by highly random and subjective variables. In the final analysis, they declared:

> The only other factor generally entering into parole decisions is the appearance, personality, or general demeanor of the applicant. Truthfulness, square shoulders, a good voice, or a steady eye may go far toward winning a scoundrel his freedom in more than one state. Members of parole boards are human . . . and are often inclined to congratulate themselves on their ability to read character at a glance. And so, shrewd but experimental guesswork, prejudices, and hunches many times decide whether a boy is to spend another two or three years behind prison walls.[46]

Wickersham committee members failed to analyze parole boards' attitudes toward female offenders. Nor did they speculate how such elusive factors as appearance and character were interpreted when applied to women. The questions about "morality"—such as those involving promiscuity, public drinking, having illegitimate children, common-law marriages, and interracial relationships—that permeated women's parole hearings were entirely missing from men's examinations. Perhaps such sexist treatment was eminently rational: society at large, not the parole board, decreed that the rules that governed proper male behavior were far more flexible than those that governed women's lives. A woman whom local authorities and community members perceived as immoral had far less chance of "making good" on parole than did a man. Indeed, whatever her previous reputation, a woman branded with the label "ex-convict" faced enormous social prejudices. Closely supervised after her release, she risked return to prison for any transgressions of the norms of proper femininity. Parole boards, fully cognizant of these realities, expressed diminishing faith in the rehabilitative powers of reformatory regimes. Growing disorder at the Illinois State Reformatory for Women between 1930 and 1954 further fueled their disillusionment.

PART V

MANAGING WAYWARD WOMEN AT THE ILLINOIS STATE REFORMATORY FOR WOMEN, 1930–1972

CHAPTER TWELVE

"DISCIPLINE AND MORALE HAVE NOT BEEN SATISFACTORY"

The Rise and Fall of the Domestic Ideal, 1930–1954

On January 1, 1944, Mrs. Miller, a cottage warder, reported: "In one day here, I have found Frances Grayson, second cook, runs the kitchen as she pleases. I heard her say she would butter up Mrs. Miller as she had Mrs. Orr and she would run the kitchen." Miller had no intention of allowing "her girls" to do as they pleased. She gave Grayson a demerit for impudence. One week later she wrote a note to Dwight's acting superintendent Elizabeth Mann. Warder Miller explained that at the dinner table she had seen inmate Ruby Sanders pass a green and white handkerchief to Crystal Hunter, who later used it to sneak a piece of cake upstairs. Miller dryly remarked: "I noticed Crystal's bust being terribly large, but didn't say anything." She concluded, "I don't believe Crystal will ever make her grade, is one of the most untruthful girls I have ever had in my cottage." Miller recommended that both Crystal Hunter and Ruby Sanders spend two days in isolation as punishment. Three days later she reported:

> Crystal was very haughty when I locked her up. . . . She didn't know that I had seen her passing the cake in the handkerchief. It was a big surprise to all girls and after breakfast about four of them came to my office and said Mrs. Miller— "We want to hold court with you"—Allison Jefferson doing the talking. I said

what for, and she said we don't want these girls in punishment and want you to have Mrs. Mann come to the cottage right away. I told them I was still running the cottage and I wasn't going to call Mrs. Mann and for them to go back to their work at once. They all went back upstairs without another word. They would run me if they could.[1]

This brief confrontation between inmates and their cottage warder reflected the deepening tensions at the reformatory during the 1940s. Cottage life rarely matched the tranquil domestic visions of the reformatory's founders. Warders and their "girls" competed daily over who would "run the cottage." In this instance, the women appropriated the concept of "holding court" (referring to the institution's disciplinary process) when they protested what they perceived as warder Miller's overly harsh reaction: assigning an inmate to two days in isolation for making off with an extra piece of cake. Miller refused to compromise. A few months later she reprimanded three inmates for failing to perform the housework according to her exacting standards:

> They haven't taken any interest in the kitchen. I pointed out dirty screens and windows. . . . Olga Yosinov said, I don't intend to clean them, I am not going to work myself to death. Louise Jennings said, I took care of my assignment. I asked her why the windows and bars are so dirty then. She said, I know nothing about such, that's not my job. The kitchen is filthy. I know they haven't cleaned it properly in ages.[2]

Miller concluded bitterly, "The girls in the cottage have rules of their own they live by and think I am crazy when I mention rules." Like many warders, Miller repeatedly complained that even women who showed no outward resistance needed constant supervision and surveillance. At one inmate's biannual classification meeting she offered the following assessment, "Bernice is courteous and has a cheerful disposition. She is neat and clean, spends her leisure time gossiping and crocheting." However, Miller added, "She will keep the rules only as long as you are watching her. Bernice knows how to work but has to be watched and at times made to do a good job." Similar accusations, along with the laments that "she is not too willing a worker" and "she requires close supervision" appeared over and over again in warders' reports.[3]

This chapter traces the conflicts that arose between rehabilitative ideals and institutional realities from 1930 to 1954, examining cottage life, staff-inmate relationships, discipline and morale, racial tensions, and vocational and educational programs. For the first half of the 1930s Superintendent Helen Hazard expressed an ebullient optimism, characterizing these years as "gratifying" and "unusually pleasant and satisfactory." Describing morale as "excellent," she "took great pride" in reporting the institution's accomplishments. During the 1940s, however, Hazard repeatedly complained about a growing "spirit of lawlessness, defiance, and rank discourtesy." In 1949 she resigned in despair, then returned briefly in 1953 after three superintendents had come and gone.

In their pioneering studies of the first women's reformatories, historians Estelle B. Freedman and Nicole Hahn Rafter maintain that authorities succeeded in "inculcating prisoners with the values of reformatory treatment." Both go so far as to claim that women lost a sense of themselves as prisoners. Indeed, Rafter suggests that women's prisons deserve special attention precisely because of this very "success." She argues that

> Upon occasion women's prisons have achieved the ultimate goal of social control— persuading subjects not merely to comply but to actually internalize new values, so that they come to supervise themselves by the authorities' rules. No men's prison has ever been so "successful" in the project of, literally, re-formation.

Likewise, Freedman concludes that, "the bulk of the evidence indicates . . . that most inmates complied with the official routines. . . . They seem to have become the dutiful daughters required by the institutional regimens."[4]

Rafter and Freedman acknowledge that institutional control relied on a complex system of rewards and punishments in which coercion usually played the major role. Freedman suggests that the reformatory took on the attributes of a "total institution." During their first weeks of incarceration inmates were subjected to an orientation period that consisted of solitary confinement and the loss of all personal belongings. Freedman presumes that this initiation period succeeded in "strip[ping] inmates of their normal identities" while giving their keepers "absolute power to impose their ideals on them." For unruly or recalcitrant women, reformatories employed a full range of punishments. Each institution relied on solitary confinement and restricted diets of bread and water; some even resorted to corporal punishment. Nonetheless, Freedman suggests that the "semblance of domesticity masked the fact that women were indeed prisoners: without consciousness of their position, prisoners were less likely to strike out at their keepers."[5]

Similarly, Rafter identifies a variety of disciplinary techniques that were used to induce conformity, including infantilization, disruption of inmates' ties to their families and friends, threats of loss of their children, mail censoring and visitor screening, parole policies that limited contact with family and former friends, and the threat of parole revocation if they did not maintain proper behavior. However, like Freedman, Rafter argues that reformatories also provided women with valued goods and services, including shelter, a nourishing diet, hospital and medical care (especially valued by pregnant inmates), and counseling and moral guidance, within an environment safe from "incestuous fathers, brutal husbands, and oppressive employers." Inmates' letters reveal that some were grateful for these services. Through this array of positive and negative incentives, Rafter concludes, the majority of young women "were, in fact, reformed."[6]

However, the limited evidence Freedman and Rafter present is not particularly persuasive. Recidivism rates were high at even the most "model" Progressive Era reformatories. Observers, administrators, and female social reformers were continually shocked and dismayed by the women's lack of repentance regarding their criminal, sexual, and moral transgressions. Many prisoners continued to resist and even flaunt Victorian and Progressive Era conceptions of gentility, sexual restraint, and proper feminine behavior even after their incarceration. These final chapters, which examine the evolution of a women's reformatory through the late twentieth century, offer a wealth of evidence challenging Freedman's and Rafter's conclusions.[7]

Those who championed the women's reformatory prisons created a far more oppressive and repressive institution than is commonly recognized. Even though the Illinois State Reformatory for Women was one of the best equipped and staffed of the nation's twenty women's reformatories in the 1930s, few women doubted that they were in anything other than a prison. Regardless of their "homelike" appearance, the intimate cottage living arrangement created unprecedented opportunities for surveillance and control. Warders vigilantly monitored every word and action, policing women's language, attitudes, dress, table manners, associations, and friendships. Lizzie Von Stuben, Dwight's first inmate, shocked parole board members by characterizing the institution as a prison at her first parole hearing. Most disturbing was the fact that Von Stuben was no troublemaker. Indeed, superintendent Helen Hazard described her as a "model prisoner" who had achieved "as perfect a record as I have known any woman to make in my eleven years of reformatory experience."[8]

The distinction between a reformatory and a penitentiary was entirely lost on most inmates. Paula Putnam, another model prisoner, also had bitter memories. In 1936 she was sentenced for stealing chickens in rural Illinois. In an interview sixty years later, the ailing Putnam expressed outrage over having been committed to a "penitentiary" for such a minor offense. The shame she felt was still palpable. Nor did the residents of her rural town grasp the distinction between the two types of institutions: for years after her release neighbors taunted Putnam for having "served time at the penitentiary." In nearly all their censored letters and confiscated notes, inmates referred to the institution as a prison or penitentiary, virtually never as a reformatory. As one woman bluntly wrote her mother: "I don't know how to say this but I guess it's best to get to the point. I am in the Dwight State Penitentiary for Women."[9]

• • •

This chapter begins with a critical analysis of cottage life, heralded as the foundation for women's rehabilitation. Newspapers throughout the state and the nation hailed the official opening of the Illinois State Reformatory for Women in 1931. All of the early reports stressed the pleasant and "homelike" atmosphere of the cottages, the beauty of the grounds, the quality of the construction and workmanship. As one journalist wrote, "There are no high stone walls, no armed guards, Instead there are potted plants in the women's rooms, gay colored napkins on dining room tables, and pianos with popular and classical music on the racks in cottage living rooms, which are bright and cheerful with wicker furniture." Many writers went so far as to deny the penal character of the institution entirely, drawing analogies instead to chateaux, boarding schools, or country estates.[10]

Reformatory administrators were well aware of the positive impression their institutions made on the average observer. In fact, superintendents often felt the need to defend themselves against the accusation that they di-

rected "country clubs" that merely "coddled criminals." Reformatory supporters were caught in the contradiction of having designed an institution
that would bear as little surface resemblance to a prison as possible, then being forced to defend themselves by asserting that it was, at heart, still a
prison. Dr. Mary B. Harris, Superintendent of Alderson Federal Women's Reformatory, addressed these public perceptions in her 1936 autobiography:

> "Don't they all want to stay here when their time is up?" "Probably this is better
> than anything most of them have had in their own homes." "I think I'll do
> something to get sent here myself." These are remarks and questions that recur
> so frequently from casual visitors that we always expect them; and we try not to
> appear weary when we explain that, no matter how pleasant a place is, loss of
> liberty takes away the charm; that imprisonment even under luxurious condi-
> tions would press on the nerves; and we remind our questioner that children
> run away from home and from expensive boarding schools.[11]

Even though on the outside reformatories appeared much more benign
than men's prisons—quaint cottages and unsecured housing units scattered
across a campus setting—surveillance of women within their small living
units was much more intense and invasive than that experienced by male
prisoners housed in larger and far more anonymous cell blocks. Moreover, by
the 1930s many women's institutions served as both penitentiaries and reformatories. During the Great Depression states often closed their custodial
women's units, transferring their populations to the new reformatories. Even
where this did not occur, within the space of a single decade most reformatories came to resemble the traditional custodial women's prisons in the strict-
ness of their disciplinary regimes, their lack of programs, and their difficulty
in attracting qualified personnel. In addition, the most distinct aspect of the
reformatories, their "family style" cottage architectural design, soon gave
way to dormitories and more traditional cell block units as the institutions
expanded and economics triumphed over ideology.

At Dwight a thirty-six-cell high-security unit was constructed in 1933 to
house the female felons transferred from Joliet. (In the 1950s this unit was
used to house suspected lesbians.) Meanwhile, Hazard campaigned for additional secure housing for the women who were already proving resistant to
the reformatory's regime. After forty women escaped during the institution's
first four years, a twenty-foot cyclone fence was constructed and bars were
installed on the cottage windows in 1935. The next year a forty-cell medium-
security unit was added. As a result, two-fifths (41%) of the 184 inmate
rooms were traditional cells. Ironically, the short-term misdemeanant
women, who were initially regarded as more amenable to rehabilitation,
were housed in the cell house units. The cottages were reserved as a reward
for good behavior for longer-term female felons.

Nevertheless, in their earliest accounts Hazard and her supporters repeatedly extolled the beauty, comfort, and quality of the cottage "homes," insist-
ing that the cottage system was the heart of the institution's rehabilitative
philosophy. Cottage living facilitated individualized treatment, training in

appropriate gender-role behaviors, and resocialization in group-living skills. Within this ideology, "home" was imbued with a tremendous transformative power all its own. At a 1932 convention of the Illinois Federated Women's Clubs, Hazard "gave example after example showing where the crimes for which these girls were sentenced were natural results of environment, lack of home training, or of no home at all." Hazard concluded:

> Few of the women are unhappy [at Dwight]. They cannot long resist the appeal of home life. Many of them have found a home in the institution for the first time in their lives. Others grow fond of it because of broken homes they have left. Home life is the keynote of the institution. We have found that most of the cases which come to us result from broken homes.[12]

By the mid-1930s, however, Hazard had abandoned entirely such sentimental and romanticized claims. The cottage possessed only the most tenuous relationship to a real home. In this confined and tightly controlled environment, the tensions of crowded group life were unmitigated by ties of kinship, friendship, love, or affection. Few elements of ordinary home life were permissible.

Beginning in the early 1940s women were graded daily on their attitude, work, and "citizenship," or cooperation. In 1948 a warder declared, "I am giving Jill Bruen poor for wasting food. She ate the crust off of three large rolls and left the centers. She does her toast in the morning just the opposite, eats only the centers." In another typical case, a warder noted, "I am giving Shirley Wilkins poor for her attitude at the breakfast table this morning."

> Shirley is just spoiling for trouble, nothing is ever right. If we don't have one particular kind of food Shirley wants it very bad, and when we have that same kind of food she won't eat it at all. Two days last week we had hot chocolate for dinner to use up our supplies of milk. . . . Shirley wouldn't eat the dinner because she didn't have coffee. On Friday we had coffee but Shirley didn't want any. A few mornings ago she wanted a glass to squeeze her grapefruit in. When they didn't get it for her she squeezed it in her cereal bowl and watched to see that I saw her drink it from the bowl.[13]

Shirley's refusal to drink coffee when it was provided, followed by her open defiance of table manners, resulted in an additional demerit. This example, culled from hundreds of similar incidents, reveals both the inordinately high levels of surveillance that female convicts endured and their equally determined resistance. Shirley, well aware that her every act was being carefully monitored, very deliberately "watched to see" that the warder observed her offending behaviors.

By the 1950s the phrase "I observed her closely," appeared frequently in warders' accounts. In a common example from a disciplinary ticket, one warder wrote: "Gertrude Jennings took 23 minutes to wash 1 pair underwear and 1 pair socks, shower, and use wash room. Takes more time than is necessary. Always has to visit and refuses to leave wash room any sooner." Two years later another warder reported the same problem: "Gertrude Jennings and Edna Millbanks are in and out of the bathroom 4 or 5 times. . . .

I've warned them that they are to have their washing and showers over in 20 minutes. They stand in there with a pair of socks or bra, and pretend to be washing them so that they can talk." The warder noted that both women were "very resentful this evening when I stood in doorway." Nearly 10 percent of women's rule violations involved "tardiness, loitering, and lagging." As in Jennings's case, these usually involved efforts to "visit" or communicate with other prisoners. During the 1950s women's friendships and interactions were closely scrutinized and duly recorded even if their actions did not result in tickets, for which women were punished with demerits, loss of privileges, time in segregation, or loss of good time.[14]

Whereas reformers had envisioned the formal cottage dining rooms as essential to women's rehabilitation, warders faced recurring conflicts over table manners, seating preferences, kind of food, quantity of food eaten, and style of preparation. During the 1950s warders' daily reports were filled with notes concerning inmates' conversations, actions, and attitudes during meal times. In fact, inmates experienced the most intense levels of surveillance at meals. In another classic example, one warder complained:

> Betty Worrell never drinks her first cup of coffee at breakfast until she has eaten her food. She day dreams, then finally gets her second cup. But says it is hot, so she can't finish it before the 20 minutes time is up. I kept the girls in the dining room 22 minutes. All was [sic] dismissed. Betty stayed at her table as she has done several times. I told her she was dismissed. She was very angry and said "I'll see the superintendent why I can't have time for my second cup of coffee." Betty intends to live by her own rules.[15]

Worrell received a demerit for "impudence" and "not finishing breakfast coffee on time." Three weeks later the exasperated warder sent her to two days in segregation for the same offense.

Living by one's own rules could mean little more than asserting one's preferences. Warders interpreted these assertions as direct challenges to their authority, which they often were. Although the issues were seemingly trivial, the contestations for power they represented challenged and threatened to undermine warders' control. Simply altering one's routines was grounds for suspicion. In 1956 a warder noted in her daily report: "Eggs sent back to kitchen this A.M. by Priscilla Cooney, Sally Daniels, and Faith Brunner to be fried hard. Their eggs have always been soft and they never complained before."[16]

Prisoners had little respite from the confines of cottage life. Despite the beauty of the "campus" setting, inmates were almost never allowed to enjoy it. Unlike the Joliet Women's Prison, whose securely enclosed yard enabled staff to offer daily recreation periods without undue supervision, Dwight allowed its inmates no regular "yard time," outdoor exercise, or recreation period until the 1980s. All movement across the grounds had to be strictly monitored. During the 1930s Grade A prisoners wore white stockings and were allowed to travel unescorted, although only to specified locations. If a woman did not reach her destination in the allotted time, an alarm was sent out. By the 1950s even this privilege was rescinded. As ex-inmate Jamella Reynolds recalled, "We had to walk in silence two-by-two. Take a certain route even if another way was closer." They were escorted by male guards. She continued, "The only way we could talk to each other was mumbling. You'd learn to keep your head looking straight and talk out of the side of your mouth."[17]

For all their attention to detail, Dwight's architects had overlooked another critical need: the cottage rooms were designed without toilets, sinks, or running water, amenities that the women had enjoyed in their cells at Joliet. Former inmates and staff vividly recalled the stench from the "pot brigade": inmates lining up every morning to empty their chamber pots. Conditions grew worse after 1940, when prisoners were locked in their cells at 6:00 every evening due to personnel shortages. Overcrowding, which led to double and triple celling, compounded the problem. In 1958 Yvette Emmerson wrote a bitter letter to her sister. Because it failed to pass the mailroom censors, it was preserved in her prison file:

> I've been polishing brass all weekend. Maybe you can explain this one to me. Why would the state take so much pains to in-lay brass on every door trying to make the doors look pretty? Seemingly to me they would have spent that money putting toilets in these rooms. Can you imagine been [sic] locked up in a room all night (2 or 3 women in a room) with a slop jar in this day and age?[18]

This gross oversight makes sense when viewed in light of the distorted vision of the reformatory's founders. Because they refused to acknowledge the institution's inherently penal character, they failed to recognize that prisoners, unlike residents of the boarding schools or colleges to which the institution was frequently compared, would need to be locked in their rooms at night. It wasn't until the 1970s that the women's cells were remodeled to include toilets and sinks.

Although the reformatory's advocates had strongly condemned work assignments in traditional women's prisons for failing to provide relevant vocational or educational training, from 1930 to 1960 roughly one-half of jobs at Dwight involved institutional maintenance. Most consisted of routine domestic tasks such as housework, cooking, waitressing, and yard work. During the 1930s the educational staff consisted of one elementary school teacher, even though 55 percent of prisoners had completed grade school. For several years this teacher offered "commercial" courses in typing, filing, and shorthand during the evening for a select group of "advanced" women. However, she left in 1942 and was not replaced until 1952. No educational program existed during most of the 1940s other than that offered by inmate tutors.

Dwight's vocational programs were equally limited. A large "industrial building" was part of the original design. One section housed the laundry, which employed roughly 10 percent of the women. In her 1931 report Hazard praised the equipment as "probably the finest of its kind in the state." Inmates, however, regarded laundry work as the least desirable job assignment. In later decades it served as a punishment detail. In 1935 the Singer company donated three power sewing machines. By 1938 a full-fledged garment industry was operating, receiving orders from other state institutions. Sewing was the only paid job. It employed 15 percent of inmates and was a popular work assignment. Ironically, like the more desirable cottage housing, this job was reserved as a reward for good behavior for long-term felons rather than assigned to short-term misdemeanants.

Other programs came and went. A nurse's assistant course in the mid-1930s was highly prized by the five inmates allowed to participate. Indeed, one woman asked that her parole be denied so she could complete the year-long course. In 1938 a "beauty culture" training program was begun, but it lasted only a few years. It was reinstated in the 1960s. Similarly, a course in "home economics" survived for a few years in the 1930s, was revived in 1951, then was quickly abandoned. Classes in sewing, knitting, crocheting, millinery, and "fancy work" (embroidery) were offered sporadically through the 1960s.[19]

From 1930 to 1960 fieldwork accounted for another 15 to 20 percent of job assignments. The women tended a herd of cattle; raised, slaughtered, butchered, and dressed dozens of pigs, chickens, hens, and turkeys; and cultivated fifty acres. During the winter months field-workers were reassigned to "occupational therapy": arts and crafts or sewing classes. By 1960 farming operations were mechanized to such an extent that the operation was run by a head farmer and a farmhand and employed only eight inmates. In 1967 the farm was closed.[20]

To the administration's credit, Dwight did provide exceptional medical services during the 1930s. There was a full-time resident female physician in addition to three registered nurses. A dentist and an eye, ear, and throat specialist provided services one full day each week. The hospital was equipped for major surgery. Most women entered the institution in poor health; few had ever had access to proper medical or dental care. Yet after Dr. Eva Wilson left in 1942, Dwight never again succeeded in attracting a full-time resident physician. Health services became mediocre, at best. Women imprisoned during the 1950s and 1960s complained bitterly about the poor quality of medical care and personnel. Referring to the hospital as "just a first aid station," a former nurse corroborated prisoners' allegations, including rumors of drunk, incompetent, and callous doctors.

• • •

During the reformatory's first two decades Helen Hazard's commanding personality shaped all aspects of institutional life. Only thirty-five when she became superintendent, Hazard was a tall, slim, attractive, and uniquely accomplished woman. A native of Rockford, Illinois, she had begun her professional career as a high school principal. In 1920 she went to Columbia College for a master's program in social work. There she spent one summer interning at the New York State Reformatory for Women at Bedford Hills and another at Pennsylvania's Sleighton Farms Girl's Reformatory. After graduating she served as education director and then superintendent at the newly established Connecticut State Farm for Women at Niantic. In 1926 she left due to poor health. After a short rest she embarked on a "seven-month tour of the penal institutions of Europe," visiting prisons in eleven countries. In 1928 Dr. Mary B. Harris hired her as assistant superintendent of the new federal women's reformatory at Alderson, West Virginia.[21]

Deeply religious, Hazard conveyed an unassuming yet forceful presence. Throughout her career outsiders and staff described her in terms of similar dualities: idealistic but practical, sympathetic but not sentimental, demanding but reasonable, fair but a strict and exacting disciplinarian. Yet Hazard's background was limited by the fact that she had worked only at fledgling reformatories where a high level of enthusiasm and camaraderie reigned during the early years. Neither staff nor inmate subcultures had crystallized or become entrenched. Thus, Hazard had never experienced the process of institutionalization that confronted and ultimately defeated her. By the late 1940s, her style of administration, based on an appeal to personal authority, decorum, and traditionalism, was no longer capable of winning the respect or adherence of her charges, while her failure to allow corporal punishment alienated many warders.

During Dwight's early years Hazard regularly referred to morale as "excellent." Rules and routines had not yet become institutionalized. There was plenty of work, including construction and landscaping, to keep the women busy. Each year inmates received new privileges, further contributing to high spirits. The Depression may have also helped foster a greater sense of camaraderie. However, the greatest contributor to high morale was most likely the fact that 75 percent of prisoners were misdemeanants who faced only six months behind bars. After 1935, when the state legislature increased misdemeanor sentences from six to twelve months, discipline became increasingly problematic. Overcrowding exacerbated the situation. The reformatory, designed to house 184 women in single rooms, had an average population of 244.

By the mid-1930s, Hazard began hinting that inmate morale was less than satisfactory. In 1936 she succeeded in hiring a recreational director, who stayed but a year. Despite a seemingly a broad array of activities—game nights, dramatic groups, chorus, newspaper, holiday pageants, and so on—Hazard admitted that "institutional programs are as a rule as stilted and drab as the lives of the women who follow them." The next year the Department of Public Welfare (DPW) donated a film projector, which was especially appreciated by the long-term women. As one inmate explained, "For an hour and a half I forgot I was doing time." Three years later Hazard continued to express appreciation for this gift and repeatedly decried the "monotonous nature" of prison life.[22]

Despite her best efforts, in 1938 Hazard admitted that the problems facing the institution tended to "become more intensified each year." She interjected a note of caution: "Whether or not the morale which was established in the early years . . . is sufficiently strong to carry on year after year remains to be seen." Hazard reiterated a point that she made in nearly all her annual reports: "Every year the institution finds itself facing a more difficult problem." There were fewer short-term women and more long-term prisoners who faced "little, if any hope for ultimate release." Roughly 30 to 40 percent of the daily population between 1935 and 1970 was composed of women who were serving sentences for murder or manslaughter. Hazard concluded, with perhaps some exaggeration, that the reformatory "receives women sentenced for longer periods than any other Institution for women in the world."[23]

In 1938 Hazard raised the issue of race relations publicly for the first time: "This year also indicates a slight increase in the colored population." Previously four of the eight cottages had been "reserved for colored women." Hazard viewed their increasing numbers with alarm, remarking cryptically, "Because of the type of colored woman who comes to the Reformatory, it has always been considered inadvisable to house more than twenty to a cottage. . . . This population, without any question, gives the reformatory its greatest problems." Hazard never elucidated the specific problems that African American women posed, aside from noting that sixty percent of them were committed for murder or manslaughter and thus faced many years behind bars. Hazard's own actions may have fueled the rising discontent. Although she asked visiting ministers not to use racial or "dialect" jokes, it was she who established and maintained the system of segregated cottages. More significantly, Hazard actively discouraged even qualified African American women from participating in the institution's few meaningful vocational programs.[24]

In a paper she wrote for a graduate course, Hazard offered the following example to illustrate Dwight's practice of vocational guidance: "It is not at all unusual to find rather average grade colored girls wanting to be placed in the commercial classes." In some cases "conversation is enough to persuade them that their schooling has been insufficient." If verbal persuasion failed, Hazard would give the inmate a clerical test "in order to demonstrate the woman's lack of preparedness." Yet even when African American women "measured up to the prescribed standards," Hazard still presumed it necessary to "guide their work interests into other channels." She boasted of her success in convincing most that "their chances of employment are very much greater in such fields as laundry or maid work rather than offices." Indeed, when praising the institution's laundry Hazard observed, "This department makes possible a type of training for which a number of our women are so admirably suited."[25]

Other staff harbored equally racist views. In personal interviews many white employees who worked at Dwight between 1930 and 1975 expressed thinly concealed racial prejudices. Even compliments often included invidious racial comparisons: "There were some very beautiful girls, even the colored ones," or "We had some very talented artists and ladies who could embroider beautifully, but most of these were not the colored from Chicago." Other staff voiced a deep sense of difference: "I couldn't even understand their talk. Not just their accent but the words they used." Many spontaneously commented, "it was the first time I ever came into contact with colored people."[26]

Although local women from Dwight had always worked as clerks and secretaries, they usually had little contact with inmates. As office workers, they were confined to the front administration building; none worked in the cottages. Aside from four or five African American women, all from Chicago, most warders were older white widows, patronage appointees from rural areas. However, due to severe personnel shortages during World War II, Hazard tried to persuade some local women to serve as relief warders. Several described their initial fears about "being around colored people." Martha Howard quit twice. On her first night in an all-black cottage she was "so scared and nervous" that she called a girlfriend to come and take her home. Hazard, desperate for personnel, persuaded Howard to return and assigned her to deliver goods from the prison store to the cottages. Howard quit a second time, still too frightened by the inmates to travel the grounds. Finally Hazard gave her a job that required little contact with prisoners, observing, "That's where I should have put you in the first place."[27]

Surprisingly, in 1941 Hazard made no reference to the "racial problems" to which she had alluded the year before. Instead, she concluded that "discipline and morale have been very satisfactory on the whole." However, the next year her tone darkened. Although many inmates had supported the war effort by donating blood and purchasing war bonds, she sensed "definite unrest":

> This is especially so among the colored population. Numerous instances have been reported where some of them have been very outspoken regarding the war and its outcome. They are resentful of every discrimination against members of their race. They see little use in fighting for the Chinese, Czechs, and Poles when freedom and equality are not given members of their own race.

Hazard blamed the discontent on "a few agitators whose constructive contributions have been negligible." Even as she averred that "every effort has been made and will be made to handle this matter in an intelligent manner," she hinted that the situation was proving difficult to manage, adding a cryptic aside: "In an Institution of this type one is always conscious of racial problems."[28]

Because the DPW published no annual reports between 1942 and 1947, conditions at Dwight remain obscure. In August 1943 Hazard took her first leave of absence to serve as a lieutenant in the Women's Auxiliary Corps (WAC). Elizabeth Mann of nearby Kankakee was appointed acting superintendent. Although Mann had worked as a county juvenile probation officer, her main qualification for the job was the fact that she was "one of the most active women in politics and women's affairs in the state," having served as local county chairwoman for the Republican women's central committee for twenty-five years. Despite her experience in probation work, several employees asserted that Mann simply wasn't up to "running the institution as a 'tight ship' the way Hazard had."[29]

In May 1946 Hazard returned to Dwight, bringing renewed enthusiasm and dedication. Her 1947 annual report describes an ambitious new program of recreational activities: summer baseball games, calisthenics classes, plays and theatrical performances, monthly parties for inmates who had maintained a record of good behavior, biannual concerts to which the public was invited, and a July 4 "county fair." Her high hopes were quickly shattered. In 1948 Hazard wrote bluntly, "Discipline has not been acceptable. The excellent morale which has been the pride of the institution has not been in evidence. A spirit of lawlessness, defiance, and rank discourtesy has been more marked than at any previous period." In 1949 she repeated this condemnation.[30]

Hazard blamed the growing "spirit of lawlessness" on factors beyond her control. First and foremost was the state's new "minimum-maximum" sentencing law (the Ward-Rennick legislation passed in 1943), which allowed judges to select lower maximums. According to Hazard the new sentences made it "in most cases unnecessary for the girl to co-operate or try to become an acceptable member of our community. The 'maximums' are so short that the women realize they cannot possibly be paroled and, therefore, any incentive for high standards of citizenship is eliminated." As was discussed in chapter 11, the parole board responded to the new law by denying parole outright to over half of the women after their first hearing. In

GRAPH 3

Total Women Sentenced for Felonies, Misdemeanors, and Drug Offenses, 1860–1970

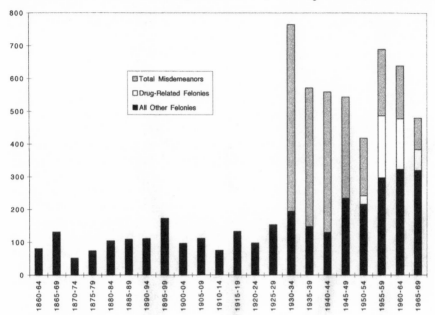

Source: Alton, Chester, and Joliet convict registers; Dwight inmate jackets; Annual Statistical Reports.

the 1930s only 31 percent of prisoners had been held until their maximum; this number doubled to 66 percent in the 1940s.[31]

Long-term women were most adversely affected. Previously a woman who was denied parole could look forward to another hearing after a year. Now she was required to serve out her maximum sentence minus good time. Poor conduct in prison and loss of good time could extend a woman's sentence, but nothing she could do would lessen it. Although it was still in inmates' best interest to remain cooperative, some women responded to parole denials with anger and defiance. In a representative example, a mental health officer observed that Sharon O'Conner's "conduct record during the past year shows that her behavior was unfavorable after she learned that her application for parole was denied." Meanwhile, as the share of misdemeanor offenders fell from roughly 75 percent of total commitments between 1930 and 1944, to 38 percent in the 1950s, more inmates came under the control of the parole board (graph 3). The new law also generated significant discontent among "old timers," who continued to serve under the previous maximums. Hazard cited the cases of two women sentenced to "1-to-1.1" years for manslaughter while thirty other women at Dwight faced "1-to-14" year sentences for the same offense.[32]

Growing inmate discontent in the late 1940s was fueled not only by external factors, such as these changes in parole board policies, but also by the increasingly repressive character of institutional life. During the war the reformatory suffered severe staff shortages from which it never fully recovered. Overworked warders had short tempers that wartime tensions exacerbated. Without staff and functioning educational, vocational, or recreational programs, there was little to keep prisoners constructively occupied. Instead, women were locked in their rooms at 6:00 every evening and for nearly the entire weekend. This situation persisted into the late 1950s. However Hazard could not blame overcrowding for the decline in discipline. With fewer misdemeanor commitments, Dwight's average daily population fell from 256 in 1940 to 168 in 1951.

In 1949 several warders described almost constant turmoil in their cottages. In May Mrs. Wright, a relief warder, found a large quantity of "hootch" (a fermented, alcoholic drink) in a woman's closet. Over the next few months she regularly referred to "disturbances" and "rebellions" in the dining room. The following account was representative:

> I am giving Ernestine Ewing, Caroline Hauser, Jackie Mae Lewis, and Edith Morris a demerit each for rudeness in the dining room and for using vulgar language. These four girls and Gracie O'Connell are in a gang that gives trouble in the cottage and especially the dining room. Ernestine Ewing referred to the food as "s—" at supper tonight. I have tried to reason with her. She says she does not care what happens. [In conversation] Caroline Hauser openly abused one of the staff members at supper. I asked her not to and suggested she go [talk] to this staff member, but she just kept on. Jackie Mae Lewis got up and walked from one table to the other and said she is "evil" and don't [sic] care what happens. Edith Morris continues to talk from table to table in the dining room. . . . I have talked with these girls at different times. They have promised to do better. They have not improved.[33]

These words underscore warder Wright's utter ineffectiveness in disciplining her unruly charges. Ignoring her pleas, the women continued to swear, verbally abuse staff, and roam from table to table during mealtimes.

• • •

According to official reports, Helen Hazard took a leave of absence for health reasons beginning on July 3, 1949. Institutional storekeeper Rose Anne McPherson offered a very different explanation. McPherson recalled that Hazard "left on a Friday night in April and did not return to duty after that. Rumor had it that her 'Lifers' had gotten the best of her, hence her resignation. The institution was certainly in a bit of an uproar at the time, so there must have been some truth to the rumor." Another staff member offered similar recollections, describing a group of "lifers" (long-term women) who "defied Hazard all the way down the line."[34]

Earlier that spring the DPW had brought in O. H. Lewis, former warden of the nearby Pontiac men's reformatory, to serve as assistant superintendent, evidence that conditions had already seriously deteriorated. Elevated to acting superintendent, Lewis confronted a "sit down strike" by prisoners in October. The surviving records offer no clue as to the strike's cause or character. Unrest continued throughout the fall. In early 1950 Lewis left Dwight to head the Sheridan boys' reformatory. The DPW then turned to Clarence L. Farber, former head of military police in Italy during World War II, to restore order. Farber was a strict disciplinarian who condoned the use of shackles and other physical restraints. According to storekeeper Rose Anne McPherson, "the institution promptly came under control."[35]

McPherson, who worked closely with the cottage warders in her position as storekeeper, believed that most warders respected Farber for "finally getting the staff in charge instead of the inmates." According to McPherson, Hazard had completely lost her warders' support. "Most complained of no backing from Hazard or her assistants Schlosser and Eyer. She would take the word of an inmate over her compensated employees any day." Although McPherson admitted that most employees had received their positions through patronage appointments and "came in very green where their jobs were concerned," she sided with the warders, who "definitely thought the inmates were being coddled because of Hazard's attitude."[36]

Farber left that summer. Although after 1950 a male always served as assistant superintendent, the law establishing the reformatory mandated that a woman be superintendent. In the spring of 1950 the DPW conducted a national search and hired Doris S. Whitney in July. Whitney had a master's degree in sociology from New York University. She had worked as the assistant educational director at Rikers Island Penitentiary in New York from 1934 to 1942, had served as a social worker during the war, and was then director of the women's division at the Detroit House of Correction from 1947 to 1950. When asked why she had chosen to accept the job at Dwight with its low salary, she responded, "I love this work. It's my life." A firm believer in rehabilitation and "modern penology," Whitney immediately came into open conflict with her cottage warders.[37]

Whitney moved quickly to implement her ideals, rarely consulting staff. She immediately hired a local teacher to resurrect the dormant educational program and hired an out-of-state woman as educational director, a move that angered local politicians. She reintroduced classes in typing, millinery, dressmaking, beauty culture, weaving, and arts and crafts; established a nurse's aid training program in conjunction with the American Red Cross; and reinstated a formal orientation program for newly admitted women. After their two-week quarantine, all new inmates were to receive a month-long series of classes in "homemaking, waitress work, cleaning, cooking, personal laundry, personal grooming and craft work" along with a "course in human relations" (see photograph, p. 88). Whitney expanded extracurricular activities involving sports, music, and band activities and succeeded in hiring a full-time female psychiatric social worker, the first to fill this position since the 1930s. All of these new programs disrupted routines and imposed many new responsibilities on warders.[38]

Whitney began her first annual report in 1951 by claiming that there had been a "definite improvement of morale" over the previous year. In a veiled allusion to allegations of corporal punishment under Lewis and Farber, she asserted, "Self-discipline and self-control have been emphasized and there is no physical punishment." Like Hazard, Whitney made clear that she was not impressed with the quality or training of most of her staff. One of Whitney's first moves was to set up an in-service training program. In an effort to attract more qualified personnel, she asked the state civil service commission to reclassify, or upgrade, the position of cottage warder. The only qualification for the position had been a high school diploma. Her warders quickly retaliated. In April 1951, only nine months after Whitney was hired, Republican state senator Fred J. Hart, citing "numerous complaints by employees," initiated a probe of conditions at Dwight. Although reporters quickly exposed the investigation's blatantly political motivations and Whitney was absolved of all charges, this was only the first battle in an all-out war between Whitney and her warders.[39]

The investigation was sparked by an inmate attack on a warder, who was subsequently hospitalized. Whitney asserted that 15 to 20 percent of inmates exhibited serious mental or emotional disturbances and blamed the incident on inadequate facilities and a lack of qualified personnel. Because resources were lacking Whitney's predecessors had resorted to housing troubled inmates in solitary confinement for long periods of time. Whitney admitted that this was "an undesirable treatment because it only increases tension" and added that "many disgruntled employees contributed to the poor state of affairs."[40]

Charges and countercharges flew during the ten full days of public hearings. Perceptive reporters quickly surmised that the "major bone of contention" was "Whitney's new education and rehabilitation system." As one journalist observed, "After the opening day's testimony the gist of the complaint is that the inmates are gaining too many benefits from the education and rehabilitation program. They are taught typing, hat designing, figurine painting and the like." Warder Alice Boyden was one of many who claimed that morale was low and that most employees were dissatisfied with Whitney's new programs: "It is glorifying the inmates and they are now telling the warders what to do. It has been a state of confusion here since the program started." Mona Harris, the warder victimized in the inmate assault, complained that "the girls are not able to do their regular work along with the educational program imposed by Miss Whitney. . . .They are more impudent. They now feel as though they're your equal." Similarly, a clerk who had been employed less than two years testified that "the girls were not as obedient as they used to be," and another warder maintained that the inmates were "violating rules with impunity."[41]

Whitney herself concluded that twelve of the thirty-four warders on her staff wer "disgruntled about their work and the reformatory program" but that there was "nothing she could do about it except to accept them as employees." Whitney's words echoed Elinor Rulien's 1926 testimony before the Will County grand jury concerning the three "disgruntled" matrons who had testified against her management of the Joliet Women's Prison. Hazard herself had confronted these same conflicts with her warders throughout the 1930s. Despite her best efforts, which included lecture series and regular staff meetings, most warders failed to forgo their "conventional" attitude toward punishment in favor of a more enlightened "psychiatric" approach.[42]

Both Fred Hoehler, director of the DPW, and Max Weston, chairman of Dwight's advisory board, strongly defended Whitney, testifying that, "Our rehabilitation program was practically collapsed until Miss Whitney arrived."

Whitney retorted that her goal was to "teach a new life to the inmates without harsh discipline," but that there were many untrained people on her staff who "would like to take a whip to them." She reasserted her conviction that corporal punishment played no part in "a modern penal program" and that the "girls" must be taught self-control and self-discipline. Whitney further antagonized local party loyalists by openly attacking the patronage system and criticizing the civil service regulations that made it "almost impossible" for her to fire incompetent employees.[43]

Nearly all of the complainants were employees or townspeople with close ties to the Democratic party. Much of their testimony was quickly revealed to be based on hearsay, gross exaggeration, or outright distortion. Although in the end Whitney was completely exonerated, the investigation exposed the chasm that existed between herself and virtually all her employees: warders, guards, and office staff. Whitney may have been tactless and lacking in political savvy. She had hastily implemented her new programs without ever consulting with the cottage warders. Nor, according to her secretary, did Whitney ever attempt to take the warders into her confidence. Nevertheless, it is probable that employees would have resisted her new programs no matter how slowly she made changes. Whitney was committed to Hazard's rehabilitative vision, which many warders rejected. Hazard had been protected by the fact that despite her equally vocal protests over patronage hiring, over the years she had earned the respect of most of her office and professional staff (if not of her warders), as well as that of townspeople and local politicians. An outsider, Whitney never succeeded in winning either employee or local community support. Allegations that she was often away from her desk, off the grounds, or impossible to reach, along with rumors about excessive drinking, haunted her short-lived administration.[44]

Less than two years later, in January 1953 when a new Republican governor was elected, Senator Hart initiated a second round of public hearings. He resurrected earlier accusations that the "prisoners were glorified by pampering" and leveled new charges of leniency and mismanagement. This time Whitney was afforded very little opportunity to defend herself and she was fired. The fifty-seven-year-old Hazard returned as acting superintendent. Four months later Hazard suffered a heart attack and resigned. She died the following year at her childhood home in Rock Island, Illinois.[45]

This time there was no national search for a new superintendent. Mary Powers, a twenty-year veteran of the Chicago police force and president of the Illinois Policewomen's Association, was offered the job. Powers's appointment represented a lasting shift from superintendents with backgrounds in social work and education to those trained in law enforcement and corrections. Yet Powers served only nine months, resigning in June 1954. Even though poor health was publicly cited as the reason for her resignation, many former employees claimed that she was "not up to the job." Others maintained that she had "simply lost it," as evidenced by her many questionable behaviors, including sneaking an inmate off the grounds in the trunk of her car. Assistant State Superintendent of Prisons John McNamara temporarily took charge.[46]

The year 1954 was a critical turning point in the reformatory's history. That summer jurisdiction over the institution was transferred from the DPW to the Department of Public Safety (DPS), which had administered the state's male prisons since 1941. No reason for the transfer was given publicly. One could speculate that after six years of controversy and turmoil, the DPW no longer felt capable of effectively managing the women's prison. DPS director Joseph D. Bibb immediately attacked conditions at Dwight, lashing out at its allegedly lax security and "low rate of rehabilitation." Claiming that "99.5% of women returned to criminal or delinquent ways," he asserted that far tighter security was needed due to the "large number of murderers and sexual perverts [i.e., lesbians] sent to the institution." His new security measures symbolized the beginning of a long-term policy of bringing the administration of the women's institution more into line with that of the state's male prisons. Bibb also noted that annual per capita costs at Dwight were $3,000 per inmate, compared to $400 for each of the state's male prisoners. Declaring that costs could be slashed a full 50 percent, Bibb proposed to replace the "wasteful" individual cottage kitchens with a central dining hall, but this would not be accomplished until 1967. Bibb, a tough "law and order" man who had been appointed after a series of riots swept the state's men's prisons in 1952, expressed no interest in or appreciation for the reformatory's raison d'être, its specifically feminine and domestic character.[47]

Bibb was responsible for hiring Dwight's next superintendent. The two finalists could not have been more opposite from each other. Similar to the short-lived Mary Powers, forty-four-year-old Ruth L. Biedermann was a seventeen-year veteran of the Chicago police force who had worked as head of its women's division for the previous eight years. Although she had a Bachelor of Arts degree in sociology from Northwestern University and had taken graduate courses in social work, Biedermann stressed efficiency, economy, security, and discipline as her primary goals. In contrast, forty-three-year-old Mary Ellen Krum, a teacher who had served as assistant superintendent under Hazard in the mid-1940s, shared Hazard's and Whitney's commitment to rehabilitation. Convinced that only a "no-nonsense" policewoman was capable of managing the institution, Bibb endorsed the selection of Biedermann. The following year Bibb praised Biedermann's economy, claiming that she had cut per capita expenses nearly in half. Biedermann herself campaigned, though unsuccessfully, for a new prison, built according to a traditional penal design, to replace Dwight's far-flung and "inefficient" cottage system. Eight years later Biedermann was forced to resign under charges that she was "unreasonably harsh to prisoners."

• • •

This chapter has traced the contradictions that emerged between rehabilitative ideals and institutional realities during the reformatory's early decades. Hazard's efforts to develop a model institution where treatment goals and rehabilitative care predominated over custodial and security concerns failed. Within Dwight's first decade inmate morale declined as an inescapably penal environment quickly emerged. Despite the beauty of the campus-style setting, the intimate cottage living units facilitated an unprecedented degree of surveillance and control. Beginning in the early 1940s women were graded daily on attitude, work, and citizenship. Cottage warders routinely recorded all incidents that occurred on their shifts. By the 1950s their daily reports documented a wide range of "disturbances," from the most trivial—a woman's failure to eat her breakfast toast—to the most serious—open defiance, physical fights, unladylike language or behavior, possession of contraband goods, or suspected "unwholesome" friendships. There is little evidence that inmates lost a sense of themselves as prisoners or ever believed that they were being housed in anything other than a prison.

Women's resistance to the countless restrictions and controls that circumscribed every aspect of their daily lives took many forms. Several inmates mounted legal challenges. In response to one appeal the Illinois Supreme Court was forced to concede in 1938 that legally the reformatory was an "institution of the class or grade of penitentiary." However, when Eleda Stella Lewis challenged her sentence to a penitentiary on a misdemeanor shoplifting charge in 1952, the supreme court justices offered a novel opinion:

> The Illinois Women's Reformatory may be a prison of the class or grade of penitentiary as to those committed to that institution for felonies, . . . but it does not follow that it is a penitentiary as to *all* offenders committed there. That a penal institution may be a prison of a certain class or grade as to some of its inmates and of a different class or grade as to others has been recognized by this court in several prior opinions.[48]

The justices reasoned that women sentenced to Dwight on misdemeanor charges were "technically in jail." As we have seen, however, all women were incarcerated under virtually the same conditions and were subject to the highest level of security and supervision. Even though the various cottages were nominally designated minimum, medium, or maximum security, this classification referred to little more than their distance from the highway. Ironically, the few privileges that were available—a paid job in the sewing factory or housing in a cottage rather than a cell house unit—were reserved as incentives for good behavior that were available only to long-term women, not misdemeanants. As Helen E. Gibson notes, "While convention requires women's prisons to *look* like minimum security institutions, economic realty decrees that they cannot *be* minimum security." Because all female prisoners in a state were housed in the same institution, "all must live by rules which are established for the control of a very few." Under the administration of Ruth L. Biedermann (1954–1962), these rules grew increasingly draconian.[49]

CHAPTER THIRTEEN

"I HAVE TROUBLE GETTING HER TO LIVE BY THE RULES"

Surveillance and Control, 1954–1962

On August 6, 1961, Captain Irwin, one of the Dwight reformatory's handful of male guards, reported Belinda Wilson for "using profanity Sunday afternoon en route to Protestant Services." On Monday morning Anne Wagner, the reformatory's new and relatively inexperienced disciplinarian, interviewed Wilson only to report that the "inmate denies the use of profanity at this or any other time." Wagner next interviewed the other inmates in Captain Irwin's Sunday group, all of whom denied overhearing any profanity. Two days later Margaret Schlosser, Dwight's seasoned business manager and a veteran of thirty years, took over the investigation. In a carefully typed report, which was copied and placed in the files of all six members of the group, Schlosser explained that she had personally interviewed Belinda Wilson "in an endeavor to obtain *truth* from inmate." Failing in her mission, she had proceeded to escort Wilson ("amid tears and continuous denial") into the superintendent's office. Ever defiant, Wilson again declared that she "did not use profanity and did not use the term 'G-- D---' " Superintendent Biedermann ordered Wilson to segregation "until others could be called into office to confront said inmate." Schlosser concluded her report: "Grapevine reports she has used profanity many other times, and she does have a poor attitude about doing time our way and not her own."[1]

Thursday at 8:00 A.M. Wilson and the five inmates who had accompanied her that Sunday were escorted back to Superintendent Biedermann's office and threatened with two days each in isolation if they failed to confess. Inmates Lola Marshall and Lettie Sellinger immediately admitted they had heard Wilson say "hell" several times. Marcia Jackson then "spoke up and said 'YES, DEFINITELY,' Belinda Wilson did use that profanity on Sunday and that she is accustom [sic] to using such language." Indeed, Jackson alleged, she had overhead Wilson declare "G-- D---" that very morning on their way to the superintendent's office "with reference to not caring about losing any Statutory Good Time, demotions, isolation, or anything else the superintendent might try to do to her." Rachel Berry, the fourth inmate, "adamantly denied hearing anything in reference to profanity." However, when she was later questioned privately she "admitted that Belinda Wilson is always cursing, swearing, using vulgarity and profanity." Schlosser explained that Berry was "afraid to make such statement in the group as she has now attained Grade 'A' and does not wish to lose her grade because of any inmate hitting her for what she might say." Likewise Emily Deslauries "evidently was afraid to say much" when questioned in public. "Says she did not hear remark."[2]

Superintendent Biedermann then warned the women that "in this institution we would NOT tolerate profanity." Belinda Wilson, a thirty-year-old African American woman recently admitted for narcotics possession, lost all commissary and recreation privileges for two weeks. A few months later Wilson received another demerit for "language unbecoming a LADY." Slang words, no matter how innocuous, were not considered appropriate feminine speech. According to Schlosser:

> Inmate admitted she used the word "Stud" in talking about the men at Cook County Jail—she was shown the definition in Webster's dictionary-that the word should be used only to referring [sic] to "special breed of horses used primarily for breeding purposes"—and inmate was advised it is not the practice at [the reformatory] to make use of such a word, when speaking of or referring to "Male Human Beings."[3]

The administration's response to these relatively minor verbal transgressions exposes the extraordinarily tight levels of surveillance and control that Superintendent Ruth Biedermann maintained at the women's reformatory between 1954 and 1962. Staff rigidly enforced proper standards of femininity in terms of language, dress, and behavior. According to many, an atmosphere of paranoia and suspicion prevailed. Relying on both staff and inmate informants, Biedermann zealously investigated, documented, and punished every violation of prison rules or suspicion thereof that came to her attention, no matter how trivial. Lesbianism was the greatest violation of all. Biedermann took the lead in carrying out surveillance and personally recording details of inmate friendships and interactions, regularly placing notes in women's files concerning whom they sat next to at special events or walked with on their way to their assignments. Biedermann was also accused of being arbitrary and autocratic in her actions toward staff. In 1962 she was asked to resign after a sociologist and psychologist initiated a newspaper investigation, charging her with "brutal" treatment of inmates and with creating an "atmosphere of unbearable tension for staff members."[4]

Thirty-five years after Biedermann's resignation former employees still harbored strong opinions. One former warder asserted, "You either liked her or you hated her." Some employees, especially office and clerical workers, were devoted to Biedermann, whereas others chafed under her autocratic regime and well-known system of staff and inmate informants. Warder Martha Howard (1943–1983) recalled, "For the most part they were pleasant years, except under Biedermann. You stuck it out, but a lot of times I came home and swore I wouldn't go back. You just dread working for somebody like that. But I needed the job and had to put in the years."[5]

Former inmates spoke even more bitterly of Biedermann's administration: One reported, "She ran it like a concentration camp; she had her own Gestapo." Another described her as a "terrible lady." A third recalled, "Her first thing was always homosexuality. She watched you, she had people watching you, especially inmates." Jamella Reynolds, incarcerated shortly after Biedermann left, vividly remembered other prisoners' "horror stories." When she complained about current conditions, "They would always remind me how much better off things were now." Many inmates genuinely feared and hated Biedermann. Their distrust and anxiety was so great that when Gloria Van Overbake, a particularly defiant and openly lesbian prisoner, committed suicide in 1959, rumors immediately circulated that Biedermann had murdered the woman.[6]

• • •

Virtually no historical studies have analyzed the evolution of women's prisons after 1930. It was not until the 1960s that the first sociological studies of female prisons appeared. David Ward and Gene Kassebaum's *Women's Prisons: Sex and Social Structure* (1965) and Rose Giallombardo's *Society of Women: A Study of a Woman's Prison* (1966) focused almost exclusively on female inmate homosexuality, role playing, and pseudofamily formation. Although these remain central elements of female prisoner subcultures, they have been studied to the exclusion of many other issues of equal, if not greater, significance. As a result, we know surprisingly little about disciplinary practices and social control within mid-twentieth-century women's prisons. Likewise, we know little about prisoners' strategies of resistance and accommodation, of staff-inmate relationships, or of how these evolved and changed over time.

A wealth of evidence exists about disciplinary practices at Dwight. Beginning in the early 1940s, cottage warders wrote out daily reports in which they recorded all incidents that occurred on their shifts, along with unsubstantiated suspicions, rumors, and gossip. These reports were later typed and included in inmates' biennial classification reports, some of which were subsequently preserved on microfilm. Biedermann also had prisoners' disciplinary tickets, originally handwritten by warders, typed and inserted in women's files, along with a brief account of the prisoner's response when called to "court." In addition, Biedermann included accusations from her various informants, typically identified as "inmate anonymous." Finally, confiscated notes and letters that failed to pass the prison censors were also placed in women's files.[7]

These sources reveal the extraordinarily high levels of surveillance to which female prisoners were subjected. Inmates' correspondence was routinely censored for a wide range of reasons: if a letter's author was overly critical or complaining, expressed negativity toward staff or institutional programs, used sexual innuendo, requested money, or tried to relay messages to third parties. The following note from Biedermann was typical: "Your Sunday letter was held. Cheerful and uncomplaining letters will pass censorship. Matters concerning your health are a medical problem and not for correspondence." A lengthy set of rules was printed on Dwight's stationery. The first rule baldly asserted, "Inmates may not write any news concerning the institution."[8]

In 1958 Yvette Emmerson, the woman who had complained about polishing brass, wrote a second letter that failed to pass the censors. In it she declared that "Illinois has always had a name for treating women the worst in the U.S. in penal institutions, I must admit its [sic] true." Emmerson, who had been incarcerated in women's prisons in four different states, concluded that "the terrible Illinois is tops." Describing conditions in the segregation unit, she charged: "This place needs investigating. Women in punishment laying on the floor in below zero weather. On a naked floor. No food for 10 days. I'm trying so hard to stay out of trouble." Although Emmerson exaggerated slightly, she was not far from the truth. Inmates received only bread and water for their first three days in segregation (although many other prisoners complained that it was for much longer). Provided with only three blankets and a Bible, they slept on the floor in an unlit and unfurnished cell. The only light was from a small window. Early in her administration Biedermann sanctioned the use of shackles and leather restraints, a practice initiated by her male predecessors. When prison sociologist Albert Lassuy filed a complaint, "Springfield [referring to the Department of Public Safety's headquarters] told them this was cruel and unusual punishment" and prohibited the use of such devices.[9]

In addition to controlling communication into and out of the institution, staff sought to limit contact between prisoners. The disciplinary files are full of confiscated messages ("kites" in prison slang). In 1961 Edna Wyeth admonished a new inmate:

> Do you know if it wasn't for Phyllis Adams we'd both be on the floor [in segregation] right now? Mrs. W went through the garbage and picked up a piece of my kite to you. Phyl reached & took it out of her hand, said it was a letter from home she had torn up! Then Phyl went through the trash & picked out all the pieces & brought them to me & I flushed them. . . . Do you know these screws and guards go through the garbage regularly? Tear them up in small pieces & flush them down the toilet.

Even this precaution had to be undertaken with great care. Wyeth continued:

> Don't flush a whole piece of paper either, as they have a big wire screen at the disposal plant & paper hits it & can't pass through if it is too big, & they have dried paper out & pasted kites together & Mrs. B [Biedermann] has mailed them to girl's familys [sic].

It was true that staff regularly went through inmates' garbage pails and carefully pieced together any notes they discovered, going to great lengths to identify the authors. Every incoming prisoner was required to provide a handwriting sample. It is far-fetched to imagine that notes flushed down a toilet could be recovered at the waste disposal plant, but Biedermann's regime fostered such unbridled paranoia among prisoners that rumors like this one appeared fully believable. What is more, the punishment that Biedermann imposed—sending copies of confiscated notes (including love letters) to the inmates' families—was so deeply humiliating that inmates sought to avoid it at all costs. Wyeth concluded her instructions:

> Either tear them up real small and flush them, or burn them, & you do the same. Those things you have simply *got* to learn to be careful about angel. . . . The only way we should ever get busted over kites is if they shake us down & we have them on us right then. It is my fault you had no way of knowing they are garbage freaks around here & I should have thought to tell you before.[10]

In such a closely monitored environment many prisoners found it impossible to avoid rule violations. As one clerk-typist declared, Biedermann had "too many rules"; in fact, she "had rules about rules." New inmates learned the hard way. One woman received a demerit for hanging a towel and pair of socks over her door to dry. After she appeared in "court" for this infraction, the disciplinarian noted: "Attitude good. Lucy said yes, the towel and socks were on the door drying. Lucy said she knew they could not be on the radiator or bed, but did not know about the door. She said she sure knew now." The disciplinarian appears not to have caught the note of sarcasm in the inmate's response. Another inmate's letter was returned because she had underlined some words for emphasis, also against the rules. The inmate responded with a conciliatory note to Biedermann: "I have been here over eighteen months, and almost every letter, I have wrote, I invariably underline some word or other, I always have done this, as a habit, and I did not know this was against writing rules. . . . I try to keep to the rules in every way. May I please have permission to rewrite it?"[11]

Rules could change unexpectedly. In 1959 a distraught Martha Ainsworth wrote a letter directly to the superintendent regarding a recent rule change. "Dear Mrs. Biedermann," she began, "A notice came to-day concerning colored sox [sic]." Ainsworth and her warder disagreed about how the notice should be interpreted. Her warder believed it "to mean that all colored sox are contraband." However, "when I read the notice I understood it to say only white sox to J. A. Hall and outside recreation. But [wearing colored socks] in the cottage or just having them in your room was not mentioned."

Ainsworth then revealed the underlying cause of her anxiety: "It is too warm to wear knit sox much now but I do have several pair I have made here in my room. I can account for the yarn and it represents a lot of work so I would hate to have them confiscated from my room as contraband. Will you please clarify this for me?" Biedermann's response was not recorded.[12]

Virtually any item could be contraband. Exchanging or sharing food, candy, cigarettes, toiletries, clothing, books, paper, or other goods was strictly forbidden. The administration went to extraordinary lengths to track down the source of all such items. The following report was personally recorded by Biedermann. She had heard through an inmate informant that Nadine Lorimar had passed two pieces of fudge to June White when they were together at the school building. Biedermann personally "shook down the room of Nadine, Harriet, and Annette." This search set off another round of investigations. Biedermann found "pants, socks and bra drying at end of bed" which Harriet claimed were hers—it was a violation of rules to hang them there. However, after being confronted with the fact that "the socks were marked Penny Foley #3648," Harriet admitted that "three months ago Penny bought socks for her in exchange for cigarettes, as Harriet doesn't smoke much and Penny smokes over 7 packs a week." When called to the superintendent's office the next day, Penny initially "denied all knowledge of exchange of clothing with Room 13." She finally confessed after being threatened with loss of good time but "still claim[ed] no knowledge of the fudge being passed at Jane Addams Hall." Biedermann continued her efforts to track down the source of the contraband fudge, calling in girls from several cottages, all to no avail. However, the following week she reported the following rumors:

> Grapevine and gossip are accusing Penny of trying to get the fudge to Sandra DeLorean, who was in June's cottage. June would be the go-between. Two inmates at Jane Addams confirmed this gossip and said that Penny was very friendly with Sandra. However, Penny herself was at Jane Addams Hall and would not have needed Nadine as an in-between in this case. Nadine insisting that she alone was involved and responsible.[13]

Although the source of the fudge was never discovered, reports of unsubstantiated accusations were included in the offending inmates' files for the next month. In a final entry a cottage warder reported overhearing women in the bathroom saying that, "June had got a bad play, that the fudge was not for her. That Penny walked up and gave it to her to give to Sandra and she could not give it back as she was being watched."[14]

As this example suggests, rarely were suspected rule violations allowed to pass unpunished, no matter how trivial. One warder reported that she had searched an inmate's closet and "found in a dress pocket two peppermint candies & wrappers from butterscotch candies, also wrapper from a candy bar." She surmised that, "as per rumor, these things got into Joan's room by way of transom" during her stay in the segregation unit. Burns received twelve additional days in isolation. In another typical food-related incident, three inmates received demerits for "conspiring to exchange food." Stephanie Janowski had requested a second piece of pie during desert one night. The inmate waitress promptly responded and "brought her Callie Wilson's." The warder, "suspecting that Stephanie and Callie had arranged for Stephanie to have her piece of pie, and that the waitress knew of this," gave them all demerits. Likewise, Elsa Robbins received a demerit for "waste of food" for "failing to eat all her French Toast." Prison disciplinarian Margaret Schlosser recorded Jansen's response: "Inmate's attitude very good—says she was sorry about it. Advised that so long as food is edible it must be eaten when served." Schlosser then added one of her typically scathing comments: "Told her in the future not to order French Toast—for fear it will not be cooked to suit her fastidious taste."[15]

In contrast to Jansen's "good attitude" (whether genuine or feigned), other inmates responded with hostility, venting their frustrations over "all these petty rules." In 1957 a warder reported: "Gerda Villanova has been sneaking food upstairs in her napkin. Today she had cookies in her pocket. I told her I knew she had been carrying food upstairs, but if she would stop, I'd give her a pass on the cookies." Rejecting this offer of leniency, Villanova allegedly retorted, "I am paying for my crime by being sent here and I can't stand all these petty rules." The warder concluded, "She is very resentful and against warders. She has a chip on her shoulder all the time. Certainly wants to do as she pleases."[16]

Such high levels of surveillance generated bitter resentment and increased resistance. Indeed, if female prisoners did not suffer under such onerous levels of scrutiny, many of their behaviors—sneaking cookies, exchanging desert pies, failing to drink a cup of coffee, not eating all their French toast— would have passed undetected. Such actions, which would not normally signify defiance, became acts of resistance solely as a result of the rigid disciplinary regime to which the women were subjected.

Inmates bombarded Biedermann with notes protesting rules and punishments they felt were unfair. Although most of the notes were conciliatory in tone, some inmates openly expressed their hostility. In 1961 an African American prisoner wrote:

> This is the third time I've written you. . . . Is it because I'm Negro and a prisoner here that justice here means nothing? Is it that a prisoner is wrong because they are prisoners? Is it that you have warders here that think they can do no wrong? If we have to follow rules why don't warders follow yours? And why does a prisoner have to be locked up and can't even see anyone to ask why and to try to defend themselves? . . . Twice I have been thrown in lock up and given demerits and my good time taken from me just because I reported sick to my warder and she wanted to have her say about who is sick or not.[17]

As in most cases, Biedermann's response was not preserved. Nor is it possible to gauge whether African American prisoners were unduly singled out for punishment. After 1954, when the state passed a revised Narcotics Control Act, the number of African American inmates increased rapidly, from 36 percent of all commitments to 70 percent by 1960. Only a handful alluded to race relations in their censored letters. Most knew better, but two referred to Dwight as "Little Mississippi."

In such a repressive setting "domestic training," trumpeted as the heart of women's rehabilitation, became "merely a hollow simulation." As historians Russell and Emerson Dobash and Sue Gutteridge point out, creativity, decision making, and the possibility of failure are essential elements of real homemaking. In the prison environment, however, obedience, not decision making, was the "skill" that was taught. Under Biedermann's administration there was a right and a wrong way to do everything. Menus, recipes, routines, timing, and procedures were all established by the institution. Any deviation or mistake could be cause for a demerit, as inmate disciplinary reports amply document. In a typical example, when one inmate was questioned about why she "had been putting pickle lilly [relish] in the potato salad," she responded that "she does the best she can, and tries to prepare the food the way the girls like it." The warder called two other warders to confirm that "they do not add pickle lilly to the potato salad." Because hers was interpreted as an "honest mistake" rather than a "willful act of defiance," the inmate was only reprimanded.[18]

Likewise, in 1961 another cook received a reprimand rather than a demerit for burning the dinner rolls. Her warder explained: "It was the first time she had burnt the rolls, was sorry, and said she did not do it on purpose." In a similar case a warder concluded, "If I thought for one minute she was forgetting these things purposely she would receive a demerit." Although warders occasionally praised their cooks, the disciplinary records are replete with conflicts and criticism, as this example attests:

Gwendolyn was told that there was devels [sic] food cake mix to make the chocolate cake for dinner tonight. . . . When I came down-stairs later found her using regular flour to make a white coconut cake. She lied to me and said she didn't know there was devel's food cake mix. I issued a ticket and made her add cocoa to the mixture.

The frustrated warder concluded, "Gwendolyn will not listen to instructions. . . . She is supposed to be the second cook here but does not even know how to cook dried fruit. Does not try to learn and shows no interest." Gwendolyn was eventually transferred to another job.[19]

In addition to the hollowness of the cottage's approximation to the environment of a real home, cottage life was extremely isolating. For the sake of efficiency most women in a cottage were given the same work assignment. This limited even further the utility of cottage classification for "individualization." As Hazard euphemistically explained, "The group to which she is assigned lives together, works together, attends services and recreational activities together, and is always under the eye of the warder assigned to the cottage." Inmates spent all day with the same women and had few opportunities to form relationships with others outside of their cottage. Tensions often ran high. At the same time, Biedermann's administration operated within a context of severe overcrowding. From a low of 168 in 1951, Dwight's daily population nearly doubled, peaking at 316 in 1961 (see graph 4). Warders who had previously supervised cottages of fifteen to twenty women were responsible for thirty women in the late 1950s. Positions often

GRAPH 4

Average Daily Population, Female Prisoners in Illinois, 1900–1985

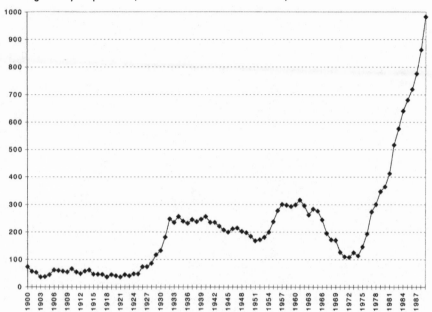

Source: Department of Public Welfare, 1926 *Annual Report*, 358; 1940 *Report of Statistician*, 162; Dwight, *Annual Statistical Reports*; 1984 *Human Services Report*.

went unfilled, and warders went weeks without a day off. Like her predecessors, in her annual reports Biedermann frequently alluded to the difficulty of finding qualified personnel.[20]

Some women regarded cottage cooking and housekeeping assignments as the least desirable placements. Cooks and housekeepers were confined inside all day under the ever-watchful eye of the warder. In 1962 one warder reported, "Gloria Hubbard was angry and impudent when I told her she had been reassigned to work in the kitchen. She said, 'Well, I won't do anything. . . . I am sick of these women and this place.'" One week later the warder continued, "Gloria is still conniving to get put out of the kitchen. . . . She is just as unhappy as before. So hard to tell what she will figure out to do tomorrow." The next day the warder observed, "Gloria has been very sassy and obstinent today." After two more weeks of detailing Hubbard's daily acts of insolence and her shirking of kitchen duties, the warder begged that "something be done":

> This morning Gloria didn't seem to be feeling good, I asked what was wrong. She said my head hurts and I feel like I did when I lost my mind. . . . She went on talking, said at times she just had an urge to hurt someone. She said I get so mad at you and Mary Ann [another kitchen worker] I would just like to hurt you. . . . Says she is just tired of looking at the same people all day and feels a change to another cottage and a change of job assignment would do her good.

Hubbard's veiled threats and her poorly cooked meals eventually succeeded in winning her a transfer to the greenhouse, although her request for a new housing assignment was not honored.[21]

Likewise, Beulah Roberts sought every means to get out of her kitchen assignment. In 1958 her warder reported: "Beulah Richards is not interested in kitchen work, does not take hold and try. Makes it too hard on the other girls to do their work. Beulah just is not kitchen material." The next week the warder again complained: "Beulah Richards is not happy in the kitchen. . . . Never sees anything to do and when someone asks her to do something, she becomes angry."[22]

One week later Richards wrote a letter directly to sociologist Bernard Robinson: "You saw the need to place me in the kitchen and now I hope you see the need to take me out. I have tried with the best of my ability to cope with this situation, but it is really getting the best of me." Claiming to have "grown very nervous," and to be "having restless, sleepless nights" and "moods of depression," she described the joys of her previous job assignment:

> When I was working on the [delivery] truck, we stayed so busy all the time working, plus the fact that I was working with a nice crew of girls, that had a gift of gab and lively singing voices, and with me trying to learn the art of singing, turned work into pleasure. And on the days when one was feeling depressed, we all had a sense of humor and some one would say something funny and you would forget all your troubles. In other words I now have plenty of time to do nothing but think about the past. . . . Being locked up all day is about to drive me insane. . . . So Mr. Robinson I hope you see fit to review my case and pray that you give me a reprieve, if not back to the truck to any outside assignment.

Richards concluded with a postscript: "P.S. Mr. Robinson I feel just like an animal being caged in." Although she was not reassigned to the truck, Richards was eventually transferred from kitchen duty. Women who refused to cooperate frequently got their way. Few warders or supervisors relished working with disruptive or recalcitrant inmates.[23]

Biedermann had no use for the reformatory's cottage architectural style or the feminine, familial ideals it was intended to embody. Throughout the 1950s she campaigned unsuccessfully for an entirely new women's prison, one built upon a traditional penal design. The legislature's Commission to Visit and Examine State Institutions echoed Biedermann's complaints. In 1959 the commission reported,

> The most serious problem . . . is the housing situation. The layout of the institution follows the design of a resort rather than a prison. . . . It is difficult to understand why a woman who has committed a very serious crime should not be confined to a cell block just the same as a man who has committed a similar crime.

The commission also pointed out that the overcrowded cottages and bathrooms created "an ideal setup for sex perversion." Although Biedermann had hoped that "in putting three girls in a room the homosexual activities would be reduced," the commission concluded that "it has not." Bieder-mann and the commission requested that, if a new prison could not be built, funds be allocated for the construction of a one-hundred-unit cell block, with toilet facilities in each cell, along with a new wall that would more securely enclose the grounds. Tighter security, discipline, control, and cost efficiency were their overriding objectives.[24]

• • •

During the 1950s the average inmate received eight to twelve disciplinary tickets a year. Although most tickets resulted only in demerits, all were reported to the parole board. Table 9 provides a representative example from one woman's official conduct record. Table 10 quantifies the most common types of rule violations. Sharon Hunter's tickets involved relatively innocuous viola-tions, few of which could be construed as willful acts of resistance. Most were due to untidiness, carelessness, and forgetfulness. There does not appear to be a clear consistency in the punishments imposed. Hunter received five days in isolation for "taking cigarettes that did not belong to her," "stealing items from warder's office" (which turned out to be a pen and several pieces of paper), and sneaking food to her room. In contrast, several incidents of "untidiness" re-sulted in loss of good time. Women's prisons have traditionally imposed exag-gerated standards of neatness and cleanliness. Every piece of clothing had to be folded in an exact way ("even the bras"). Ruffled curtains had to be washed and ironed monthly. Not a speck of dust was tolerated. As Helen Gibson observes, "Inmates perceive these duties as feminine versions of the 'rock pile.'"[25]

Were such exacting standards unique to women's prisons? To what extent were male prisoners disciplined for similar infractions in the 1950s and 1960s? Many observers claimed that under the legendary warden Joseph E. Ragen (1936–1961), the nearby Stateville-Joliet penitentiary complex was governed by an equally exacting and all-encompassing set of rules. The press lionized Ragen, lauding Stateville as the "tightest prison in the US." Accord-ing to a typical *Chicago Tribune* report, "Discipline . . . is not merely strict, it is absolute. . . . Profane or abusive language is not tolerated. Neither is inso-lence." As in Biedermann's regime, informers were the backbone of his sys-tem. One of Ragen's favorite quotes was, "Whenever you see three inmates standing together, two of them are mine." Academic researchers uncritically accepted these claims. Sociologist James B. Jacobs asserted that Ragen ruled Stateville "with an iron grip. Strict rules governed every aspect of inmate life. Inmates were not allowed to talk in the dining hall or while marching from one assignment to another, which they did in precise formation. . . . Not even the slightest infraction of prison rules went unpunished."[26]

These reports suggest that the strict control Biedermann wielded at Dwight reflected the tenor of the times, rather than the gendered nature of the refor-matory regime. Despite these apparent similarities, however, in practice discipline was less exacting at Stateville than it was at Dwight. Although such actions as "having top button of shirt unbuttoned" were prohibited at both institutions, men were disciplined for only the most serious violations. Stat-eville sociologist Nathan Kantrowitz (1957–1963) argues that descriptions

Table 9

INMATE CONDUCT RECORD, 1964–1966

1/13/64	Bedspread not on bed at P.M. room check.	1st ticket
2/27/64	Dirty socks found in dresser drawer.	4 days recreation denied
	Consultation with superintendent about not keeping her clothes clean. Promised to try and be more neat.	
4/6/64	Dirty clothes in lock-box.	Reprimanded & excused
4/22/64	Warning inmates that warder was coming.	1 week recreation denied
5/11/64	Left radio on while at assignment.	1 week radio denied
5/11/64	Taking cigarettes that did not belong to her.	5 days in isolation
6/16/64	Had dirty clothes in drawer and room left untidy.	1 week rec. denied and 2 days Statutory Good Time lost
11/3/64	Dust on transom.	Reprimanded and excused
11/4/64	Stealing items from warder's office.	5 days in isolation
1/13/65	Taking extra grapefruit and making juice.	4 days recreation denied
1/18/65	Putting wet clothing in laundry basket.	5 days Statutory Good Time lost
3/15/65	Very untidy with self and room.	1 week recreation denied
6/8/65	Talking in line, pushing and slapping partner.	1 week recreation and 1 week commissary denied
6/16/65	Using too much sugar at breakfast.	Reprimanded and excused
8/3/65	Loud talking and laughing during letter writing.	1 week recreation denied
9/21/65	Late coming to dinner.	1 week recreation denied
10/14/65	Late for supper and bed unmade at recreation time.	2 days Statutory Good Time lost
1/12/66	Playing radio loud enough to be heard in hall.	1 week radio denied
3/9/66	Not waiting for breakfast line.	1 week recreation and 1 week commissary denied
4/4/66	Visiting at D. Murphy's door w/o permission.	2 weeks recreation denied
4/8/66	Dirty ash tray in room.	Reprimanded and excused
4/15/66	Contraband lipstick and deodorant found in room.	1 week recreation and 1 week commissary denied
6/3/66	Taking food to her room and other inmate's jeans found in room.	4 days in isolation
7/30/66	Candy in mouth on assignment.	1 week recreation denied
10/15/66	Not standing in hall as told by warder while waiting for C-1 girls to come from assignment.	2 weeks polishing brass on warder's door

Source: Dwight #4217, conduct record, Microfilm Reel C9-026, Illinois State Archives (restricted access). An example from the 1960s is used because conduct records from the 1950s rarely included the specific punishments.

Table 10

RULE VIOLATIONS AT DWIGHT, 1954–1967

15%   Talking, laughing, yelling, loudness ("talking in line," "constantly giggling," "yelling across kitchen")

11%   Impudence, disrespect, insubordination, rudeness to staff

9%   Tardy, loitering, lagging ("tardy for breakfast," "loitering in hall")

9%   Contraband (sneaking or exchanging food, cigarettes, candy, cosmetics, etc.)

8%   Clothing-related violations (altering or destroying clothing, wearing another inmate's clothing, dirty socks, washing without permission, "not wearing dress to job assignment")

8%   General disobedience, uncooperativeness (not following rules and regulations, uncooperative, refusing to follow an order, poor attitude or conduct, "creating a disturbance")

5%   Seeking to contact or communicate with other inmates (visiting another's room, talking in doorway, signaling, passing notes)

5%   Job assignment (poor cooperation or conduct, failure to perform tasks)

4%   Going somewhere without permission ("taking the wrong road")

4%   Room (not tidy, ashtray full, bed unmade, dust, leaving lamp on, radio loud)

3%   Profanity, vulgarity ("foul language," "language unbecoming a lady")

3%   Verbal argument with another inmate

3%   Smoking

3%   Food or dining-room related violations (complaining, "using too much sugar in coffee," "poor table manners")

2%   Washroom (not following rules, loitering, "taking an extra shower")

2%   Sleeping (napping or being in bed during the day, no lights out)

2%   Sexual misconduct (embracing, kissing, in bed together, in shower)

1%   Physical fights

Source: Sample of sixty Dwight inmate conduct records, microfilmed files, Illinois State Archives (restricted access).

such as Jacobs's are "nonsense." Male inmates routinely "violated many of warden Ragen's trivial rules." They regularly argued; used profanity; conversed in line; walked to their assignments "side-by-side in a slow shamble" rather than in the "precision march" for which reporters lauded Ragen; exchanged cigarettes, food, and other items; and mouthed off to staff.[27]

Men's disciplinary records provide striking evidence that women experienced higher levels of surveillance and were punished more severely for relatively minor transgressions. Nearly one-third of men's punishments were for engaging in physical fights with other inmates (18%) or verbally threatening staff (11%). Other infractions included: refusing to work (9%); serious misbehavior in segregation—such as throwing objects or feces at guards (9%); insolence (9%); homosexuality (7%); and possessing contraband (3%). Another 18 percent of disciplinary referrals were for "continuous minor punishment reports." This nebulous category could include many of the minor acts of rebellion (talking back, repeatedly using profanity, being in another inmate's cell) for which women were routinely punished, but men were disciplined only after accumulating a lengthy list of such infractions. Similar to nineteenth-century authorities, prison officials in the 1950s and 1960s viewed men's resistance to penal authority as natural and normal. Male prisoners were supposed to mouth off, shirk work, fight, gamble, and otherwise attempt to "get over" on their keepers. When women engaged in the same behaviors they defied not only prison rules, but also social definitions of proper womanhood.[28]

Moreover, even when men were ostensibly penalized for the same violations as women, their actions were often more serious. For example, men who were punished for using "profanity" had used vulgarity toward staff, not just in conversations with other prisoners. Likewise, men's "contraband" infractions typically were more serious acts involving "trafficking"—stealing a large quantity of food or goods from the commissary or kitchen, then selling, bartering, or gambling it away in the inmate black market. Male prisoners were hardly ever disciplined for sneaking a few cookies, a piece of candy, or a single sandwich. Similarly, although it was against regulations for male prisoners to exchange items of personal property, their cells were not inspected on a daily basis. When "shakedowns" did occur, correctional officers searched for weapons, drugs, and major contraband. In contrast, Carol Rawlings recalled bitterly, "They weren't searching our rooms for knives or weapons, they were searching our bras and panties, searching our pockets for candy and gum, counting our barrettes and hair bands."[29]

The much greater staff-inmate ratio and the architecture of men's prisons—five-hundred-man cell blocks, central cafeterias, factory-size industrial work sites—mitigated against the possibility of such tight control. However, architecture and scale alone cannot account for the differences. In prison as in the free world women were, and are, expected to acquiesce to a level of social control that would be deemed utterly unacceptable by men.

Dana Michelle Britton points out that the crucial issue is not which mode of incarceration is more repressive: "If men and women in prison are subjected to different types of discipline, the question then becomes one of the types of human subjects who are produced by these disciplines." Supervision and surveillance in men's prisons fulfills Foucault's prerequisites for a panoptic regime. In the large, anonymous cell block where a single correctional officer may supervise over a hundred male prisoners, "interaction between inmates and staff is minimized and supervision is likely to be impersonal." The goal is to reconstruct male offenders "in the model of the self-policing, atomized individual," whereas errant women are to be "reconstructed in a more relational mold, akin to the family." Of course, neither mode of discipline succeeded.[30]

• • •

At Dwight as at many mid-twentieth-century women's prisons, lesbianism represented the greatest transgression of norms of proper feminine behavior. Such relationships and activities carried an array of meanings and reflected a wide range of behaviors; it is impossible to ascertain the number of women who participated in them. Ward and Kassebaum (1965) estimated on the basis of official reports at the prison they studied that 19 percent of women were involved. However, more than half of both staff and inmates they interviewed gave larger estimates, varying widely from 30 to 70 percent. Whatever the exact percentages at Dwight, during the 1950s Biedermann's obsession with suspected homosexuality permeated all aspects of institutional life. Former teacher Edward Reis readily admitted: "There was a tremendous obsession with homosexuality. The joke was that any time two inmates looked at each other it was homosexuality. And if anything actually happened they threw them in the hole for months."[31]

Warders and staff vigilantly monitored all inmate friendships, as the following notes from the warders' daily reports indicate: "Alberta Lacy is very interested in Lena Raetz." "Mrs. Lee advised me to watch Ola Mae Hahn, due to sex reasons; as yet I have seen nothing out of the way, but will immediately report it if it so happens." Using rather old-fashioned language, another read: "Warder questions the relationship of Lucille Edelberg and Pearl Fells. Warder feels that it is not what it should be to be referred to as wholesome." Often a warder reported that even though she had no evidence that there was "anything wrong" about a particular friendship, she felt that the women "bear watching." Gossip, rumors, and unsubstantiated allegations were routinely included in women's files: "Grape Vine: Beulah Moss is supposed to have said Sarah Stearns told her Bessie Thorp stopped going with Sandra Ewing and started going with Rachel Willoughby. Sandra Ewing denied this said it wasn't true."[32]

Even the most innocuous behavior—walking or sitting regularly with another woman—was suspect. Under Biedermann's administration, warders' daily reports were filled with notes such as the following: "Sadie Cochran walked with Hattie Tucker going to their assignment this afternoon. Hattie lives at Frances Willard cottage. They both make it a point to meet up the road a ways." Another warder warned, "Trudy Jo and Lillian walked to and from Bible Class and Church service today, always try to be in the bathroom at the same time, also enter and leave the dining room together." Exchanging or sharing contraband—whether candy, cosmetics, or clothing—was interpreted as a sign of a potential lesbian relationship. Any open show of affection was grounds for punishment; all physical contact was strictly prohibited. One warder's report included the request, "Give Mary Ellen a demerit for having her arm on Dale McNeal's shoulder while walking on the road to television." Similarly, being in another inmate's room was strictly forbidden, regardless of whether there were any hints of sexual misconduct:

> Am writing a ticket for Marcia for being in Patricia's room. My opinion Marcia is always hanging around Pat. She wants to room with her. I didn't see anything wrong when I saw Marcia in the room. She was sitting on one bed and Patricia on the other. I have had no trouble at all with Patricia. With Marcia I have trouble getting her to live by the rules. She will not cooperate.[33]

Superintendent Biedermann took the lead in ferreting out suspected lesbian liaisons. The following were among the hundreds of incidents she personally recorded (always writing in passive voice or third person). "Superintendent has observed Viola Marks and Ernestine Muller work side by side at laundry, sit together at rest periods. Advised Mrs. Scott to change station assignment of one and keep them apart as much as possible." The next day the laundry supervisor reported: "Ernestine Muller looked like a thundercloud when I put Viola Marks on another assignment. However, she said nothing and soon cheered up." Four months later Biedermann added another note to Marks's file regarding another suspected love interest: "At the movie tonight Cheryl Ranney had curls and heavy make-up on her lips and walked with and sat by Viola Marks. Viola had her hair pulled back tight and no make-up."[34]

As this example attests, staff were particularly suspicious of friendships in which one woman appeared to play the masculine role. Yet even though Cheryl Ranney was assumed to be the more feminine partner because of her heavy makeup and curls, her demeanor and behavior was far from submissive. The next day her cottage warder sent a note to Biedermann: "Cheryl Ranney is so demanding, bold and independent. She is impudent at the table. . . . Instead of talking to all, her conversation is always with Viola. . . . I can't say there is anything between them but they are quite friendly. . . . I am separating them at the table today."[35]

Suspicions were easily aroused. In 1956 Delores Marshall and Beatrice Wolf both received demerits for "walking together from Mass and not with their cottage group." Two weeks later the baseball coach, who had been warned of their possible relationship, reported, "At the ball game Beatrice Wolf was disrespectful to me and I am giving her a demerit. She dropped her umbrella three times so she could get down [from the bleachers] and talk to Delores Marshall. I told her that was enough of that moving around and she just screamed at me." Six months later Biedermann personally recorded the following: "Delores Marshall managed to slip in seat next to Beatrice Wolf at entertainment at Jane Addams Hall this evening. There were many other seats available." She ordered Delores to move and gave her a demerit. In her note Biedermann explained that she had recently transferred Delores from Beatrice's cottage after "the warder verbally reported to the Superintendent [Beatrice's] interest toward Delores."[36]

In 1958, Billie Franklin, an African American woman, lost six months good time for being caught in an "unnatural act" with another woman. She wrote her mother:

> These people make me think I am some kind of a sex feind [sic]. I can't under-
> stand their reason. . . . I guess it's because I wear my hair short. . . . This is little
> Mississippi here, so go [figure it out] from there. It hurts me so, because I am so
> friendly. And friendship here is always taken for a romance. Well my precious
> mother, I feel so despondent but soon it will be over. I hate to write you like
> this, but these things are happening to me. . . . Even a smile here is forbidden.[37]

This growing obsession with prison homosexuality after World War II re-flected broader cultural fears. In *Intimate Matters: A History of Sexuality in Amer-ica*, John D'Emilio and Estelle B. Freedman argue that, "Even as some sexual boundaries were dissolving [at mid-century], others grew tighter. Hand in hand with the more permissive attitudes of sexual liberalism toward most forms of heterosexual expression went an effort to label homosexual behavior as de-viant." As homosexuality became more visible after World War II, "federal, state, and local governments mobilized their resources against this under-ground sexual world." The military service, migration, and expanded work op-portunities of the war years uprooted literally millions of young men and women. As young people were freed from the constraints of parents and small-town life and often segregated in same-sex institutions, the war became a water-shed in the emergence of gay and lesbian subcultures in major American cities. After the war, Cold War politicians smeared homosexuals as "moral perverts and national security risks." During a decade when many Americans believed their cherished institutions of marriage, home, and family were under attack from international communism, those who resisted tradition were regarded as dangerous subversives: "Just as hidden traitors were undermining the nation's physical security, so too did sexual deviants deplete its moral resources."[38]

During the war military psychiatrists routinely questioned inducted men about homosexuality. Although they failed to identify most cases, their ques-tioning helped "propagate psychiatric definitions" of homosexuality. Like mili-tary authorities, prison sociologists in the 1950s routinely questioned women regarding same-sex relationships. The following assessments were typical: "She claims heterosexual satisfaction and denies homosexuality." "She admits to sex-ual promiscuity and prostitution, but denies ever having a venereal disease or ever participating in homosexual activity." In the case of a young woman who "admit[ted] to sexual promiscuity, both heterosexual and homosexual, since the age of fourteen," the sociologist recommended that "housing be away from the more improvable and impressionable offenders." The label *homosexual* car-ried many negative consequences. Staff checked off a box prominently marked "homosexual" on the woman's admission card (the only other such box was for "escape risk"). Automatically defined as beyond rehabilitation, suspected les-bians were regarded as morally corrupting influences. They endured greater sur-veillance and were housed in the least desirable unit.[39]

Academics and outside observers have been fascinated by prison lesbian-ism, which remains a central feature of pulp novels and Hollywood B movies about women's prisons. Assuming a model of "heteronormativity," sociologists and criminologists have traditionally analyzed prison lesbianism as a response to the "pains of imprisonment" and deprivation from "natural" heterosexual contacts. Others have endorsed the stereotype of the predatory and masculine lesbian who "turns out" vulnerable, newly arrived "normal" women (who become "institutional" or "situational" lesbians). Yet as Dana Michelle Britton perceptively argues, "It is also possible . . . to read these relationships as resistance." Through their lesbian involvements, female prisoners challenged the rigid gender dichotomies upon which women's prisons were premised. By creating their own world of primary relationships, close friendship networks, and "pseudofamily" formations, they collectively resisted socially sanctioned definitions of proper femininity. Indeed, through their prison "families" female prisoners subverted the very vision of domesticity that women's prisons were designed to inculcate. Instead of becoming socialized in proper "ladylike" behavior, some prisoners actively perfected an ostensibly "masculine" style, which some may have found liberating.[40]

Biedermann and her staff fully subscribed to the stereotype of the predatory, masculine "real" lesbian. However, many of their own reports challenge this simplistic dichotomy. In 1958 a warder wrote Biedermann requesting that she "separate Gail Ames and Quincy Taylor." The warder explained:

> I do not want them both in the same cottage. Gail is young and foolish but I believe she can be a pretty good young lady if she is not influenced by wrong doing people. I have known or thought for quiet [sic] some time that she and Quincy Taylor were too close. . . I have talked to Gail and she would say she was sorry and did not know she was doing wrong, and that she was going to be a good girl. I honestly believe she would too, if she wasn't afraid to refuse to do Quincy's bidding.

The warder construed Ames's participation as the result of fear and intimidation. Therefore, she was able to continue defining her as a basically "nice girl" and "pretty good young lady." She continued:

> I have tried to catch them in an awkward position, but I feel I'm either too late or too early. I don't think I need to tell you what a sex maniac Quincy Taylor is . . . but there are no one here who doesn't think that Gail would be a nice girl if she wasn't influenced.[41]

The warder's tone darkened perceptibly after Quincy Taylor was transferred and gossip continued to link Ames with suspected lesbian activities. Six months later Ames was caught in the shower with another woman. Rejecting her claims that she was simply washing the other inmate's back, Biedermann demoted Ames to B grade and gave her fifteen days in segregation. Two months later the nurse reported a "new romance started between Gail Ames and Yvonne Roberts."[42]

Similarly, in 1959 another frustrated warder identified Laurie Zecher as the "aggressor" in a series of liaisons in her cottage, only to find that her partners were equally active participants: "When I came back today I found

Laurie and Tricia Jean real palsy-walsy, walking together to the dining room. Tricia would stall around until Laurie could get close enough to walk out of the dining room with—meet in the bathroom, etc. So I got after them." One week later the warder wrote Biedermann:

> I am not going to have any romances going on. . . . Before Laurie got to playing around with Tricia Jean—she and Emma were walking to meals, etc., but that didn't last long—Emma being upstairs they didn't have any chances to get together. As I said, I don't care. I'll battle with her until she gets tired of romancing. If you move her any where [sic], just move her away from here. She is too masculine for my old ladies.[43]

Zecher, identified as the masculine aggressor, was singled out for punishment. Four days later Biedermann personally called her into her office "to be advised that she would be moved to Jessie Hodder Hall." Again writing in the third person, Biedermann explained that she had "advised" Zecher that:

> the superintendent had noticed her attentiveness to Emma Schumacher and more recently to Tricia Jean. . . . For the past three weeks Laurie has walked with Tricia Jean every chance she got. Superintendent noticed how very close they walked and Laurie taking a masculine attentive role. She saw that Tricia Jean sat down first, held the Hymnal for her etc.[44]

Despite Zecher's transfer, the warder in her former cottage continued to report problems. Tricia Jean Williams and Emma Schumacher, originally perceived as more innocent because they assumed the "feminine" role in their relationships, were soon involved in an affair of their own. Two months later the warder discovered them together in the bathroom and reported: "They stayed in washroom long. I went in and looked and said, 'What are you girls doing?'" Tricia unabashedly replied, "'I am kissing her.'" Both received two weeks in isolation and were transferred to Jessie Hodder Hall (known as J.H.H.)[45]

Although some inmates vociferously protested a transfer to J.H.H., asserting that they "weren't homos," a few expressed a preference for the high-security cell house (which had originally been built for the female felons transferred from Joliet). Remarking on its architectural advantages, one woman wrote her lover: "That's something else over there, you got all kinds of chances to take care of business. The way the building is arranged, there's no chance of a warder slipping up on you, you can see her coming a mile away, plus the doors open out instead of sliding like these & you can make [escape to] another room easy." Another warder reported overhearing the following conversation: "Demetria and Gail were talking about what they are going to do at J.H.H. Said they were going to live up to the reputation of the cottage, be homos, said they'd tried to be good but it doesn't pay."[46]

Although former prisoners described the existence of pseudofamilies, virtually no references to these appear in the warders' daily reports. Instead, staff exhibited a single-minded obsession with real and suspected lesbianism. Of course, not all prisoners condoned lesbian relationships, especially if the lovers were too open in their sexual expression. Warder Parkinson believed that her efforts to "keep things decent" reflected the wishes of most cottage residents. On December 1, 1957 she observed that "Gladys Billings is getting too thick with Frannie Bruhl. Can't turn without her." Three weeks later Parkinson described their affair as "out of hand."

> Gladys and Frannie are together constantly. All the girls are disgusted, think it should be stopped. I talked with both but they just go on the same. . . . I have tried to catch them together, Gladys being an old hand at such, certainly is sly. . . . Everything is fine on the cottage except these two.

The next day Parkinson reported:

> Gladys and Frannie still going strong. Frannie was mad and said, "I am going to go to Mrs. Biedermann about Mrs. Parkinson." Her idea of a warder is for them to sit downstairs and never go up to see what goes on. She was furious because I sit in the day room with them to keep things decent for the other girls. They know I am on to them.

On Christmas day warder Parkinson voiced even greater exasperation. Nothing seemed to deter the two women, and Parkinson could not be everywhere "keeping things decent" for the other residents. Her notes continued:

> Gladys and Frannie are incorrigible. They are so bad I have to supervise constantly. When girls were ready to go to the movie Gladys was standing in Frannie's door, had her hands on Frannie's breasts. When she saw me was quick to grab her sleeve, pretending she was rolling it up. Every time I go upstairs, Gladys makes a run for her room. . . . The girls in cottage complain constantly how rotten they are and how something ought to be done. . . . The girls tell me they catch them hugging and kissing.

Parkinson ignored this overt physical display. Instead, she hoped to catch the two in an even more unambiguously "compromising" situation: "I think in time I'll be able to catch them. If they get so carried away, they can't hear me go upstairs. I hope something can be done about this situation." A week later Parkinson acknowledged plaintively that because Gladys's "outdate" was only four months away, "little could be done."[47]

Even though Gladys Billings didn't have anything to fear from the parole board, given that she had already received her "maximum X" outdate, Frannie Bruhl did. Inexplicably, at her biennial classification meeting six months later warder Parkinson seemed willing to overlook her earlier misbehaviors:

> Frannie is trying to be good so she can get home as soon as possible. I had some trouble with Frannie last year but none since. She has improved. She is congenial with warder, wants to do the right thing. She has learned to knit and crochet. Makes lovely things to send home. Attends Bible class and vespers service. Missed very few Sundays. Attends and participates in most sports. Doing well as assistant cook. Helps with extra work in kitchen and yard.[48]

Despite the administration's obsession with suspected homosexuality, overt sexual misconduct—such as embracing, kissing, or being found in bed together—accounted for barely 2 percent of women's punishments, although suspicions about lesbian relationships may have been a factor in a far larger percentage. As several former warders recalled, "They were good at not getting caught." At the same time, not all warders were intent upon monitoring women's every deed. Some preferred to "look the other way," as long as inmates weren't too blatant in their actions. Others disliked enforcing the myriad petty rules. Although one warder reported that she "always tried to wear shoes with rubber soles so that the girls couldn't hear me coming," another explained that "a correctional officer who was more tolerant would manage to jangle her keys or in some way make a noise when she was approaching a group of women, so they could change any behavior that would get them in trouble." Warders had to reach some accommodation with "their girls" in order to be effective. However, even the most sympathetic could only go so far; they too were under constant close surveillance.[49]

· · ·

The autocratic and repressive nature of Biedermann's regime first came to the public's attention in 1961 when staff psychologist Arthur E. Ellerd was fired after accusing her of negligence in the 1959 suicide of Gloria Van Overbake. At a state Civil Service Commission hearing, Ellerd accused Biedermann of treating inmates "sadistically." At the same time Dwight sociologist Albert Lassuy (1953–1960) wrote Governor Otto Kerner charging Biedermann with being a "dictator and tyrant" who was "inordinately punitive" toward inmates. In February 1962 the *Chicago American* newspaper launched a full-scale investigation. Instead of immediately reporting its findings, however, the paper complied with Department of Public Safety (DPS) director Joseph Ragen's request that it withhold publication until he could conduct his own inquiry. Ragen, a Democrat, had recently been appointed the department's director and was already filling prison positions across the state with his loyal followers. Ragen had proven as authoritarian as Biedermann in his twenty-five year career as warden at Stateville-Joliet and harbored no philosophical objections to her system of staff and inmate informants. However, he saw no compelling reason to defend Biedermann, an active contributor to Republican campaigns. Ragen quickly pressured her to resign. The *Chicago American* praised his "prompt action."[50]

The newspaper's major charges against Biedermann involved cruel and excessive use of solitary confinement. Inmates routinely spent up to 25 or 30 days in the unfurnished and unlit segregation cells despite a DPS rule limiting segregation to fifteen consecutive days. The keys to the segregation cells were kept at the main administration building, one-quarter mile away. Biedermann ignored staff fears (prompted by Van Overbake's suicide) that inmates might injure themselves before their cells could be unlocked. The report also alleged that an inmate with a broken jaw had been denied medical treatment; that other inmates were denied religious privileges; that staff used "humiliating" methods of searching prisoners for notes and contraband, sometimes in the presence of male guards; and that Biedermann exhibited rampant favoritism, punishing some inmates for petty infractions while ignoring more serious offenses committed by many others.[51]

The state employee's union termed Dwight "our main trouble spot." For over a year the union had been negotiating, unsuccessfully, for a grievance procedure for employees who wished to "contest discipline slips." Biedermann opposed all efforts by employees to gain union recognition. Staff complained about Biedermann's inconsistency in applying rules and "excessive use of discipline slips for staff infractions," which resulted in days off without pay. Others repeated widespread allegations that Biedermann "maintained a system of informers among staff members who say they were required to report on one another for rule infractions."[52]

Referring to the investigation as a "frame up" and "so many lies," Biedermann's supporters rallied to her defense. They pointed to political party differences as the main reason Ragen "abandoned Biedermann." Others claimed that sociologist Lassuy had ulterior motivations; they alleged that he had chafed under the leadership of a female supervisor and wanted the position of superintendent for himself. However, unlike the charges against Whitney a decade earlier, the complaints against Biedermann appear well-founded.[53]

• • •

Drawing conclusions about the nature of social control, staff-inmate relationships, and daily life from discipline reports requires caution. The records obviously reflect the actions of the most troublesome, hostile, and actively resistant inmates and those of the most vigilant, demanding, and uncompromising warders. Nor was it possible to balance the written record with oral testimony. Although I conducted many interviews with employees who worked at Dwight in the 1940s and 1950s, several of whom testified to the repressive character of Biedermann's regime, nearly all were office, clerical, or professional staff. Most cottage warders, who were typically in their fifties and sixties when they worked at Dwight, have long since passed away. However, interviews with a younger generation of warders hired after the change to eight-hour shifts in 1962 offer a more nuanced portrait of cottage life.

Although four-fifths of new warders quit within their first few months, several of those who stayed spoke of enjoying their work and finding it deeply gratifying. They described a relaxed atmosphere in the cottages during the 1960s: evening card games, snacks of popcorn, and leftover cake shared in the day room; time spent gossiping, exchanging recipes and knitting patterns, and watching soap operas with "their girls" after household chores were done; serving as a confidante when time allowed. These employees remembered few serious conflicts. They claimed that warders wrote few tickets and that most inmates were respectful and well-behaved until discipline started to deteriorate after 1972. However, former inmates continued to express less rosy views. The next chapter, which draws extensively from interviews with former staff and inmates, analyzes the character of Margaret Morrissey's administration during the institution's final decade as a reformatory (1962–1972).

CHAPTER FOURTEEN

"PUNISHED FOR VULGARITY AND UNLADYLIKE BEHAVIOR"

Dwight's Final Decade as a Reformatory, 1962–1972

In 1967 Jacqueline Warner wrote a breezy letter to a friend two months after she had arrived at Dwight: "It is said I have made a good adjustment here, thats [*sic*] the terminology, and it means I am doing my work the best I can. I am getting along well with everyone, agreeable and friendly and creating no problems." Warner, a white woman convicted of credit card fraud, was assigned to work in the hospital, which she found "pleasant-enough" and "not too strenuous." Her assorted duties included: "Learning x-ray, painting furniture, serving meals, cleaning, doing dishes, washing windows when the weather permits." Warner's morale had much improved since her transfer from Cook County Jail, "I had been there just about as long as I could possibly endure. . . . It was so filthy a place."

In the late 1960s Dwight's daily population averaged 180; the reformatory was only at two-thirds capacity (see graph 4). Physical conditions were much improved. Warner appreciatively detailed the furnishings in her "rather large" single room, although her reference to the "quite modern arrangement of toilet and washbowl" revealed more than a hint of sarcasm: chamber pots were still in use. Warner was further impressed with the "well stocked commissary" where she had recently purchased "loafers and tennis shoes, bra and panties and knee socks, and cologne (at last)." She had just had her first appointment at the beauty shop. Explaining that she was "blue . . . but in there trying,"

Warner concluded: "I guess I am getting along as well as I can. It certainly isn't the movie prototype of a women's prison, altho [sic] I kid you not, it isn't a girls finishing school either."[1]

Warner's summation—that Dwight was neither a "movie prototype" nor a "girl's finishing school"—strikingly captures the contradictions of reformatory life. No matter how outwardly pleasant the reformatory was, or how many amenities or "feminine" touches it offered, the institution's inherently penal nature could not be disguised. This last chapter explores Dwight's final decade as a distinctly reformatory women's institution, evaluating treatment programs, staff perspectives, race relations, inmate morale, and disciplinary practices. As in previous decades, Dwight failed to fulfill its founders' vision. Discipline remained exacting. There was little evidence of flexibility or individualization. As Sociologist Lois Green surmised, "Control of the inmates had long since replaced therapeutic programming."[2]

* * *

On May 12, 1962, two months after Biedermann's resignation, Department of Public Safety (DPS) director Joseph Ragen appointed fifty-year-old Margaret D. Morrissey the reformatory's new superintendent. Morrissey, a widower and one of Ragen's wife's best friends, had worked at Stateville since 1949 as chief clerk. Although she had taken classes at Joliet Junior College, she never completed her associate's degree. Ragen selected Morrissey over twenty-five applicants, many with advanced degrees in education and social work, because of her "general knowledge of the rules and regulations pertaining to prisons, and her knowledge of . . . security concerns." Ragen, who demanded absolute loyalty, knew that Morrissey would remain firmly under his control.[3]

Despite the fact that Morrissey was as strict a disciplinarian as Ruth Biedermann had been, many former prisoners and staff agreed that the overall atmosphere improved significantly after Biedermann's departure. Most notably, the level of paranoia declined. Ex-inmate Carol Rawlings declared, "The whole atmosphere just changed. The tension was gone. . . . When Morrissey came we were so glad to be able to breathe without always looking over our shoulders." Part-time evening school instructor Edward Reis concurred: "The tension at the prison diminished considerably. The difference between Biedermann and Morrissey was this. You see two inmates talking. Biedermann's first reaction would be, 'Ah ha, something is up. Either some lesbian liaison is being set up or they're making hootch.' Morrissey would have thought, 'Forget it.'" Although Morrissey maintained a "modified grapevine" for keeping tabs on prisoners, none accused her of planting informants among staff.[4]

Morrissey's administration (1962–1972), whose philosophy was closely allied to that of DPS director Joseph Ragen, left a contradictory legacy. Even though Morrissey continuously exhorted women to maintain "ladylike" standards of behavior, language, dress, housekeeping, and attitude, her policies helped pave the way for the establishment of a purportedly gender neutral coeducational correctional facility in the 1970s. As one employee recalled, Morrissey "wanted everything to be done the way it was at Stateville." She tightened security, introduced new procedures, and renamed the cottages, which had originally been named after prominent women who might inspire the inmates and serve as role models for them. Morrissey implemented a simple numbering system (C-1, C-2, and so on) instead. A central dining hall was opened in 1967, replacing the individual cottage kitchens and dining rooms, which were remodeled into five-bed dormitories. Morrissey also campaigned to close the prison nursery because she was convinced that babies had no place in a modern correctional facility. Yet she also took pride in introducing secretarial, charm school, and "body dynamics" courses that reflected traditional ideals of proper femininity.

Newly hired sociologist Lois Green (1964–1977) respected Morrissey, despite their major philosophical differences: "She was decent, honest, basically kind. She did what she thought was her job. She was in over her head. The joke was that she called Ragen every hour. The job was larger than her experience or education, yet she did it." Morrissey "did it" by ruling strictly by the book. Green explained, "She was often overly rigid and unreasonable. She didn't know how to rule so she tried to keep everything under her thumb." According to a secretary, "Morrissey never delegated work. She wanted everything to go over her desk. She had to see everything." Lieutenant Ester Dodge agreed: "She ruled with an iron hand. Took care of every detail herself. There was very little chain of command." Nor was there any room for debate: "When she put out a directive it had to be followed."[5]

Those who harbored less favorable opinions used different words to describe Morrissey: "timid," "hesitant," "petty," "insecure," "standoffish," "never seemed confident," "not quite sure of herself," and "scared of the inmates." Some office staff regarded Morrissey as little more than a "glorified secretary" who "wasn't really qualified for the job." Many noted that she was in nearly daily telephone contact with DPS Director Ragen, as was his male protégé who had replaced him at Stateville. Ragen also regularly visited Dwight. Others believed that Morrissey relied heavily upon assistant superintendent Russell Powers, another Ragen protégé and appointee.[6]

Security and custodial priorities continued to override treatment goals. Like Biedermann, Morrissey was wary of treatment staff. Lois Green recalled: "We were at loggerheads most of the time. A treatment philosophy may have been there in her annual reports, but it was a long way from what happened on the cell block. Security was the official and unofficial agenda." For her first six months Green received the "silent treatment": Morrissey and most warders simply ignored her presence. There was a great deal of suspicion about treatment. . . . It took them a long time to realize that I wasn't a threat."

Green speculated that this attitude stemmed from an underlying sense of insecurity among the members of the administration. Of all Dwight's employees, only two or three had college degrees. "The administration wasn't professional. They were political appointees who felt threatened by any and everything." An atmosphere of distrust and suspicion prevailed. Morrissey "operated on the basis of a worst-case scenario. There was precious little flexibility." Green was reprimanded and eventually "locked out" for several days after she began offering group counseling sessions. Green contended that "the standard operating procedure was 'don't deal with inmates in groups.'

Their basic attitude was, 'If you put a bunch of inmates together what they're going to do is plot against the administration.'" Yet because sociologists were hired and supervised by the DPS Office of the Criminologist, Green was effectively outside the superintendent's control.[7]

Despite her suspicion of treatment staff, Morrissey was committed to broadening the reformatory's educational programs, which she could both control and take full credit for. During her first year Morrissey expanded the part-time TV College program to full time, enabling women to earn an associate's degree. In 1964 the beauty school received official accreditation. In 1968 she brought in IBM keypunch classes, and the following year she initiated a secretarial school through Joliet Junior College. Morrissey also supported the W. Clement and Jessie V. Stone Foundation's programs, including its charm school and courses in "body dynamics" and "positive mental attitude." While the latter classes provided a welcome break from the tedium of institutional life, they were far removed from women's real needs. No drug treatment programs were offered. "Black studies" were explicitly forbidden, as were magazines such as *Ebony* and *Jet*.

Over half of the inmates were single parents. The law that established the reformatory mandated that it include a nursery and specified that women could keep their infants until they were one year old. This applied both to women who gave birth in prison and to new mothers who wished to bring their infants with them. Theoretically at least, it appeared that the dilemma of pregnant women that had confounded nineteenth-century prison officials was finally resolved. Yet even though 225 women gave birth at Dwight between 1931 and 1971, few kept their infants for long. In the 1960s mothers were permitted only a single hour-long visit each week with their babies, who were cared for by civilian nurses. Inmate mothers were encouraged to find an outside placement—with relatives or in foster care—within the first month.[8]

The tension between women's dual status as mothers and convicts remained intractable. Despite the stress on inculcating appropriate gender-role behaviors, no one championed mother-infant bonding or the fostering of female convicts' mothering skills as central to their rehabilitation. One administrator expressed views that may have been widely shared: "Many inmates had so many kids they really didn't care about their new child. Many were bad mothers when they were out; their children were raised by their grandparents." Dismissing the pain many women expressed over their separation from their children, she concluded, "Most women only claimed they were interested in their children when they were incarcerated, not when they really had the chance." According to this perspective, female convicts, condemned as "bad mothers," were by definition beyond rehabilitation.[9]

Most women's prisons in the 1960s revealed the same lack of commitment to treatment goals. In 1966 there were fifty-four state and federal correctional facilities housing women nationwide. Thirty (55%) were separate prisons; twenty-four (45%) remained divisions of male correctional institutions. Doctoral student Kathleen G. Strickland, after surveying the thirty independent women's prisons, concluded that 50 percent of them were exclusively or strongly "custody oriented," employing almost no treatment staff whatsoever; 18 percent were "mixed"; 14 percent were "treatment oriented"; and only 18 percent could be classified as "treatment institutions."[10]

Strickland's rankings, based almost exclusively on staff-inmate ratios, reflected the most minimal definition of treatment. Nor did she try to assess the quality of the services offered. Although 29 percent of institutions reported that "group counseling" was "widely used," such sessions were often conducted by correctional officers, most with only a high school diploma. Individual psychotherapy was "regularly used" at only one institution (4%); intake diagnosis (i.e., "classification") at two (7%); and "casework" at four (18%). Two institutions—Dwight was one of them—sponsored Alcoholics Anonymous, but only "occasionally." None offered drug treatment programs.[11]

Dwight fell within the 50 percent of women's institutions that were exclusively or strongly custody oriented. The John Howard Association, a prison reform watchdog group, consistently decried the absence of counseling programs in Illinois's prisons. A 1968 reported argued that "as far as it is known, Illinois is the only major state where formal counseling services are relatively non-existent." In 1970 the John Howard Association commended Dwight for its varied educational programs but criticized the dearth of clinical, counseling, and social work services. Dwight employed only one sociologist (compared to an average 2.2 social workers at comparably sized women's prisons), a visiting psychiatrist who provided services one day a month, and no part-time psychologist. In 1970 the new Illinois Department of Corrections (D.O.C.) created the position of counselor. However, in 1972 an investigator discovered that many staff at Dwight were asked to perform "double and triple duty." As a result, poorly qualified personnel provided many treatment services: a switchboard operator was "pressed into service as a group therapist while the woman who supervises the sewing industries serves as an occupational therapy [i.e., art] teacher and room counselor." The wives of male guards were hired for similar positions.[12]

Despite their name, the counselors hired after 1970 were not trained to provide individual psychotherapy. Their role was solely to help resolve inmate problems or grievances relating to job, housing, or roommate assignments; staff members; and disciplinary procedures. Less frequently they acted as intermediaries in women's interactions with state foster care or welfare agencies or with the courts. Nor did they possess any formal authority: they could only make recommendations regarding prisoners' needs or grievances. Until the mid-1970s, counselors' offices were in the main administration building. Ex-counselor Sue Welch remembered, "I wanted to move out on the grounds. Inmates didn't like to go to the administration building, as other residents would think they were stool pigeons." More significantly, counselors' ability to represent the needs of inmates over those of the administration was further compromised by the fact that they wrote recommendations for the parole board.[13]

Eileen Fitzpatrick (1952–1978), who became Dwight's first counselor in 1970, was a long-time staff member and a former disciplinarian. Although she was one of the handful of employees with a college degree, in inmates' eyes she was thoroughly identified with the administration. Sue Welch (1971–1977), Dwight's second counselor, was a newcomer with a master's degree in psychology. She had recently married a chaplain who worked at the nearby Pontiac Correctional Center. Welch accepted the position only after failing to find another professional job in the area. Unlike Fitzpatrick, she perceived a sharp division between custodial and professional staff: "My greatest frustration was that I was naive about prisons. I was accustomed to treatment. I had absolutely no interest in security. Everyone else had a security orientation." Welch was also frustrated that few inmates seemed eager to confide or wanted what she considered real counseling services. Instead, Welch concluded, "Most just came to us because they wanted a different job or cottage assignment." Jeanie Fairman, an African American parole agent, was equally struck by prisoners' reserve, "They were very distrustful of staff. They weren't quick to confide or open up in conversations."[14]

Such transfers became easier to arrange under Morrissey's administration, which was spared the extreme overcrowding that had strained resources and personnel under Biedermann. By the mid-1960s, Dwight's daily population was in sharp decline (see graph 4). In Illinois a new generation of criminal justice professionals stood at the forefront of a developing national movement in favor of community corrections and alternative sentencing. After 1962 the parole board reversed its twenty-year policy of holding most prisoners to their maximum, nearly doubling the number of women it paroled each year. In 1965 the state legislature created a new conditional release program, and shortly thereafter a furlough program. These enabled dozens of women to be released each year before their maximum. Meanwhile, more liberal drug laws resulted in fewer commitments for low-level narcotics offenses. Whereas in 1965, 40 percent of Dwight's daily population had been sentenced for drug law violations (and three-quarters of these for simple possession), by 1970 their share of the reformatory population had declined to 15 percent. In 1968 a women's halfway house opened, accepting women who had served part of their sentences. As a consequence, Dwight's daily population plunged from a historic high of 316 in 1961 to an unprecedented low of 90 in 1972. Rumors abounded that the institution would be closed and the remaining women moved to local jails or new community correctional facilities.[15]

Despite the decline in the prison population, which might have facilitated greater flexibility, discipline remained strict and unyielding. Like Biedermann, Morrissey rigorously enforced all rules, relying heavily upon segregation and loss of good time as punishments. An initial report by the Illinois League of Women Voters noted that "any deviation from the rules and regulations, including the use of profanity, can be a cause for isolation." Morrissey personally oversaw women in segregation and included verbatim notes of their conversations in their files. In a typical case that clearly reflects Morrissey's priorities she reported:

> Ellen Sandige assured me that she was just fine and was doing her time in isolation all right and looking forward to coming out and conforming to the rules and regulations and making more of an effort to control her emotions and temper. She agreed that nothing is gained or settled by fighting. The interview lasted three to four minutes.[16]

Penelope Castle, who was serving four days in segregation for "vulgarity and unladylike conversation to an officer," was less docile. Castle "flatly refused" to leave the segregation unit when her time was up. Morrissey wrote a detailed account of their interaction:

> Penelope Castle was sitting on the bed. I asked her if she would please stand up and talk to me as a lady. Penelope replied, "I am a lady. I'm tired and I don't want to talk to anybody. I've had it." Penelope proceeded to explain how she wanted to spend her remaining fourteen months in isolation and had absolutely no intention of following any more rules: "I do not intend to get up at the prescribed times. I will not be in line for head counts, nor will I turn my lights out at the prescribed time." . . . These are my feelings and I don't intend to change them.

Morrissey recorded no immediate rejoinder, reporting only that Castle "went on and on, very politely asserting that she didn't want to make trouble but that she had no intention of following any more rules and just wanted to be left alone to complete the remainder of her sentence in segregation." Equally polite, Morrissey allowed Castle to finish, then calmly yet firmly reminded her that "this was her release date with all good time given to her," which she would lose if she chose to remain in segregation. This was no idle threat; Morrissey relied upon revocation of good time as a punishment even more frequently than Biedermann had. Castle promptly got up, took her shower, dressed, and reported to her new work assignment. Although Castle had received twenty-five demerits during the previous three years, she received only two in the year following this incident.[17]

Even model inmates found Dwight's rules and regulations repressive. Jamella Reynolds (1963–1966), who later earned a degree from Roosevelt University and became a community organizer, declared emphatically, "there was definitely *not* a reformatory atmosphere. [Morrissey] ruled strictly by the book. I never saw any sign of compassion." Reynolds vividly remembered several incidents that illustrated the administration's refusal to bend any rules regardless of the individual circumstances. Because inmates were only allowed to write one letter a week, Reynolds explained, "This one write out, you had to use it very wisely. You had to choose the family member very carefully. Chose one sister this week, mother the next. . . . If you wrote a letter that didn't get past the desk [the mailroom censor], you really blew it." Reynolds was the oldest of six and came from a large extended family. When she requested an "extra write out" the week before Christmas, Morrissey purportedly responded, "'I'm sorry, that would be impossible. See, the state only allots us so many sheets of paper per year,' blah, blah, blah." Reynolds was enraged: "They made it out to be such a privilege to get one sheet of paper. I went berserk. You mean you're telling me that this state can't give me another sheet of paper to write my family?" She confessed that "the only way I could get anything was to act wild. Because I was usually a model inmate. I went into this go-off mode." Reynolds was not punished for her angry outburst, but she never received her extra write out either.[18]

Reynolds also testified to the administration's continuing obsession with lesbianism: "Any touch or hug meant homosexuality. Fastening a cross for another inmate meant homosexuality. We'd get in trouble for Kleenex. Girls would take boxes of Kleenex and make tissue paper flowers. Arrange them in little jars and give them to someone. That was contraband." Reynolds's anger and resentment were still palpable. She felt that she had been unfairly labeled "homosexual" after another prisoner wrote her a love letter during her first week in orientation. Reynolds tore the note up and left it in her wastebasket. Staff subsequently pieced it together and "assumed I had done something to provoke the girl's advances."[19]

Nevertheless, under Morrissey the single-minded obsession with monitoring women's friendships eased substantially. Warders' daily reports rarely included the kind of unsubstantiated rumors, gossip, and observations concerning who regularly sat, walked, or talked with whom that had been so prevalent under Biedermann. Indeed, many former staff claimed that lesbianism "wasn't a big problem." Others maintained that "there were a few lover's quarrels now and then, but for the most part if they were involved, the girls kept it well-hidden." Some staff preferred to downplay or overlook the evidence. Denial could make their jobs easier, but it was not always possible. Former warder Helen Lithgow laughed uproariously as she recalled her embarrassment the first time she had to write up a ticket detailing what she had seen when she found two women in bed together. Her first attempt included "a lot of blank lines and spaces. I just couldn't bring myself to put it down in words." After reading the ticket Morrissey called Lithgow into her office and told her, "Helen, you have to write out exactly what you saw." It wasn't until her third effort that her report was deemed satisfactory.[20]

• • •

One of Morrissey's most far-reaching changes was to place cottage warders on eight-hour shifts, which made the job much more attractive to local women. Over the next few years, there was a dramatic changeover in personnel as nearly a hundred new warders (called correctional officers, or COs, after 1967) were hired. Despite the fact that the new employees' union had won increased pay and benefits, four-fifths left within six months. In 1963 Morrissey reported, "We continue to find it difficult to secure competent help." Due to the new eight-hour shift and work weeks limited to forty hours, at least four warders were needed to replace the single warder who had previously supervised a cottage.[21]

Warders' reasons for leaving are revealing. One short-lived employee explained that she "didn't have the patience to work there." Another noted, "It was nerve-racking. You had to count and keep track of everything. There were so many rules I kept calling the office several times a day." For another it was "just too scary being in those cottages at night." Nor did she like "searching women all the time" or "dealing with all the homosexuality." Female staff were also expected to serve as role models. Helen Lithgow reported, "In those days you could be fired for any type of moral infraction. If you got off work and went to the local tavern you could get fired. On Fridays

[Assistant Superintendent] Russell Powers used to go around checking out the bars."[22]

Other women left because they never became comfortable with or lost their fear of working with African American women. Betty Swearingen (1966–91) recalled that on her second day another warder asked, "You ever been around black people before?" and then left her alone upstairs in a cottage. Swearingen "flew down those stairs two at a time." Many employees reported similar stories. Swearingen never fully enjoyed the job, which she characterized as "very strenuous and stressful. There were a 'lot of trying times.' I tried to quit several times, but they kept upping my wages." Those who stayed were often single mothers. Swearingen confessed, "I wasn't working there by choice. I had a son to support." Gwen Edwards concurred, "For pay and benefits and just a high school education, it's the best job there was." Linda Senter, a nurse, confessed that she was "petrified. I had seen too many movies about prison, but I was getting divorced and had to get a job." Swearingen, Edwards, and Senter all had mothers who had worked at Dwight. They could turn to them for advice and reassurance when problems arose. Others who stuck it out often had husbands or sons who worked at nearby men's prisons.[23]

Helen Lithgow (1962–1986), barely thirty years old when she applied for a position, boasted that she was "the youngest one ever hired to work as a warder." Morrissey didn't think she was old enough, but Lithgow's mother, Dwight's head farmer since 1938, convinced Morrissey "how much I needed the job." Lithgow acknowledged:

> I might not have stayed, except for my mother working there. I was so afraid I'd do something wrong. And then you were running all day long. Watching the girls. Supervising. Counting. But I needed the job so bad. I'd call Mrs. Morrissey three or four times a shift. She always said to call if you were in doubt. She would say, 'Think about it Helen, think about it.' And I'd just figure it out.[24]

According to Lithgow, Morrissey exhorted warders that their role was above all "security and observation." "First and most important was your security. Head counts was security. You called in about five head counts every shift. You had to know where all your girls were at all times." Yet security did not entail physical intervention. Female warders called male guards if a woman needed to be restrained or forcibly moved. Nor did female staff receive any weapons training until the mid-1970s. Several former warders confessed they were afraid of guns. Lithgow laughingly explained, "I worked there for nearly twenty years before I had to go [for weapons training], but they couldn't fire me if I didn't pass the test because I was hired under the old law."

A few warders loved their job, which was far more challenging and interesting than most other work available for high school graduates in their rural towns. Lithgow commented, "Every day was a different day. You never got bored." Gwen Edwards used the same words, "It was fascinating. There was something different every day." Others felt that the job enabled them to "help people." Nurse Linda Senter, who also emphasized her feelings of stress and being ill-prepared for her position, responded, "If I didn't think I was doing some good I wouldn't have stayed." Lieutenant Ester Dodge observed that what she liked the most was "being able to help someone. Just sitting and talking. They had to have someone to talk to. 'I didn't get a letter from my kids this week.' But we weren't supposed to offer advice, just listen."[25]

In contrast, Georgia Perisee (1957–1992), an African American warder, maintained, "You didn't like none of it. But it was a job. It paid well after a while." Betty Swearingen concurred, "The idea of being in a cottage and all those doors locked. Spookier than hell. I knew I had too, but it wasn't a pleasurable time." Despite her twenty-five years' service, she added, "I never did actually relax. I never forgot I was in a prison. Just a little leery all the time." Although Swearingen believed she had done a good job, she admitted that "it's hard to be a CO. Hard to find that middle ground—not too lenient or too strict." "Too lenient" meant failing to enforce rules. "Too strict" was "just writing them up constantly, the least little thing. Inmates hated their damned guts."[26]

Former warders were divided over their evaluations of their fellow colleagues. Warder Sarah Ruddell (1961–1973) declared, "As far as I was concerned, the inmates were human beings first. The main thing was to be fair. That went over big with them." Ruddell felt that many warders didn't share her view. "For most, jobs were scarce and it was a job. That's all they cared about." Ruddell, hired in 1961, was chosen to train new warders. She was convinced that her appointment reflected the DPS's tacit acknowledgment that Biedermann's warders, who had far more seniority than she did, included many "rotten apples." After Biedermann's resignation, DPS officials spent several months investigating Dwight before Morrissey was appointed. Assistant Superintendent of Prisons Hollis McKnight purportedly told Ruddell, "I've been on the grounds several months now and I've been asking around and all the inmates say, 'She's the only warder that we could call a lady on this campus.'"[27]

Ester Dodge (1962–1992), who advanced to the position of first (and only) female lieutenant in the 1970s, agreed with Ruddell's negative assessment. Dodge bluntly asserted that "25 to 30 percent weren't worth a shit. What can you expect," she asked, "if you take a farmer's wife or a country housekeeper and put her in a prison, who doesn't know anyone who had ever known anyone who had ever been in trouble? How is she going to relate?" Lois Green agreed. In the 1960s when there was plenty of local factory work, "Dwight was at the very bottom of the employment ladder. We got women who had to support their families, farmers who had gone bust, guys who couldn't get jobs elsewhere. We were a retirement home for old guys [who served as guards, patrolling the grounds at night]."

A few offered more positive assessments. Anna Cook (1963–1986) felt that most warders treated the women fairly. Those who didn't rarely lasted long: "Being ornery didn't get you any place with anybody." Cook claimed she didn't need to write many tickets, "If you tried to work with them they didn't give you much problem." Likewise, Vicky Washton (1962–1987) thought that "most COs were good. Most treated their girls with respect. They overlooked a lot of minor things, didn't have to write many tickets. It was rewarding if you could keep your cottage happy." Delores Gilbert, a prisoner who served three sentences at Dwight, also expressed fond memories. She proudly recalled the "homelike atmosphere" in the cottages: "Everything was immaculate. That was the word. At that time the CO lived with her girls. She knew her girls and was for them." In the 1970s COs rotated assignments every few months, which made it much more difficult for them to establish ongoing relationships with inmates.[28]

Ex-prisoner Jamella Reynolds (1963–1966) offered a more embittered perspective: "We didn't trust anyone there. They didn't care about our welfare or our health. Everything was 'you're a criminal, you're an inmate.'" Although Reynolds greatly appreciated the institution's educational programs, she remembered only one correctional officer who "treated us as human beings." She concluded bitterly, "What did these women know about women who came out of the inner city? Basically they saw us as criminals who had to be dealt with in a criminal way. I think with them we were all criminals and we were all prone to homosexuality."

Although the cottages were officially desegregated in 1960, Reynolds charged that a de facto segregation continued to operate:

> Blacks did the serious manual labor. We worked outside. We were the garbage collectors, worked on the laundry truck. The white girls had the light jobs, while they treated us like men. So it was basically segregated cottages. If you worked on the same assignment then you lived together.

As other studies of women's prisons have found, African American prisoners contended that there was little racial animosity between black and white inmates. However, they felt that many staff harbored deeply racist attitudes. Although virtually all white employees denied that any racial tensions or issues existed at the reformatory, Jeanie Fairman, Dwight's first Director of Family Services (1980–2001), agreed with Reynolds. As a parole agent in the late 1960s Fairman had regularly attended meetings at the reformatory. She recalled the overall atmosphere as:

> Very sad and depressing, dismal. No sense of humanity. No warmth. It just seemed like a very sterile environment. Control clearly belonged to staff, no doubt about that. Not that this was necessarily wrong, but the control orientation was not balanced by any humanity. There was no room for compassion. People seemed to feel that compassion was the worst thing you could do. 'These people are convicted felons.' That was their attitude.[29]

Fairman concluded, "I wouldn't have come here to work in 1970. I wouldn't have fit in. It was just too dismal." Nor would she have fit in as a professional African American woman: "The first thing you noticed was the white staff and black inmates. I don't remember any black staff in 1970." Sheila Bennet, a black counselor hired shortly after 1970, stayed only a few years. Herbert Bailey, Fairman's Chicago neighbor, was appointed assistant superintendent in the mid-1970s. According to Fairman, "when Bailey found out he had to come down here to Dwight he had a fit. Of course, he came down. He was a trooper. Did what he had to. But his wife absolutely refused to come live here." Bailey stayed in the former staff quarters in the administration building, commuting home to Chicago and his family on weekends. Fairman and her husband (then warden at Pontiac) visited whenever they could: "Culturally it was truly a shock to him. It was a white community with totally conservative views." In 1980, when Fairman accepted a job as a counselor, 13 percent of employees were African American. She felt that the overall atmosphere had improved greatly. Nevertheless, few black employees chose to live in the town of Dwight.[30]

Unlike Jeanie Fairman and sociologist Lois Green, many long-term white employees characterized Morrissey's administration as the "good old days" before prisoners gained too many rights and a "new breed" of inmate entered in the 1970s. Helen Lithgow maintained:

> You never had any trouble in those days. If there was a rule there was a rule. If you broke a rule you knew what was going to happen. They didn't talk back then. Never cussed and never did nothing. They used to respect you. The inmates were more mature then. We rarely had to deal with nineteen, twenty, twenty-one-year-olds.

However, she also admitted that "they were slick. There were a lot of things you might not know about that was going on." Her daughter, Susan Lithgow, also a correctional officer, concurred:

> If someone got put in seg, that was a big thing then. They were older women and you didn't have as many problems. There were only four rooms for segregation and that was enough. There would be days and weeks you had nobody in segregation at all. Later, we had to use more rooms than the original four, which were built in the back all by themselves. Then they built C-12 and the number jumped to thirty.[31]

Imogene Becker (1966–1984) echoed their sentiments, "It was very nice in the 1960s. Nothing stressful. The girls usually abided by the rules. They had a lot more maturity then. In the 1970s the new inmates started getting a lot more aggressive. Now it's out of this world."[32]

Similar to many long-term staff, these women felt that "everything went downhill" after Morrissey left. Lithgow provided a litany of complaints: the laws changed, inmates gained more rights, a "new type" of younger inmate appeared who was less respectful and more difficult to deal with, there were more physical fights, "wishy washy" superintendents weren't strict enough. Other warders objected to the end of the "no contact" rule, which had prohibited all physical touch between inmates; the decision to allow women to purchase their own clothes; and the establishment of difficult-to-supervise outdoor recreation periods. Lithgow concluded, "It got so I just couldn't handle the cottages. I was trying to run a cottage the way I had been taught to run it, but I just couldn't. There was no backup. All the rules had changed." Betty Swearingen agreed, "Under Morrissey a rule was a rule. Inmates knew where they stood then. They knew what they could and couldn't do. In the 1970s it got to be so that one officer enforces the rules, the next doesn't."

Many long-term employees also noted that a "new breed" of younger, less mature staff added to the difficulties. After 1970, correctional officers were often only nineteen or twenty years old themselves. Meanwhile, rapidly growing overcrowding severely strained personnel and resources. Whereas Dwight's population had plummeted to ninety in 1972, in late 1980 it topped four hundred, and by 1990 it had doubled to nearly eight hundred.[33]

• • •

Margaret Morrissey served as superintendent until her retirement in 1972. In 1970 the Illinois Department of Public Safety was dissolved. As in many other states, all prisons (adult and juvenile) were transferred to the new Department of Corrections (D.O.C.). The institution's name was officially changed to Dwight Correctional Center, similar to the names of the state's male facilities. Under the aegis of the D.O.C., the reformatory's founders' vision of a specifically feminine form of "disciplinary treatment and care," inherently flawed and never realized in practice, was officially abandoned. Yet many contradictions remained.

The D.O.C. exhibited no unified or clearly articulated policy regarding female offenders. Due to Dwight's plummeting population, in 1973 the department announced that it would become a co-correctional facility. In 1976 a legislative committee described Dwight's population of 105 women and 48 men as "a rather strange mix of inmates." The men were mostly nonviolent offenders, typically fifty years of age or older. Many had serious medical problems. Despite this, several female prisoners became pregnant each year. Concurrently, Vienna Correctional Center in southern Illinois was also transformed into a co-correctional facility. Fifty-eight women were housed there; most participated in a special work-release program.[34]

During the 1970s and 1980s many states experimented with co-correctional prisons, which were championed by a diverse group of advocates. Some saw them as a humane reform that would help to normalize the prison environment. However, movement and interaction between the sexes was tightly controlled. Although men and women shared the same facilities—such as the dining hall, library, classrooms, and work sites—often they did not use them at the same time. Other supporters assumed that the presence of women would act as a "softening" influence, resulting in improvements in male inmate behavior and, specifically, decreased levels of violence. Some feminists viewed co-correctional facilities as the only way to provide female prisoners access to the far superior educational, vocational, and employment facilities that male prisons offered. In 1984 nearly two-thirds (61%) of the nation's female offenders were housed in co-correctional facilities.[35]

At Dwight, co-corrections resulted in major changes in personnel. Between 1972 and 1977 male wardens replaced female superintendents. At the same time, nearly all upper-level correctional staff—lieutenants, sergeants, and captains—were men brought in from the male system. Dwight's first wardens, Robert Buchanan (1973–1974) and John Platt (1974–1977), were extremely liberal reform administrators who inaugurated sweeping changes. However, many of their male staff, an unprecedented 20 percent of correctional officers, showed little respect to female prisoners and staff. According to correc-

GRAPH 5

Average Daily Population of Female Prisoners in Illinois, 1930–2000

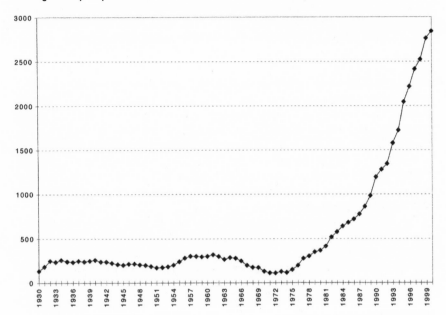

Source: Department of Public Welfare, 1926 *Annual Report*, 358; 1940 *Report of Statistician*, 162; Dwight, *Annual Statistical Reports*; Department of Corrections, *Five-Year Reports*.

tional officer Susan Lithgow, their dominant attitude was that "Dwight isn't a real prison. It's just pretend. And besides, you should be home cooking."[36]

Dwight's experiment in co-corrections was abandoned in 1977, although Vienna remained co-correctional until 1999. With the return to a tougher, law-and-order philosophy during the mid-1970s, Dwight's female population began its meteoric rise (see graph 5). In 1979 two fifty-bed housing units were added, identical in design to new cell houses built in the state's men's prisons. That same year the first of several major sex scandals unfolded, this one involving the sexual abuse of female prisoners by two high-ranking male officers. Newly appointed warden Charlotte Sutliffe-Nesbitt (1977–1979) resigned and was replaced by Jane Higgins (1982–1991), who received rave reviews from many former prisoners as well as women's groups and prison reform organizations. Higgins introduced many innovative programs in her effort to liberalize and humanize prison conditions. Nonetheless, a 1984 study revealed that Dwight issued the highest number of disciplinary tickets per prisoner of any institution in the state (1.9 versus a male average of 0.9 per prisoner). The study's authors speculated that Dwight was experiencing "either unusual disciplinary problems or high staff-inmate tension." Letters to the John Howard Association revealed that at Dwight, unlike at a comparable male prison, there were "continual complaints about grievance procedures, calculation of 'good-time,' segregation and disciplinary policies, staff-inmate tensions, and general administrative procedures." Women inmates also filed a disproportionate number of complaints regarding lack of programs.[37]

In 1986 female prisoners sued the D.O.C., charging that compared with male prisoners they were provided with substantially inferior educational and vocational programming and were paid lower wages for similar work. Dwight offered no bachelors-level college program, employed no trained law librarian, and offered only a rudimentary law library. The women also alleged that they were adversely impacted by the lack of a minimum-security facility. Male inmates could request transfers to a dozen prisons of various security classifications, each one offering a different variety of educational, vocational, and treatment programs. In 1991 the D.O.C. entered into a consent decree, promising new training programs for women in business and computer technology. That same year the Kankakee minimum-security unit opened as a satellite of Dwight.

Meanwhile, to ease the continued overcrowding at Dwight, whose population was now close to eight hundred, and to give women access to a broader array of programs, two medium-security male facilities were turned into co-gender institutions: Logan Correctional Center in 1987 and Dixon Correctional Center in 1989. However, female inmates were not given a choice about whether they wanted to be housed in a co-gender facility, where they often suffered greater surveillance and harassment. As in the nineteenth century officials disproportionately blamed female convicts for creating sexual disturbances. Lydia Townsend, one of the first women transferred to Dixon, recalled bitterly, "We were the ones they watched. We were the ones they blamed for being provocative. We were the ones who could no longer wear open-toe sandals or sleeveless blouses."[38]

In the 1990s women prisoners in Illinois, like their counterparts nationally, were primarily guarded by male staff. In 1992, 71 percent of correctional officers working in the four Illinois institutions housing women (Dwight, Logan, Dixon, and Kankakee) were male. When women brought charges of sexual abuse against male staff, they were the ones who faced punishment or retaliation. A 1996 investigation by Human Rights Watch titled *All Too Familiar: Sexual Abuse of Women in U.S. State Prisons* revealed that sexual abuse of female prisoners was a serious problem nationwide. Illinois was one of five states singled out for an in-depth investigation. The report's authors concluded that there existed "a serious problem with sexual misconduct in Illinois correctional facilities for women, including frequent privacy violations and sexually explicit verbal degradation of female prisoners, inappropriate sexual contact, and, at times, rape and sexual assault." The report's authors observed, "Neither Illinois prison rules nor [Illinois] criminal law expressly prohibits such abuse. When female prisoners have attempted to report sexual misconduct, they have faced a biased grievance and investigatory procedure and often have suffered retaliation or even punishment by prison staff."[39]

With 2,760 women behind bars in 1999, Illinois had the seventh-largest female prison population in the nation. Nearly one-half (48%) of the women were sentenced for drug violations and another one-third (35%) for property offenses, most commonly retail theft or check fraud. Only 12 percent were incarcerated for violent crimes. Three-quarters (76%) were African American or Latina. Most served less than a year, contributing to a constant turnover: 2,642 women were admitted annually. Such short sentences meant that few could participate in meaningful educational or vocational training programs. For many, incarceration's major cost was the tremendous hardship it imposed on their families. Seventy-one percent were single mothers who risked losing custody of their children as a result of their imprisonment.

Feminist criminologist Pat Carlen concludes, "Overall, the dominant meaning of women's imprisonment . . . is that it is imprisonment denied: it is denied that the woman's prison is a 'real prison,' it is denied that the women are 'real prisoners,' it is denied that the prisoners are 'real women.'" The founders of the Illinois State Reformatory for Women failed to envision the singularly repressive character of the institution they had so ardently championed and lovingly designed. At Dwight women were told that they were being held not in a real prison, but at a school, hospital, treatment center, or training program. They were instructed to view themselves as "residents" rather than "prisoners," connoting the status of students, patients, or willing subjects of a voluntary treatment regime. But the very fact of their incarceration meant that they had failed both as real women and as good mothers. At the same time, women's experiences of incarceration and the close homosocial and homosexual ties they created with other women only served to further mark them as deviant and beyond the bounds of normal womanhood.[40]

CONCLUSION

Lessons for the Twenty-First Century

In contemporary American society, prisons play a historically unparalleled role in official policies of race, class, and gender control. The United States imprisons more people than any other nation in the world. According to the U.S. Department of Justice, 1.1 percent of women and 9 percent of men will be incarcerated at some point during their lifetime. These odds vary enormously by race: 3.6 percent of adult African American women will be imprisoned, compared to 1.5 percent of Latina and 0.5 percent of white women. For men, the figures are even more shocking: 28.5 percent of African American men, 16 percent of Latino, and 4.4 percent of white men will serve a prison sentence during their adult lifetimes. These extraordinary statistics do not include the far greater numbers who will serve time on probation or in local jails.[1]

Before 1970 neither the penitentiary nor the women's reformatory was central to the social control of women. Between 1835 and 1930 only 1,653 women were sentenced to prison in Illinois—fewer than twenty annually—in contrast to over 70,000 men. Women represented only 2.4 percent of the state's prison population. Although women's commitments, including those of both felons and misdemeanants, increased to roughly 1,200 per decade after the Illinois State Reformatory for Women at Dwight opened in 1930, women still represented less than 4 percent of the state's penal population. Nationally, female incarceration rates actually fell during most of the twentieth century, from 4 percent of all prisoners in 1900 to 3 percent in 1970. Reflecting on her three years' imprisonment for a narcotics violation in the early 1960s, Jamella Reynolds observed, "Women did not go to prison. Who knew that we even existed? Men went, not women. So this to me was like a double strike. You're not only a woman, but you've been to prison. And then if you're black, that's a third strike."[2]

Reynolds's words cogently capture the many contradictions female prisoners confronted throughout the last two centuries. The penitentiary was never considered an appropriate place for punishing "proper women." In 1878 Joliet's penitentiary commissioners complained that "only the most depraved women are sent here." One hundred years later ex-counselor Sue Welch observed, "In the 1970s, judges sent to Dwight only those they considered hopeless." Sociologist Lois Green concurred, "The women were in bad shape. Women did not get sent to prison unless they were pretty dysfunctional." Such moralistic evaluations—most depraved, hopeless, dysfunctional—fail to acknowledge the crucial fact that only certain groups of women risked being branded with such labels.

Like their counterparts in previous centuries, women sentenced to prison today are overwhelmingly poor, marginalized, and disadvantaged. Nationally in 1999, 67 percent were African American or Latina. White women, constituting 33 percent of the female prison population, were nearly twice as likely to be on probation (62%). As in the past, three-quarters of female inmates were incarcerated for nonviolent crimes: drug offenses (34%), property offenses (27%), and public order offenses (13%). Most were single mothers; two-thirds had minor children. Sixty percent were unemployed at the time of their arrest. Of those who were working 37 percent earned less than $7,200 per year. More than half had histories of physical and sexual abuse. Compared to their male counterparts, female prisoners admit to more severe drug and substance abuse problems. Indeed, over half were under the influence of drugs or alcohol at the time of their offense. Of the total, one-third committed their crimes in order to obtain money for drugs.[3]

Although today's female offenders share many similarities with women prisoners from earlier eras, they are being incarcerated in historically unprecedented numbers. In virtually every year since 1970 the number of women sentenced to prison has increased at a faster rate than that of men. In 1972, 6,269 women and 189,823 men were incarcerated in approximately two hundred state and federal prisons nationwide. In mid-2000 there were 92,688 women and nearly 1.3 million men in 924 adult correctional facilities. Another 70,000 women were incarcerated in local jails, and 800,000 were serving time on probation. Since 1970 women's share of the nation's prison population has doubled from 3.1 percent to 6.7 percent.[4]

These extraordinary increases in rates of imprisonment for both men and women are a product of increasingly draconian criminal justice policies, rather than changes in criminal behavior. Women have been disproportionately affected by the war on drugs and mandatory sentencing laws that give judges little to no discretion. Narcotics offenders are the fastest growing category of female prisoners, nearly tripling from 12 percent in 1986 to 34 percent in 1999, one-third of whom were sentenced for possession. Meanwhile, between 1979 and 1999 the proportion of women inmates incarcerated for violent offenses declined from 49 to 28 percent. At the same time, the proportion sentenced for less serious, public order offenses (driving while intoxicated, morals and decency, and commercialized vice offenses) increased from 5.1 to 13 percent. These statistics suggest that higher rates of incarceration reflect not increasing rates of serious female criminality, but states' willingness to incarcerate women, including first offenders, in unprecedented numbers. Whereas in 1991, 28 percent of female prisoners had no prior criminal record, by 1999 this proportion had increased to 35 percent. Indeed, more female than male inmates were first offenders (35% versus 23%), suggesting that the criminal justice system continues to view the average female offender as worse than a male offender.[5]

• • •

Throughout this study I have argued that both crime and criminality are socially constructed categories. Positivist views that regard crime as an objective social fact ignore the powerful role that discretion plays in processing individuals into and through the various levels of the criminal justice system. For every theft, robbery, assault, burglary, murder, or other possibly criminal legal transgression that was committed by a convicted woman in Illinois, at least another hundred, if not another thousand, identical acts were committed under similar circumstances, but the perpetrators' actions were not prosecuted as crimes, or if prosecuted, did not result in a penitentiary sentence. Few of their crimes were heinous enough to demand state intervention or necessitate a penal response. Women and men in Illinois often did get away with murder—and with larceny, robbery, forgery, assault, and many other crimes—but *some* women, and a larger number of men, had to be punished and held accountable for their actions.

The few female convicts provided an example that women were neither completely above the law nor completely beyond the power of the state to punish. Not every woman, however, was equally vulnerable to becoming a living example of the rule of law. Those who were selected for prosecution and punishment were typically the most socially and economically marginal. During the nineteenth century, these were disproportionately Irish and other European-born immigrant women. However, by 1890 the percentage of foreign-born women had reached parity with their share in the state's general population. In place of ethnicity, race became central to the social definition of female criminality. From 1890 to 1950 African American women, averaging approximately 4 percent of the state's female population, were sentenced for 70 percent of all serious assaults, 57 percent of all robberies, 66 percent of all manslaughter deaths, and 53 percent of all murders. These racial disparities are so enormous that they seriously challenge the assumption that differences in rates of incarceration reflect real differences in rates of criminality.

Regardless of race or ethnicity, the majority of female convicts were unskilled and poorly educated working-class women. They were twice as likely as nonincarcerated women to have been born outside of Illinois, and hence less likely to have deep community or familial roots. Many female felons failed to conform to conventional notions of proper femininity. Despite an average age of thirty, they were less likely to be married than women in the state's general population and ten times more likely to be separated or divorced. Over half were childless. Most were burdened with the stigma of immoral and disreputable women who had led "improper lives." Whatever the nature of their legal transgressions, it was others' estimate of their character and moral standing that most often determined their fate within the criminal justice system.

• • •

None of the dominant interpretations of the history of the prison adequately account for women's experiences of incarceration. Progressive historians interpreted the penitentiary as a more humane and enlightened method of punishment, yet women in nineteenth-century Illinois were rarely subjected to corporal forms of punishment. Nor were women viewed as the ideal objects of the new rehabilitative technology. Instead, ideological supporters of the penitentiary regarded criminal women as beyond redemption; none imagined that the penitentiary would inspire their reformation.

As in most states no sustained ideological debate accompanied the transition from corporal to incarcerative modes of punishment in Illinois. Nor were there any extended philosophical discussions of the merits of competing rehabilitative regimes or visions of penal reform. Pecuniary rather than philosophical or ideological motives fueled the evolution of the penitentiary. In the antebellum period the warden of the penitentiary was the lessor of the convicts' labor; in the post–Civil War period the state managed the penitentiaries and prisoners' labor was leased to private contractors. In both systems profit was the overriding motive, and the quality of the care and treatment prisoners—both male and female—received suffered accordingly.

During the nineteenth century female convicts were incarcerated alongside of men at Alton (1835–1858), Joliet (1859–1896), and Chester (1878–1889) penitentiaries. There they suffered under the same wretched living conditions as men while often experiencing more extreme neglect. Despite the fact that a one-hundred-cell unit at Joliet was originally designed for them, between 1870 and 1896 the women were locked away on the fourth floor of the "Warden's House," or main administration building. Their feet "never touched the ground" except once a year. From the limited remarks of wardens and penitentiary commissioners, it is clear that success was measured solely in terms of the amount of profit that could be extracted from the women's labor, the cleanliness of their quarters, and the effectiveness of the discipline that matrons maintained.

In their pardon petitions women voiced their utter desperation. The executive clemency files also reveal local officials' ambivalence over their incarceration. Nevertheless, in Illinois no outside women's, religious, or reform groups expressed interest in the plight of the state's female felons. Instead, at the end of the century male prison administrators in many states began to advocate for separate women's units to house the growing numbers of female convicts and eliminate the "pernicious influence" of these supposedly depraved and degraded women. In 1896 Illinois's female convicts were removed from inside the state's male penitentiaries and housed in their own unit. The Joliet Women's Prison (1896–1933), standing directly across the street from the men's institution and mirroring it in architectural design, typified this first generation of custodial women's prisons.

Throughout the nineteenth century, women's forms of resistance to penal authority proved particularly troubling for their male captors, who were continually frustrated in their efforts to effectively manage, control, and discipline them. These attitudes persisted into the twentieth century. In 1960 famed Joliet warden Joseph P. Ragen, appointed a few months before the closing of the Women's Prison in 1933, reminisced, "even though my association with the Women's Branch was brief, . . . I knew enough about it to be thankful that this additional problem was not added to the many which fell to me during my first trying days." Ragen then added a revealing aside: "With the removal of the last eight women from Joliet to Dwight on June 30, one day before the deadline, there ended a problem that had been a thorn in the side of every warden since Warden Buckmaster's time [the 1850s]." Likewise, contemporary surveys of correctional officers reveal that many continue to regard female prisoners as more troublesome, demanding, and difficult to handle than male.[6]

The history of women's imprisonment in Illinois is fully representative of national trends. Until World War I the majority of female prisoners did their time in such custodial units. During its first two decades Joliet Women's Prison was administered as a subdivision of the male penitentiary. Little was heard from Chief Matron Maria S. Madden (1888–1914) or her charges, most of whom labored nine hours a day in either contract labor or the prison's "modern" steam laundry. In 1913 a new warden inaugurated sweeping changes, including the appointment of the first college-educated chief matron the following year. Grace Fuller (1914–1921), a national leader in domestic science education, entered Joliet with an ambitious reform agenda. She was convinced that even the "hardest" prisoners could be reformed through a regime of domestic training. Both Fuller and her successor, Elinor Rulien (1921–1929), expressed an unwavering faith in the possibility of women's reformation.

In striking contrast, superintendents and staff at the Illinois State Training School for Delinquent and Dependent Girls at Geneva freely characterized the girls under their care as incorrigible, degenerate, feeble-minded, and in need of permanent custodial care. Instead of expressing optimism over the possibility of their reformation, staff repeatedly portrayed the girls as a menace to society, the potential mothers of a "very undesirable grade of population." In 1911 Geneva Superintendent Ophelia Amigh, accused of frequently flogging the girls with heavy rawhide whips, was forced to resign. Yet her views, if not her methods, remained deeply entrenched. Through the mid-1920s Geneva superintendents and staff continued to write disparagingly about the possibility of reforming wayward girls.[7]

No similar scandals occurred at Joliet until 1926, when a grand jury investigation of the Joliet penitentiary revealed the existence of an inmate subculture that had not previously been exposed to public view. Like their nineteenth-century counterparts, female inmates in the 1920s were neither docile nor dutiful subjects. Whether pursuing same-sex romances or illicit contact with male prisoners, distilling alcohol, swearing, fighting, or talking back, women prisoners challenged their keepers', and society's, notions of propriety, modesty, morality, and proper femininity. Nationally reformatory and prison officials expressed increasingly negative attitudes, often within the first decade of their institutions' founding. By the 1920s optimism and high hopes had already given way to derogatory assessments of the character, mental ability, and rehabilitative potential of female prisoners. Ironically, at the Joliet Women's Prison, where rehabilitative hopes were never as high, superintendents never publicly denounced their charges. Whereas officials at the Geneva girls' reformatory publicly and repeatedly condemned the girls' alleged resistance, willful moral degeneracy, and perverted sexual practices, Elinor Rulien's studied silence and lenient treatment incurred the wrath of both outside investigators and some of her own staff.

Although most of the female superintendents at the Joliet Women's Prison appear to have been sympathetic to the plight of their charges, prison psychiatrists and parole board members expressed little optimism about the possibility of the inmates' reformation. After 1920 the Illinois parole board was one of the most restrictive in the country. In addition to doubling time served, the board denied parole outright to over half of women, allowing them to be released only after they had served their full sentence. Board members characterized the majority of female convicts as immoral, sexually promiscuous women who had led improper lives. Parole evaluations typically concluded with the standard phrase "success upon parole is doubtful" and recommended permanent institutionalization for women who did not succeed on parole.

Although conflicts often emerged among the recommendations of parole board members, mental health officers, prison staff, judges, and state's attorneys, all parties assessed female criminality in highly gendered and moralistic ways. Even though they might disagree over whether a particular woman was "criminalistic in nature" or had led an otherwise "proper life," all agreed that a woman's adherence to conventional standards of proper femininity was critical for assessing her worthiness for parole. In their decision making officials' concern about a woman's past sexual propriety, marital fidelity, drinking habits, children's legitimacy, family's respectability, presence of venereal disease, and general reputation in her local community frequently overshadowed legal factors, such as the seriousness of her crime, prior record, or institutional conduct.

• • •

Conflicting and competing discourses on the nature of female criminality emerged after 1900. Even as the female superintendents at Joliet repeatedly referred to their charges as these "poor unfortunates" and instituted domestic training programs designed to awaken dormant feminine sensibilities, staff at the Geneva girls' reformatory portrayed the young women sentenced there as feeble-minded, defective, degenerate, and incapable of reformation, views that were shared by parole board members and prison psychiatrists. During the 1920s these two discourses became intertwined. The Illinois club women who campaigned for a new state reformatory for women argued that those female inmates deemed capable of reformation deserved a higher level of "treatment and care" than that provided at Joliet Women's Prison, whereas those judged to be incapable of reformation required permanent commitment to "farm colonies" for the feeble-minded. Only the scientific assessment and classification of prisoners by prison psychiatrists, sociologists, and physicians could determine which category a particular woman should be placed in. Classification, however, remained crude. Female prisoners were routinely labeled as psychopathic, feeble-minded, and borderline defective; none of these diagnoses offered much hope of a cure. The birth of the prison evolved out of the competing and contradictory ideologies of reform and social control. The history of the movement to establish the Illinois State Reformatory for Women clearly embodies this dualism.

Although women's prisons are commonly viewed as more benign and treatment-orientated than men's institutions, the history of the Illinois State Reformatory for Women at Dwight from 1930 to 1972 reveals an institution that came to rely on a rigid system of discipline and control and failed to offer significant treatment programs. Reformers' visions quickly collided with the realities of day-to-day prison administration, including inmate resistance to a program that trained them for little more than domestic service. Within the first decade of the reformatory's operation, its rehabilitation and treatment goals gave way to an increasingly draconian emphasis on security, custodial care, and control. Simultaneously, larger numbers of women were sentenced to prison than ever before. Whereas 252 women had been committed to Joliet Women's Prison in the 1920s, over 1,300 were sentenced to the new reformatory in the 1930s, 75 percent of whom were misdemeanor offenders. As late as the early 1980s, 10 percent of female prisoners in Illinois were still misdemeanants. Convinced that "residents" were receiving only beneficial protection, treatment, training, and care, reformers failed to acknowledge the coercive character of these new reformatory institutions.

In *Partial Justice: Women, Prisons, and Social Control*, Nicole Hahn Rafter observes, "Women's prisons required obedience not only to prison rules (generally more numerous for women) and criminal laws (also more numerous until recently), but also to cultural standards for femininity that fluctuated by race and social class." Women at Dwight were held to strict standards of femininity in regard to their language, dress, attitudes, and behavior. Forced to live among strangers, when they did develop affectionate or caring relationships, they risked being labeled homosexual. They were graded daily on their attitude, work, and citizenship. Warders' daily reports are filled with accounts of women's failure to conform to the myriad rules that governed every aspect of daily life. During World War II an extreme shortage of personnel developed that plagued the institution over the next two decades. Virtually all organized educational and recreational programs were eliminated. Instead, women were locked in their rooms by 6:00 every evening.[8]

By the late 1940s Superintendent Helen H. Hazard was complaining that "discipline and morale" were at an all-time low. Changes in the state's sentencing laws and parole board policies further reduced incentives for cooperation. After 1944 the board gave two-thirds (66%) of prisoners a "Maximum X," denying parole completely after their first year in prison. Warders, all patronage appointees with no specialized training, continued to resist Hazard's "psychiatric" approach and resented her failure to allow corporal punishment. In 1949 Hazard resigned in despair. The Department of Public Welfare brought in two male wardens in an effort to restore order and control. They were followed by Doris Whitney, a short-lived reform superintendent. She was fired in 1953 as a result of warders' resistance to both her purported "leniency" and her new educational programs, which were perceived as "glorifying inmates." Another unsuccessful superintendent resigned nine months later.

In 1954 the reformatory was transferred to the Department of Public Safety, which governed the state's male prisons. During the next two decades Dwight superintendents came from backgrounds in law enforcement or corrections, rather than education or social work. Under the administrations of Ruth L. Biedermann (1954–1962) and Margaret D. Morrissey (1962–1972) discipline became increasingly exacting and security and custodial concerns dominated institutional life. Contrary to the idealized vision of the reformatory's founders, cottage living bore no resemblance to ordinary home life. Instead, the small, intimate cottage housing units facilitated an unprecedented degree of surveillance and control.

• • •

In 1999 the Illinois Department of Corrections established a separate Women and Family Services Division. Its stated mission is to provide "a continuum of programs and services . . . which address the unique medical, social, psychological, and educational needs of the committed female offender" and to develop "special programs that recognize, support, and maintain her parental roles and responsibilities." The report's authors highlight women's special needs relating to substance abuse treatment; histories of physical, sexual, and domestic abuse; unique medical and mental health issues; family reunification services; and affordable housing after release. Although the authors outline many new and innovative programs, they fail to address either the pragmatic question of funding or the more profound question of the ability of prisons to serve as sites of genuine rehabilitation.[9]

Despite the best of its founders' intentions, the history of the Illinois State Reformatory for Women suggests that the concept of a humane or therapeutic prison remains a contradiction in terms. In a reflective article titled, "Why Study Women's Imprisonment? Or Anyone Else's?" Pat Carlen reaches a similar conclusion. She observes, "All criminologists seeking research access to prisons are required to collude in the liberal myth that, 'We all want prisons to be more humane places, don't we?'" Instead, Carlen argues that we must admit precisely the opposite. Pain is not an unintentional byproduct, but the sine qua non of imprisonment. Researchers need to investigate prisons and theorize about them "as deliberate and calibrated mechanisms of punishment inflicting state-legitimated pain."[10]

The purpose of imprisonment is punishment. After two hundred years of failed experiments in prison reform, it is time to admit that prisons simply cannot be reformed. Nor can they serve as genuine instruments of rehabilitation. Of course, some prisons and some administrations are better than others: more humane, more concerned with meeting prisoners' needs, more vigilant in monitoring or responding to staff abuses. Nevertheless, outside of a narrow range of possibilities, history suggests that little can be done to alleviate the prison's inherently oppressive and repressive nature, its degrading and often brutal realities. Nor can even the most seemingly attractive prison or well-intentioned staff compensate for the pains of imprisonment that incarceration, by its very definition, involves: the profound loss of freedom, autonomy, individuality, and self-respect; severed connections to family, friends, and loved ones; and deprivation of valued goods and services.

In her final reflection, ex-prisoner Lydia Townsend, another model inmate, voiced a sentiment shared by many others:

> The hardest part of doing time is the dehumanization. It's not physical, it's mental. Telling you when to move; eat when you're not even hungry; sleep and you're not even sleepy. Talking down to you like you're nothing but a child, or a number. The games they play. It might be easier just to be beaten. Then at least they'd stop for a while. Instead it's an every day, constant, mental abuse. And your children, your family, they have to go through it too when they come to visit.[11]

Townsend's off-hand proposition, "It might be easier just to be beaten," suggests the worlds of pain that incarceration entails.

NOTES ON ARCHIVAL SOURCES

Convict Registers, 1835–1933

Statistical and demographic data on female prisoners were compiled from the convict registers located at the Illinois State Archives (RG 243.200 and RG 243.001). No sampling methods were used. All statistical calculations are based upon the total female convict population. For the period between 1835 and 1933 a total of 1,670 women prisoners were identified at Alton, Joliet, and Chester (Menard) penitentiaries. Because female convicts were processed with the men, no separate registers were kept for them. Thus, every page of the six-hundred-page volumes had to be searched. Before the 1890s female convicts were identified on the basis of their feminine names. In cases of doubt, such variables as occupation, height, and weight were considered. After 1890, the designation "Female Department" was frequently written in under the section titled "Assignment." In all, a total of forty-two volumes of convict registers were searched. As a check for accuracy, some volumes were examined twice. (The Illinois State Archives is currently developing an online database for the convict registers.)

Only the third and fourth volumes of the Alton Convict Registers have survived. A typewritten transcript exists of the first register (1833–1842) in the Joseph E. Ragen Collection at the Illinois State Historical Library. Only two women were sentenced to prison during these early years. The second volume (1842–47) has been completely lost. The evidence suggests that at most only a half-dozen women were sentenced during this missing five-year period.

In 1895 the newly established State Board of Pardons and Parole significantly revised the format of the convict register books. The earliest versions included spaces for only eighteen variables, including the prisoner's offense, sentence, county, age, nativity, marital status, occupation, education, religion, physical description (hair, eye, and skin color), and "habits of life" (temperate or intemperate). After 1895 prison clerks were required to collect data on over fifty variables. In addition to demographic information, clerks provided a brief description of the prisoner's offense, along with an assessment of her "general reputation," "disposition," "industriousness," and "habits"; the "character" of her "associates"; and whether her crime was "attributable to use of liquor."

It is not at all obvious how the prison clerk arrived at these judgments. In most cases the clerk offered only an innocuous "fair," a begrudging "not bad," or a far less common "good" or "excellent." In other cases he offered a few telling details. One clerk reported that Lena Dunn, a young housekeeper, was "generally regarded as a prostitute." However, he admitted, "I know very little about her except from reputation. I understand she is from a good family but like many other girls took the wayward path." In the case of another nineteen-year-old housekeeper convicted of stealing candlesticks from her employer, he noted only, "Family good. Respectable colored people." After 1911 clerks ceased all such commentary, leaving these spaces blank. For a more detailed description of the convict registers, see Dodge, "'Her Life Has Been an Improper One,'" 732–46.

Pardon Petitions, 1835–1911

Pardon letters and clemency petitions are located under Secretary of State, Executive Section, Executive Clemency Files, RG 103.096, at the Illinois State Archives. There is no index for cases prior to 1912. Pardon petitions from 1835 to 1861 are filed by year in neatly labeled individual manila folders. From 1861 to 1911 they are jumbled together in large file boxes labeled alphabetically. These files also include petitions from prisoners incarcerated in county jails and workhouses. Clemency files from years after 1911 must be requested individually and by name. Approximately one hundred clemency petitions from women have been preserved from the nineteenth century. Twenty-five pardon files were examined from the years 1900–1940.

These files are very inconsistent in their contents. Most contain just one or two items. In cases of pregnancy, illness, or insanity the warden and prison physician each wrote brief notes. Between 1860 and 1900 roughly one-third of the files included a letter from the prisoner herself. The most complete files also contained actual petitions signed by family, friends, or town officials along with letters from the prosecuting judge or state's attorney. Notes from wardens, matrons, or prison commissioners verifying good conduct in prison were relatively rare. Although the prisoner's name is always indicated in the files, convict numbers are not. Nor was there any consistent documentation about the actual offense, sentence, or whether the pardon was granted or denied. In cases in which a woman was released early (before her sentence would have expired), I simply assumed that her pardon had been granted. However, no reasons were provided as to why a particular request was granted or denied.

Inmate Jackets: Joliet Women's Prison, 1920–1933

All inmate jackets are located at the Illinois State Archives (RG 403: Parole and Pardon Board, restricted access). Complete jackets were maintained beginning in 1920. All of the demographic information (crime, judge, sentence, race, age, nationality, nativity, marital status, prior arrests, and so on) recorded in the convict registers was now simultaneously transcribed on the outside of the inmate's jacket. Inside the jackets are copies of women's admissions, classification, and mental health officers' reports; parole board transcripts; legal papers; and the "Statement of Fact" signed by the trial judge and prosecuting attorney. The amount and type of material varies greatly, depending upon the number of appearances the prisoner made before the parole board. By the mid-1960s the parole board began to tape record hearings and no longer prepared typed transcripts.

Unfortunately, most inmate jackets dating from the 1920s were destroyed. The extant jackets are those of Joliet women who were transferred to Dwight at the closing of the Joliet women's prison in 1933 or of prisoners who remained under active parole supervision at that time. Only seven jackets exist from 1920–1924; 102 from 1925–1929; and 43 from 1930–1933. Both Anne Hinrichsen and Superintendent Grace Fuller refer to social histories of female prisoners conducted during 1920 and 1921, but none have survived.

Dwight (Illinois State Reformatory for Women) Inmate Jackets, 1930–1963

The Dwight convict register books are no longer in existence. Demographic data is available for female prisoners incarcerated at Dwight from 1930 (when the institution opened) to 1963 (after which none of the original inmate jackets were preserved). Because felons came before the parole board, two duplicate sets of jackets were maintained: one at the institution and a second set that was forwarded to the board. The latter set is now housed at the Illinois State Archives. (The first set of jackets, which was maintained at the reformatory, were destroyed in the 1970s.) The jackets at the state archives are numbered 1 to 4235; roughly 25 percent are missing. These missing files represent misdemeanants for whom duplicate jackets were not maintained. Incarcerated under a "flat," one-year sentence, misdemeanants were automatically released after twelve months. Thus their cases did not appear before the parole board. Nevertheless, it was possible to reconstruct a limited profile of misdemeanants (including race, crime, age, marital status, number of children, nationality, and county) from a set of alphabetized index cards covering the time period 1930–1975, located in the admissions office at Dwight.

Because the surviving felony jackets include only those for women who were paroled or released during the 1930–1963 period, data after 1955 becomes problematic: I estimate that roughly 15 to 20 percent of women committed between 1955 and 1960 were not released until after 1963. Thus, the statistical data presented in chapters 6 and 7 focuses on the 1890–1950 time period, for which the most complete information is available. Limited data for 1963–1974, including annual commitments, daily population, and crimes, was compiled from the unpublished *Annual Statistical Reports*, discovered in basement filing cabinets at Dwight.

Microfilmed Inmate Jackets, 1937–1968

Although the original set of inmate jackets maintained at Dwight was destroyed, roughly 250 have been preserved on microfilm. Unfortunately, this microfilming was done in random order. Thus, for example, Microfilm Reel (MR) B9–016 includes eight inmate jackets filmed in the following order (date of entrance given in parentheses): #1238 (1937), #1892 (1943), #1884 (1943), #1321 (1938), #4586 (1967), #4613 (1967), #4597 (1967), and #4591 (1967). Although housed at the Illinois State Archives, there is no index or RG number for this collection, for which access remains restricted.

These microfilmed jackets were invaluable. They cover both felony and misdemeanor cases and include a wealth of material that was not submitted to the parole board: medical records; disciplinary tickets; the progress cards on which warders graded women daily on attitude, work, and citizenship; censored or confiscated letters; personal notes inmates sent staff (requesting favors; counseling sessions; and changes in assignment, cottage, or room-mate); and internal memos or reports staff wrote regarding specific inmates. The microfilmed files also contain the notes on women's behavior that were transcribed from the warders' daily reports, which are no longer in existence. Most microfilmed jackets date from the 1954–1968 period; only four survive from the 1930s and roughly forty from the 1940s.

Restricted Access and Confidentiality

The Joliet and Dwight inmate jackets are not available to the general public. Although housed at the Illinois State Archives, they belong to the Illinois Department of Corrections. Special permission must be obtained to use these materials. (Refer to Public Act 77-2197 and State Record Act of 1957, as amended.)

Illinois law further requires that information regarding individual cases remain confidential and sealed for a period of seventy-five years. Thus, to protect prisoners' anonymity, the convict numbers and names of inmates who entered prison after January 1, 1925, were altered according to the following method. First, a fixed number (less than thirty) was added to each prisoner's convict number. This system was chosen in order to maintain as close a relationship as possible between the prisoner's fictitious convict number and the year in which she was actually incarcerated (convict numbers were assigned in order of admission, beginning with Joliet inmate #1 in 1859 and Dwight inmate #1 in 1930). Second, prisoners' names were also disguised, but their real initials have been used. Thus, Mattie Watkins (Joliet prisoner #7454c) became Mildred Williams (prisoner #74—c). In a few instances, however, a prisoner's real name has been used. In these cases the woman's name had already become part of the public record as a result of extensive media publicity surrounding her case (for example, the six women who received the death penalty in Illinois in the 1920s and 1930s).

INTERVIEWEES

Professional Staff

1980–2001	Jeanie Fairman	Counselor; Director of Family Services
1971–1977	Sue Welch	Counselor
1964–1973	Linda Senter	Nurse
1964–1977	Lois (Green) Guyon	Sociologist
1957–1963	Nathan Kantrowitz	Sociologist (Stateville)
1952–1978	Eileen Fitzpatrick	Office worker; disciplinarian; counselor
1952–1972	Edward Reis	Part-time teacher; softball coach
1951–1972	Harriet Steiger	Teacher
1945–1970	Stowe SymonS	upervising sociologist
1930–1937	Dorothy Burkhardt	Music teacher

Office, Secretarial, and Clerical Staff

1957–1985	Ann Wagner	Office worker; disciplinarian
1953–1978	anonymous	Ruth Biedermann's secretary
1951–1981	anonymous	Bernard Robinson's secretary; office worker
1951–1954	Gwen Edwards	Clerk
1951–1953	Charlene Berry	Clerk
1949–1952	anonymous	Doris Whitney's secretary
1949–1950	anonymous	Storekeeper
1948–1949	Rose Ann McPherson	Storekeeper
1935–1946	Marian Conrath	Helen Hazard's secretary

Warders and Correctional Officers

1981–1995	Gwen Edwards
1978–1989	Pam Neal
1976–1978	Susan Lithgow
1966–1991	Betty Swearingen
1966–1984	Imogene Becker

1966	Thena Thom
1964	Mary Jean Scoles
1963–1986	Anna Cook
1962–1992	Esther Dodge
1962–1987	Vicky Washton*
1962–1986	Helen Lithgow
1962	Mildred Viles
1961–1972	Sarah Ruddell
1959–1963	Robert Skonetski (guard sergeant)
1958–1971	Harriet Hoffman (greenhouse/commissary)
1957–1992	Georgia Perisee
1943–1983	Martha Howard*

Prisoners

1980–1993	Lydia Townsend*
1968–1971	Emma Sales*
1962–1966	Delores Gilbert* (also 1975, 1995–1996)
1963–1966	Jamella Reynolds*
1958–1963	Marcia Miller*
1955–1963	Carol Rawlings*
1936–1937	Paula Putnam*

*pseudonyms; anonymous individuals quoted by position only

Not all interviewees were quoted. Altogether forty-four staff were interviewed: nineteen warders and correctional officers, eight secretaries and clerks, three sociologists, three teachers, three counselors, two nurses, two male guards, two maintenance workers, and two store supervisors.

Current staff helped me locate former employees, who generously referred me to others. Former prisoners were located by word-of-mouth and connections with prison reform organizations. Prison records were not used to locate ex-inmates. Three-fourths of interviews were conducted in person, one-fourth by phone. Fourteen people were interviewed more than once. Most interviews were conducted during the 1995–1996 academic year.

NOTES

Pseudonyms have been used for all women committed to prison after 1925. See appendix A for details on archival sources.

ABBREVIATIONS

DIJ   Dwight inmate jackets (Illinois State Archives, Record Group 403: Parole and Pardon Board [restricted access])

DPS   Illinois Department of Public Safety annual reports (Springfield: State of Illinois, 1942–1970)

DPW   Illinois Department of Public Welfare annual reports (Illinois Department of Public Welfare, *Administrative Report of the Directors of Departments* [Springfield, Ill.: State of Illinois], 1917–1954)

ECF   Executive clemency files (Illinois State Archives, Record Group 103.096: Secretary of State, Executive Section)

ISP   Illinois State Penitentiary (Joliet) biennial reports (*Report of the Commissioners of the Illinois State Penitentiary at Joliet* [Springfield, Ill.: State Journal Company], in separate volumes 1861–1914; included in DPW beginning in 1917)

ISRW   Illinois State Reformatory for Women (at Dwight) annual reports (in DPW, 1930–1952; and DPS, 1954–1970)

IWP   Illinois [Joliet] Women's Prison annual reports (in DPW, 1919–1932)

JCR   Joliet convict registers (Illinois State Archives, Record Group 243.200)

LWV   League of Women Voters materials on the Illinois State Reformatory Women's Campaign (Chicago Historical Society, Manuscript Division)

MHO   Mental health officer

MR   Microfilm reel (of Dwight inmate jackets [Illinois State Archives])

PBH   Transcripts of parole board hearings (in DIJ)

RGA   *Reports Made to the [Illinois] General Assembly* (slightly different titles and different publishers over the years, 1839–1890; all are bound together at most state libraries)

WDR   Warder's Daily Report (from microfilmed inmate jackets [Illinois State Archives])

INTRODUCTION

1. See appendix A for a complete description of sources and appendix B for a list of all interviewees. Employees' real names are used unless they requested anonymity. Pseudonyms are always used when quoting from interviews with former prisoners.

2. Bureau of Justice Statistics, *Bulletin: State and Federal Prisoners, 1925–1985* (Washington, D.C.: Government Printing Office, 1986), 2. Bureau of Justice Statistics, *Bulletin: Prison and Jail Inmates at Midyear 2000* (Washington, D.C.: Government Printing Office, 2001), 1.

CHAPTER 1

1. Sally Jefferson (Alton #23), typed transcript of the First Alton Convict Register (1833–1842), Joseph E. Ragen Collection, Illinois State Historical Library. No newspaper reports could be found covering Jefferson's arrest or trial; nor was her pardon request preserved. For a full description of archival sources see appendix A.

2. Lucia Zedner, "Wayward Sisters: The Prison for Women," in *The Oxford History of the Prison: The Practice of Punishment in Western Society,* ed. Norval Morris and David J. Rothman (New York: Oxford University Press, 1995), 331.

3. N. E. Hull, *Female Felons: Women and Serious Crime in Colonial Massachusetts* (Urbana: University of Illinois Press, 1987), 125. Mary Beth Norton, "Gender, Crime, and Community in Seventeenth-Century Maryland," in *The Transformation of Early American History: Society, Authority, and Ideology,* ed. James A. Henretta, Michael Kammen, and Stanley N. Katz (New York: Alfred A. Knopf, 1991), 123–50.

4. Samuel Walker, *Popular Justice: A History of American Criminal Justice* (New York: Oxford University Press, 1998), 180–81.

5. Incarcerative institutions such as jails, workhouses, and bridewells had existed in Europe since the tenth century. However, these differed radically from the nineteenth-century penitentiary ideal. Jails were designed for the short-term detention of individuals awaiting trial, punishment, or execution. Located in the center of urban areas, jails held prisoners in large, congregate rooms and sleeping areas. Men, women, and children were intermixed; serious offenders shared space with a motley assortment of debtors, vagrants, drunkards, and disorderly and mentally ill persons. Jailhouse keepers made no effort to segment or control space, time, or movement. See David J. Rothman, *The Discovery of the Asylum: Social Order and Disorder in the New Republic,* 2nd ed. (Boston: Little, Brown and Co., 1990), and "Perfecting the Prison: United States, 1780–1865," in *The Oxford History of the Prison: The Practice of Punishment in Western Society,* ed. Norval Morris and David J. Rothman (New York: Oxford University Press, 1995), 111–30.

6. U.S. Superintendent of the Census, *Statistical View of the United States* (Washington, D.C.: A. O. P. Nicholson, 1854), table CLXXXI, p. 167, and table CLXXIX, p. 166. Percentages are my calculation from raw data on the number of women in state penitentiaries; prisoner populations in city and county jails were omitted. Significant international differences existed. During the first half of the nineteenth century women made up 20 to 25 percent of the prison population in England and Wales, 33 percent in Scotland, and from 14 to 20 percent in France. By the 1850s England had two national penitentiaries for women that housed approximately six hundred prisoners each. Ireland opened a similar six-hundred-cell female-convict prison in the 1850s. Statistics from Zedner, "Wayward Sisters," 331.

However, by the late nineteenth century the number of women in European prisons declined sharply. In one of the few comparative studies, "The Vanishing Female: The Decline of Women in the Criminal Process, 1672–1912," *Law and Society Review* 25 (1991), 719–57, Malcolm M. Feeley and Deborah L. Little argue that the great disciplinary achievement of the nineteenth century was not the invention of the penitentiary, but a shift in and intensification of "private patriarchal control of women within the household." In a follow-up article Feeley found a similar pattern of the "vanishing female" in a half dozen other European cities and jurisdictions ("The Decline of Women in the Criminal Process: A Comparative History," *Criminal Justice History: An International Annual* 15, 235–74). Lucia Zedner also documents a dramatic decline in the number of women prisoners in England between 1857 and 1913. She attributes this to the "medicalization" of female deviancy: criminal women were seen not so much as "bad," but as "mad." See Zedner, *Women, Crime, and Custody in Victorian England* (Oxford: Oxford University Press, 1991).

7. W. David Lewis *From Newgate to Dannemora: The Rise of the Penitentiary in New York, 1796–1848* (Ithaca, N.Y.: Cornell University Press, 1965), 162 and 217. Chaplain B. C. Smith, quoted in W. David Lewis, *From Newgate to Dannemora*, 164 (emphasis in original).

8. Nicole Hahn Rafter, *Partial Justice: Women, Prisons, and Social Control*, 2nd ed. (New Brunswick, N.J.: Transaction Publishers, 1990). New York's Mount Pleasant Female Prison, which operated from 1839 to 1877 at Sing Sing, was the first separate women's unit. However, it can not be classified as an independent institution. See Rafter, *Partial Justice*, 16–20, and W. David Lewis, *From Newgate to Dannemora*, 166–77.

9. Barbara Welter, "The Cult of True Womanhood: 1820–1860," *American Quarterly* 18 (1966), 151–74. Historians have debated whether the doctrine of separate spheres represented an advance or loss for women. See Nancy F. Cott, *The Bonds of Womanhood: "Woman's Sphere" in New England, 1778–1835* (New Haven: Yale University Press, 1977), and Gerda Lerner, "The Lady and the Mill Girl: Changes in the Status of Women in the Age of Jackson," *Mid-Continental American Studies Journal* 10 (1969), 5–15.

10. William Acton, quoted in Nancy Wolloch, *Women and the American Experience* (Boston: McGraw Hill, 2000), 127. Nancy F. Cott argues that this redefinition of women's nature as more moral than that of men strongly appealed to women, offering as it did "a distinctly improved view of women's character and social purpose" (Cott, "Passionlessness: An Interpretation of Victorian Sexual Ideology, 1790–1850," in Nancy F. Cott and Elizabeth H. Pleck, *A Heritage of Her Own: Toward a New Social History of American Women* [New York: Simon and Schuster, 1979], 168). See also Daniel Scott Smith, "Family Limitation, Sexual Control, and Domestic Feminism in Victorian America," in *Clio's Consciousness Raised*, ed. Mary Hartman and Lois Banner (New York: Octagon, 1974), 119–36; Estelle Freedman, "Sexuality in Nineteenth-Century America: Behavior, Ideology, and Politics," *Reviews in American History* 10 (1982), 196–215; Carroll Smith-Rosenberg, "Beauty, the Beast, and the Militant Woman: A Case Study of Sex Roles and Social Stress in Jacksonian America," *American Quarterly* 23 (1971), 562–84, and Smith Rosenberg, *Disorderly Conduct: Visions of Gender in Victorian America* (New York: Oxford University Press, 1985).

11. Welter, "Cult of True Womanhood," 151. Unnamed novelist quoted in John D'Emilio and Estelle B. Freedman, *Intimate Matters: A History of Sexuality in America* (New York: Harper and Row, 1988), 69.

12. Lucia Zedner, "Women, Crime, and Penal Responses: A Historical Account," in *Crime and Justice: A Review of Research*, vol. 14, ed. Michael Tonry (Chicago: University of Chicago Press, 1991), 320.

13. W. David Lewis, *From Newgate to Dannemora*, 159, and Russell P. Dobash, R. Emerson Dobash, and Sue Gutteridge, *The Imprisonment of Women* (London: Basil Blackwell, 1986), 45.

14. Zedner, "Women, Crime, and Penal Responses," 320.

15. Elizabeth Fry and unnamed reformer, quoted in Dobash, Dobash, and Gutteridge, *Imprisonment of Women*, 43–44.

16. Cesare Lombroso and William Ferrero, *The Female Offender* (1895; reprint, New York: D. Appleton and Co., 1900), 187. For a critique of Lombroso see Mary S. Gibson, "The 'Female Offender' and the Italian School of Criminal Anthropology," *Journal of European Studies* 12 (1982), 155–65, and Nicole Hahn Rafter, "Criminal Anthropology in the United States," *Criminology* 30 (1992), 525–45. Gibson argues that Lombroso's views were particularly influential because few other theorists addressed the topic (165). By 1911 *The Female Offender* had already gone through six reprints.

17. According to the 1850 census, women were 2.5 percent of the daily prison population but 16.1 percent of the population in local jails and houses of correction.

See U.S. Superintendent of the Census, *Statistical View,* 167–168. In 1880 and 1890 female prisoners represented the following percentages (respectively): prison, 4.6 percent and 4 percent; county jail, 11.8 percent and 14.1 percent; city jail, 15.4 percent and 18.0 percent; and workhouse, 24.2 percent and 19.9 percent. Percentages are my calculations based on raw numbers from Frederick Howard Wines, *Report on the Defective, Dependent, and Delinquent Classes . . . As Returned at the Tenth Census: 1880* (Washington, D.C.: Government Printing Office, 1888), 484–90, and *Report on Crime, Pauperism, and Benevolence . . . at the Eleventh Census: 1890* (Washington, D.C.: Government Printing Office, 1895), Part II, General Tables: tables 4, 13, 14, 19, 20, 29 and 30.

18. Marcus Kavanaugh, *The Criminal and His Allies* (Indianapolis: Bobbs-Merrill, 1928), 149. All quotes from chapter 12, "The Bad Woman." Kavanaugh tied for fifth place out of 228 Illinois judges in the number of women he committed to prison.

19. Ibid., 149–50.

20. Otto Pollak, *The Criminality of Women* (New York: A. S. Barnes & Co., 1950), 3–4. For incisive critiques of traditional criminology's perception of women see Dorie Klein, "The Etiology of Female Crime: A Review of the Literature," in *The Female Offender,* ed. Laura Crites (Lexington: D. C. Heath, 1976), 5–32; Eileen B. Leonard, *Women, Crime, and Society: A Critique of Criminology Theory* (New York: Longman, 1982); Ngaire Naffine, *Female Crime* (Sydney, Australia: Allen & Unwin, 1987); Joycelyn M. Pollock, *Criminal Women* (Cincinnati: Anderson, 1999); Carol Smart, *Women, Crime, and Criminology: A Feminist Critique* (London: Routledge & Kegan Paul, 1976); and Richard A. Wright, "From Vamps to Tramps to Teases and Flirts: Stereotypes of Women in Criminology Textbooks, 1956 to 1965 and 1981 to 1990," *Journal of Criminal Justice Education* 3 (1992), 223–36.

21. Elizabeth Chace, letter to E. Wines, quoted in Estelle B. Freedman, *Their Sisters' Keepers: Prison Reform in America, 1830–1930* (Ann Arbor, Mich.: University of Michigan Press, 1981), 53.

22. Rafter, *Partial Justice,* 49.

23. Indiana prison officials quoted in Rafter, *Partial Justice,* 30. On the Indiana Reformatory Institution for Women and Girls see Rafter, *Partial Justice,* 29–33, and Freedman, *Their Sisters' Keepers,* 51–52. On the Massachusetts Reformatory Prison for Women see Rafter, *Partial Justice,* 34–44, and Freedman, *Their Sisters' Keepers,* 67–106.

24. Western House of Refuge for Women, *1894 Annual Report,* 7, quoted in Rafter, *Partial Justice,* 35. On the first reform school for girls see Barbara Brenzel, *Daughters of the State: A Social Portrait of the First Reform School for Girls in North America, 1865–1905* (Cambridge, Mass.: MIT Press, 1983). On young women's reformatories see Ruth M. Alexander, *The "Girl Problem": Female Sexual Delinquency in New York, 1900–1930* (New York: Cornell University Press, 1995), and Mary E. Odem, *Delinquent Daughters: Protecting and Policing Adolescent Female Sexuality in the United States, 1885–1920* (Chapel Hill: University of North Carolina Press, 1995).

25. For exact dates of the establishment and opening of women's reformatories see Rafter, *Partial Justice,* table 3.1. I have used the dates of the institutions' opening, rather than the date of their legislative establishment. A reformatory sometimes existed on paper for several years before a state's legislature was finally persuaded to appropriate the funds for its construction and operation. This was the case in Illinois. For a massive overview see Eugenia C. Lekkerkerker's six-hundred-page *Reformatories for Women in the United States* (Gronigen, Netherlands: J. B. Wolters, 1931).

26. Kathleen Daly and Meda Chesney-Lind, "Feminism and Criminology," *Justice Quarterly* 5 (1988), 513. These statistics are my calculations from raw numbers supplied in Bureau of the Census, *Prisoners 1923* (Washington, D.C.: Government Printing Office, 1926), 52, table 24. Offenses categorized as "unclassified" or "unknown" were excluded. In 1923 women represented 3.3 percent of all prisoners committed to state prisons; of those 15.1 percent had been committed to reformatory prisons (47).

27. Joanne Belknap, *The Invisible Woman: Gender, Crime, and Justice* (Belmont, Calif.: Wadsworth, 1996), 68. During the 1970s women's activists and feminist legal

reformers campaigned to abolish state laws mandating differential sentencing for men and women, most of which disadvantaged women.

28. David A. Ward and Gene G. Kassebaum, *Women's Prisons: Sex and Social Structure* (Chicago: Aldine-Atherton, 1965), and Rose Giallombardo, *Society of Women: A Study of a Woman's Prison* (New York: Wiley & Sons, 1966).

29. Helen E. Gibson, "Women's Prisons: Laboratories for Penal Reform," in *The Female Offender*, ed. Laura Crites (Lexington, Mass.: Lexington Books), 98.

30. In 1971 the first co-correctional federal prison opened in Ft. Worth. In 1984 approximately 61 percent of adult female offenders were housed in co-correctional facilities. Claudine Schweber, "Beauty Marks and Blemishes: The Coed Prison as a Microcosm of Integrated Society, *The Prison Journal* 64 (1985), 3–15. No current national statistics are available. The 2002 directory of the American Correctional Association lists 87 all-female institutions, 31 co-gender facilities, and 806 all-male adult prisons.

31. For a classic progressive view see Blake McKelvey's *American Prisons: A History of Good Intentions* (1936; reprint, Montclair, N.J.: Patterson Smith, 1977). For historiographies of the penitentiary, crime, and punishment, none of which takes gender into account, see Alexander W. Pisciotti, "Corrections, Society, and Social Control in America: A Metahistorical Review of the Literature," *Criminal Justice History: An International Annual* 2 (1981), 109–30; Robert Weiss, "Humanitarianism, Labor Exploitation, or Social Control? A Critical Survey of Theory and Research on the Origin and Development of Prisons," *Social History* 12 (1987), 331–50; Michael Ignatieff, "State, Civil Society, and Total Institutions: A Critique of Recent Social Histories of Punishment," in *Crime and Justice: An Annual Review of the Literature*, ed. Michael Tonry and Norval Morris (Chicago: University of Chicago Press, 1981), 153–91; Michael S. Hindus, "The History of Crime: Not Robbed of Its Potential, But Still on Probation," *Criminal Review Yearbook* 1 (1980), 217–42; John A. Conley, "Criminal Justice History as a Field of Research: A Review of the Literature, 1960–1975," *Journal of Criminal Justice* 5 (1977), 13–28; and Paul Takagi, "Revising Liberal Conceptions of Penal Reform: A Bibliographic Overview," *Crime and Social Justice* 5 (1976), 60–65.

32. Michel Foucault, *Discipline and Punish: The Birth of the Prison*, trans. Alan Sheridan (New York: Pantheon, 1977). For an outstanding critique of Foucault see Adrian Howe, *Punish and Critique: Towards a Feminist Analysis of Penality* (New York: Routledge, 1994). For key reviews of the debate over the social-control paradigm see Anthony M. Platt, "Rethinking and Unthinking 'Social Control,'" in *Inequality, Crime, and Social Control*, ed. George S. Bridges and Martha A. Myers (San Francisco: Westview, 1994), 72–79; Stanley Cohen "The Critical Discourse on 'Social Control': Notes on the Concept as a Hammer," *International Journal of the Sociology of Law* 17 (1989), 347–57; Stanley Cohen and Andrew Scull, "Introduction: Social Control in History and Sociology," in *Social Control and the State*, ed. Stanley Cohen and Andrew Scull (New York: St. Martin's Press, 1983), 1–14; David J. Rothman, "Social Control: The Uses and Abuses of the Concept in the History of Incarceration," in *Social Control and the State*, ed. Stanley Cohen and Andrew Scull (New York: St. Martin's Press, 1983), 106–117; and William A. Muraskin, "The Social-Control Theory in American History: A Critique," *Journal of Social History* 9 (1976), 559–69.

33. Sherrill Cohen, *The Evolution of Women's Asylums Since 1500: From Refuges for Ex-Prostitutes to Shelters for Battered Women* (New York: Oxford University Press, 1992), 4–6.

CHAPTER 2

1. Mary Wiser (Alton #198), typed transcript of the first Alton Convict Register (1833–1842), Joseph E. Ragen Collection, Illinois State Historical Library.

2. Only five of the seventy-nine women (6%) convicted of murder or manslaughter during the nineteenth century are known to have used poison. Elizabeth Reed's public hanging in 1845 drew several thousand spectators. John W. Allen, *It Happened in Southern Illinois* (Johnston, Ill.: A. E. R. P., 1968), 275–76; "Mrs. Elizabeth Reed Hung," *Sangamon Journal* (Springfield, Ill.), June 12, 1845; and "Execution

of Mrs. Reed," *Western Sun and General Advertiser* (Vincennes, Ind.), May 31, 1845. See also George Robb, "Circle in Crinoline: Domestic Poisonings in Victorian England," *Journal of Family History* 22 (1997), 176–90.

3. Although Buckmaster acted as both lessee and warden from 1839 to 1861, during some years he appointed others to serve as warden. See William R. Greene, "Early Development of the Illinois State Penitentiary System," *Journal of the Illinois State Historical Society* 70 (1977), 185–95.

4. Dorothea L. Dix, "Memorial in Relation to the Illinois Penitentiary," February 5, 1847, *RGA* 1947, 111, reprinted in David L. Lightner, *Asylum, Prison, and Poorhouse: The Writings and Reform Work of Dorothea Dix in Illinois* (Carbondale: Southern Illinois University Press, 1999). Dix spent eight months in Illinois. Her first visit to Alton, in May 1846, clearly aroused concern in the state legislature, which quickly dispatched a special joint select committee to render its own investigation. While this committee noted many of the same problems, its tone was laudatory rather than condemnatory. The committee concluded that overall the convicts were well-fed, well-clothed, and well-treated, and it expressed only the highest confidence in and praise for Warden Buckmaster (*RGA* 1846, 119). Physician's testimony from "Report of the Select Committee on the Penitentiary," *RGA* 1839, 11.

5. Wiley B. Sanders, "The History and Administration of the State Prisons of Illinois" (Ph.D. diss., University of Chicago, 1929), 220.

6. Anne M. Butler, *Gendered Justice in the American West: Women Prisoners in Men's Penitentiaries* (Chicago: University of Illinois Press, 1997), 72.

7. Committee on the Penitentiary, January 12, 1843, *RGA* 1843, 324; Dix, "Memorial," 106.

8. Dorothea L. Dix, *Prisons and Prison Discipline in the United States*, 2nd ed. (Philadelphia: Joseph Kite & Co., 1845), 107–8. Committee on the Penitentiary, February 21, 1843, *RGA* 1843, 1, 182.

9. Inspector's Report, December 6, 1844, *RGA* 1845, 5; Minority of the Penitentiary Committee, February 14, 1845, *RGA* 1844, 239–40; Inspector's Report, December 5, 1846, *RGA* 1846, 78; and Dix, "Memorial," 106.

10. Letter from prosecuting attorney to governor regarding Mary Perry (Alton #718a), May 15, 1848, ECF.

11. Commissioner's Report, *RGA* 1878, 8C. Throughout the nineteenth century the profiles of male and female convicts differed in significant ways. Although the overwhelming majority of both men and women had been committed for property crimes (89% of women and 76% of men), male convicts were far more representative of the state's general population. In the 1850s fewer than half (45%) of male convicts were foreign born, compared to 74 percent of female convicts, and only 16 percent were Irish, compared to 55 percent of the women. Male convicts were more skilled in terms of occupation, more likely to have been born in Illinois, and more likely to report being married than female convicts. Two competing explanations could account for these differences. Given that law-breaking was so contrary to the dominant norms of respectable femininity, only the most desperate and impoverished women might have engaged in criminal activity. On the other hand, judges and juries might have been willing to sentence only the most socially marginal and defenseless of criminal women to the penitentiary, whereas they were willing to sentence men from a broader range of social strata. Evidence presented in chapters five through seven favors the second explanation.

12. Inspector's Report, January 16, 1851, *RGA* 1851, 62–63. In 1857 a new chaplain was the first and only official to indicate interest in the moral reformation of the female convicts: he reported that he conducted two services every Sunday, one for the women and one for the men (Chaplain's Report, *RGA* 1857, 452).

13. Minority of the Penitentiary Committee, February 14, 1845, *RGA* 1845, 239–40.

14. Undated letter quoted in Nancy J. Harm, "Women Incarcerated in Illinois

State Prisons, 1843–1915: An Exploratory Study in Social Policy" (Ph.D. diss., University of Illinois at Chicago, 1989), 102.

15. Joy Damousi, *Depraved and Disorderly: Female Convicts, Sexuality, and Gender in Colonial Australia* (Cambridge: Cambridge University Press, 1997), 22 and 48. For other analyses of nineteenth-century women's strategies of resistance to penal authority see Butler, *Gendered Justice*, and Mary Ellen Curtin, "The 'Human World' of Black Women in Alabama Prisons, 1870–1900," in *Hidden Histories of Women in the New South*, ed. Virginia Bernhard (Columbia: University of Missouri Press, 1994), 11–30.

16. Frederick W. Robinson, *Female Life in Prison, by a Prison Matron* (London: Hurst and Blackett, 1862), 68. For the reactions of one British prison reformer to these views, see chapter 4, "Female Convicts," in Mary Carpenter, *Our Convicts*, vol. 2 (1864; reprint, Montclair, N.J.: Patterson Smith, 1969), 105–176.

17. Ibid.

18. 1827 law quoted in Sanders, *History and Administration*, 38. Before 1827 women in Illinois could legally be subjected to corporal punishment. However, in practice they were rarely whipped. In his doctoral study of 1820s court records Michael Lee Siegfried found only one example of a woman subjected to corporal punishment. Designated simply as "Phebe, a Woman of Color," she was sentenced in 1828 to twenty lashes for the vague offense of "Misbehaviorin" (*sic*). This was the only recorded case of punishment for such an ill-described crime (Michael Lee Siegfried, "Crime and the Institutionalization of the Penitentiary in Illinois, 1818–1841: A Study in Penal Change" [Ph.D. diss., Southern Illinois University at Carbondale, 1992], 32).

19. Sidney W. Wetmore, *Behind the Bars at Joliet: A Peep at a Prison, Its History, and Its Mysteries* (Joliet, Ill.: J. O. Gorman and Co., 1892), 119.

20. Inspector's Report, *RGA* 1855, 125. This concern over pregnant women was repeated verbatim in the 1857 Inspector's Report (*RGA* 1857, 442). Warden's Report, *RGA* 1855, 297.

21. Joint Committee on the Penitentiary, *RGA* 1855, 294. Warden's Report, November 1858, *RGA* 1858, 319.

22. Letter from warden to governor regarding Anna Roach (Joliet #1620a), May 1, 1862 (emphasis in original); judge's letter, June 17, 1862, ECF.

23. The physician's reports occasionally listed "childbirth" among services rendered. According to Sidney W. Wetmore, prison officials allowed a woman to keep a child born in the penitentiary with her until the child reached four years of age. Wetmore's photograph of "Little Dorrit," shown on the book jacket, testifies to such a penitentiary birth (Joliet Prison Collection, Prints and Photographs Division, Chicago Historical Society).

24. Estelle B. Freedman, *Their Sisters' Keepers: Prison Reform in America, 1830–1930* (Ann Arbor: University of Michigan Press, 1981), 16.

25. Bronwyn Dalley, "Following the Rules? Women's Responses to Incarceration, New Zealand, 1880–1920," *Journal of Social History* 27 (1993), 312.

26. Warden Samuel S. Buckmaster, letter regarding Gertrude Wolfe (Alton #3080), October 8, 1859, ECF.

27. Warden's letter regarding Caroline Meyer (Joliet #1509a), June 10, 1862, ECF.

28. Warden Robert W. McClaughry, letter regarding Rose Slocum (Joliet #2524b), February 28, 1882; letter from a friend regarding Ellen McCarthy (Alton #2467a), April 3, 1857, ECF.

29. Joint Committee on the Penitentiary, January 1, 1855, *RGA* 1855, 293; and Joint Select Committee, January 5, 1857, *RGA* 1857, 244.

30. Architect's Report, January 1, 1859, *RGA* 1859, 189–91. See also Reverend S. G. Lathrop, *Crime and Its Punishment and Life in the Penitentiary* (Springfield, Ill.: n.p., 1866).

31. Catherine Sweeney (Alton #2468; Joliet #203); Warden's Report, May 31, 1858, and August 31, 1858, *RGA* 1858, 299 and 305. Although abandoned by the state in 1860, Alton served as one of the largest federal military prisons during the Civil War, housing Confederate prisoners. Overcrowding and inadequate sanitary facilities

resulted in one of the worst smallpox epidemics in southern Illinois history. Between 1862, when it reopened, and its final closing in May 1865, it has been estimated that 1,500 to 2,300 prisoners died. The prison was finally torn down in the late 1860s.

CHAPTER 3

1. Mary Brennan (Joliet #2321a), letter to the governor, July 25, 1864, ECF.

2. Ibid.

3. Ibid.

4. Mary Brennan, letter to the governor, October 20, 1864, ECF.

5. Architect's Report, January 1, 1859, *RGA* 1859, 189–91. The original female cell house at Joliet was officially referred to as the Female Prison, even though it was only a single building located within the male prison compound.

6. See Edith Abbott, "The Civil War and the Crime Wave of 1865–1870," *Social Service Review* 1 (1927), 212–34, and Estelle B. Freedman, *Their Sisters' Keepers: Prison Reform in America, 1830–1930* (Ann Arbor: University of Michigan Press, 1981), 13.

7. Commissioner's Report, December 1862, *RGA* 1861–1862, 220.

8. Letter from warden to governor regarding Mary Murphy (Alton #2518a), July 3, 1858, ECF.

9. A list of all Joliet wardens, commissioners, and inspectors can be found in the 1927–1928 *Illinois Blue Book* (Springfield, Ill.: State Journal Printing Company, 1928), 421. Illinois General Assembly, *Report of the Joint Committee of Investigation into the Affairs of the Illinois State Penitentiary* (Springfield, Ill.: Illinois Journal Printing Office, 1872).

10. "Guard's Duty," *RGA* 1861, 80. 1867 *Laws of the State of Illinois* (Springfield, Ill.: n.p.), 24. Matron Paris was succeeded by Sadie Brown (1867–1871), Katie Grace (1871–1873), Mrs. Judson (1873–1878), Mrs. Benjamin L. Mayhew (c. 1880), Mrs. S. H. Ayers (c. 1882), and Maria S. Madden (1888–1913). No complete listing of matrons exists.

11. Report of the Penitentiary Commissioners, *RGA* 1869, 71, and Chaplain's Report, *RGA* 1869, 187.

12. Physician's Report, *RGA* 1869, 189–90 (emphasis in original).

13. Letter from the warden to the governor regarding Mary Kelly, March 13, 1868 (Joliet #2978a), ECF.

14. Chaplain's Report, *RGA* 1870, 70. In 1884 an anonymous speaker observed that most convicted women were sentenced to local jails, which also lacked adequate facilities. As a consequence, "judges frequently suspend sentence, in case of female convicts, and turn them loose upon the world." In the speaker's opinion, "The tendency of this policy is to defeat every end of justice." The speaker concluded with a plea for the "erection of a separate prison for women by the state of Illinois." This plea, the only reference to female prisoners in all of the reports of the Illinois State Board of Charities, went unheeded ("Female Law-Breakers," *1884 Biennial Report* [Springfield: Illinois Board of Charities], 162).

15. Unattributed Executive Clemency file quoted in Nancy J. Harm, "Women Incarcerated in Illinois State Prisons, 1843–1915: An Exploratory Study in Social Policy" (Ph.D. diss., University of Illinois at Chicago, 1989), 100. The percentage of African Americans in the male prison population also increased immediately after the Civil War, but not as dramatically. Black men, 2 percent of the prison population in the 1850s, constituted 8 percent for the 1860s as a whole (in comparison to 18% for black women). Although in name a free state, Illinois had never welcomed African Americans. In 1812 the territory had adopted an "Act to Prevent the Migration of Free Negroes and Mulattoes," which mandated that African Americans register and show a certificate of freedom. Nor was an African American allowed to vote, serve on a jury, testify against a white person in court, serve in the militia, or marry a white person.

16. Laura T. Fishman, "Slave Women, Resistance, and Criminality: A Prelude to Future Accommodation," *Women and Criminal Justice* 7 (1995), 35–65; Elizabeth Fox-Genovese, "Strategies and Forms of Resistance: Focus on Slave Women"; Darlene Clark Hine, "Female Slave Resistance"; and Mary Ellen Obitko "'Custodians of a House of Resistance':

Black Women Respond to Slavery," all in *Black Women in American History: From Colonial Times through the Nineteenth Century,* ed. Darlene Clark Hine (New York: Carson, 1990).

17. Chaplain's Report, *RGA* 1870, 7. See also Report of the Commissioners, *RGA* 1874, 12–13; "Death of Convict Williams," *Signal* (Joliet), December 23, 1873; "Prison Discipline: The Cold-Bath Case," *Chicago Daily Tribune,* December 28, 1873; and "The Penitentiary Bath," *Chicago Daily Tribune,* December 31, 1873. Both the Chicago and Joliet papers characterized the death as a "murder" and the result of "atrocious cruelty," but the possibility of partisan motives on the part of the papers' publishers cannot be entirely dismissed. Nineteenth-century prison "reform" included lurid descriptions of investigations of egregious abuses. Investigators were often motivated as much by a desire to discredit a particular administration as by genuine concern for prisoners' treatment.

18. Brockway's speech is reported in Blake McKelvey's *American Prisons: A History of Good Intentions* (1936; reprint, Montclair, N.J.: Patterson Smith, 1977), 90–92. For a critical assessment of the first male reformatory prison, which Brockway established, see Alexander W. Pisciotti, *Benevolent Repression: Social Control and the American Reformatory-Prison Movement* (New York: New York University Press, 1994).

19. Margaret Dorsey Phelps, "Idled Outside, Overworked Inside: The Political Economy of Prison Labor during Depressions in Chicago, 1871–1897" (Ph.D. diss., University of Iowa, 1992), 262. For more on McClaughry's career see Henry L. Kamerling, "'Too Much Time for the Crime I Done': Race, Ethnicity, and the Politics of Punishment in Illinois and South Carolina, 1865–1900," (Ph.D. diss., University of Illinois at Urbana-Champaign, 1998). However, even under McClaughry, accusations of physical brutality persisted. In 1878 legislative investigators interviewed prisoners and prison personnel. They left a handwritten transcript titled "Joliet Penitentiary: Testimony on Inhuman Treatment of Prisoners." The results of this investigation were never published, and an official report was never made. McClaughry, who was not directly implicated in the unofficial report, may have succeeded in suppressing its publication (Special Collections Department, Regenstein Library, University of Chicago).

20. Warden's letters to the governor regarding Alice Mayor (Joliet #699b), April 18, 1877 and May 15, 1877, ECF.

21. Warden's Report, *RGA* 1874, 563, and Commissioner's Report, *RGA* 1876, 14.

22. Commissioner's Report, *RGA* 1876, 14, and Commissioner's Report, *RGA* 1878, 7–8C.

23. Illinois Department of Public Charities, *1882 Biennial Report of the Illinois Board of Charities* (Springfield: Illinois Department of Public Charities), 1888.

24. Sidney W. Wetmore, *Behind the Bars at Joliet: A Peep at a Prison, Its History, and Its Mysteries* (Joliet, Ill.: J. O. Gorman and Co., 1892).

25. Ibid., 46.

26. Ibid., 42.

27. Ibid., 43–45. See also pages 44–45 of Wetmore's unpublished typewritten notes in the Wetmore Collection at the Manuscript Division of the Chicago Historical Society.

28. Wetmore, *Behind the Bars at Joliet,* 45.

29. Ibid., 43–44.

30. Wetmore, *Behind the Bars: Life and Times in Joliet Prison* (Chicago: Ottaway Printing Co., 1883), 10.

31. Wetmore, *Behind the Bars at Joliet,* 45–46.

32. Chester Penitentiary, *RGA* 1878, 17D and 38D.

33. Report of the Commissioners (of the Chester penitentiary), *RGA* 1882, 17–18H.

34. 1884 *Report of the Commissioners of the Southern Illinois Penitentiary* (Chester), 6. Male convicts at Chester were governed by an eleven-page list of regulations that was so detailed as to prohibit "spitting upon the floor in the Cell House" by both convicts and officers. Yet none of these rules made even a passing reference to Chester's female convicts. See *Rules for the Government of Officers and Employees of the Southern Illinois Penitentiary* (St. Louis: Globe-Democrat Job Printing Co., 1879), 10.

35. Enoch C. Wines, *The State of Prisons and of Child-Saving Institutions in the*

Civilized World, (Cambridge: University Press, John Wilson and Son, 1880), 172.

36. 1887 *Laws of the State of Illinois*, 320, and 1889 *Laws of the State of Illinois*, 218.

37. "New Prison Now Ready: Women Convicts at Joliet Will Move into Fresh Quarters," *Chicago Tribune*, November 15, 1896.

38. Warden's Report, ISP 1894, 16–17.

39. Warden Allen's Report, ISP 1896, 14. Quote regarding "cat calls" from unpublished manuscript by Joseph E. Ragen on the history of the Joliet penitentiary, *The Devil Stoned: The History of an Institution*, circa 1960, Box 4, TS, p. 175, Joseph E. Ragen Collection, Illinois State Historical Library, Springfield; Maggie Tiller (Joliet #4266c), letter to Mrs. Wiens, June 11, 1899.

40. 1895 *Laws of the State of Illinois*, G. A., 1st Sess., June 24, 1895, p. 54; Nicole Hahn Rafter, *Partial Justice: Women, Prisons, and Social Control*, 2nd ed. (New Brunswick, N.J.: Transaction Publishers, 1990), 239 (n. 1). Similarly, in the Declaration of Principles adopted at the 1870 National Prison Congress, which concluded with a call for independent women's prisons staffed entirely by women, the only rationales emphasized the managerial and health problems of housing male and female prisoners within the same institution (McKelvey, *American Prisons*, 90).

41. Anne M. Butler, *Gendered Justice in the American West: Women Prisoners in Men's Penitentiaries* (Chicago: University of Illinois Press, 1997), 34.

CHAPTER 4

1. Mary Kelly (Joliet #2978a), letters to the governor, March 8, 1868 and June 26, 1868; letter from Commissioner Reid, July 7, 1868, ECF (emphasis in original).

2. Mary Brennan (Joliet #2321a), letter to the governor, April 25, 1864; Louise Mc-Neil (Joliet #5082a), letter to Commissioner Edwards, July 4, 1875. Nancy J. Harm quantified women's pardon letters for the 1843–1915 time period. According to her categorization, the most common rationales included mitigating circumstances of the crime (32%), pregnancy (19%), illness (17%), needed at home to care for children (16%), good conduct in prison (10%), "weak-minded" or "insane" (3%), and advanced age (3%). Petitioners, who included the prisoners themselves and their supporters (such as family, friends, local townspeople, and prosecuting officials), along with the prison warden or matron, frequently offered more than one rationale. Harm failed to include a category for "moral character." As will be discussed later in this chapter, virtually all female prisoners sought to portray themselves as women of virtuous character and good reputation prior to the "unfortunate" (and presumably uncharacteristic) action that resulted in their incarceration ("Women Incarcerated in Illinois State Prisons, 1843–1915: An Exploratory Study in Social Policy" [Ph.D. diss., University of Illinois at Chicago, 1989], 99).

3. Essie Stewart (Joliet #4838c), letter to the Board of Pardons, March 19, 1900, ECF.

4. Letter from warden to the governor regarding Mary Cassidy (Joliet #4833a), November 21, 1868; matron's letter to the governor regarding Kitty Brine (Joliet #7928a), May 17, 1875, ECF (emphasis in original).

5. Governor Oglesby, letter regarding Rosetta Callahan (Chester #1215), April 13, 1888; Matron Ives, letter, April 10, 1888, ECF.

6. Governor Oglesby, letter regarding Rosetta Callahan (Chester #1215), April 13, 1888.

7. Matron Katie Grace, letter regarding Mary Weber (Joliet #3336a), November 26, 1872, ECF (emphasis in original).

8. The 1870 National Prison Congress denounced the overuse of pardons, as did Illinois reformers. See the "Report of the Joint Committee of Investigation into the Affairs of the Illinois State Penitentiary" (Springfield, Ill.: Illinois Journal Printing Office, 1872), 26–27. Prison officials also had economic reasons for opposing pardons. Once Warden McClaughry had succeeded in turning Joliet's convict labor into a profitable economic venture, prisoners became a financial asset rather than a burden. Short sentences and early releases threatened profits. See Henry L. Kamerling, "'Too Much Time for the Crime

I Done': Race, Ethnicity, and the Politics of Punishment in Illinois and South Carolina, 1865–1900" (Ph.D. diss., University of Illinois at Urbana-Champaign, 1998), 125–38.

9. Unattributed clemency file quoted in Harm, "Women Incarcerated," 102.

10. Petition regarding Mary Cassidy (Joliet #4833a), November 2, 1868; petition to the Board of Pardons regarding Louise Jackson (Joliet #3168d), April 18, 1917; state's attorney's letter regarding Almira Humphry (Joliet #1231a), March 4, 1861, ECF.

11. Letter from state's attorney regarding Jennie Rose (Joliet #3136), February 3, 1868; letter from judge, June 8, 1866; undated petition, c. 1868, ECF. Throughout this text, the word "mulatto" is employed whenever this was the description used in the original sources.

12. Letter from state's attorney regarding Mary McWilliams (Joliet #2113c), November 25, 1892; letter from judge, December 23, 1892; undated petition, c. 1892, ECF.

13. Letter from judge regarding Essie Stewart (Joliet #4838c), October 5, 1897, ECF. For more on Essie Stewart see "Fired from her Window," *Chicago Daily News*, July 3, 1895.

14. Mary King (Joliet #5721e) and Annie O'Daniels (Joliet #5766e), both convicted in 1897, were the only other African American women convicted of murder who succeeded in winning a pardon before 1930. O'Daniels's sentence represented the greater travesty of justice; the state's attorney himself eventually acknowledged that her imprisonment was a "great mistake." O'Daniels had been frightened into pleading guilty to her husband's murder, even though she had played no role in it whatsoever. An acquaintance, Henry Miller, had shot her husband during a quarrel and then buried the body. Miller had then threatened that he would kill O'Daniels if she went to the authorities. O'Daniels remained quiet for two weeks before revealing her husband's death, at which point she was arrested, jailed, and charged with the murder. "Pretended friends" advised her that she would be assured a light sentence if she pled guilty to murder, "but that if she made a defense she would receive a heavier punishment and might be hanged." "Terrified" and "influenced by ignorance, fear, and hope," she agreed. Although from a "colored family of good reputation," O'Daniels, like many other African American women, feared risking her life before an all-white jury (ECF). O'Daniels was released after serving ten years in prison.

15. Penitentiary Commissioner John Reid, letter to the governor regarding Sally Bentley (Joliet #4009a), March 3, 1869; Mrs. John Reid, letter, March 21, 1869, ECF.

16. Louise McNeil (Joliet #5082a), letter to former warden Edwards, July 4, 1975; Edwards, letter to the governor, July 13, 1875, ECF.

17. Undated petition regarding Mary Cosgriff (Joliet #3807a), c. 1868, ECF.

18. Petition for Lydia Ann Starks (Joliet #2855a), September 16, 1865, ECF. Although Starks was pardoned, her apparent accomplice, eighteen-year-old Sophia Miner, was forced to serve her full one-year sentence. Miner had no children. Both were listed as "Indian." They were the only two Native American women known to have been incarcerated in Illinois between 1835 and 1963.

19. Petition for Henrietta Reese (Joliet #3577a), October 16, 1866; state's attorney's letter regarding Ann Manning (Joliet #2894a), May 24, 1867, ECF.

20. Natalie Zemon Davis, *Fiction in the Archives: Pardon Tales and Their Tellers in Sixteenth Century France* (Stanford, Calif.: Stanford University Press, 1987), 15.

21. Lena Schreiner (Joliet #9041b), statement of petitioner, June 22, 1891, and letter from judge, July 8, 1891 (emphasis in original), ECF.

22. See "A Wretched Woman Confesses to a Barbarous Deed," *Joliet Republic and Sun* (July 8, 1888), and "Lena Schreiner's Terrible Crime," *Chicago Herald* (September 27, 1888).

23. Letter from juror regarding Mamie Starr (Joliet #3953d), January 29, 1896, EFC.

24. Letter from defense attorney regarding Mamie Starr (Joliet #3953d), c. 1895; letter from juror, January 29, 1896, ECF. For more on Starr's case see "Mamie Starr on Trial," *Chicago Daily News*, December 4, 1890; "Mamie Starr Sheds Tears," *Chicago Daily News*, December 5, 1980; "Help for Mamie Starr," *Chicago Daily News*, December 13, 1890; "Behind Bars for Life," *Chicago Tribune*, January 4, 1891; and "Mamie Starr in Joliet," *Chicago Daily News*, January 4, 1891.

25. Confession letter to governor dictated by Kate Williamson (Chester #1734,

Joliet #9632b), September 10, 1888. It appears that Williamson's lawyer transcribed her words. The letter is written on the stationery of "Law Office of William C. Mulkey" and is signed "W. C. Mulkey on behalf of Kate Williamson, Petitioner." Governor Altgeld, letter, June 17, 1893, ECF. In 1888, after Williamson had been in prison for five years, Matron Kate Mitchell failed to fully endorse Williamson's request, maintaining that she didn't "think she has been here long enough to get out." Instead of recommending a direct pardon, Mitchell suggested that the governor commute Williamson's life sentence to a fixed number of years. While the matron's suggested sentence of "twenty-five or even *fifty*" years was draconian, she reasoned that this might "provide at least a 'hope'—for what is life to any one without *one hope?*" (Acting Matron Kate Mitchell, in a letter on behalf of fifteen-year-old Elvira Wilburn [Chester #1385], June 8, 1888 [emphasis in original], ECF).

26. Letter from Governor John Altgeld concerning Kate Williamson (Chester #1734, Joliet #9632b), June 17, 1893, ECF.

27. Undated petition for Margaret McAnally (Joliet #3057a), ECF; Undated petition by "Ladies of the City of Chicago" on behalf of Mary Cosgriff [also known as Mary Trussell] (Joliet #3807a), ECF. For extensive coverage of Cosgriff's case see "The Randolph Street Homicide," *Chicago Times*, December 15, 1866, and "The Trussell Manslaughter," *Chicago Times*, December 16, 1866.

CHAPTER 5

1. Maggie Tiller (Joliet #4266c), letter to Mrs. Wiens, June 11, 1899, ECF.

2. Illinois Association for Criminal Justice, *Illinois Crime Survey* (Chicago: Blakeley Printing, 1929), table A-3, p. 35.

3. For dismissal rates on the basis of type of offense see the *Illinois Crive Survey*, table B-5, p. 63.

4. Danielle Laberge, "Women's Criminality, Criminal Women, Criminalized Women? Questions in and for a Feminist Perspective," *Journal of Humanistic Justice* 2 (1991), 50; Piers Beirne and James Messerschmidt, *Criminology* (New York: Harcourt Brace Jovanovich, 1991), 51.

5. *Chicago Tribune,* July 17, 1936. For a critique of the Cook County coroner's system see the *Illinois Crime Survey,* 272–73, 377–92, 596–98, and 632. In 1926 and 1927 police filed charges of murder or manslaughter against 401 persons who were later released upon an exonerating verdict by the coroner's jury. Sixty-three percent of these cases involved automobile-related deaths. Coroner's juries ruled the remaining 134 deaths as "justifiable" homicide (596 and 601).

6. In July 1890 the *Chicago Tribune* reported on the dissimilar fates of two women—one white, one black—on trial for similar deeds. Channie Robinson, an African American woman, was found guilty of manslaughter in her husband's shooting death, which she claimed was accidental. The judge admitted her husband was a "thoroughly worthless fellow" who "lived off her earnings," was involved in an affair with a "dissolute negress," and had attempted to extort money from her. Despite these and other mitigating circumstances, Robinson was convicted and served three years. Four days later the newspapers reported that Ada Barrett, a white woman, was acquitted in the shooting death of her husband. Her claim of self-defense was accepted despite conflicting testimony. While some witnesses portrayed Barrett as a loving and devoted wife, others testified that she "frequently abused her husband" and had often "pledged to poison or shoot him." ("Said He Was No Gentlemen," *Chicago Tribune,* July 29, 1890). Barrett's case was covered in the *Chicago Daily News* through August 3, 1890.

7. See the following articles in the *Chicago Daily News:* "Hope for Maggie Tiller" (April 27, 1895), "Talk of Maggie Tiller" (April 29, 1895), and "She Will Go to Joliet" (May 4, 1895). Before 1890 African American women prisoners were disproportionately from southern Illinois. During the 1890s the percentage of African American female convicts committed from Cook County doubled (from 31% to 61%).

8. "Talk of Maggie Tiller." After Tiller's 1895 case, no other woman received a death sentence in Cook County until 1923.

9. Maggie Tiller (Joliet 4266c), letter to Mrs. Wiens, June 11, 1899 (emphasis in original).

10. These estimates of felony convictions statewide are based on numbers provided in Chicago police reports published between 1890 and 1930; Anne Hinrichsen's study, "The Criminal Statistics of Illinois," *Institution Quarterly* 8 (1917); and the *Illinois Crime Survey*. In extrapolating statewide estimates, several assumptions were made. For 1890 the only available statistic is that 10,592 women were arrested in Chicago. The assumption that 92 percent of these arrests were for misdemeanors (a ratio based on numbers first reported for the 1910s), leads to an estimate of 847 felony arrests in Chicago. Assuming that 35 percent of these arrests resulted in convictions (a ratio based on Hinrichsen's 1915 figures), Chicago saw about 297 felony convictions. If 90 percent of the state's convictions occurred in Chicago (as suggested by Hinrichsen's study), then an estimated 330 women were convicted of felonies statewide in 1890.

11. Garry L. Rolison, "Toward an Integrated Theory of Female Criminality and Incarceration," in *Women Prisoners: A Forgotten Population*, ed. Beverly R. Fletcher, Lynda D. Shaver, and Dreama G. Moon (Westport, Conn.: Praeger, 1993), 136–37.

12. For the most-frequently cited studies of police dismissal of felony arrests, see Donald Black, *The Manners and Customs of the Police* (New York: Academic, 1980), 85–108, and "Production of Crime Rates," *American Sociological Review* 35 (1970), 733–48.

13. Chicago Commission on Race Relations, *The Negro in Chicago: A Study of Race Relations and a Race Riot* (Chicago: University of Chicago Press, 1922), 345.

14. Ibid., 352, 345, and 335. The commission failed to offer a gender analysis. It only noted the great prejudice "against colored girls who are ambitious to earn an honest living." More recent studies suggest that African Americans continue to be arrested on weaker evidence than whites. See Joan Petersilia, *Racial Disparities in the Criminal Justice System* (Santa Monica, Calif.: Rand, 1983), 21–26, and Samuel Walker, Cassia Spohn, and Miriam Deleone, *The Color of Justice: Race, Ethnicity, and Crime in America* (Belmont, Calif.: Wadsworth, 1996), 98–104. Studies of the impact of gender on police decision making offer mixed results. Some conclude that police treat female suspects more leniently than men, while others suggest that women are treated more harshly. See Joanne Belknap, *The Invisible Woman: Gender, Crime, and Justice* (Belmont, Calif.: Wadsworth, 1996), 78.

15. Percentages of arrests and convictions in Chicago courts are my calculations from raw numbers compiled from the annual reports of the Chicago Department of Police, *Report of the General Superintendent of Police . . . to the City Council* (Chicago: Department of Police), 1913–1925.

16. Ibid.

17. Mark H. Haller, "Historical Roots of Police Behavior: Chicago, 1890–1925," in *Police, Prison, and Punishment: Major Historical Interpretations*, ed. Kermit L. Hall (New York: Garland, 1987), 339.

18. Ibid., 335, 323; *Illinois Crime Survey*, 393–419.

19. Hinrichsen, "Criminal Statistics," 116. In 1909 the Illinois General Assembly authorized the State Charities Commission to establish a Bureau of Criminal Statistics that would collect and publish annually a complete report on crime in the state. However, no appropriation was made until 1915, and the amount proved inadequate. Outside of Chicago no towns or cities published annual police reports. Hinrichsen's data were collected directly from the sheriff's logs, the police chief's "day books," jail registers, and court files. See Hinrichsen's "Pitfalls in Criminal Statistics," *Institution Quarterly* 7 (December 1916), 7–12, and "Update on Criminal Statistics," *Institution Quarterly* 8 (March 1917), 17. Hinrichsen completely disregarded race as a variable.

20. Hinrichsen, "Criminal Statistics," 117, 124. Only three counties had a commitment rate that averaged more than one woman per year: Vermilion County; St. Clair County, which includes East St. Louis; and Cook County. The number of women sentenced to prison bore little relation to a county's population. Eight counties among the

top 25 percent for female commitments ranked in the bottom 60 percent in population. Seven of these were rural counties in southern Illinois, which historically committed disproportionate numbers of African American women. From 1860 to 1930, 90 percent of the women sentenced from Pulaski County were African American, as were 80 percent from Alexander and Jackson counties and 56 percent from Williamson County.

21. Numbers are my calculations from the Chicago House of Correction, *Annual Report of the Board of Inspectors and the Superintendent* (Chicago: Chicago House of Correction), compiled from reports for the years 1911–1919. See also City of Chicago, *The House of Correction of the City of Chicago: A Retrospective, 1871–1921* (Chicago: City of Chicago, 1921). For a description and photos, see Mary Baber, Head Matron, "The Women's Department," in *The House of Correction of the City of Chicago*, World's Fair Edition (Chicago: City of Chicago, 1933), 80–86.

22. *Illinois Crime Survey.* See also Chicago Community Trust, *Reports Comprising the Survey of the Cook County Jail* (1922; reprint, New York: Arno, 1974). For an analysis of the ideological assumptions behind these national crime surveys see Samuel Walker, "Origins of the Contemporary Criminal Justice Paradigm: The American Bar Foundation Survey, 1953–1969," *Justice Quarterly* 9 (1992), 201–30.

23. Chicago Department of Police, *Report of the General Superintendent,* for the years 1926 and 1927.

24. *Illinois Crime Survey,* 268.

25. *Illinois Crime Survey,* table 165, p. 627. Percentages are my calculations from raw numbers. In contrast, grand juries exonerated 19 percent of white men and 16 percent of African American men prosecuted for murder. Murder and manslaughter were the only crimes for which data were presented by both gender and race.

26. Ibid., 94. For a critique of Cook county's criminal defense attorneys, see pp. 408–10. Aside from the analysis of homicide in Cook County, none of the *Crime Survey's* one-hundred-odd tables used race, ethnicity, or gender as a variable. Defense attorney's letter on behalf of Louise Jackson (Joliet #3168d), May 18, 1917, ECF.

Hinrichsen's 1915 study uncovered intriguing differences in conviction rates for male and female offenders. On average, women were *more* likely to be found guilty than were men. Of 1,315 women arrested for felonies, 35 percent were convicted (versus 30% of men). Likewise, of 16,038 women arrested on misdemeanor charges, 48 percent were convicted (versus 40% of men). A similar but more disparate pattern emerged from Chicago police records. Women arrested for felonies were one-third more likely to be found guilty: averaging 43 percent versus 32 percent for men.

There are several possible explanations for women's higher conviction rates. First, women may have been arrested only when the evidence against them was fairly strong. Conversely, the fact of arrest itself might have more deeply prejudiced a judge or jury against a woman than a man, and hence they may have been more likely to find a woman guilty. Finally, given that incarcerated women were more economically and socially disadvantaged than men, female defendants may have had fewer financial and social resources to marshal in their defense. As a consequence, a greater proportion may have been found guilty by virtue of their greater poverty and social marginality.

However, even when a woman was convicted of the same crime as a man, a Chicago judge was less likely to sentence her to the penitentiary. Between 1913 and 1930, 2 percent of men convicted of larceny, but only 0.3 percent of female thieves, received a prison sentence. Most men (60%) were sentenced to the Chicago House of Correction while most women (70%) received probation. This disparity may be explained by either judicial leniency or the relative seriousness of their offenses. Women's larcenies may have averaged lesser value than men's, or the women may have had less extensive prior records and thus were more deserving of probation. However, it is also possible that regardless of the value of the goods stolen, judges simply did not consider female thieves to be as threatening to the social order as male offenders.

27. *Illinois Crime Survey,* table E, p. 87.

28. *Illinois Crime Survey,* 84.

29. PBH for Dwight #489 (Joliet #2147e), October 22, 1929, DIJ. After 1930 this racial disparity was eliminated; roughly one-half of both white and black female felons pleaded not guilty.

30. Case Summary for Dwight #157, c. 1939, DIJ. Defendants who maintained their innocence had the right to choose whether to be tried by a jury or by a judge in a bench trial. Defendants convicted by juries risked harsher penalties. Recent studies document the existence of this so-called "jury tax": defendants who take their cases before juries—a costly and time-consuming process—and are found guilty receive longer prison sentences than those who are convicted of similar offenses in bench trials.

31. PBH for Dwight #2611, November 30, 1955, and letter from state's attorney regarding Dwight #1177, March 13, 1937, DIJ.

32. Laberge, "Women's Criminality," 53.

33. Beirne and Messerschmidt, 53.

34. My calculations are from the 1913–1925 Chicago police reports. Likewise, of 1,391 white men arrested for manslaughter, only 24 (1.7%) were found guilty. In comparison, 115 African American men were arrested for the same crime and 10 (8.7%) found guilty.

35. Undated petition regarding Maggie Tiller (Joliet #4266c), c. 1900, ECF.

36. Letter to Governor Tanner regarding Maggie Tiller, December 18, 1899, ECF.

37. Statement by the Board of Pardons regarding Maggie Tiller, October Term 1900, ECF.

CHAPTER 6

1. Grace Wilder (Joliet #7786c), JCR. Note: throughout this study, a convict's real name (taken from the convict registers) is used for anyone incarcerated before 1925. Because pseudonyms are used for women after that date (see appendix A for Illinois laws regarding privacy and confidentiality of state records), only their convict numbers are cited in these notes.

2. Prior to 1895 the convict registers did not record any details about prisoners' crimes. Between 1895 and 1911 clerks included one- or two-sentence descriptions, along with the exact value of any stolen goods. Women's inmate jackets preserved from 1920 to 1963 include women's legal commitment papers, which offer detailed descriptions of their crimes. See appendix A for a complete description of these sources.

3. All statistics related to female prisoners in Illinois are my own calculations based on data compiled from the inmate convict registers (see appendix A).

4. Judith A. Allen, *Sex and Secrets: Crimes Involving Australian Women since 1880* (New York: Oxford University Press, 1990), 8.

5. Ibid., 31.

6. Minnie Waller (Joliet #5915c), JCR. Prison sentences for larceny were extremely rare, and their application was arbitrary. In Chicago in the 1910s and 1920s, seven hundred to one thousand women were arrested for larceny every year. Over half were found guilty, yet each year only five or six were sentenced to Joliet. Larceny figures compiled from the annual reports of the Chicago Department of Police (*Report of the General Superintendent of Police . . . to the City Council* [Chicago, Department of Police]) from 1913 to 1930.

7. PBH for Dwight #142 (Joliet #3582e), January 22, 1931, and MHO Report, December 1, 1930, DIJ. For a study of nineteenth-century shoplifting, see Elaine Susan Ableson, *When Ladies Go A-Thieving* (New York: Oxford University Press, 1992).

8. Statement of Fact, Dwight #352, September 4, 1931, DIJ.

9. Mahalia Lewis (Joliet #9778c), Inga Nelson (Joliet #6692c), and Blanche Benboy (Joliet #9190c), JCR.

10. Rosa Kling (Joliet #8693c), Bessie Small (#839d), and Mamie Hyatt (#9470c), JCR.

11. Pearl McLaughlin (Joliet #6840C), Pauline Smiley (Joliet #6453C), Laura Williams (Joliet #6108c), Maggie Young (Joliet #6109c), Mollie Steel (Joliet #4770c), and Mary Sommers (Joliet #8061c), JCR. Last quote from case summary for Dwight #1263, c. 1938, DIJ.

12. May Allen (Joliet #9408c); Mamie Ray (Joliet #5445c), JCR. All but one of the robberies for which details were provided were committed by black women; hence, no racial comparison of the amounts stolen is possible.

13. Letter from state's attorney regarding Dwight #551, June 22, 1928; and statement of fact from state's attorney regarding Dwight #1108, c. 1937, DIJ.

14. Letter from the Illinois Banker's Association regarding Dwight #115, February 6, 1929, DIJ.

15. Mean values refer to the 1895–1911 period, the only time when the value of stolen goods was recorded in the convict registers.

16. Annie Jackson (Joliet #4540c) and Annie Smith (#6410c), JCR.

17. Flora Childs (Joliet #2282d); MHO Report on Dwight #552, (Joliet #3408e), September 30, 1930, DIJ.

18. African American women in Chicago were also more likely to be charged with felony assault than with misdemeanor assault: 42 percent of women's felony assault cases involved African American defendants, compared to 34 percent of misdemeanor assault cases. Black women were also more likely than white women to be convicted: 10 percent of black women were found guilty in felony assault cases versus 3 percent of white women; 43 percent versus 18 percent in misdemeanor cases. My calculations are from Chicago annual police reports, 1913–30. Similarly, between 1930 and 1960 African American women made up 73 percent of women sentenced to Dwight for felony assaults, although they accounted for only 16 percent of those committed for misdemeanor assault.

19. Jessie Davis (Joliet #7933c); Laura Gardner (Joliet #5019c); Lizzie Briton (Joliet #8215c), JCR.

20. Stella Dixon (Joliet #7787c), JCR.

21. 1889 *Laws of the State of Illinois* (Springfield, Ill.: n.p.), 112; 1899 *Laws of the State of Illinois*, 125.

22. Ella Wagenar (Joliet #4706c), JCR. Convicted in 1930, Wagenar was the last woman sentenced for the crime of harboring. Lina Plank (Joliet #4706c). Between 1900 and 1914 an average of 2.2 men per year were sentenced to Joliet for this offense.

23. Roger Lane, *Violent Death in the City: Suicide, Accident, and Murder in Nineteenth-Century Philadelphia* (Cambridge, Mass.: Harvard University Press, 1979), 99. See also Peter C. Hoffer and N. E. H. Hull, *Murdering Mothers: Infanticide in England and New England, 1558–1803* (New York: New York University, 1981).

24. Anna Smith (Joliet #9702c), JCR.

25. Illinois Association for Criminal Justice, *Illinois Crime Survey* (Chicago: Blakeley Printing, 1929), 636.

26. Emma Hicks (Joliet #6595c), JCR; Statement of Fact, Dwight #131, June 8, 1931, DIJ.

27. Letter from state's attorney concerning Dwight #1292, March 23, 1938, DIJ.

28. *Chicago Times*, "The Evil and the Remedy," December 13, 1888. Reporting continued through January 23, 1889. For an analysis of this exposé, see Leslie J. Reagan, *When Abortion Was a Crime: Women, Medicine, and Law in the United States, 1867–1973* (Berkeley: University of California Press, 1997), 46–61. Male doctors were also rarely sanctioned. Between 1890 and 1914 only eight men were committed to Joliet for manslaughter by abortion.

29. *Illinois Crime Survey*, 604, 117–18. See also Leslie J. Reagan, "'About to Meet Her Maker': Women, Doctors, Dying Declarations, and the State's Investigation of Abortion, Chicago, 1867–1940," *Journal of American History* 77 (1991): 1239–64.

30. Parole board case summary, c. 1937, and letter from the state's attorney, August 9, 1937, regarding Dwight #1159, DIJ.

31. Reagan, *When Abortion Was a Crime*, 114.

32. Ian Taylor, *Crime, Capitalism, and Community: Three Essays in Socialist Criminology* (Toronto, Ont.: Butterworths, 1983), 91; Anne Hinrichsen, "The Criminal Statistics of Illinois," *Institution Quarterly* 8 (1917), 94. Women's homicide patterns of the past appear similar to those of the present. Women who kill are most likely to kill inti-

mates. Of the thirty-three murder cases between 1895 and 1911 for which the convict registers supply details, men were the victims in twenty-one (64%), women in eight (24%), children in three (9%), and a married couple in one (3%). Of the twenty-six cases for which the killer's method is indicated, the victim was shot in eighteen (69%), stabbed with a knife in six (23%), and poisoned in two (8%).

33. See raw numbers for 1913–1925 in Chicago Department of Police, *Report of the General Superintendent.*

34. In many other cases of calculated, cold-blooded murder, white women managed to escape conviction. For example, on October 31, 1912, after a well-publicized trial, Louisa Lindloff was acquitted of killing her insured son with arsenic (*Chicago Daily News*). In 1919 famed attorney Clarence Darrow successfully defended Emma Simpson using the insanity defense. Simpson, a white woman, was charged with shooting her husband in cold blood, purportedly because she was jealous over a recent affair. Darrow concluded his appeal to the all-male jury: "You've been asked [by the prosecutor] to treat a man and a woman the same—but you can't. No manly man can." The jury agreed. Their verdict stated that even though they found that the defendant "committed the act charged in the indictment . . . at the time of said act she was a lunatic or insane person" ("Mrs. Simpson Found Insane," *Chicago Tribune,* September 26, 1919). The Broadway hit musical *Chicago* celebrates two such cases from the 1920s.

35. "Find Cook County Juries Kind to 'Lady Killers': Seven out of Every Nine Women Acquitted Since 1906," *Chicago Tribune,* July 28, 1935, and "Women Killers Go Free," *Chicago Tribune,* 1927. An undated copy of the 1927 article was found in an old file at Dwight Correctional Center. The original source could not be located. See also "26 Women Freed, 3 Convicted as Slayers in 12 Years," *Chicago Tribune,* September 26, 1919. Compared with the typical white female prisoner, white women convicted of murder were older (35 versus 29 years of age), significantly more likely to be foreign born (32% versus 17%), and twice as likely to separated or divorced (24% versus 11%). 1939 *Laws of the State of Illinois,* 691.

36. Interview with Jamella Reynolds, May 23, 1996. Sentence severity provides additional evidence for these qualitative differences. Whereas only 5 percent of African American women convicted of murder between 1920 and 1950 received sentences of fifty years or more, 34 percent of white women received such harsh sentences. Even when white women were convicted of manslaughter, the character of their crimes was usually much more extreme than those of black women convicted of the same offense. African American women were typically charged with manslaughter in situations for which white women would escape prosecution entirely.

37. For a discussion of victim devaluation theory see Darnell F. Hawkins, "Black and White Homicide Differentials: Alternatives to an Inadequate Theory," in *Homicide among Black Americans,* ed. Darnell F. Hawkins (Lanham, Md.: University Press of America, 1986), 109–36, and Coramae Richey Mann, "Black Female Homicide in the United States," *Journal of Interpersonal Violence* 5 (1990), 176–201.

38. Steven R. Belenko (ed.), *Drugs and Drug Policy in America: A Documentary History* (Westport, Conn.: Greenwood Press, 2000), 183–209. See also Eva Bertram et al., *Drug War Politics: The Price of Denial* (Berkeley: University of California Press, 1996), 78–87.

39. Margaret E. Hall, "Mental and Physical Efficiency of Women Drug Addicts," *Journal of Abnormal and Social Psychology* 33 (1938), 332–45.

40. Adrian Howe, *Punish and Critique: Towards a Feminist Analysis of Penality* (New York: Routledge, 1994), 116.

41. Nicole Rafter uncovered a similar pattern of increasing admissions for interpersonal and violent crimes. As in Illinois, by 1900 approximately one-third of women committed to custodial prisons in New York, Tennessee, and Ohio had been sentenced for crimes against persons. In contrast to my argument, Rafter contends that "in all probability, these patterns [of incarceration] reflected actual patterns of offending." Rafter also argues that the disproportionate sentencing of African American women for violent offenses reflects "higher rates of offending for some serious crimes." Nicole

Hahn Rafter, *Partial Justice: Women, Prisons, and Social Control,* 2nd ed. (New Brunswick, N.J.: Transaction Publishers, 1990), 114, 136, and 134.

42. Judith A. Allen, *Sex and Secrets,* 9.

43. African American men were also overrepresented in violent crime commitments, although to a far lesser degree than were black women. Between 1906 and 1912 African American males were 16 percent of men sentenced to Joliet for murder (commitments to Chester and Pontiac penitentiaries were not reported by race). Between 1925 and 1935 this figure doubled to 36 percent (Joliet, Chester, and Pontiac penitentiaries), while the overall percentage of male prisoners who were black held steady at 20 percent (data from 1906 to 1914 compiled from table 16 of the Illinois State Penitentiary biennial reports; data from 1925 to 1935 compiled from the *Annual Report of the Statistician* [Illinois Department of Public Welfare]). In an article titled "'The Negro Would Be More Than an Angel to Withstand Such Treatment': African American Homicide in Chicago, 1875–1910," Jeffrey S. Adler documents a dramatic increase in homicide rates in Chicago after 1890. At the same time, the character of homicide also changed in significant ways. Although the same trends occurred within Chicago's white and ethnic communities, they were most pronounced among African Americans. Before 1890 most African American homicides (like most white homicides) resulted from fights involving young, impoverished, and unattached men that took place in barrooms and brothels. After 1890, however, African American homicide was increasingly domestic in character: 38 percent took place within the home, and wives and girlfriends were the primary victims. Adler argues that this sharp increase in African American homicide overall, and domestic homicide in particular, must be correlated with Chicago's deteriorating racial climate and the forced making of Chicago's black ghetto. Lack of jobs, severely overcrowded housing, and an increasing climate of racial hostility generated growing stress and tension within African American households, tension that was more likely to erupt in lethal violence. Although Adler thoughtfully explores the reasons for the increase in domestic homicide after 1890, he says nothing about whether the number or character of homicides committed by African American women followed these same patterns (in *Lethal Imagination: Violence and Brutality in American History* [New York: New York University Press, 1999], 295–314).

44. For more on Susie Lattimore's case, see L. Mara Dodge, "'Our Juvenile Court Is Becoming More Like a Criminal Court': A Century of Reform at the Cook County (Chicago) Juvenile Court," *Michigan Historical Review* 26 (2000): 60–61; and Lauren B. Lipson, "'No Haven for Criminals': The Susie Lattimore Case and the Gradual Decline in Juvenile Justice" (Senior thesis, Northwestern University, 2001).

CHAPTER 7

1. Anne Hinrichsen, "The Women's Prison," *Welfare Bulletin* (February 1942), 8. Hinrichsen's first professional position was with the then-new Chicago Department of Welfare, in 1914. In 1915 the State Charities Commission appointed her Inspector of Institutions responsible for investigating the state's jails, almshouses, insane asylums, and orphanages. In 1918 Hinrichsen became executive secretary to the state's Board of Commissioners of Public Welfare. She later worked as the Department of Public Welfare's "informational officer" from the 1920s to the mid-1940s. Her reports appeared regularly in *Institution Quarterly, Welfare Magazine,* and *Welfare Bulletin.*

2. Ibid.

3. Moheb Ghali and Meda Chesney-Lind, "Gender Bias and the Criminal Justice System: An Empirical Investigation," *Sociology and Social Research* 70 (1986), 164. For reviews of the chivalry hypothesis see Joanne Belknap, *The Invisible Woman: Gender, Crime, and Justice* (Belmont, Calif.: Wadsworth, 1996), 64–90, and Joycelyn Pollock, *Criminal Women* (Cincinnati: Anderson, 1999), 87–97.

4. Belknap, *Invisible Woman,* 70, 80, 85.

5. Ilene H. Nagel and John Hagan, "Gender and Crime: Offense Patterns and Criminal Court Sanctions," in *Crime and Justice,* vol. 4, ed. Michael Tonry and Norval

Morris (Chicago: University of Chicago Press, 1983), 116. See also Ngaire Naffine, *Female Crime* (Sydney, Australia: Allen & Unwin, 1987), 36. Virtually all criminologists agree that female juvenile delinquents are sanctioned more severely than male. Girls are far more likely than boys to be arrested, prosecuted, and sentenced to a reformatory on minor charges, particularly those involving sexual improprieties. For a historical study see Steven Schlossman, *Love and the American Delinquent: The Theory and Practice of 'Progressive' Juvenile Justice, 1825–1920* (Chicago: University of Chicago Press, 1977).

6. Most Progressive Era investigators found that 40 to 80 percent of female prisoners had been employed as domestic servants. Nicole Hahn Rafter, *Partial Justice: Women, Prisons, and Social Control,* 2nd ed. (New Brunswick, N.J.: Transaction Publishers, 1990), 141.

7. Anne Worrall, *Offending Women: Female Lawbreakers and the Criminal Justice System* (London: Routledge & Kegan Paul, 1990), 88. The relationship between legal decision making and class has long been a major focus of social science studies on the treatment of male offenders, and a voluminous literature exists on the subject.

8. Belknap, *Invisible Woman,* 84. See also Keith B. Crew, "Sex Differences in Criminal Sentencing: Chivalry or Patriarchy?" *Justice Quarterly* 8 (1991), 59–84.

9. Letter from state's attorney regarding Anna Ostroska (Joliet #2945c), April 17, 1917, ECF.

10. Belknap, *Invisible Woman,* 73, and Diane K. Lewis, "Black Women Offenders and Criminal Justice: Some Theoretical Considerations," in *Comparing Female and Male Offenders,* ed. Marguerite Q. Warren (Beverly Hills, Calif.: Sage, 1981), 102. For stereotypes about African American women see Patricia Morton, *Disfigured Images: The Historical Assault on Afro-American Woman* (New York: Greenwood Press, 1991), and Jacklyn Huey and Michael J. Lynch, "The Image of Black Women in Criminology: Historical Stereotypes as Theoretical Foundation," in *Justice with Prejudice: Race and Criminal Justice in America,* ed. Michael J. Lynch and E. Britt Patterson (Guilderland, New York: Harrow and Heston, 1996), 72–89. Additional recent studies of racial discrimination include Gary Hill and Elizabeth Crawford, "Women, Race, and Crime," *Criminology* 28 (1990), 601–26; Marvin D. Krohn, James P. Curry, and Shirley Nelson-Kilger, "Is Chivalry Dead? An Analysis of Changes in Police Dispositions of Males and Females," *Criminology* 21 (1983), 417–47; Cassia Spohn, John Gruhl, and Susan Welch, "The Impact of Ethnicity and Gender of Defendants on the Decision to Reject or Dismiss Felony Charges," *Criminology* 25 (1987), 175–91; and Vernetta D. Young, "Gender Expectations and Their Impact on Black Female Offenders and Victims," *Justice Quarterly* 3 (1986): 305–28.

11. Rafter, *Partial Justice,* 146. Race was less central to the social construction of male criminality. Between 1890 and 1940 African American men averaged only 19 percent of the male prison population in Illinois, a proportion comparable to national rates, while black women averaged 42 percent of the female prison population. One could hypothesize that African American men engaged in far less criminal activity than did their black sisters, but this is not plausible. Instead, racial stereotypes regarding the naturally hardened character, inherent immorality, and innate criminality of black women most likely played a determining role. When this factor was coupled with the preferential treatment white women experienced in the courts, African American women came to constitute a much higher proportion of the female prison population than did black men of the male prison population.

12. Kavanaugh, *The Criminal and His Allies* (Indianapolis: Bobbs-Merrill, 1928), 149.

13. This analysis of growing fears of the criminality of "newly liberated" females in the 1920s is based on my reading of newspaper accounts. I have been unable to uncover any secondary sources analyzing this phenomenon. During the 1970s similar fears were unleashed by mainstream criminologists, who posited that women's participation in crime, particularly violent crime, was increasing as a result of the women's liberation movement. Though the press widely publicized these predictions, they were unfounded. Women's violent crime rates remained stable. Although women's property crime rates did increase after 1970, more thoughtful researchers attributed this to women's worsening economic plight—the increasing feminization of poverty—rather than to a new generation of "emancipated" female criminals. For critiques of 1970s "liberation theory," see Belknap,

Invisible Woman, 37–39; Carol Smart, "The New Female Offender: Reality or Myth?" in *The Criminal Justice System and Women*, ed. Barbara R. Price and Natalie J. Sokoloff (New York: Clark Boardman, 1982), 105–116; and Pollock, *Criminal Women*, 81–87.

14. The six condemned women were: Sabel Nitti (1923), Catherine Cassler (1927), Gertrude Pulse (Dwight #989) (1935), Mildred Bolton (Dwight #1218) (1936), Minnie Mitchell (Dwight #1219) (1937), and Marie Porter (1938). Although the governor granted a last-minute stay of execution for both Pulse and Mitchell, their male accomplices were executed. Pulse died after two years in prison, and Mitchell was paroled after six years. Nitti and Cassler were granted new trials and were subsequently acquitted. Mildred Bolton received the death penalty for shooting her ex-husband in his office in the middle of the day. She is purported to have remarked, "They can't convict women of murder in Cook County" and accurately predicted that the governor would offer a last-minute reprieve ("Widow: 'I Killed Him,'" *Chicago Daily Tribune*, July 17, 1936). Bolton served ten years.

Sarah Ruddell, a correctional officer at Dwight from 1961 to 1972, claimed that her husband had "died because of putting people to death. He put to death the first and only woman in Illinois [in the twentieth century: Marie Porter], and that worked on him. He was the one who tried to stop the execution." Since 1933 he had served as chief guard at Menard Correctional Center, where all executions took place. According to Ruddell, both she and her husband were "great believers in justice and treating inmates with humanity." During the Depression, jobs at Menard were among the few available in their rural area (Interview with Ruddell, April 3, 1996).

15. Chicago Commission on Race Relations, *The Negro in Chicago: A Study of Race Relations and a Race Riot* (Chicago: University of Chicago Press), 351. Additional evidence of female convicts' "friendless" status and weak community ties comes from the convict registers. Between 1890 and 1930, when asked to provide a close reference, one-fifth (21%) of the white women and one-third (34%) of African American women named someone who was living in another state, intimating that they did not have close relatives or friends in the local community. Although several dozen women were classified as "mulatto" and "creole" in the convict registers (1935–1963) and Dwight inmate jackets (1930–1963), no more than eight were identified as "Indian" or "Mexican." Even though Illinois had large Mexican and Puerto Rican communities, less than a dozen women with Spanish surnames appeared in the records.

16. Pollock, *Criminal Women*, 144. Several studies have found that married women are significantly less likely than their unmarried counterparts to receive a prison sentence, but marital status had no effect on the sentencing of male offenders. See Ilene Bernstein, N. J. Cardascia, and C. E. Ross, "Defendant's Sex and Criminal Court Processing," in *Discrimination in Organizations*, ed. R. Alvarez (San Francisco: Jossey-Bass, 1979), 329–54, and Edna Erez, "Dangerous Men, Evil Women: Gender and Parole Decision-Making," *Justice Quarterly* 9 (1992), 105–26. However, Chicago police reports from 1913 to 1930 reveal that single men were more likely to be convicted than married men (36% versus 27%), just as single women were more likely to be convicted than married women (47% versus 41%).

17. Letter from state's attorney regarding Dwight #565, June 8, 1930, DIJ. Several researchers have argued that rather than treating women more leniently than men, court officials exhibit a form of "familial paternalism." Kathleen Daly contends that "protecting women" in so-called chivalrous sentencing primarily serves to protect their children ("Discrimination in the Criminal Courts: Family, Gender, and the Problem of Equal Treatment," *Social Forces* 66 [1987], 152–75, and "Structure and Practice of Familial-Based Justice in a Criminal Court," *Law and Society Review* 21 [1987], 267–90). See also Mary Eaton, *Justice for Whom? Family, Court, and Social Control* (Philadelphia: Open University Press, 1986).

18. Mothers have not universally benefited from preferential treatment during sentencing. In her study of courts in Ontario, Canada, from 1871 to 1920 Helen Boritch concluded that "judges appeared to view women's criminality as prima facie evidence of their inadequacy as mothers and showed little hesitancy in removing them from their child-care roles" ("Gender and Criminal Court Outcomes: An Historical Analysis," *Criminology* 30 [1992], 319).

19. For example, in 1910 over half (54%) of adult white women in Illinois were 35 or older in contrast to 49 percent of black women. Department of the Interior, Census Office, *Reports of the Thirteenth Census: Population,* vol. II (Washington, D.C.: Government Printing Office, 1913), table 7, p. 478. Nancy Brooks, a fourteen-year-old African American girl, was the youngest female sentenced to prison during the entire period of this study. In 1908 Brooks received a forty-five year sentence for first-degree murder. During a quarrel over a dress she had stabbed her sister in the thigh with a pen knife; the knife struck an artery and the wound proved fatal. Brooks later stated that at her trial "she was not advised, and did not know the difference between murder and manslaughter." After serving ten years in prison she was freed as a result of the intercession of Ella Hamlin, a prominent local woman. In an impassioned letter to the parole board Hamlin wrote: "I can not understand how any jury of even half intelligence could have given this child this sentence—even though she is black." However, the state's attorney remained adamantly opposed to Brooks's release, characterizing her as "a very ignorant negro, and one of the vicious class we have to deal with." The parole board disregarded his objections. Frankly exposing his own racial prejudices, the chairman of the parole board concluded, "She is bright, courteous and polite, apparently the product of superior negro stock." Nancy Brooks (Joliet #1006d), 1917, ECF.

20. Pre-Parole Report on Dwight #1214, December 30, 1937; Letters from state's attorney regarding Dwight #518 (Joliet #497e), January 25, 1929; PBH for Dwight #150, September 27, 1932, DIJ.

21. PBH for Dwight #762, February 27, 1935, DIJ. Joliet #4856c. Before 1920 white women were substantially more likely to have a husband in prison than were African American women: 10 percent versus 2 percent. Judges displayed fewer qualms over sending a white woman to prison if her family had already been disgraced, believing that her claims to respectability and patriarchal protections were compromised beyond repair. After the 1920s the percentage of white women with a husband in prison declined; white female offenders were increasingly sentenced on their own, regardless of their husband's status.

22. Joliet #6184c and #6789c, JCR; Sociologist's Report for Dwight #2264, March 6, 1947; Sociologist's Report for Dwight #3165, October 2, 1956, DIJ. For a more recent study see Candace Kruttschnitt, "Respectable Women and the Law," *Sociological Quarterly* 23 (1983), 221–34. Kruttschnitt's indicators of respectability included prior criminal record, drug or alcohol abuse, prior psychiatric care, employer censure (such as being fired from a job), and peer deviance (defined by the reputation of her associates). She found that "respectable" women received the lightest sentences. Interestingly, women who had prior criminal records but were otherwise perceived as "generally respectable" were treated slightly better than those who had *no* prior record but were considered "generally disreputable." Those characterized as "totally disreputable women" received the harshest sentences. Unfortunately, Kruttschnitt did not analyze race as an independent variable.

23. Nicole Hahn Rafter, "Hard Times: Custodial Prisons for Women and the Example of the New York State Prison for Women at Auburn, 1893–1933," in *Judge, Lawyer, Victim, Thief: Women, Gender Roles, and Criminal Justice,* ed. Nicole Hahn Rafter and Elizabeth A. Stanko (Boston: Northeastern University Press, 1982), 245.

24. PBH for Dwight #126 (Joliet #3481e), November 6, 1930, DIJ. In *The Roots of Justice: Crime and Punishment in Alameda County, California 1870–1910,* Lawrence M. Friedman and Robert V. Percival reach similar conclusions regarding the social disadvantages of most prosecuted offenders and the minor nature of their offenses (Chapel Hill: University of North Carolina Press, 1981).

CHAPTER 8

1. "Grand House Warming," (Joliet) *Daily Republican,* November 23, 1896; "New Prison Now Ready," *Chicago Tribune,* November 15, 1896; and "Inspect the Prison," (Joliet) *Weekly News,* November 26, 1896.

2. "New Prison for Women," (Joliet) *Daily Republican,* November 12, 1896.

3. Ophelia Amigh, *Biennial Reports of the Illinois State Training School for Girls* (Springfield, Ill.: n.p., 1904), 6. For more on female juvenile delinquency in Illinois, see Anne Meis Knupfer, *Reform and Resistance: Gender, Delinquency, and America's First Juvenile Court* (New York: Routledge, 2001).

4. A. L. Bowen, "Ten Years Ago and To-Day: Joliet State Prison," *Welfare Magazine* 19 (1928), 574–76.

5. *Chicago Tribune,* November 15, 1896. PBH for Ethel Kryzak (Dwight #604, Joliet #6172d), January 1920, DIJ.

6. "Commissioner's Report," ISP 1906, 5. In 1908 the Illinois General Assembly authorized a commission to design a new penitentiary. However, construction at Stateville did not begin until 1916 and the facility was not completed until 1925. In 2001, the Illinois Department of Corrections finally announced that it was closing Joliet.

7. Maggie Tiller (Joliet #4266c), letter to Mrs. Wiens, June 11, 1899, ECF.

8. Eliza Ingersoll (Joliet #6652c), pardon petition, January 13, 1907, ECF. On the WCTU see "Chaplain's Report," ISP 1906, 11–12; "Chaplain's Report," ISP 1912, 12; "Chaplain's Report," ISP 1914, 27; and IWP 1931, 354.

9. Philip S. Foner and Sally M. Miller, eds., *Kate Richards O'Hare: Selected Writings and Speeches* (Baton Rouge: Louisiana State University Press, 1982), 297; Florence Northridge Beatty, "The Woman's Prison," *Welfare Magazine* 18 (1927), 925

10. "Miss Maria S. Madden: Managing Matron of the Women's Prison," *Joliet Prison Post* 1 (1914), 56 (emphasis in original).

11. Ophelia Amigh, *Biennial Reports,* 1902, 6. Geneva's inmates, who averaged fifteen years of age, were sentenced for less serious crimes than were the women at Joliet. These included minor misdemeanors such as petit larceny; "chastity" offenses including premarital sex, attending dance halls unsupervised, and unwed pregnancy; and underage "status" offenses such as incorrigibility, drinking, running away, and "willful stubbornness." Geneva also housed large numbers of nondelinquent, orphaned, abused, and neglected girls, some victims of incest or rape, when no other placement could be found for them. Geneva's large size may have contributed to the greater difficulties its staff experienced. The institution, founded in 1894, saw its daily population increase from one hundred in 1900 to roughly five hundred in 1910. As Amigh reported in the latter year, "We can't build cottages fast enough." Geneva's cottage housing and open campus setting also made supervision more difficult.

12. Olga Bridgman, "Juvenile Delinquency and Feeble-Mindedness," *Institution Quarterly* 5 (March 1914): 166–67.

13. Dr. Esther H. Stone, "Plea for an Early Commitment to Correctional Institutions of Delinquent Children," *Institution Quarterly* 9 (1918): 64–65. For similar views, see June Purcell-Guild, "Study of One Hundred and Thirty-One Delinquent Girls Held at the Juvenile Detention Home in Chicago, 1917," *Journal of the American Institute of Criminal Law and Criminology* 10 (1919), 468.

14. Mary G. Peck, "Race Betterment," *Welfare Magazine* 18 (1927), 1477–82; Frank Dikotter, "Race Culture: Recent Perspectives on the History of Eugenics," *American Historical Review* 103 (1998), 467; Nicolas Hahn Fischer [Nicole Hahn Rafter], "Too Dumb to Know Better: Cacogenic Family Studies and the Criminology of Women," *Criminology* 18 (1980), 3. The literature on the eugenics movement is voluminous. See Daniel J. Kevles's *In the Name of Eugenics: Genetics and the Uses of Human Heredity,* 2nd ed. (Cambridge: Cambridge University Press, 1995). For the profound influence of "eugenics jurisprudence" in Chicago, see Michael Willrich, "The Two Percent Solution: Eugenics Jurisprudence and the Socialization of American Law, 1900–1930," *Law and History Review* 16 (1998), 63–111.

15. Nicole Hahn Rafter, *Creating Born Criminals* (Urbana: University of Illinois Press, 1997), 94.

16. Katherine Bement Davis, "The Duty of the State to Its Delinquent Women," *Institution Quarterly* 5 (1914), 116. For more on Davis see Nicole Hahn Rafter, *Partial Justice; Women, Prisons, and Social Control,* 2nd ed. (New Brunswick, N.J.: Transaction Publishers, 1990), 65–73 and 79–80, and Freedman, *Their Sisters' Keepers: Prison Reform in America, 1830–1930* (Ann Arbor: University of Michigan Press, 1981), 116–42.

17. Mabel Ruth Fernald, Mary Hayes, and Almena Dawley, *A Study of Women Delinquents in New York State* (New York: The Century Company, 1920). See also Jean Weidensall, *The Mentality of the Criminal Woman* (Baltimore: Warwick & Work, 1916), and Edith R. Spaulding, *An Experimental Study of Psychopathic Delinquent Women* (1923; reprint, Montclair, N.J.: Patterson Smith, 1969).

18. "The Training School for Girls," *Institution Quarterly* 2 (1911): 55–56. Geneva's next managing officer, Dr. Clara B. Hayes (1917–1921), complained repeatedly about the girl's "low mental grade" and predicted that most would "soon become victims of society and a further menace to the state." Like others before her, she called for a state institution where such girls could be maintained "during their entire lives" (Clara B. Hayes, "1917/18 Geneva Annual Report," *Institution Quarterly* 9 [1918]: 167–68). See also Clara B. Hayes, "Segregation of Mental Defectives as a Preventive of Crime, Immorality, and Inefficiency," *Institution Quarterly* 6 (1915), 96–101, and "Our Work as Seen from Geneva," *Institution Quarterly* 10 (1919), 116–20.

19. In 1920 Illinois became one of the few states to establish a state farm for male misdemeanants. Located at Vandalia, the farm housed men who previously would have been committed to local county jails for misdemeanor offenses. In contrast to the women who were committed to reformatories, male misdemeanants were rarely sentenced for chastity offenses such as adultery and fornication. See Hinrichsen, "State Penal Farm Displaces County Jail," *Institution Quarterly* 7 (1916), 44–49, and articles in *Institution Quarterly* 11 (1920): 47–48, and *Institution Quarterly* 8 (1917): 173–77.

20. "Change of Management at Women's Prison," *Joliet Prison Post* 1 (1914), 303–4, and "Interview: Miss Frances Cowley," *Joliet Prison Post* 1 (1914), 110. There is no information about when or why Cowley left Joliet. The Illinois State Library holds the only extant copies of the remarkable *Joliet Prison Post,* which was initiated under Warden Allen. The library's holdings include volume 1 (1914) and scattered issues from 1916. See also "Former Matron of Woman's Prison Dies in Kansas," *Joliet Evening Herald,* May 20, 1914.

21. "Instructs Convicts in Home Sciences," *Joliet Evening Herald,* August 20, 1914; "Class of 1910—Dedication to Grace Fuller," *Aurora* (Michigan State Normal College Yearbook), 8–9 (in "Grace Fuller" folder, Eastern Michigan University Archives, Ypsilanti, Michigan).

22. "Instructs Convicts in Home Sciences," *Joliet Evening Herald,* August 20, 1914. Likewise, at the New York State Prison for Women at Auburn, described as "nominally a state prison," chief matron Anna Welshe successfully introduced "reformatory measures." See Jeanne Robert, "The Care of Women in State Prisons," *The American Review of Reviews* 44 (1911), 80.

23. "Convicts to Cook: Matron to Instruct," *Joliet Evening Herald,* September 3, 1914. Formal domestic science classes were begun at Geneva in the late 1920s. Investigator June Purcell-Guild observed that most girls were "frankly scornful of domestic accomplishments. They knew little of such things [cooking and sewing] and had no desire to become proficient in them" ("Study of One Hundred and Thirty-One Delinquent Girls," 456) By far the greatest benefit of Fuller's domestic science classroom was the fact that the Women's Prison now had a fully functional kitchen. During the previous two decades the women's food had been carried over from the men's institution, arriving, at best, in a lukewarm state.

24. "The New Superintendent," *Joliet Prison Post* 1 (September 1914). Since the 1880s male prisoners had been provided with elementary-level classes and their own library.

25. Grace Fuller, *Too-Loo Byrd: The Story of a Little Negro Waif* (Macon, Ga.: J. W. Burke Co., 1924), 13, 15–16, 74. In the book Aunt Phebe, who finds the orphaned boy, Too-Loo, readily agrees that it would be the "best thing for the chile" to be raised by the Byrds, a prominent white family. Fuller characterizes Mrs. Byrd as a "born mistress of the art when it came to handling negroes." Too-Loo quickly becomes the "best trained little negro for miles around" and "utterly devoted" to his white masters. Uncle Phineas concludes with admiration, "'Yes, sir, dat chile's got de makin's of a real gentleman's nigger.'" The fact that neither Fuller nor her successors wrote any pardon recommendations for African American women is equally telling. As in the past, white women were more than twice as likely to receive a pardon, commutation, or special discharge.

26. "Convicts to Cook: Matron to Instruct," *Joliet Evening Herald,* August 20, 1914. In Illinois no centralized investigative body monitored conditions at the state's penal institutions, another factor that contributed to the lack of outside awareness of, and interest in, the plight of female prisoners. Although Illinois was among the first to organize a board of charities, in 1879, the state's prisons were outside its mandate. There is only one reference to Joliet's female prisoners in Henriette Frank and Amalie Jerome's history, *Annals of the Chicago Woman's Club for the First Forty Years of Its Organization, 1876–1916* (Chicago, Ill.: The Chicago Women's Club, 1916). In 1890 the Philanthropy Committee reported its concern that although there was a "home" in Chicago for male ex-convicts, there was no home to aid the dozen women released annually from Joliet (75). No further discussion was reported. In 1900 sociologist Frances A. Kellor conducted one of the first research studies designed to replicate and challenge Lombroso's theories. Kellor compared female prisoners at Joliet with female students on a broad range of sensory and physiological measures. Concluding that there were no significant biological differences between the two groups, she argued forcefully in favor of social and environmental causes of criminality (Kellor, "Psychological and Environmental Study of Women Criminals," *American Journal of Sociology* 5 [1900], 527–43 and 671–83). Kellor moved to New York soon after her studies were published and never became active in prison reform in Illinois. See also Freedman, *Their Sisters' Keepers,* 111–15.

27. For the 1917 Joliet riot see Gladys A. Erickson, *Warden Ragen of Joliet* (New York: E. P. Dutton & Co., 1957); *Joliet Evening Herald-News* (June 1917); A. L. Bowen, "Ten Years Ago and To-Day: Joliet State Prison," *Welfare Magazine* 19 (1928), 574–83; and "Disorder in Prison and Reformatory," *Institution Quarterly* 8 (1917), 69–71.

28. DPW 1918, 232. Although the institution was renamed the Illinois Women's Prison in 1919, I will continue to refer to it as the Joliet Women's Prison.

29. "'Fugitives Will Return' Says Prison Chief," *Joliet Evening Herald-News,* June 30, 1920; "Woman Convict Tells How Three Escaped Prison," *Joliet Evening Herald-News,* July 1, 1920. Fuller further defended herself by pointing out that male escapes from the honor farm at Stateville averaged two to three a month and were so commonplace as to cause little reaction.

30. For more on these escapes, see L. Mara Dodge, "Her Life Has Been an Improper One: Women, Crime, and Prisons in Illinois" (Ph.D. diss., University of Illinois at Chicago, 1998), 479–88.

31. In 1910 61 percent of the nation's female offenders were sentenced to state prisons as opposed to women's reformatory institutions; by 1923 this proportion had declined to 40 percent (Bureau of the Census, *Prisoners, 1923* [Washington, D.C.: Government Printing Office, 1926], 47, tables 19 and 20). Nevertheless, new custodial units continued to be constructed throughout the 1920s. See Paul W. Garrett and Austin H. MacCormick, eds., *Handbook of American Prisons and Reformatories* (New York: National Society of Penal Information, 1929), 159, 222, 795, and Ellen C. Potter, "Women in Correctional Institutions," in *1933 Annual Proceedings* (Indianapolis: American Prison Association, 1933), 105.

CHAPTER 9

1. Sarah M. Victor, *The Life Story of Sarah M. Victor* (Cleveland, Oh.: Williams Publishing Co., 1887), 346–47.

2. "New Chief Will Take Charge of Women's Prison," *Joliet Evening Herald-News,* September 10, 1929.

3. PBH for Dwight #604 (Joliet #1788e), February 5, 1929, DIJ. Despite many effusive promises, Foster continued her criminal career after her release. In 1931 a warrant was issued for her arrest "on account of disappearing for parts unknown and being accused of stealing $58.00 from her employer." Foster fled to New York, where she was arrested for another theft and sentenced to the Auburn Women's Prison. Released in 1935, she failed to make her monthly reports and was declared a parole violator three months later. During this time Foster returned to Chicago, where she was ar-

rested and convicted of three new charges of theft. After serving one year at the Chicago House of Correction she was returned to Dwight to serve out her time for her original parole violation. She was released in 1938. Illinois authorities immediately returned her to New York to complete her time for her parole violation from that state.

4. Quoted from IWP 1925, 259, and IWP 1926, 258–59. For Rulien's appointment see "Joliet Woman Is Appointed Prison Matron," *Joliet Evening Herald-News*, September 20, 1921, and "Mrs. Frank Rulien New Superintendent," *Joliet Daily Times*, September 20, 1921.

5. IWP 1928, 313, and IWP 1925, 259.

6. PBH for Dwight #503 (Joliet #4488e), March 1, 1932, and Dwight #552 (Joliet #3408e), October 1, 1930, 10, DIJ. African American parole violators were more likely to be apprehended and returned to prison than white parole violators: 46 percent versus 36 percent from 1895 to 1920 and 88 percent versus 74 percent in the 1920s. This disparity suggests that paroled black women encountered greater suspicion and police surveillance. By the 1940s and 1950s, virtually all parole violators were apprehended. Indeed, in several cases middle-aged women were returned after more than a decade and forced to complete the remainder of their prison sentences, even though they had lived law-abiding lives during the entire period of their "parole violation."

7. IWP 1922, 581. Information on Rulien's accomplishments were compiled from the IWP annual reports from 1921 to 1928.

8. In 1894 the Illinois General Assembly, pressured by organized labor, voted to gradually phase out the profitable contract labor system in existence since 1867. In its place, prisoners manufactured goods for "state use." Although contract labor was not completely abolished until 1931, this was the beginning of the end of the private "factory prison." The expanded educational, vocational, and recreational programs for male prisoners implemented after 1900 were less a response to a new reform philosophy than to a pragmatic need to fill the time of growing numbers of unemployed and idle prisoners. In 1932 nearly one-half (48%) of male inmates had no job assignment. See Albert Tilendis, "The Prison Labor Problem in Illinois" (Ph.D. diss., University of Illinois, Urbana, 1941), 9.

9. See "The Full Text of the Grand Jury Report," *Joliet Evening Herald-News*, May 26, 1926, and the *Chicago Daily Tribune*, May 27, 1926.

10. Florence Monahan, "Separate Penal and Reformatory Institutions for Women," *Woman's City Club Bulletin* 15 (1925), 135–6.

11. Florence Monahan, *Women in Crime* (New York: Washburn, 1941), 139.

12. "The Full Text of the Grand Jury Report," *Joliet Evening Herald-News*, May 26, 1926, and Wiley B. Sanders, "The History and Administration of the State Prisons of Illinois" (Ph.D. diss., University of Chicago), 524.

13. "The Full Text of the Grand Jury Report," *Joliet Evening Herald-News*, May 26, 1926.

14. Margaret A. Otis, "Perversions Not Commonly Noted," *Journal of Abnormal Psychology* 8 (1913), 112–14, and Charles A. Ford, "Homosexual Practices of Institutionalized Females," *Journal of Abnormal and Social Psychology* (1929), 442–49. For an incisive historical overview see Estelle B. Freedman, "The Prison Lesbian," *Signs: Journal of Women in Culture and Society* 21 (1996), 248–80.

15. Stone, Esther H., "Plea for an Early Commitment to Correctional Institutions of Delinquent Children," *Institution Quarterly* 9 (1918), 63. Eugenia Lekkerkerker, in her exhaustive 1931 survey of women's reformatory prisons, reported that many institutions justified racial segregation in cottages and housing units as a means of inhibiting interracial lesbian relationships. *Reformatories for Women in the United States* (Gronigen, Netherlands: J. B. Wolters, 1931), 234, 396–402, 435.

16. Unnamed "delinquents" quoted in Philip Morris Hauser, "Motion Pictures in Penal and Correctional Institutions: A Study of the Reactions of Prisoners to Movies" (Ph.D. diss., University of Chicago, 1933), 38. Charlotte Ruth Klein also documented and denounced girls' same-sex attractions. See "Success and Failure on Parole: A Study of 160 Girls Paroled from the State Training School at Geneva, Illinois" (Master's thesis, University of Chicago, 1935), 66–75.

17. Hauser, "Motion Pictures," 39, and Stone, "Plea for an Early Commitment," 64–65.

18. Stone, "Plea for an Early Commitment," 64–65.

19. MHO Report on Dwight #604 (Joliet #1788e), January 1, 1929; MHO Report on Dwight #448 (Joliet #3286e), May 31, 1930; and MHO Report on Dwight #563 (Joliet #3522e), November 4, 1930, DIJ.

20. "Woman's Prison Superintendent Has Resigned," *Joliet Evening Herald News*, September 8, 1929. See also "John L. Whitman—Dreamer and Doer," *Journal of Criminal Law and Criminology* 18 (1927), 5–10. Nearly three-quarters (73%) of the women who entered Joliet in the 1920s maintained perfect institutional records. Another 15 percent received but one or two demotions, after which they quickly earned their way back up to A grade. Only 12 percent received three or more demotions. Even of these "incorrigible" inmates, only five were ever demoted to the lowest grade of E.

21. Whereas the average white woman served 1.6 years in the 1910s, she served 3.3. years in the 1920s. Likewise, in the same period African American women's sentences more than doubled, from 2.2 to 5.2 years. In the 1920s 16 percent of all female convicts served eight years or more.

22. "Takes Charge of Women's Prison," *Joliet Evening Herald-News*, September 12, 1929, and "Joliet Woman Is Appointed Prison Matron," September 20, 1921.

23. PBH for Dwight #559, December 13, 1930, DIJ; IWP 1931, 353. No newspapers reported on the 1930 "riot." Information on it could only be gleaned from the few references found in parole board transcripts.

24. Whereas Chicago's leading female reformers, social welfare professionals, and women's clubs ceaselessly championed and vigorously supported the juvenile court from the 1890s through the 1930s, the reformatory movement failed to capture the imagination of prominent activists. Almost none of Chicago's leading female reformers, scholars, or social welfare professionals played significant roles in the reformatory campaign. Indeed, recent studies of female reform in Progressive Era Chicago completely fail to mention this movement. The Chicago Historical Society, Manuscript Division, holds the correspondence and reports from the Illinois State Reformatory Women's Campaign. For published summaries, see "New Reformatory Ready for Women," (Bloomington) *Pantagraph*, November 6, 1930; Helen H. Hazard, "Services of Dedication at the Illinois State Reformatory for Women," *Welfare Bulletin* (1942): 8–12; and the booklet "Dedication: Oakdale Reformatory," 1932, LWV. The League of Women Voters also played an instrumental role in establishing the California women's reformatory.

25. A 1920 study of morals courts in four cities revealed that only 19 percent of women arraigned in Chicago were convicted, compared to 63 percent in Philadelphia, 68 percent in New York, and 81 percent in Boston. Moreover, only 2.3 percent of Chicago convicts were sentenced to a penal or reformatory institution. In contrast, 25 percent of the women convicted in Boston, 44 percent in Philadelphia, and 53 percent in New York were incarcerated (George E. Worthington and Ruth Topping, *Specialized Courts Dealing with Sex Delinquency: A Study of the Procedures in Chicago, Boston, Philadelphia, and New York* [1923; reprint, Montclair, N.J.: Patterson Smith, 1969]).

26. Nineteenth-century female reformers shared similarly dualistic views. Rafter reports that Josephine Lowell, a key crusader for the pioneering Massachusetts Women's Reformatory Prison, originally called for the establishment of two separate women's institutions—"a reformatory prison for those who might be salvageable and a custodial asylum for the feebleminded who by definition were not" (Rafter, *Creating Born Criminals* [Urbana: University of Illinois Press, 1997], 40–41).

27. Anne Hinrichsen, "The Women's Prison," *Welfare Bulletin* (February 1942), 7.

28. Charlotte S. Butler, "The Woman Recidivist in Illinois," *The Clubwoman* (March 1926), 12–13, LWV.

29. Charlotte S. Butler, "Annual Report of the Courts Committee," *Women's City Club Bulletin* 16 (1927), 11, LWV. See also the statements (with no author indicated), "Farm Colony for Women, c. 1924, and "A State Reformatory for Women in Illinois," c. 1925, LWV.

30. Hazard, "Services of Dedication," 8–12.

31. Hinrichsen, "Women's Prison," 8. Prison reformers Austin H. MacCormick

and Paul W. Garrett offered a similar assessment. Although they acknowledged that the Joliet Women's Prison was "very well kept," the diet "good," and the recreation "reasonably adequate," they criticized its custodial character and traditional penal philosophy, concluding: "This institution, more than almost any other institution for women in the country, appears to be run according to the concepts and regimen of institutions for men" (*Handbook of American Prisons* [New York: G. P. Putnam's Sons, 1926], 276).

32. "Farm Colony for Women," undated letter circa 1926, LWV. The Will County Women's Christian Temperance Union (WCTU), remaining the only women's group to express any interest in the plight of Joliet's female felons, continued its program of annual Christmas-gift giving and monthly chapel services.

33. Senate Bills 91 and 92 passed unanimously. House bills 160 and 161 passed the house with only two dissenting votes. Superintendent Helen Hazard and Advisory Board members Emma Mason and Elizabeth Lewis fondly recalled this early period. In 1943 Hazard wrote, "And then came the long and delightful days and weeks spent with architects . . . and the contractors, and the selecting of the types of buildings, and plans of every kind." These three women were responsible for almost every detail, beginning with the design and decoration of the buildings. Their early correspondence reveals virtually no concern with penological issues, but solely a preoccupation with the proper outfitting and decor of the cottages: the choice of a color scheme for the rooms, the design of the woodwork, the selection of matching shades, lamps, curtains, and pictures. In a typical letter Hazard observed to Lewis, "Yes, I am watching the plaster and will keep you informed regarding it. That which we saw has cracked terribly but on another wall they have tried a different material. Yesterday it was all right." Three months later she wrote: "I am wondering if you would want to come in order to see the paint which they are putting on Cottage One? I thought you might have an idea as to the color. Of course it isn't essential and I don't want you to put yourself out terribly in order to get here but of course you know I would like to have you come" (Letters from Hazard to Lewis, July 31, 1930 and October 21, 1930, LWV). Lewis became superintendent at Geneva in the 1940s.

34. "No Trouble at Women's Prison: Tear Gas Bombs Are Sent There to Use in an Emergency," *Herald-News*, March 19, 1931; "Subpoena Three Members of Parole Board," *Joliet Evening Herald-News*, March 22, 1931; MacCormick and Garrett, *Handbook* (1926); Austin H. MacCormick and Paul W. Garrett, *Handbook of American Prisons and Reformatories* (New York: National Society of Penal Information, 1929). See also Illinois Association for Criminal Justice, *The Illinois Crime Survey* (Chicago: Blakely Printing), 490–500.

35. State Reformatory for Women, 1932–1935 combined report, DPW 1935, 325. "Plan Transfer of Women to Dwight Prison: Building Will Be Used as Hospital for Men Prisoners," *Joliet Evening Herald-News*, March 22, 1931. Since the mid-1970s the former Joliet Women's Prison has served as the receiving and diagnostic center for all males admitted to prison in Illinois.

36. PBH for Dwight #3636, February 1, 1960, DIJ.

37. Misdemeanor offenses during the 1930s included drug possession (21%), petit larceny (16%), public drunkenness (16%), prostitution (15%), vagrancy (14%), adultery and fornication (7%), contributing to the delinquency or to the dependency of a minor (7%), and simple assault (2%). During the 1950s, the last decade for which such detailed data were preserved, far fewer women were sentenced for morals and sex-related misdemeanors. Twenty percent of committed misdemeanants were sentenced for child-related offenses (contributing to the dependency or to the delinquency of a minor), 17 percent for petit larceny, 17 percent for check fraud, 16 percent for prostitution or vagrancy, 10 percent for drug offenses, 5 percent for assault, 4 percent for adultery or fornication, and 4 percent for driving under the influence. Between 1980 and 1982, the last years for which data are available, misdemeanants accounted for 10.6 percent of female commitments.

38. Letters from trial judge regarding Dwight #19, May 11, 1932 and April 30, 1933, DIJ. Although Sophie Danzer was actually a minor felony offender, I have used her case to illustrate attitudes toward minor offenders more broadly defined (i.e.,

misdemeanants). Because misdemeanor offenders did not appear before the parole board, none of their inmate jackets have been preserved (see appendix A for further explanation). Thus, no detailed statements of fact, letters from judges or state's attorneys, MHO reports, or transcripts of parole board hearings exist for their cases. Consequently, no descriptive data is available on the exact character of their crimes.

CHAPTER 10

1. MHO Report on Dwight #494, April 19, 1928, DIJ. For reproductions of ten complete MHO Reports see L. Mara Dodge, "'Her Life Has Been an Improper One': Women, Crime, and Prisons in Illinois, 1835–1933" (Ph.D. diss., University of Illinois at Chicago, 1998), 784–801. Because pseudonyms have been used for all women sentenced to prison after 1925, only their convict numbers are cited in these notes.

2. MHO Report, April 18, 1932, and PBH, May 3, 1932, on Dwight #494, DIJ.

3. PBH, April 16, 1937, and MHO Report, March 30, 1937, both regarding Dwight #494, DIJ.

4. Michel Foucault, *Discipline and Punish: The Birth of the Prison,* 2nd ed., trans. Alan Sheridan (New York: Vintage, 1995), 16 and 9.

5. Harold S. Frum, *Fifty-Year History of the Division of the Criminologist* (Springfield, Ill.: State of Illinois, 1968). See also Wiley B. Sanders, "The History and Administration of the State Prisons of Illinois" (Ph.D. diss., University of Chicago, 1929), 460–70, and Illinois Prison Inquiry Commission, *The Prison System in Illinois: A Report to the Governor* (Springfield, Ill.: State of Illinois, 1937), 454–92.

6. Anne Hinrichsen, "Social Histories in the Women's Prison," *Institution Quarterly* 9 (1918), 250. Before 1917 inmates' prison files contained almost no information.

7. Report of the Criminologist, DPW 1920, 346. Dr. Adler described how the girls at Geneva "in spite of every effort, promptly dubbed the mental health officers 'brain touchers'" (John A. Larson and Herman M. Adler, "Lie Detection Tests with Prisoners: A Preliminary Communication," *Institution Quarterly* 16 [1925], 118–19.

8. MHO Report on Dwight #141, November 4, 1930, DIJ. State Criminologist Dr. Herman Adler, one of the few to question the presumed relationship between criminal activity and mental inferiority, authorized a careful study of all men and women admitted to prison between 1920 and 1927. Using individual intelligence tests, this study revealed that nearly two-thirds (61%) of the women scored in the average or above-average range. However, female prisoners were more likely to be classified in the inferior range than were male prisoners (39% versus 24%). Dr. Adler speculated that it was "quite likely that the high percentage of women with inferior ratings is a result of the selective process, so that more of the inferiors are given penitentiary sentences, while the woman offenders with superior intelligence are placed on parole." Reported in Simon Tulchin, *Intelligence and Crime: A Study of Penitentiary and Reformatory Offenders* (Chicago: University of Chicago Press, 1939), 138–40. After the 1930s the attribution of criminality to feeble-mindedness gradually lessened, although it never entirely disappeared. In the 1950s and 1960s half of female prisoners (51%) were classified as below average in intelligence, versus only 28 percent of men (DPS 1955–1969 Annual Reports).

9. Excerpts from MHO Reports on Dwight #631, March 29, 1932; Dwight #572, September 17, 1931; Dwight #553, December 1, 1930; Dwight #141, November 4, 1930; and Dwight #439, October 31, 1931, DIJ.

10. Sheldon Glueck and Eleanor T. Glueck, *Five Hundred Delinquent Women* (New York: Alfred A. Knopf, 1934; reprint, Krauss Reprint, 1971), 299.

11. Allison Morris, *Women, Crime and Criminal Justice* (Oxford: Basil Blackwell Ltd., 1987) 52.

12. MHO Report on Dwight #504, October 26, 1932, DIJ.

13. MHO Report, December 6, 1927, and PBH, December 7, 1927, on Dwight #503 (Joliet #990e), DIJ. Board members became antagonistic when they realized that Harden was not really a "white" woman. The following absurd exchange fully reveals their racism. At the

end of her hearing examiner Benson asked, "He [her husband] was a colored man, wasn't he?" Harden replied, somewhat evasively: "Well, he was colored and Irish." Another board member interjected, "Red hair?" Harden answered that "he was not red haired. He was mixed." Benson responded caustically, "You mean he was black and green." Harden replied, "No, he was red complexion, but he was not dark." She added, perhaps somewhat defiantly, implicitly rejecting the board's racial bigotry, "Of course, I have done more wrong after I married him than I ever did before." A third board member then interjected, "Are you colored blood too?" Harden admitted that her mother was "Indian," a fact that she could have denied given that her prison records listed her as "white." After this exchange the board summarily dismissed Harden. In the brief summary of their deliberations, Benson recapitulated the facts of her case, reiterating the legally irrelevant point that Harden was "part Indian" and "her husband was a colored man," although he duly noted that "she says he was colored and Irish."

14. Excerpts from mental health officer reports in Joliet male inmate jackets: #6106e, May 8, 1936; #4129e, April 13, 1931; #3910e, February 21, 1933; #7890d, March 23, 1928. Male inmate jackets for Joliet have been preserved and are at the Illinois State Archives (restricted access). In another typical case the mental health officer characterized a male convict as someone who had "never been industrious," had led a "nomadic existence," and had "hoboed all over the country for years." Nevertheless, he concluded that "extended supervision is not necessary" and recommended parole (MHO Report on Joliet male #9045e, January 12, 1941).

15. MHO Report on Joliet male #7890d, March 23, 1928.

16. MHO Report on Dwight #439, October 31, 1931, DIJ.

17. MHO Report on Dwight #432, September 17, 1931, DIJ.

18. Admission Report on Dwight #2456, November 26, 1947, DIJ.

19. Pre-Parole Report on Dwight #2456, November 9, 1948, DIJ.

20. Herman M. Adler, "The Criminologist and the Courts," *Journal of the American Institute of Criminal Law and Criminology* 11 (1920), 423–24. Anne Meis Knupfer, *Reform and Resistance: Gender, Delinquency, and America's First Juvenile Court* (New York: Routledge, 2001); for incisive analyses of the construct of "psychopathy" see Elizabeth Lunbeck, *The Psychiatric Persuasion: Knowledge, Gender, and Power in Modern America* (Princeton, N.J.: Princeton University Press, 1994), and Ian Parker, Eugenie Georgaca, David Harper, Terence McLaughlin, and Mark Stowell-Smith, eds., *Deconstructing Psychopathology* (London: Sage, 1995).

21. Glueck and Glueck, *Five Hundred Delinquent Women*, 299 (emphasis in original).

22. ISRW 1936, 469.

23. Harriet J. Comstock, "The Woman Offender in Illinois," *Welfare Bulletin* (1927), 312; Audrey B. Bower, "Classification in Penal Institutions with Special Reference to the State Reformatory for Women, Dwight, Illinois (M.A. thesis: University of Illinois, 1942), 5.

24. ISRW 1940, 769. Six psychiatrists were employed at Dwight between 1932 and 1942; four stayed for only a year. The reformatory's founders had also hoped to interest universities in conducting research at the institution. However, lack of housing facilities prevented the utilization of more than one intern at a time. Staff lived on the second floor of the administration building. In the 1940s the superintendent finally acquired her own residence, a farmhouse one-quarter mile from the institution.

25. Psychiatric Progress Notes on Dwight #2023, September 18, 1945 and April 23, 1946, Dwight #2173, DIJ.

26. MHO Report on Dwight #508, December 3, 1941. Majeski was released in 1950 after serving twenty-four years. In another case, after six months of outbursts, complaints, observation, interviews, and hospitalization, Dr. Fishback still was not sure whether a woman's behavior "was entirely feigned [in an attempt to receive a transfer to another job assignment] or whether she had a brief psychotic episode." Again Fishback concluded the obvious: "At any rate she is a very unstable person who reacts out of proportion to the situation" (Progress note #2, January 7, 1942, reproduced in Audrey B. Bower, "Classification in Penal Institutions with Special Reference to the State Reformatory for Women, Dwight, Illinois" [M.A. thesis, University of Illinois, 1942], 51.)

27. ISRW 1940, 769. Dorothy Burkhardt, a part-time music teacher from 1930 to 1937, noticed this tension between treatment and custodial staff: "My friends were shocked that they hired me. 'How come you're working at the reformatory? Those girls shouldn't have music.' Even a lot of the warders felt that way. But Miss Hazard wanted to provide as much to build them up morally as she could." Illinois women's clubs maintained an active interest in Dwight during the 1930s. One club paid Burkhardt's salary. However, in her seventh year the state took over funding, and the position "got to be a political job." Burkhardt was replaced by a woman who "knew nothing about music aside from how to play the piano." Burkhardt regarded her seven years as a "real learning opportunity." Like most former employees, she admitted that it was her "first time working with black girls." She was impressed by their spirituals. "I didn't know a thing about them. It was amazing to me, how each girl, no matter where they came from, each knew those spirituals and they could all harmonize beautifully. . . . I just sat there and listened" (interview, December 17, 1995).

28. ISRW 1936, 460; ISRW 1938, 611; ISRW 1939, 560; ISRW 1940, 877. Dwight's assistant superintendent during the 1930s was a patronage appointee who provided Hazard with little help.

29. IRSW 1938, 609–12. Hazard took graduate classes in psychology at Illinois State University and the University of Chicago during the late 1930s.

30. Kathleen G. Strickland, "Correctional Institutions for Women in the United States," (Ph.D. diss., Syracuse University, 1967), 166.

31. Classification Report on Dwight #3099, July 18, 1959, DIJ.

32. Case Summary for the Parole Board on Dwight #2717, 6, Nov. 29, 1952, DIJ.

33. Interviews with Dr. Lois Green, Dwight sociologist from 1964 to 1977, April 27, 1996, and Dr. Nathan Kantrowitz, Stateville sociologist from 1957 to 1963, April 18, 1996. Kantrowitz wrote parole prediction reports on thirty to forty prisoners a week, spending an average of a little over an hour each. After interviewing the prisoner he immediately dictated his reports, which were typed by inmate clerks. "No observation, just one interview. Pretty superficial." This was his only responsibility. The state's male prisoners all spent their first month at the Joliet Diagnostic Center, where their admissions reports were prepared. Kantrowitz, *Close Control: Managing a Maximum Security Prison* (New York: Harrow and Heston, 1996), 1–2.

34. Illinois Department of Public Safety, *Annual Report of the Statistician* (Springfield: State of Illinois, 1942), 200. Classification percentages are my calculations from the raw numbers presented in DPS annual reports from 1957 to 1969.

35. Classification Report on Dwight #3668, June 1, 1959, 3, DIJ.

36. Interview with Carol Rawlings, December 14, 1995.

37. Sociologist's Report on Dwight #3602, July 13, 1960, and Admission Classification Report on Dwight #3721, August 18, 1961 (emphasis in original), DIJ.

38. Letter from Dwight #3551, December 18, 1958, MR C9-024; interview with Rawlings, December 14, 1995; interview with Wagner, December 16, 1995. Some of the blame may lie with the sheer number of reports—admissions, classification, pre-parole—that Robinson had to complete. The flood of new commitments after 1954 meant that Robinson, Dwight's single sociologist, though occasionally aided by Pontiac sociologist Albert Lassuy, was swamped. His secretary reported, "We were behind on our work all the time. Many days I stayed to 9:00 at night typing reports. It was crazy, but the work had to be done" (anonymous interview, September 30, 1995). Likewise, sociologist Lois Green's assessments fail to reveal her deep empathy and advocacy for the women she evaluated.

CHAPTER 11

1. PBH for Dwight #540 (Joliet #9384d), October 23, 1929, DIJ. Before 1917 each prison had a single parole agent who was responsible for prisoners paroled throughout the state. Real supervision was minimal. The Department of Public Welfare increased the number of parole agents and assigned them to specific counties, enabling them to develop much closer relationships with local authorities. As Superintendent Will Colvin euphemistically

explained, "The more persons in each locality who can be interested in looking after people on parole makes better the chance that the prisoner will successfully go through the parole period" (Report of the Division of Pardons and Paroles, DPW 1923, 481). This increased surveillance also made "better the chance" that parole violators would be apprehended. After 1917 women who broke their parole were far more likely to be returned to prison than was the case during previous decades. Whereas between 1895 and 1910 fewer than half (43%) of female parole violators were apprehended and recommitted, in the 1920s 83 percent were returned, and by the 1950s 96 percent were sent back to prison.

2. By the mid–1960s the Parole Board began to tape record hearings and no longer prepared typed transcripts.

3. PBH for Dwight #540 (Joliet #9384d), October 23, 1929, DIJ.

4. Ibid.

5. MHO Report on Dwight #540 (Joliet #9384d), August 29, 1925.

6. MHO Report on Dwight #540 (Joliet #9384d), June 29, 1933.

7. 1895 *Laws of the State of Illinois*, (Springfield, Ill.: n.p.), 158.

8. David J. Rothman argues that nationally sentence lengths increased after the introduction of indeterminate sentencing (*Conscience and Convenience: The Asylum and Its Alternatives in Progressive America* (Boston: Little, Brown, and Co., 1980), 194–98.

9. PBH for Dwight #127 (Joliet #9737d), March 1926, DIJ. Only a dozen transcripts have been preserved for hearings held before the Colvin board.

10. Hinton G. Clabaugh, quoted in Andrew A. Bruce, "A Study of the Indeterminate Sentence and Parole in the State of Illinois," *Journal of the American Institute of Criminal Law and Criminology* 19 (1928), 85; DPW 1941, 499. A version of Bruce's two-hundred-page study is included in Illinois Association for Criminal Justice, *Illinois Crime Survey* (Chicago: Blakely Printing, 1929), 427–537. While nationally the average prisoner served 19.2 months in the 1930s, in Illinois the typical inmate served over five years. For most offenses men served slightly longer sentences than women: for murder, 10.0 years for men versus 9.7 for women; for manslaughter, 6.4 versus 5.9; for assault to kill, 6.6 versus 5.1; for a con game, 4.7 versus 3.1; for forgery, 4.4 versus 2.3; and for larceny, 4.1 versus 3.1. However, women served longer for bigamy, 2.3 years versus 1.8 years; for burglary, 4.6 versus 2.7; and for robbery, 4.6 versus 4.3 (DPW 1941, 499). Although women's shorter sentences may have reflected greater leniency or chivalrous treatment toward female offenders, legal factors were also involved. First, the average male convict had a more extensive prior criminal record than did the average female convict. Second, the character of women's offenses was often less serious than that of men's. Even though judges sentenced far fewer women than men to prison, many women were sentenced for crimes, particularly larceny or shoplifting, for which men often received only probation or short jail sentences. Thus, women were actually penalized more severely for lesser offenses.

11. Bruce, "Study of the Indeterminate Sentence," 199.

12. PBH for Dwight #358 (Joliet #2041e), November 1, 1933, and Dwight #2903, November 12, 1955, DIJ.

13. PBH for Dwight #429 (Joliet #1844e), February 5, 1929, DIJ. In other equally prejudiced exchanges Thompson focused on prisoners' ethnicity and religious customs, as the following excerpt suggests: "Q. What are you, Polish? A. Yes, sir, Polish descent. Q. Born in this country? A. Yes, sir. Q. What is your husband's nationality? A. Polish descent. Q. Any Jewish in your family? A. No, sir" (Dwight #550 [Joliet 1505e], September 10, 1930, DIJ).

14. PBH for Dwight #524 (Joliet #2995e), June 8, 1929, DIJ.

15. Interview with Dr. Nathan Kantrowitz, April 18, 1996.

16. "New Parole Board Is Appointed," *Joliet Evening Herald-News*, September 13, 1929.

17. Progressive Era legal reformers campaigned unsuccessfully to give the parole board the right to subpoena witnesses at their hearings, thereby condoning the board's practice of retrying prisoners' cases.

18. PBH for Dwight #627 (Joliet #3250e), June 4, 1930, DIJ.

19. PBH for Dwight #1104, November 2, 1938, and Case Summary for Dwight #3100, April 4, 1957, DIJ.

20. MHO Report on Dwight #131 (Joliet #4006e), March 25, 1931, DIJ.

21. Statement of Fact for Dwight #131 (Joliet #4006e), April 1, 1931, DIJ; PBH for Dwight #131 (Joliet #4006e), April 1, 1931 (emphasis in original).

22. PBH for Dwight #138 (Joliet #315e), December 1, 1930, and Dwight #1361, September 10, 1941, DIJ.

23. PBH for Dwight #126 (Joliet #3481e), November 6, 1930, DIJ.

24. PBH for Dwight #446 (Joliet #2792e), March 5, 1930, DIJ. To be declared clean, female prisoners had to receive ten consecutive negative results of a G.C. smear (a test that was administered weekly) and a negative Wassermann test.

25. The Illinois Prison Inquiry Commission complained that despite the creation of the ten-member board in 1927, men's parole hearings continued to be perfunctory (Illinois Prison Inquiry Commission, *The Prison System in Illinois: A Report to the Governor* [Springfield, Ill.: State of Illinois, 1937], 506–7). In an effort to make board decision making more scientific, the state's first Sociologist Actuary developed an instrument to predict parole success for male prisoners in 1933; it was revised periodically and used through the 1970s (Sam Daykin, "The Use of Prediction Techniques in Parole Administration," *Welfare Bulletin* 11 [1938], 1).

26. Quotes from PBH for Dwight #544 (Joliet 1785e), October 1, 1930; Dwight #49, March 30, 1932; Dwight #50, March 30, 1934; Dwight #1919, October 5, 1945; Dwight #1562, March 13, 1941; and Dwight #3368, December 3, 1956, DIJ.

27. Letter from state's attorney, April 29, 1952, and PBH for Dwight #1252, October 5, 1938, DIJ.

28. PBH for Dwight #550 (Joliet #1505e), September 10, 1930, DIJ.

29. PBH for Dwight #550 (Joliet #1505e), March 25, 1932, DIJ.

30. Interview with Jamella Reynolds, May 23, 1996.

31. Adelaide Johnson (Dwight #544, Joliet #1785e), letter to Irene M. Gaines, September 23, 1928, Irene McCoy Gaines Papers, Box 1 (Folder 8), Chicago Historical Society. Johnson, an eighteen-year-old African American college student, represented the rare case of a woman who was twice able to convince the board to grant her parole. Johnson was convicted of a "confidence game" for cashing a check she claimed to have found. The mental health officer observed that "the girl seems greatly disgraced by her imprisonment. She has rather high standards, both moral and social, and has suffered because of these in her relations with other inmates of the Women's Prison. They have made fun of her personal appearance and consider her 'stuck up' and superior in her attitude." The board, equally impressed, paroled Johnson. She was returned eighteen months later after another check-cashing attempt failed. At her second hearing the board's questioning began on an accusatory note, but Johnson quickly charmed them and was paroled again, only to be returned for cashing another check, this time stolen from a mailbox. Because theft from a mailbox constituted a federal offense, she was sentenced to a year at the federal reformatory for women at Alderson, West Virginia. Afterward she was returned to Dwight to serve four more years on her original parole violation (MHO Report, January 2, 1929, and PBH, October 1, 1930 and September 28, 1932, DIJ).

32. PBH for Dwight #49, September 6, 1933; Dwight #949, January 9, 1936; Dwight 1396, November 27, 1939, DIJ.

33. Case Summary for Dwight #19, May 11, 1932, DIJ.

34. PBH for Joliet male #3797e, February 4, 1932, DIJ.

35. Letter from state's attorney and trial judge regarding Dwight #1953, July 31, 1941, DIJ.

36. PBH for Dwight #1953, February 3, 1946, DIJ.

37. PBH for Dwight #1386, October 3, 1939, DIJ.

38. In *Stateville: The Penitentiary in Mass Society,* James B. Jacobs reports that in 1960 Illinois prisoners were serving the second longest sentences in the nation (48). In 1969 Peter B. Bensinger, the first director of the Illinois Department of Corrections, observed that Illinois prisoners were "incarcerated for periods longer than 45 other states" (*Chicago Sun-Times,* December 14, 1969). For national statistics see the annual

reports titled *Prisoners Released from State and Federal Prisons and Reformatories*, published by the Bureau of the Census.

The Ward-Rennick Act has a long history. In 1937 the Illinois Senate, expressing strong hostility toward the parole board in its debates, passed an earlier version of the act. However, it was defeated in the House by a few votes. In 1939 both the Senate and the House approved the bill, but it was vetoed by the governor. It was reapproved by the Illinois Senate later that year but then failed to pass the House. See "Vote Parole Curb in Senate," *Chicago Tribune*, April 19, 1939. Throughout the 1930s the *Chicago Tribune* fueled hostility toward the parole board.

39. PBH for Dwight #2134, April 23, 1946; and Dwight #3048, June 12, 1956, DIJ.

40. Case Summary for Dwight #2173, March 4, 1947, DIJ. Women dismissed at their maximum were free from parole supervision; parole only applied in cases in which a prisoner was released early.

41. PBH for Dwight #2611, November 30, 1955, DIJ.

42. Letter written by Dwight #3212, December 1, 1957, MR B9-044.

43. Wickersham Commission, *Report on Penal Institutions, Probation, and Parole*, vol. 9 (1931; reprint, Montclair, N.J.: Patterson Smith, 1968), 133.

44. Pre-Parole Report on Dwight #1325, March 5, 1948, DIJ.

45. In *Conscience and Convenience*, historian David J. Rothman credits the parole boards he studied with greater rationality than that with which I credit the Illinois parole board. He concludes that despite numerous flagrant instances of capricious and discriminatory decision making, "parole outcomes were not invariably devoid of reason" (176). According to Rothman, parole boards focused on four common factors: developing their own estimates of the seriousness of the offense, establishing the prisoner's institutional conduct record, determining whether the prisoner had an acceptable parole sponsor, and ascertaining the extent of the prisoner's past criminal career. However, the first three of these factors were highly subjective. Rothman studied only men; he failed to examine women's parole hearings.

46. Wickersham Commission, *Report on Penal Institutions*, 134-35.

CHAPTER 12

1. Note to Acting Superintendent Mann regarding Dwight #1921, January 9, 1944, MR B9-014. All quotes from warders' daily reports and discipline tickets are from the microfilmed copies of women's inmate jackets (see appendix A). Only four jackets from the 1930s and roughly forty from the 1940s were microfilmed. Most microfilmed jackets date from the 1954-1968 period. Therefore, jackets from the 1950s are disproportionately quoted in this chapter.

2. Warder's Daily Report (WDR) on Dwight #1955, June 22, 1944, MR B9-014. Mildred Viles, a warder for two months in 1962, echoed Miller's complaints: "You had to get down on your hands and knees to get them to do something. I would have to practically do it myself." The inmates were "slow, so slow. They didn't really work them. Took them half an hour just to wash one window." Viles quit, figuring that "my temper would soon get the better of me" (telephone interview with Viles, April 8, 1996).

3. Classification Report on Dwight #2015, March 13, 1945, MR B9-023.

4. Estelle B. Freedman, *Their Sisters' Keepers: Prison Reform in America, 1830-1930* (Ann Arbor: University of Michigan Press, 1981), 101 and 100, and Nicole Hahn Rafter, *Partial Justice: Women Prisons, and Social Control*, 2nd ed. (New Brunswick, N.J.: Transaction Publishers), xii. For a more extensive critique of their conclusions see L. Mara Dodge, "'Her Life Has Been an Improper One': Women, Crime, and Prisons in Illinois, 1835-1933" (Ph.D. diss., University of Illinois at Chicago, 1998), 58-78.

5. Freedman, *Their Sisters' Keepers*, 101-102. The concept of prisons as "total institutions" derives from the theory of sociologist Irving Goffman (*Asylums* [New York: Anchor, 1961]). Despite their anger, humiliation, and apprehension over incarceration, none of the former inmates I interviewed felt that they had been "stripped of

their normal identities" during the month-long orientation period. One retorted, "A whole thirty days in pajamas in a room with a Bible. And they called that orientation" (interview with Jamella Reynolds, May 23, 1996).

6. Rafter, *Partial Justice*, 303, 307. For a similar argument see Nicole Hahn Rafter, "Chastising the Unchaste: Social Control Functions of a Woman's Reformatory, 1894–1931," in *Social Control and the State: Historical and Comparative Essays,* ed. Stanley Cohen and Andrew Scull (Oxford: Martin Robertson, 1983), 288–311.

7. The question of "reformation" must be conceptually separated from that of "compliance" and even more from that of "conformity." To the extent that reformatories succeeded, it was not simply their internal regimes of domesticity and proper femininity that tamed these young women, but broader social, economic, political, and cultural forces that constrained and in some cases overpowered their youthful resistance to social norms. For a particularly thoughtful analysis see Ruth M. Alexander, *The "Girl Problem": Female Sexual Delinquency in New York, 1900–1930* (Ithaca: Cornell University Press, 1995).

8. PBH for Dwight #1, May 26, 1931, DIJ. In 1930 the reformatory's advisory committee sent letters to Illinois's judges extolling the new institution and encouraging them to sentence only young first offenders "amenable to rehabilitation." Lizzie Von Stuben, the reformatory's first inmate, was a nineteen-year-old white woman with no prior criminal record. Judge Mathews explained, "I sentenced this girl to Dwight for her own good." Von Stuben and a group of friends had engaged in an unplanned burglary of a house on their way home from a dance, stealing clothes and other small items. Von Stuben participated after her boyfriend "called me yellow because I didn't want to go." The state's attorney wrote that her associations, "particularly association with one John B.," had "demanded that she be imprisoned at least for a sufficient length of time until she could, in a measure, adjust and find herself." Thus, instead of viewing a reformatory sentence as a punishment, some officials fully subscribed to the theory that Dwight was a benign, treatment-oriented institution.

9. Telephone interview with Paula Putnam, August 16, 1995; letter from Dwight #3617 to her mother, May 16, 1963, MR A9-025.

10. *Rock Island Argus,* December 2, 1932. The following headlines were representative: "Governor Finds No Cell Blocks in Reformatory," "State Building Laboratory to Reclaim Women," "Reformatory is Monument to Social Workers," "'Sister' to Greet Women in New Reformatory," "Illinois Leads in Care of Women Offenders," and "New Women's Prison Like Chateau: Hope of Redemption, Experiment for First Offenders."

11. Mary B. Harris, *I Knew Them in Prison* (New York: Viking, 1936), 386.

12. "Reformatory Superintendent Speaks," *Decatur Herald and Review,* December 13, 1932. Hazard used these exact words in several speeches and interviews.

13. WDRs on Dwight #1905, April 19, 1948, MR B9-014, and Dwight #3116, July 3, 1956, MR A9-003.

14. WDRs on Dwight #3445, December 6, 1958 and March 1, 1960, MR C9-021.

15. WDR on Dwight #3635, May 23, 1959, MR A9-025.

16. WDR on Dwight #3693, May 29, 1960, MR A9-015.

17. Interview with Jamella Reynolds, May 23, 1996. A former switchboard operator reported, "The warder would have to call the switchboard when the inmate left the cottage. Then another warder would have to call when she got to the destination. That went on all day. You nearly broke your neck on that switchboard. I tried to get out of there fast" (anonymous interview, April 5, 1996).

18. Dwight #3551, letter to sister, November 30, 1958, MR A9-003.

19. PBH for Dwight #562, March 3, 1936, DIJ.

20. Although Hazard repeatedly stressed the "therapeutic value of outdoor work," urban women often failed to appreciate it. In a typical note a warder reported in 1957: "While we were cleaning up after dressing chickens at the farm I overheard Mildred Arthur discussing her dislike of the farm. . . . Mildred said, 'I am a city girl, a dope fiend and I am going back to using dope when I leave this place. I am going to steal or do anything I can to get off this farm assignment. I would even go to the "hole" for five

months.'" Despite her vocal complaints, the staff refused to heed Mildred's request for reassignment. However, two months later she was transferred after Superintendent Biedermann noted in her file "frequent reports" of a suspected homosexual relationship between Mildred and another farm worker (WDR on Dwight #3440, August 19, 1957, MR A9-022).

21. At a speech in Chicago in the winter of 1929 Mary B. Harris recommended Hazard to the club women of Illinois. Although she was "loath to see her go," Harris "could not think of a more qualified woman." In 1932 the vocal support of Illinois club women saved Hazard from dismissal after fall elections brought in a Democratic administration. For Hazard's background see the *Rock Island Argus,* February 7, 1930 and November 19, 1931; the *Davenport* (Iowa) *Times,* July 20, 1930; the *Pontiac* (Illinois) *Daily Leader,* November 24, 1930; the (Bloomington) *Daily Pantagraph,* 6 and November 15, 1930; and the *Chicago Daily News,* April 15, 1932.

22. ISRW 1936, 465; ISRW 1937, 608; ISRW 1940, 877.

23. ISRW 1938, 612.

24. Ibid.

25. Helen Hazard, graduate paper for SSA Course #341, February 25, 1938, 6, provided by Marian Conrath, Hazard's secretary.

26. Staff often expressed contradictory racial attitudes. The employee who voiced one of these disparaging comments was also quick to note that "black inmates were not worse than the white. I got more respect from my black girls than the whites." Several warders agreed that they would "take a black inmate over a white one any day."

27. Interview with Martha Howard, May 4, 1996. Howard eventually overcame her racial fears and became a warder. She worked at Dwight for forty years and was one of the few townspeople to befriend African American employees in the early 1970s.

28. ISRW 1942, 116–17.

29. Interview with Marian Conrath, October 5, 1995. Mrs. Mann died suddenly in October 1948 of a heart attack while on her way to a Republican party gathering. In public hearings in 1951 Superintendent Doris Whitney blamed some of the institution's problems on war-time laxity and Hazard's absence, during which "the place was allowed to deteriorate through lack of proper supervision." "Open Probe of Conditions at Dwight Prison," *Streator Daily Times-Press,* April 12, 1951.

30. ISRW 1948, 135. For a more positive portrayal of Dwight in 1947 see "Oakdale Prison for Women High on Penal Scale," *Chicago Sunday Tribune,* March 23, 1947. For the 1940s see also: Leonor Campbell's six-part series in the (Bloomington) *Daily Pantagraph,* 4–December 11, 1941, and Edan Wright, *Chicago Daily News,* 10–August 15, 1949 and 10–November 12, 1948 (a "girl undercover" series).

31. ISRW 1948, 135. At the same time, a new parole board ruled that inmates were eligible to appear for their hearings whether or not they were in "A grade," thereby eliminating another powerful incentive to good behavior. This policy was reversed in 1952, but not before it had wreaked havoc with discipline.

32. MHO Report on Dwight #1900, June 3, 1952, DIJ.

33. WDR on Dwight #1921, September 26, 1949, MR B9-014.

34. Rose Anne McPherson, storekeeper (1948–1950), letter to author, October 5, 1995. Her views were supported by two other former staff members, who requested complete anonymity.

35. Rose Anne McPherson, letter to author, October 5, 1995. Farber continued on to a controversial career in Illinois corrections. At one point he was forced to resign as superintendent of the Sheridan State Training School for Boys as a result of accusations of brutality. See *Chicago Tribune* and *Streator Daily Times-Press,* 20 February to March 10, 1961.

36. McPherson, telephone interview, October 14, 1995, and letters to author dated October 5, 1995 and April 8, 1996. McPherson was "mercifully thankful" to leave her job after two years when her husband was transferred out of state. McPherson's negative assessment of Hazard reflected the views of warders and newer staff. Younger employees who knew Hazard only at the end of her career tended to describe her as an overly strict and iron-willed "battle ax," unyielding, stubborn, humorless,

old-fashioned, "strait laced," and set in her ways. Clerk Charlene Berry (1951–1953) contended that "Hazard wanted it run the way she wanted it. As long as you did it her way it was O.K. They [Hazard and Business Manager Iris Eyer] really thought they owned the place." McPherson resented Hazard's Victorian stress on decorum ("all the yes ma'am, no ma'am rules") and the "prissy, ladylike" atmosphere she sought to impose. However, five other employees hired during the same period described Hazard much more positively. Most were professional or clerical workers whose jobs rarely involved close contact with warders. They praised Hazard in the following terms: "strict but fair," "knew her job well and did it," "no monkey business but not unreasonable," "commanded respect, maintained clear and consistent rules," and "a real lady."

37. "Doris S. Whitney Appointed Supt.," *Dwight Star and Herald,* July 23, 1950.

38. Staff who worked at Dwight in the 1950s and 1960s reported that they needed the approval of a local political committeeman to be employed. When hired, they were required to sign an undated resignation letter, which they automatically turned in when a new governor was elected. For patronage politics in Illinois's men's prisons, see James B. Jacobs, *Stateville: The Penitentiary in Mass Society* (Chicago: University of Chicago Press, 1977), 19–23 and 31–32.

39. ISRW 1951, 108. *Pontiac* (Illinois) *Daily Leader,* April 21, 1951.

40. "Open Probe of Conditions at Dwight Prison," *Streator Daily Times-Press,* April 12, 1951.

41. "Oakdale Senate Probe Opens," *Dwight Star and Herald,* April 20, 1951. For an analysis of custodial staff's similarly negative response to a new educational program at the federal woman's reformatory at Alderson, West Virginia, see Rose Giallombardo, *Society of Women: A Study of a Woman's Prison* (New York: Wiley & Sons, 1966), 57–73.

42. "Oakdale State Invetigation Opens," *Pontiac* (Illiois) *Daily Leader,* April 12, 1951.

43. "State Official Claims Von Ruden 'Lied' about Miss Whitney," *Pontiac* (Illinois) *Daily Leader,* April 21, 1951.

44. Mrs. Spandet, a member of the county Democratic central committee, claimed a waitress had told her that Whitney visited a local tavern two or three times a week. Upon cross-examination the waitress denied the statement, explaining that she had only stated that Whitney visited the tavern, which was also a restaurant, two or three times during the entire year. The reformatory's dentist (a member of the state Democratic central committee) testified that Whitney engaged in frequent drinking parties, an accusation he later admitted was based solely on hearsay. He was subsequently fired when it was revealed that he charged inmates fees for his services. Department of Public Works director Hoehler effectively refuted an allegation that Whitney had been fired from her previous position for incompetence. See extensive coverage in the *Pontiac* (Illinois) *Daily Leader,* the *Streator Daily Times-Press,* the *Dwight Star and Herald,* and the Bloomington *Daily Pantagraph,* 12–April 30, 1951.

45. "Stratton Fires Head of Dwight Reformatory," *Chicago Tribune,* January 28, 1953; "Doris Whitney Fired," *Streator Daily Times-Press,* January 29, 1953; and "Helen Hazard—New Head," *Dwight Star and Herald,* January 30, 1953.

46. *Dwight Star and Herald,* September 18, 1953 and June 11, 1954.

47. "Dwight Prison Luxuries Hit by Director," *Streator Daily Times-Press,* July 26, 1954. In 1969 per capita costs at Dwight were still two to three times higher those at the state's male penitentiaries ($6,045 versus $2,305).

48. *People v. Amore,* 369 Ill. 245 (1938), and *People v. Lewis* 108 N. E. 2d 473 (1952).

49. Helen E. Gibson, "Women's Prisons: Laboratories for Penal Reform," in *The Female Offender,* ed. Laura Crites (Lexington, Mass.: Lexington Books), 99 (emphasis in original).

CHAPTER 13

1. Ann Wagner, letter to Biedermann concerning Dwight #3904, August 1961; WDR for Dwight #3904, August 10, 1961, MR B9-047.

2. Margaret Schlosser, Special Report, Dwight #3904, August 10, 1961, MR B9-047.

3. Disciplinary Ticket for Dwight #3904, December 18, 1961, MR A9-005.

Women who used profanity toward staff were immediately sent to segregation and demoted in grade and therefore lost good time. In a typical incident from 1959 a warder reported: "Corrine Geller has been disagreeable all day and played her radio to [sic] loud and I asked her to turn it down, she didn't so I pulled out the plug. Then at dinner time she started raising Cain. . . . I asked her to stop it and she didn't. She said she was no child and she was over 18 and that I acted as if I wanted her to kick and lick my ass for the food and that dam [sic] radio . . . and these bitches this and M.F.'s that, so I called Mrs. Biedermann and she was out, so I called Capt. Fitzpatrick and told him I wanted him to send some Guards down and move the things out of her room, because I wanted her put on the floor [i.e., segregation]. So he did. Tonight at check time Corrine was or pretended to be real sweet." Geller was given a month in segregation and demoted to C grade (WDR on Dwight #3328, March 13, 1959, MR B9-039).

4. "Prison Heads Quits," *Chicago American*, March 7, 1962.

5. Linda Senter's mother worked at Dwight in the early 1950s. Senter recalled her mother's outrage that "Biedermann wanted the staff to inform on each other." Her mother quit, returning only after Biedermann resigned (interview with Linda Senter, April 26, 1996).

6. Interviews with former inmates Jamella Reynolds (May 23, 1996), Marcia Miller (December 8, 1995), and Carol Rawlings (December 14, 1995). Similarly, sociologist Lois Green (1964–1977) often heard inmates saying, "That would never have happened under Biedermann." The unusual circumstances of Gloria Van Overbake's suicide fueled rumors of foul play. Using a noose fashioned from blankets, Overbake managed to hang herself from a bar that was barely over her head on the door of her segregation cell. Warder Sara Ruddell recalled rumors that Overbake had recently completed two months in segregation after being caught in a "compromising" position (i.e., homosexual act). Ruddell speculated that "She probably thought they were going to keep her there forever" (telephone interview 4/3/96). (Ruddell was hired shortly after Biederman's dismissal.) The thirty-three-year old Van Overbake, repeatedly described as "mannish," an "avowed homosexual," and a "disciplinary problem," had served three misdemeanor sentences at Dwight in 1951, 1955, and 1957. In April 1959, she received a "two-to-eight" year sentence for burglary. Five months later she escaped but was quickly recaptured and returned to Dwight. Her suicide occurred the following evening. For newspaper coverage see: "Oakdale Inmate Recaptured," *Dwight Star and Herald* 23 September 1959; "Dwight Fugitive Returned," *Pontiac Daily Leader* 21 September 1959; "Prisoner Found Hanged at Dwight," [Bloomington] *Pantagaph* 24 September 1959; "Inmate Placed in Solitary . . . Noose Fashioned from Blankets," *Pontiac Daily Leader* 24 September 1959; and "Coroner's Juries Rule on Deaths," *Dwight Star and Herald* 15 October 1959. For Overbake's previous escape attempt see, "Inmate Uses Fake Gun to Leave Disciplinary Cottage," *Dwight Star and Herald* 28 January 1955.

7. In one case Biedermann noted: "Inmate anonymous talked about different girls but mostly about Margaret O'Malley, saying she was really smart and clever and her quiet ways and manners was just to catch some one off guard." Another informant alleged that two women "engaged in sex relations in the washroom at Jane Addams Hall during band lessons. Other inmates knew about this and some saw it happen." Not all such information proved correct. In one case a warder noted: "LaRuth Hendricks passed by and said that 'hootch' was being made at Frances Willard Cottage and supposed to be in the attic. She also reported that Ella Mason was carrying a razor blade in a cigarette package. Capt. Fitzpatrick notified at 11:05 A.M. but was unable to find 'hootch' or razor blade." If discovered, inmate informants suffered severe ostracism. In one case a warder observed, "All I could get from Virginia is that the girls don't like her. It is all over the campus that she is a 'stool pigeon,' and the girls on the truck wont [sic] talk to her" (WDRs on Dwight #3197, June 21, 1956, MR B9-044; Dwight #3351, January 3, 1958; Dwight #3204, June 20, 1957, MR B9-044; and Ann Wagner, letter to Biedermann concerning Dwight #3889, July 19, 1961, MR B9-011).

8. Ruth Biedermann, note to Dwight #3334, October 30, 1957, MR B9-014. Staff kept precise accounts of prisoners' correspondence. During the 1930s and 1940s these

reports were fairly general: "Mary hears from various members of her family." Bieder-mann demanded more exacting records: "Janet Jones writes very regularly to, and re-ceives fairly regularly letters from daughter, Anna Smith (was Anna Jones—now mar-ried). She writes and hears from daughter, Roberta, very seldom—she is a child. She writes fairly regularly, but hears only occasionally from sister, Aurelia Patterson. She sent one letter to niece, Brenda Prizen, but received none. She writes occasionally to, but seldom hears from, brother, Frank Mullen. She has received one letter from friend, Belinda Coombs—sent none. She received one letter from a nun, sent none" (Biennial Classification Reports, DIJ).

9. Dwight #3551, letter to sister, January 16, 1959, MR C9-024; interview with Stowe Symon, August 6, 1996. Review of correspondence was never perfunctory. In a case of careful sleuthing Biedermann uncovered the following "conspiracy": "Lenore Wooster and Earlie Powell had an affection for one another while both were in this in-stitution. Earlie was paroled in October. . . . It has come to light that Earlie had an ap-proved friend on her corresponding list by the name of Mrs. Rose Burroughs at 4267 S. Yale Ave, Chicago, IL. Lenore has an aunt on her approved corresponding list by the name of Mrs. Selma Burroughs. The aunt was investigated at 3235 N. Clyborne Ave, but on April 1 her letters began to come from 4267 S. Yale Avenue. . . . It is believed that this is a conspiracy for the two inmates to correspond with one another." (Names and addresses have all been changed.)

10. WDR on Dwight #3677, April 12, 1961, MR B9-011. In another instance Bie-dermann reported, "Two kites were found by Mrs. Dickson, torn in little bits under Maura O'Sheary's window. They were pieced together and checked against handwrit-ing and found to be Margaret Malloy's handwriting." The superintendent questioned Malloy, who denied writing the notes. She received eight days' solitary confinement for lying (WDR on Dwight #3197, January 7, 1957, MR B9-045).

11. "Dwight Reformatory Superintendent Quits," [Bloomington] *Pantagraph,* March 6, 1961; disciplinary ticket on Dwight #3246, September 15, 1961, MR B9-046; letter to Biedermann from Dwight #3264, March 13, 1958, MR C3-014. When outside letters sent to inmates were censored and "held," it was official policy not to inform the inmate. Nor was the sender informed that the letter was not delivered. In 1958 James Emmerson, a particularly distraught husband, wrote Superintendent Bieder-mann: "This letter is in regards to my wife. . . . I received a four line letter from her to-day stating that she has not heard from me but twice in the last two months. I have written about fifty letters (every other day) and around twenty-five Xmas cards (every day since the first of Dec.) I feel sure that my letters were in accordance with the rules." Emmerson begged Biedermann to "kindly notify her as to the facts pertaining to my correspondence." Biedermann responded that prisoners were allowed to write and receive only one letter per week per correspondent. However, because Mr. Emmer-son was being held at Cook County Jail awaiting trial, she had reduced his number to once a month (without informing him). In a contrite tone, Emmerson immediately answered that he was unaware of this rule and "never meant to abuse the privilege." Although in the future he would "be content" to write once a month, he beseeched Biedermann to give his wife all his previous letters "as she was sickly" and "close to a nervous breakdown" on account of not hearing from him. Biedermann's response was not noted. Letters from husband to Dwight #3551, December 22, 1958 and December 31, 1958, MR A9-003. A former mailroom supervisor (1962–1987) confirmed this pol-icy (interview with Vicky Washton, April 28, 1996).

12. Letter to Superintendent Biedermann from Martha Ainsworth (Dwight #3425), January 15, 1959, MR A9-022.

13. WDRs on Dwight #3648, October 25, 1960, and November 1, 1960, MR A9-026.

14. WDR on Dwight #3648, November 20, 1960, MR A9-026.

15. WDRs on Dwight #3215, November 7, 1957, MR B9-045; Dwight #3197, September 5, 1961, MR A9-034; and Dwight #3909, August 26, 1961, MR A9-009

16. WDR on Dwight #2721, September 30, 1957, MR A9-020.

17. Letter to Superintendent Biedermann from Dwight #3394, March 8, 1961, MR C9-024.

18. Russell P. Dobash, R. Emerson Dobash, and Sue Gutteridge, *The Imprisonment of Women* (London: Basil Blackwell, 1986), 176; WDR on Dwight #3829, June 22, 1961, MR A9-020.

19. WDRs on Dwight #3815, May 2, 1961, MR A9-015; Dwight #3298, April 7, 1956, MR A9-028; and Dwight #3682, April 29, 1960, MR B9-049. Staff favored certain cottages due to the reputation of their cooks. In interviews many fondly recalled the wonderful home cooking they enjoyed before the centralized dining room was constructed in 1967.

20. *Davenport* (Iowa) *Times*, "Women's Reformatory at Dwight," July 20, 1931. In 1958 Biedermann succeeded in hiring a local high school teacher who offered part-time evening courses in commercial and secretarial subjects. This expanded education program helped occupy the time of otherwise idle inmates, especially as farm work was being phased out. She also brought in a TV College program. Whereas in 1952 roughly 20 percent of inmates had been enrolled in elementary-level classes, school participation rose to 45 percent in 1961.

21. WDR on Dwight #3435, May 3, 11, 12, and 28, 1962, MR A9-006.

22. WDR on Dwight #3220, August 8, 1958, MR A9-015.

23. Letter to Bernard Robinson from Dwight #3220, August 16, 1958, MR A9-015.

24. Illinois General Assembly, Commission to Visit and Examine State Institutions, Penal Division, *Report of the Penal Division of the Legislative Commission to Visit and Examine State Institutions* (Springfield, Ill.: The Commission, 1959), 1. Throughout the 1960s the commission repeated its claims that "the institution is poorly designed and difficult to operate efficiently." It called for not only new cell blocks, but also a centralized kitchen and dining room as a major cost-cutting measure.

25. Helen E. Gibson, "Women's Prisons: Laboratories for Penal Reform," in *The Female Offender*, ed. Laura Crites (Lexington, Mass.: Lexington Books), 99. Political prisoner Helen Bryan stressed the pettiness and pervasiveness of prison rules in her account of her incarceration at the Alderson Federal Women's Reformatory in the early 1950s (see Helen Bryan, *Inside* [Boston: Houghton Mifflin, 1953]).

26. James B. Jacobs, *Stateville: The Penitentiary in Mass Society* (Chicago: University of Chicago Press), 44 and 38.

27. Nathan Kantrowitz, *Close Control: Managing a Maximum Security Prison* (New York: Harrow and Heston, 1996), 38.

28. My percentages regarding male prison infractions are from raw numbers provided by Kantrowitz, *Close Control*, 130. Another 16 percent of men's punishments referred to unspecified "other" infractions, which may have been equally minor. Recent studies suggest that women prisoners are more likely to be punished for minor rule infractions than men, and to be punished more severely. See Dorothy S. McClellan, "Disparity in the Discipline of Male and Female Inmates in Texas Prisons," *Women and Criminal Justice* 5 (1994), 71–97. McClellan found that women prisoners in Texas averaged 15.1 citations annually versus 2.9 for men. A national survey found that women averaged 2.0 annual violations and men 1.4 (Bureau of Justice Statistics, *Special Report: Prison Rule Violators* [Washington, D.C.: Government Printing Office, 1989]). In the 1990s correctional officers continued to view female prisoners as more troublesome, disruptive, demanding, and difficult to handle than male. See Joycelyn M. Pollock, *Sex and Supervision: Guarding Male and Female Inmates* (Westport, Conn.: Greenwood Press, 1990). A majority of correctional officers (66% of male and 72% of female) expressed a preference for working in men's prisons. Dana Michelle Britton reports similar findings in "Sex, Violence, and Supervision: A Study of the Prison as a Gendered Organization" (Ph.D. diss., University of Texas at Austin, 1995).

29. Interview with Carol Rawlings, December 14, 1995.

30. Britton, "Sex, Violence, and Supervision," 274–75.

31. Ward and Kassebaum, *Women's Prisons*, 90–92; interview with Edward Reis, December 3, 1995. Superintendent Hazard appears to have adopted a much more tolerant

attitude toward lesbianism. Although warders' reports in the 1940s occasionally referred to suspicions regarding "unwholesome friendships," these references were far fewer and the surveillance of inmate friendships far less intense than under Biedermann. Several younger staff members recalled being "protected" by Hazard and her chief assistants, who made veiled comments such as, "You don't need to know about that," or "You wouldn't understand." Some admitted that they were not even aware of the existence of lesbianism before they were hired.

32. WDRs on Dwight #3463, August 26, 1958, MR C9-021; Dwight #3648, September 17, 1960, MR A9-026; and Dwight #3919, August 10, 1961, MR A9-009.

33. WDRs on Dwight #1964, February 2, 1946, and Dwight #3625, May 26, 1959, MR A9-025.

34. WDRs on Dwight #3183, July 27, 1959; July 23, 1959; and November 28, 1959, MR A9-034.

35. WDR on Dwight #3183, November 29, 1959, MR A9-034.

36. WDR on Dwight #3346, June 13 and 19, 1957, MR B9-032.

37. Letter to her mother from Dwight #3361, November 30, 1958, MR A9-024.

38. John D'Emilio and Estelle B. Freedman, *Intimate Matters: A History of Sexuality in America* (New York: Harper and Row, 1988), 288 and 294. For more on the nation's increasingly hostile attitudes toward lesbianism after World War II, see Lillian Faderman, *Odd Girls and Twilight Lovers: A History of Lesbian Life in Twentieth-Century America* (New York: Columbia University Press, 1991), 130–59.

39. Admissions Report on Dwight #4278, May 28, 1964, MR B9-020.

40. Britton, "Sex, Violence, and Supervision," 219.

41. WDR on Dwight #3465, July 6, 1958, MR A9-026. See also Dwight #3455, MR A9-020.

42. WDR on Dwight #3465, January 18, 1959, MR A9-026.

43. WDR on Dwight #3186, May 14, 1959.

44. WDR on Dwight #3186, May 18, 1959.

45. WDR on Dwight #2880, July 14, 1959, MR B9-016.

46. Note to inmate from Dwight #3677, April 12, 1961, MR A9-004; WDR on Dwight #3445, June 27, 1958, MR C9-021.

47. WDR on Dwight #3466, December 11, 21, 22, and 25, 1957, MR C9-021.

48. WDR on Dwight #3466, June 6, 1958, MR C9-021.

49. Eventually, most staff who stayed developed some level of tolerance for homosexuality. Sue Welch, a counselor who was at Dwight in the 1970s, acknowledged that "working at Dwight was my first encounter with either real or 'pretend' lesbians." She recalled the first time an inmate confided in her that she had "married" another woman: "I was so horrified that I never inquired into what actually happened, but apparently they had some kind of a ceremony in their cottage day room. Apparently the correctional officer didn't 'rat' on them and the administration never found out." Over time this counselor was able to "put aside [her] dislike of homosexuality" and offer advice to a lesbian who was having problems with her lover (undated letter to author, c. May 1996).

50. "Prison Head Quits," *Chicago American*, March 5, 1962; "Ragen's Prompt Inquiry" (editorial), *Chicago American*, March 6, 1962.

51. "Biedermann Resigns Dwight Post," *Pontiac* (Illinois) *Daily Leader*, March 5, 1962; "Dwight Reformatory Superintendent Quits," (Bloomington) *Pantagraph*, March 8, 1962; "Women's Prison Chief Quits," *Chicago Daily News*, March 5, 1962.

52. "Prison Head Quits," *Chicago American*, March 5, 1962.

53. Sociologist Lois Green (1963–77) reported that her secretary, who had also been Lassuy's secretary, had told her that Biedermann "was so afraid of Lassuy that she 'bugged' his office." The secretary cautioned Green "not to consider my office secure for private conversations." Green assured me that the secretary "was a very smart woman and not at all crazy. I have no reason to believe she was not telling the truth

about the 'bugging.'" Whether the office was bugged or not, the allegation attests to the atmosphere of suspicion and paranoia that pervaded the institution during Biedermann's administration (Lois [Green] Guyon, e-mail to author, January 26, 2001).

CHAPTER 14

1. Letter to friend from Dwight #4591, March 11, 1967, MR B9-016. Warner's innocuous letter failed to pass censorship.

2. Interview with Dr. Lois (Green) Guyon, August 25, 1995. Note: Interviews cited in this chapter are footnoted only the first time they are quoted. All interviews were conducted in person unless otherwise noted. Real names are used unless the interviewee requested anonymity. See appendix B.

3. "Joliet Woman Named Dwight Prison Chief," *Joliet Herald News*, May 12, 1962.

4. Interviews with Edward Reis, December 3, 1995, and Carol Rawlings, December 15, 1995.

5. Telephone interview with a secretary, April 10, 1995; interview with Lieutenant Ester Dodge, September 1, 1995.

6. Assistant Superintendent Russell Powers was Ragen's brother-in-law. He had worked as business manager at the Menard penitentiary and the Sheridan boys' reformatory. Sociologist Lois Green characterized Powers as "a real thorn in my side for years. He was very civil, but there was a cold war between us. He had a lot of power and was constantly causing me grief. He felt that he couldn't control me and was always sure that I was going to hurt him, but I never did. . . . He was a genuine political hack." Similar conflicts had existed between Ragen and his sociologists when he was the warden at Stateville. James Jacobs reports, "Distrust engendered distrust and few professionals could tolerate more than a year or two in the Office of the Sociologist Actuary at Stateville" (*Stateville: The Penitentiary in Mass Society* [Chicago: University of Chicago Press, 1977], 94–100).

7. Green's supervisor, Stowe Symon, recalled Green's many conflicts with Morrissey. He reported, "One time I was sent down to fire Lois, but when I saw what it was about, I refused." Green's short-lived predecessor, sociologist Alice Hanrahan (1962–63), also had frequent conflicts with Morrissey (interview with Stowe Symon, August 6, 1996).

8. Nationally, about 5 to 6 percent of women enter prison pregnant. They face enormous problems. In 1991, 30 percent reported that they had received no prenatal care. In 1999, 20 percent had received no such care (U.S. Department of Justice, Bureau of Justice Statistics, *Special Report: Women in Prison* [Washington, D.C.: Government Printing Office, 1994], *Special Report: Women Offenders* [Washington, D.C.: Government Printing Office, 1999]). Most states require that inmates be shackled to a hospital bed while they give birth. Few allow women to keep their babies for more than a few hours after delivery.

9. Anonymous interview, August 16, 1996.

10. Kathleen G. Strickland, "Correctional Institutions for Women in the United States" (Ph.D. diss., Syracuse University, 1967), 206. Strickland's rankings were based on only four factors: inmate–treatment staff ratios; inmate-staff ratios; frequency of staff meetings; and administrative style. The median women's prison population was 175. Sixty-eight percent of the prisons employed part-time psychologists (averaging 18 hours per week); 61 percent employed full-time social workers (averaging 2.2 per institution); and 50 percent employed part-time psychiatrists (averaging 8.2 hours per week). One might speculate that the twenty-four women's facilities that were divisions of male institutions were even more likely to be exclusively custodial in their orientation.

11. Ibid., 188.

12. Quoted in James B. Jacobs, *Stateville: The Penitentiary in Mass Society* (Chicago: University of Chicago Press, 1977), 94; "John Howard Report Has Few Criticisms of Dwight Prison," *Pontiac Daily Leader*, March 18, 1970; Robert Getman quoted in League of Women Voters of Illinois, *Women in Prison* (Chicago, Ill.: League of Women Voters, 1973 [mimeograph]), 2.

13. Telephone interview with Sue Welch, May 2, 1996. For an insightful analysis of the contradictions of the counselor's position, see James B. Jacobs, "The Stateville Counselors: Symbol of Reform in Search of a Role, *Social Service Review* (1976), 138–47.

14. Telephone interview with Sue Welch, May 2, 1996; interview with Jeanie Fairman, September 29, 1995.

15. Whereas in the 1950s, 58 percent of women were required by the parole board to serve their full sentences, this proportion fell to 34 percent after 1965. Other factors also contributed to Dwight's population decline. Two former inmates had accused Biedermann of "holding up women's parole." It may be more accurate to say that Biedermann did little to facilitate their parole. In her 1965 annual report Morrissey acknowledged that "for a number of years there has been the problem of submerged parolees, unable to be released from the penitentiary [*sic*] because of inadequate help from family or friends to establish an approved parole sponsor" (49). Morrissey approved an innovative special release program that allowed Dwight chaplains and local volunteers to serve as parole sponsors. In the late 1960s the Department of Public Safety hired more female parole agents. Special pre-parole classes were offered at Dwight, enabling women to receive parole assistance even before their release. Pardons and commutations also increased. A former prisoner recalled that Governor Kerner "cut a lot of girls' time in the 1960s. Girls who had been here 30 years when I arrived, began to be released."

16. Margaret Morrissey, note concerning Dwight #3634, August 16, 1966, MR B9-023; League of Women Voters, *Women in Prison*, 5. The League of Women Voters found that even though regulations "forbid a stay of over 15 days in isolation, this is frequently violated by taking the woman out for one day after the 15 days and then putting her back on another charge" (4).

17. Margaret Morrissey, Report on Visits to Isolation Unit to see Dwight #3680, August 11, 1964, MR B9-047. According to Morrissey's annual reports, in 1965 the average prisoner received 3.2 disciplinary tickets; 12.4 percent of these violations were punished with segregation, which averaged 7.3 days. In 1969 average tickets increased slightly, to 3.5 per prisoner.

18. Interview with Jamella Reynolds, May 23, 1996. Ex-prisoner Delores Gilbert (1962–66) agreed, "It makes a person hard and bitter when they can't communicate. Only one letter a week. Just one sheet of paper allowed" (interview, November 12, 1995).

19. Rules against physical contact remained absolute. In the 1960s, inmates were not allowed to hold hands during Sunday night roller skating in the basement of Jane Addams Hall. Instead, both partners held onto the end of a handkerchief to prevent any physical contact.

20. Interview with Helen Lithgow, December 16, 1995.

21. In 1965 Morrissey noted that twenty-two employees had resigned that year but only eighteen had been hired. She characterized this turnover as "small" in comparison to that of the previous three years (ISRW, 1965, 47).

22. Telephone interviews with Thena Thom, April 14, 1996; Mildred Vives, April 8, 1996; and Mary Jean Scoles, April 9, 1996. Interview with Helen Lithgow, December 16, 1995.

23. Interviews with Betty Swearingen, April 26, 1996; Gwen Edwards, December 3, 1995; and Linda Senter, April 26, 1996.

24. Several women, all hired when they were in their late twenties, claimed that at the time they were hired (which ranged from 1949 to 1970) they were the youngest employee on staff.

25. However, Lt. Ester Dodge also admitted that "after a while you began to put up a shield. You did the very best you could for the eight hours you were there—it was good pay. But you tried not to take their stories to heart." Nor did Dodge share anything about herself. Many warders recalled a specific incident that led them to "put up a shield." Often it involved learning that an inmate with whom they felt unusually sympathetic had committed a particularly heinous offense, especially if it was a crime involving children.

26. Telephone interview with Georgia Perisee, September 18, 1995. Perisee's attitude was obvious to inmates. Ex-prisoner Lydia Townsend (1980–93) recalled that

Perisee was "straight up military. She didn't care. To her it was a job. She would write as many disciplinary tickets as she could. She never showed any compassion" May 9, 1996.

27. Telephone interview with Sarah Ruddell, April 3, 1996.

28. Telephone interview with Anna Cook, May 4, 1996. Interview with Vicky Washton, April 28, 1996. CO Pam Neal characterized the new policy of rotating officers' assignments in the 1970s, implemented by male wardens, as "horribly confusing and terribly stressful." She explained, "You were thrown in there in a unit with thirty-four women you didn't know from Adam, and you were responsible for their whereabouts and their assignments. The philosophy was to keep the officers and residents from becoming too close to one another. The administration felt that once a CO was on a unit too long they started getting too lenient. You can tell that this was men deciding!" (Telephone interview, May 5, 1996).

29. Interview with Jeanie Fairman, September 29, 1995.

30. Several white employees acknowledged the racial hostility local residents expressed when African Americans first moved to the town of Dwight. Martha Howard reported that she "tried to get her husband to speak to town businessmen about including Assistant Warden Herb Bailey in their business groups, but they resisted." She also tried to get the library to hire Bailey's wife as a librarian, "but they wouldn't hire her either." Howard concluded that "Dwight just wouldn't accept them. They wouldn't accept them now either" (interview, May 4, 1996).

31. Interview with Susan Lithgow, December 17, 1995.

32. Telephone interview with Imogene Becker, December 12, 1995.

33. Interestingly, several women incarcerated in the 1980s spoke of appreciating the older female correctional officers over the "young rookies." Lydia Townsend singled out correctional officers Cook, Dodge, and Helen Lithgow, characterizing them as "unique" and "compassionate." She explained: "By them being there for so long they could sort out the real from the unreal. They knew and heard who the serious inmates were. They treated them with respect." However, Townsend felt that the administration "didn't appreciate the older COs who were compassionate." Younger staff appeared more contemptuous of inmates, as well as deeply resentful of the privileges they enjoyed. Several voiced sentiments similar to the following: "It's so nice for them now. They have a bed, food, TVs, can order their clothes out of a J.C. Penney catalog. What more could they want?" (anonymous interviewee).

34. Illinois General Assembly Commission to Visit and Examine State Institutions, Subcommittee on Penal Institutions, *Report of the Subcommittee on Penal Institutions of the Legislative Commission to Visit and Examine State Institutions* (Springfield, Ill.: The Commission, 1976), 1.

35. Claudine Schweber, "Beauty Marks and Blemishes: The Coed Prison as a Microcosm of Integrated Society," *The Prison Journal* 64, 3–15.

36. Lieutenant Dodge and correctional officer Pam Neal recalled similarly contemptuous attitudes by male staff in the 1970s.

37. For coverage of the sex scandal see *Chicago Tribune*, 10 September–October 3, 1979. Anna Aylward and Jim Thomas, "Quiescence in Women's Prisons Litigation: Some Exploratory Issues" *Justice Quarterly* 1 (1984), 256.

38. Townsend vociferously protested her transfer to Dixon: "I didn't want to go. I tried everything in my power not to go. . . . You don't do human beings like that. You don't put males and females together but then say you can't be together. Women and men with hormones racing. Eighty women sitting in a cafeteria in the middle of 900 to 1,000 men. They were always staring at us. Some of the women liked it, but I didn't." There were eight pregnancies within ten months of the women's transfer. Townsend also complained that the men monopolized all the good jobs. She wrote Dixon's assignment committee, "You brought me from Dwight where women did the same jobs as the men do here—maintenance, painting, mowing lawns—but now you say women can't do those jobs." Townsend was finally assigned to the furniture shop, where she learned upholstering and was one of three women among twenty-five men (interview with Lydia Townsend, May 9, 1996).

39. Human Rights Watch, *All Too Familiar: Sexual Abuse of Women in U.S. State Prisons* (New York: Human Rights Watch, 1996), 180. Only twenty-seven states explicitly criminalized sexual contact between prisoners and prison staff (39).

40. Pat Carlen, *Women's Imprisonment: A Study in Social Control* (London: Routledge & Kegan Paul, 1983), 221.

CONCLUSION

1. Bureau of Justice Statistics, *Special Report: Women Offenders* (Washington, D.C.: Government Printing Office, 1999), 11.

2. Interview with Jamella Reynolds, May 23, 1996.

3. Bureau of Justice Statistics, *Special Report: Women Offenders*, 6–7.

4. Bureau of Justice Statistics, *Bulletin: State and Federal Prisoners, 1925–85* (Washington, D.C.: Government Printing Office, 1986), 2. Bureau of Justice Statistics, *Bulletin: Prison and Jail Inmates at Midyear 2000* (Washington, D.C.: U.S. Dept. of Justice, March 2001), 1. Of these 924 adult facilities, three-quarters had been built since 1970. Eighty-seven were all-female institutions; another 31 were co-gender correctional centers. In addition, in 2000 there were another 81 "non-institutional" facilities that housed women. These included boot camps, work release and pre-release centers (such as halfway houses), community correctional centers, substance abuse centers, and diagnostic/reception centers.

5. For comparative statistics, see the somewhat dated, but still useful study by Russ Immarigeon and Meda Chesney-Lind, *Women's Prisons: Overcrowded and Overused* (San Francisco: National Council on Crime and Delinquency, 1992). The Bureau of Justice Statistics' *Special Report: Women in Prison* (Washington, D.C.: Government Printing Office, 1994) offers statistics for 1986 and 1991. Many of Illinois's statistics exceeded national numbers: in 1999, 76 percent of female prisoners in Illinois were African American or Latina (versus 48% nationally), and 42 percent were sentenced for drug offenses (versus 34% nationally). According to the D.O.C., female inmates were less likely to have prior sentences than in previous decades; "a majority of women are first time offenders." In 1999, 59 percent were classified as minimum security. Illinois Department of Corrections, *Five-Year Plan for Female Inmates* (Springfield: Illinois Department of Corrections, 2000), 28–29.

6. Joseph E. Ragen, *The Devil Stoned: The History of an Institution,* circa 1960, Box 4, TS, pp. 172 and 183, Joseph E. Ragen Collection, Illinois State Historical Library, Springfield.

7. Ophelia Amigh, *Biennial Reports of the Illinois State Training School for Girls* (Springfield, Ill.: n.p., 1904), 6.

8. Nicole Hahn Rafter, *Partial Justice: Women, Prisons, and Social Control,* 2nd ed. (New Brunswick, N.J.: Transaction Publishers), xii.

9. Illinois Department of Corrections, *Five Year Plan for Female Inmates* (Springfield, Ill.: Illinois Department of Corrections, 2000), 3. The "deficiency model" permeates the report's description of female offenders: "The women enter the system with a myriad of long-standing deficiencies and destructive dependencies. Many are displaying the same ruinous cycles as their families." The report fails to recognize women's strengths or resiliency.

10. Pat Carlen, "Why Study Women's Imprisonment? Or Anyone Else's? An Indefinite Article," in *Prisons in Context,* ed. Roy D. King and Mike Maguire (Oxford: Clarendon, 1994), 136.

11. Interview with Lydia Townsend, May 9, 1996.

BIBLIOGRAPHY

See appendix A for notes on archival sources and appendix B for a list of interviewees.

Abbott, Edith. "The Civil War and Crime Wave of 1865–1870." *Social Service Review* 1 (1927): 212–34.

Ableson, Elaine Susan. *When Ladies Go A-Thieving*. New York: Oxford University Press, 1992.

Adler, Herman M. "The Criminologist and the Courts." *Journal of the American Institute of Criminal Law and Criminology* 11 (1920): 420–25.

Adler, Jeffrey S. "My Mother-in-Law Is to Blame, but I'll Walk on Her Neck Yet: Homicide in Late Nineteenth-Century Chicago." *Journal of Social History* 31 (1998): 253–76.

———. "'The Negro Would Be More Than an Angel to Withstand Such Treatment': African American Homicide in Chicago, 1875–1910." In *Lethal Imagination: Violence and Brutality in American History*, ed. Michael A. Bellesiles, 295–314. New York: New York University Press, 1999.

Alexander, Ruth M. *The "Girl Problem": Female Sexual Delinquency in New York, 1900–1930*. Ithaca: Cornell University Press, 1995.

Allen, Hilary. "Rendering Them Harmless: The Professional Portrayal of Women Charged with Serious Violent Crimes." In *Gender, Crime, and Justice*, ed. Pat Carlen and Anne Worall, 191–201. Philadelphia: Open University Press, 1987.

Allen, John W. *It Happened in Southern Illinois*. Johnston, Ill.: A.E.R.P., 1968.

———. "Slavery and Negro Servitude in Pope County, Illinois." *An Illinois Reader*, ed. Clyde C. Walton, 103–12. DeKalb: Northern Illinois University Press, 1970.

Allen, Judith A. *Sex and Secrets: Crimes Involving Australian Women since 1880*. New York: Oxford University Press, 1990.

Amigh, Ophelia, *Biennial Reports of the Illinois State Training School for Girls, 1900–1930* (Springfield, Ill.: State Journal Printing Company for 1909–1917, n.p. for other years).

Anderson, Etta. "The Chivalrous Treatment of the Female Offender in the Arms of the Criminal Justice System: A Review of the Literature." *Social Problems* 23 (1976): 349–57.

Arnold, Regina. "Process of Victimization and Criminalization of Black Women" *Social Justice* 17 (1990): 152–66.

Aylward, Anna, and Jim Thomas. "Quiescence in Women's Prison Litigation." *Justice Quarterly* 1 (1984): 253–76.

Baber, Mary. "The Women's Department." In *The House of Correction of the City of Chicago*, World's Fair Edition, 80–86. Chicago: City of Chicago, 1933.

Barrick, Roy G. "Classification of Prisoners." *The Welfare Bulletin* 40 (1939): 14–18.

Bartky, Sandra. "Foucault, Femininity and the Modernization of Patriarchal Power." In *Feminist Philosophies: Problems, Theories, and Applications*, ed. Janet A. Kourany, James P. Sterban, and Rosemary Tong, 105–19. Englewood Cliffs, N.J.: Prentice Hall, 1992.

Beattie, John M. "The Criminality of Women in Eighteenth-Century England." *Journal of Social History* 8 (1975): 80–116.

Beatty, Florence Northridge. "The Woman's Prison." *Welfare Magazine* 18 (1927): 920–27.

Beirne, Piers, and James Messerschmidt. *Criminology.* New York: Harcourt Brace Jovanovich, 1991.

Belenko, Steven R., ed. *Drugs and Drug Policy in America: A Documentary History.* Westport, Conn.: Greenwood Press, 2000.

Belknap, Joanne. *The Invisible Woman: Gender, Crime, and Justice.* Belmont, Calif.: Wadsworth, 1996.

Bernstein, Ilene, N. J. Cardascia, and C. E. Ross. "Defendant's Sex and Criminal Court Processing." In *Discrimination in Organizations*, ed. R. Alvarez, 329–54. San Francisco: Jossey-Bass, 1979.

Bertram, Eva. *Drug War Politics: The Price of Denial.* Berkeley: University of California Press, 1996.

Birch, Helen, ed. *Moving Targets: Women, Murder, and Representation.* Berkeley: University of California Press, 1994.

Black, Donald. "Production of Crime Rates." *American Sociological Review* 35 (1970): 733–48.

———. *The Manners and Customs of the Police.* New York: Academic Press, 1980.

Boritch, Helen. "Gender and Criminal Court Outcomes: An Historical Analysis." *Criminology* 30 (1992): 293–326.

Bowen, A. L. "Ten Years Ago and To-Day: Joliet State Prison." *Welfare Magazine* 19 (1928): 574–83.

Bower, Audrey B. "Classification in Penal Institutions with Special Reference to the State Reformatory for Women, Dwight, Illinois." Master's thesis, University of Illinois, 1942.

Branham, Charles. "Black Chicago: Accommodationist Politics before the Great Migration." In *The Ethnic Frontier: Essays in the History of Group Survival in Chicago and the Midwest*, ed. Melvin Holli and Peter d'A. Jones, 212–62. Grand Rapids, Mich.: Eerdmans, 1977.

Brenzel, Barbara. *Daughters of the State: A Social Portrait of the First Reform School for Girls in North America, 1865–1905.* Cambridge, Mass.: MIT Press, 1983.

———. "Domestication as Reform: A Study of the Socialization of Wayward Girls, 1856–1905." *Harvard Educational Review* 50 (1981): 196–213.

Bridges, George S., and G. Beretta. "Gender, Race and Social Control: Toward an Understanding of Sex Disparities in Imprisonment." In *Inequality, Crime, and Social Control*, ed. George S. Bridges and Martha A. Meyers, 158–75. San Francisco: Westview, 1994.

Bridges, George S., and Martha A. Meyers, eds. *Inequality, Crime, and Social Control.* San Francisco: Westview, 1994.

Bridgman, Olga. "Juvenile Delinquency and Feeble-Mindedness." *Institution Quarterly* 5 (1914): 164–67.

Britton, Dana Michelle. "Sex, Violence, and Supervision: A Study of the Prison as a Gendered Organization." Ph.D. dissertation, University of Texas at Austin, 1995.

Bruce, Andrew A. "The Probation and Parole System." In *The Illinois Crime Survey*, ed. Illinois Association for Criminal Justice, 519–45. Chicago: Blakely Printing, 1929.

———. "A Study of the Indeterminate Sentence and Parole in the State of Illinois. *Journal of the American Institute of Criminal Law and Criminology* 19 (1928): 1–105.

Bryan, Helen. *Inside.* Boston: Houghton Mifflin, 1953.

Butler, Anne M. *Gendered Justice in the American West: Women Prisoners in Men's Penitentiaries.* Chicago: University of Illinois Press, 1997.

———. "Still in Chains: Black Women in Western Prisons, 1865–1910." In *"We Specialize in the Wholly Impossible": A Reader in Black Women's History*, ed. Darlene Clark Hine, 321–34. New York: Carlson, 1995.

Butler, Charlotte S. "Annual Report of the Courts Committee." *Women's City Club Bulletin* 16 (1927): 11.

———. "The Woman Recidivist in Illinois." *The Clubwoman* (March 1926): 12–13.

———. "Women Delinquents: Their Custodial Care." *Welfare Magazine* 18 (1927): 438–40.

Cahalan, Margaret. *Historical Corrections Statistics in the U.S., 1850–1894.* Washington, D.C.: Government Printing Office (Bureau of Justice Statistics Publication), 1986.

Carlen, Pat. *Women's Imprisonment: A Study in Social Control.* London: Routledge & Kegan Paul, 1983.

———. "Why Study Women's Imprisonment? Or Any Else's? An Indefinite Article." In *Prisons in Context,* ed. Roy D. King and Mike Maguire, 131–40. Oxford: Clarendon, 1994.

Carlson, Shirley J. "Black Migration to Pulaski County, Illinois 1860–1900." *Illinois Historical Journal* 80 (1987): 37–46.

Carpenter, Mary. *Our Convicts.* Vol. 2. 1864. Reprint, Montclair, N.J.: Patterson Smith, 1969.

Chesney-Lind, Meda. *The Female Offender: Girls, Women, and Crime.* Thousand Oaks, Calif.: Sage, 1997.

Chicago Commission on Race Relations. *The Negro in Chicago: A Study of Race Relations and a Race Riot.* Chicago: University of Chicago Press, 1922.

Chicago Community Trust. *Reports Comprising the Survey of the Cook County Jail.* 1922. Reprint, New York: Arno, 1974.

Chicago Department of Police, *Report of the General Superintendent of Police . . . to the City Council.* Chicago: Department of Police, 1890 to 1930. Copies of these bound annual reports are located at the Chicago Historical Society and the Harold Washington Branch of the Chicago Public Library.

Chicago House of Correction. *Annual Report of the Board of Inspectors and the Superintendent.* Chicago: Chicago House of Correction, 1911–1919.

Clark, Charles L. *Lockstep and Corridor: Thirty-Five Years of Prison Life.* Cincinnati: University of Cincinnati Press, 1927.

Claussenius, G. A. *The House of Correction of the City of Chicago: A Retrospect, 1871–1921.* Chicago: City of Chicago, 1921.

Clemmer, Donald. *The Prison Community.* New York: Rinehart and Winston, 1940.

Clinton, Catherine. *The Other Civil War: American Women in the Nineteenth Century.* New York: Hill and Wang, 1984.

Cohen, Sherrill. *The Evolution of Women's Asylums Since 1500: From Refuges for Ex-Prostitutes to Shelters for Battered Women.* New York: Oxford University Press, 1992.

Cohen, Stanley. "The Critical Discourse on 'Social Control': Notes on the Concept as a Hammer." *International Journal of the Sociology of Law* 17 (1989): 347–57.

Cohen, Stanley, and Andrew Scull. "Introduction: Social Control in History and Sociology." In *Social Control and the State,* ed. Stanley Cohen and Andrew Scull, 1–14. New York: Saint Martin's Press, 1983.

———, eds. *Social Control and the State.* New York: Saint Martin's Press, 1983.

Collins, Catherine Fisher. *The Imprisonment of African American Women: Causes, Conditions, and Future Implications.* Jefferson, N.C.: McFarland and Company, 1997.

Colvin, Will. "Pardons and Commutations." *Welfare Magazine* 26 (1926): 66–68.

Comstock, Harriet J. "The Woman Offender in Illinois." *Welfare Bulletin* (1927): 312–15.

Conley, John A. "Criminal Justice History as a Field of Research: A Review of the Literature, 1960–1975." *Journal of Criminal Justice* 5 (1977): 13–28.

Cott, Nancy F. *The Bonds of Womanhood: "Woman's Sphere" in New England, 1778–1835.* New Haven: Yale University Press, 1977.

———. "Passionlessness: An Interpretation of Victorian Sexual Ideology, 1790–1850." In *A Heritage of Her Own: Toward a New Social History of American Women.* New York: Simon and Schuster, 1979.

Cox, William B., F. Lovell Bixby, and William T. Root, ed. *Handbook of American Prisons and Reformatories*. Vol. 1. New York: Osborne Association, 1933.

Crawford, William. *Report on the Penitentiaries of the United States*. 1835. Reprint, Montclair, N.J.: Patterson Smith, 1969.

Crew, B. Keith. "Sex Differences in Criminal Sentencing: Chivalry or Patriarchy?" *Justice Quarterly* 8 (1991): 59–84.

Crites, Laura, ed. *The Female Offender*. Lexington, Mass.: Lexington Books, 1976.

Curran, Debra A. "Judicial Discretion and Defendant's Sex." *Criminology* 21 (1983): 41–58.

Curtin, Mary Ellen. "The 'Human World' of Black Women in Alabama Prisons, 1870–1900." In *Hidden Histories of Women in the South*, ed. Virginia Bernhard, 11–30. Columbia: University of Missouri Press, 1994.

Curtis, Patrick A. "Eugenic Reformers: Cultural Perception of Dependent Populations, and the Care of the Feebleminded in Illinois, 1909–1920." Ph.D. dissertation, University of Illinois at Chicago, 1983.

Dalley, Bronwyn. "Following the Rules? Women's Responses to Incarceration, New Zealand, 1880–1920." *Journal of Social History* 27 (1993): 309–25.

Daly, Kathleen. "Discrimination in the Criminal Courts: Family, Gender, and the Problem of Equal Treatment." *Social Forces* 66 (1987): 152–75.

———. "Structure and Practice of Familial-Based Justice in a Criminal Court." *Law and Society Review* 21 (1987): 267–90.

Daly, Kathleen, and Rebecca Bordt. "Sex Effects and Sentencing: An Analysis of Statistical Literature." *Justice Quarterly* 12 (1995): 141–68.

Daly, Kathleen, and Meda Chesney-Lind. "Feminism and Criminology." *Justice Quarterly* 5 (1988): 497–538.

Damousi, Joy. *Depraved and Disorderly: Female Convicts, Sexuality, and Gender in Colonial Australia*. Cambridge: Cambridge University Press, 1997.

Davis, Kathleen Bement. "The Duty of the State to its Delinquent Women." *Institution Quarterly* 5 (1914): 116–19.

Davis, Natalie Zemon. *Fiction in the Archives: Pardon Tales and Their Tellers in Sixteenth-Century France*. Stanford, Calif.: Stanford University Press, 1987.

Daykin, Sam. "The Use of Prediction Techniques in Parole Administration." *Welfare Bulletin* 11 (1938): 1–4.

Degler, Carl N. "What Ought to Be and What Was: Women's Sexuality in the Nineteenth Century." *American Historical Review* 79 (1974): 1479–90.

D'Emilio, John, and Estelle B. Freedman. *Intimate Matters: A History of Sexuality in America*. New York: Harper and Row, 1988.

Dikotter, Frank. "Race Culture: Recent Perspectives on the History of Eugenics." *American Historical Review* 103 (1998): 466–93.

"Disorder in Prison and [Pontiac] Reformatory." *Institution Quarterly* 8 (1917): 69–71.

Dix, Dorothea L. "Memorial in Relation to the Illinois Penitentiary." *Reports to the General Assembly* (1847): 97–112.

———. *Prisons and Prison Discipline in the Unites States*, 2nd ed. Philadelphia: Joseph Kite & Co., 1845.

Dobash, Russell P., R. Emerson Dobash, and Sue Gutteridge. *The Imprisonment of Women*. London: Basil Blackwell, 1986.

Dodge, L. Mara. "'Her Life Has Been an Improper One': Women, Crime, and Prisons in Illinois, 1835–1933." Ph.D. dissertation, University of Illinois at Chicago, 1998.

———. "'The Most Degraded of Their Sex, If Not of Humanity': Female Prisoners at Joliet Penitentiary, 1860–1900." *Journal of Illinois History* 76 (1999): 3–28.

———. "'Our Juvenile Court Is Becoming More Like a Criminal Court': A Century of Reform at the Cook County (Chicago) Juvenile Court." *Michigan Historical Review* 26 (2000): 51–90.

———. "'One Female Prisoner Is of More Trouble than Twenty Males': Women Convicts in Illinois Prisons, 1835–1896." *Journal of Social History* 32 (1999): 907–30.

Dooley, Lucille. "The Psychopathic Woman." *Mental Hygiene* 8 (1924): 192–201.

Eaton, Mary. *Justice for Whom? Family, Court, and Social Control.* Philadelphia: Open University Press, 1986.

Erez, Edna. "Dangerous Men, Evil Women: Gender and Parole Decision-Making." *Justice Quarterly* 9 (1992): 105–26.

Erickson, Gladys A. *Warden Ragen of Joliet.* New York: E. P. Dutton & Co., 1957.

Faderman, Lillian. *Odd Girls and Twilight Lovers: A History of Lesbian Life in Twentieth-Century America.* New York: Columbia University Press, 1991.

Farnworth, Margaret, and Raymond Teske. "Gender Difference in Felony Court Processing: Three Hypotheses of Disparity." *Women and Criminal Justice* 6 (1995): 23–44.

Feeley, Malcolm M. "The Decline of Women in the Criminal Process: A Comparative History." *Criminal Justice History: An International Annual* 15 (1994): 235–74.

Feeley, Malcolm M., and Deborah L. Little. "The Vanishing Female: The Decline of Women in the Criminal Process, 1672–1912." *Law and Society Review* 25 (1991): 719–57.

Felson, Richard B., and Steven F. Messner. "To Kill or Not to Kill? Lethal Outcomes in Injurious Attacks." *Criminology* 34 (1996): 519–46.

"Female Law Breakers." In *1884 Biennial Report of the Illinois State Board of Commissioners of Public Charities,* 61–63. Springfield: Illinois Department of Public Charities.

Fernald, Mabel Ruth, Mary H. S. Hayes, and Almena Dawley. *A Study of Women Delinquents in New York State.* 1920. Reprint, Montclair, N.J.: Patterson Smith, 1968.

Figueira-McDonough, Josefina. "Gender Differences in Informal Processing: A Look at Charge Bargaining and Sentence Reduction in Washington, D.C." *Journal of Research in Crime and Delinquency* 22 (1985): 101–33.

Fishman, Laura T. "Slave Women, Resistance, and Criminality: A Prelude to Future Accommodation." *Women and Criminal Justice* 7 (1995): 35–65.

Fletcher, Beverly R., Lynda D. Shaver, and Dreama G. Moon, eds. *Woman Prisoners: A Forgotten Population.* Conn.: Praeger, 1993.

Flynn, Elizabeth Gurley. *The Alderson Story: My Life as a Political Prisoner.* New York: International Publishers, 1963.

Foner, Philip S., and Sally M. Miller, eds. *Kate Richards O'Hare: Selected Writings and Speeches.* Baton Rouge: Louisiana State University Press, 1982.

Ford, Charles A. "Homosexual Practices of Institutionalized Females." *Journal of Abnormal and Social Psychology* (1929): 442–49.

Foucault, Michel. *Discipline and Punish: The Birth of the Prison.* New York: Pantheon, 1977.

Fox-Genovese, Elizabeth. "Strategies and Forms of Resistance: Focus on Slave Women." In *Black Women in American History: From Colonial Times through the Nineteenth Century,* vol. 2, ed. Darlene Clark Hine, 409–31. New York: Carson, 1990.

Frank, Henriette, and Amalie Jerome. *Annals of the Chicago Woman's Club for the First Forty Years of Its Organization, 1876–1916.* Chicago, Ill.: The Chicago Women's Club, 1916.

Freedman, Estelle B. "The Prison Lesbian." *Signs: Journal of Women in Culture and Society* 21 (1996): 248–80.

———. "Sexuality in Nineteenth-Century America: Behavior, Ideology, and Politics." *Reviews in American History* 10 (1982): 196–215.

———. *Their Sisters' Keepers: Prison Reform in America, 1830–1930.* Ann Arbor: University of Michigan Press, 1981.

Friedman, Lawrence M., and Robert V. Percival. *The Roots of Justice: Crime and Justice in Alameda County, California, 1870–1910.* Chapel Hill: University of North Carolina Press, 1981.

Fritz, Blance. "Education and Rehabilitation: Oakdale State Reformatory for Women." *Welfare Bulletin* (March/April, 1953): 13–17.

Frum, Harold S. *Fifty-Year History of the Division of the Criminologist.* Springfield, Ill.: State of Illinois, 1968.

Fuller, Grace. *Too-Loo Byrd: The Story of a Little Negro Waif*. Macon, Ga.: J. W. Burke Co., 1924.

Garrett, Paul W., and Austin H. MacCormick, eds. *Handbook of American Prisons and Reformatories*. New York: National Society of Penal Information, 1929.

Ghali, Moheb, and Meda Chesney-Lind. "Gender Bias and the Criminal Justice System: An Empirical Investigation." *Sociology and Social Research* 70 (1986): 164–71.

Giallombardo, Rose. *Society of Women: A Study of a Woman's Prison*. New York: Wiley & Sons, 1966.

Gibson, Helen E. "Women's Prisons: Laboratories for Penal Reform." In *The Female Offender*, ed. Laura Crites, 93–120. Lexington, Mass.: Lexington Books, 1976.

Gibson, Mary S. "The 'Female Offender' and the Italian School of Criminal Anthropology." *Journal of European Studies* 12 (1982): 155–65.

Giddings, Paula. *When and Where I Enter: The Impact of Black Women on Race and Sex in America*. New York: Bantam, 1984.

Gittens, Joan. *Poor Relations: The Children of the State in Illinois, 1818–1990*. Chicago: University of Illinois Press, 1994.

Glueck, Sheldon, and Eleanor T. Glueck. *Five Hundred Delinquent Women*. New York: Alfred A. Knopf, 1934; reprint, New York: Krauss Reprint, 1971.

Granger, Bill, and Lori Granger. *Lords of the Last Machine*. New York: Random House, 1987.

Greene, William R. "Early Development of the Illinois State Penitentiary System." *Journal of the Illinois State Historical Society* 70 (1977): 185–95.

Grossman, James R. *Land of Hope: Chicago, Black Southerners, and the Great Migration*. Chicago: University of Chicago Press, 1989.

Hagan, John, and Nancy O'Donnell. "Sexual Stereotyping and Judicial Sentencing: A Legal Test of the Sociological Wisdom." *Canadian Journal of Sociology* 3 (1978): 309–319.

Hagan, John, John H. Simpson, and A. R. Gillis. "The Sexual Stratification of Social Control." *British Journal of Sociology* 30 (1979): 25–38.

Hahn, Nicolas Fischer. "Female State Prisoners in Tennessee, 1831–1979." *Tennessee Historical Quarterly* 39 (1980): 485–97.

———. "Too Dumb to Know Better: Cacogenic Family Studies and the Criminology of Women." *Criminology* 18 (1980): 3–25.

Hall, Margaret E. "Mental and Physical Efficiency of Women Drug Addicts." *Journal of Abnormal and Social Psychology* 33 (1938): 332–45.

Haller, John S., and Robin M. Haller. *The Physician and Sexuality in Victorian America*. Urbana: University of Illinois Press, 1974.

Haller, Mark H. "Historical Roots of Police Behavior: Chicago, 1890–1925." In *Police, Prison, and Punishment: Major Historical Interpretations*, ed. Kermit L. Hall, 321–39. New York: Garland, 1987.

———. "Urban Crime and Criminal Justice: The Chicago Case." *Journal of American History* 57 (1970): 619–35.

Harm, Nancy J. "Women Incarcerated in Illinois State Prisons, 1843–1915: An Exploratory Study in Social Policy." Ph.D. dissertation, University of Illinois at Chicago, 1989.

Harris, Mary B. *I Knew Them in Prison*. New York: Viking, 1936.

Hauser, Philip Morris. "Motion Pictures in Penal and Correctional Institutions: A Study of the Reactions of Prisoners to Movies." Ph.D. dissertation, University of Chicago, 1933.

Hawkins, Darnell F. "Black and White Homicide Differentials: Alternatives to an Inadequate Theory." In *Homicide among Black Americans*, ed. Darnell F. Hawkins, 109–36. Lanham, Md.: University Press of America, 1995.

———, ed. *Ethnicity, Race, and Crime: Perspectives across Time and Place*. Albany: State University of New York Press, 1995.

Hayes, Clara B. "Our Work as Seen from Geneva." *Institution Quarterly* 10 (1919): 116–20.
———. "Segregation of Mental Defectives as a Preventative of Crime, Immorality, and Inefficiency." *Institution Quarterly* 6 (1915): 96–101.
Hazard, Helen H. "Services and Dedication at the Illinois State Reformatory for Women." *Welfare Bulletin* 33 (1942): 5–7.
Heidensohn, Frances. *Women and Crime.* New York: New York University Press, 1985.
Henriques, Zelma. "African American Women: The Oppressive Intersection of Gender, Race, and Class." *Women and Criminal Justice* 7 (1995): 67–80.
Hentig, Hans Von. "The Criminality of the Colored Woman." *University of Colorado Studies in Social Science* 1 (1942): 231–60.
Hill, Gary, and Elizabeth Crawford. "Women, Race, and Crime." *Criminology* 28 (1990): 601–26.
Hindus, Michael S. "The History of Crime: Not Robbed of Its Potential, but Still on Probation." *Criminology Review Yearbook*, vol. 1, ed. Sheldon L. Messiner and Egon Bittner, 217–42. Beverly Hills, Calif.: Sage Publications, 1980.
Hine, Darlene Clark, ed. *Black Women in American History: From Colonial Times through the Nineteenth Century.* New York: Carson, 1990.
Hinrichsen, Anne. "The Criminal Statistics of Illinois." *Institution Quarterly* 8 (1917): 3–120.
———. Hinrichsen, Anne. "Pitfalls in Criminal Statistics." *Institution Quarterly* 7 (1916): 7–12.
———. "Social Histories in the Women's Prison." *Institution Quarterly* 9 (1918): 28–29.
———. "State Penal Farm Displaces County Jail." *Institution Quarterly* 7 (1916): 44–49.
———. "The Women's Prison." *Welfare Bulletin* (February 1942): 8–10.
Hoffer, Peter C., and N. E. H. Hull. *Murdering Mothers: Infanticide in England and New England, 1558–1803.* New York: New York University, 1981.
Howe, Adrian. *Punish and Critique: Towards a Feminist Analysis of Penality.* New York: Routledge, 1994.
Huey, Jacklyn, and Michael J. Lynch. "The Image of Black Women in Criminology: Historical Stereotypes as Theoretical Foundation." In *Justice with Prejudice: Race and Criminal Justice in America,* ed. Michael J. Lynch and E. Britt Patterson, 71–88. Guilderland, N.Y.: Harrow and Heston, 1996.
Hull, N. E. *Female Felons: Women and Serious Crime in Colonial Massachusetts.* Urbana: University of Illinois Press, 1987.
Human Rights Watch. *All Too Familiar: Sexual Abuse of Women in U.S. State Prisons.* New York: Human Rights Watch, 1996.
Ignatieff, Michael. "State, Civil Society, and Total Institutions: A Critique of Recent Social Histories of Punishment." In *Crime and Justice: An Annual Review of Research,* vol. 3, ed. Michael Tonry and Norval Morris, 153–91. Chicago: University of Chicago Press, 1981.
Ignatiev, Noel. *How the Irish Became White.* New York: Routledge, 1995.
Illinois Association for Criminal Justice. *The Illinois Crime Survey.* Chicago: Blakely Printing, 1929.
Illinois Blue Book. Springfield, Ill.: State Journal Printing Company, 1928.
Illinois Department of Corrections. *Annual Report.* Springfield: Illinois Department of Corrections, 1970–1990.
———. *Five-Year Plan for Female Inmates.* Springfield: Illinois Department of Corrections, 1990, 1993, 1995, 2000.
Illinois Department of Public Charities. *Biennial Report of the Illinois Board of Commissioners of Public Charities.* Springfield: Illinois Department of Public Charities, 1888.
Illinois Department of Public Safety. *Annual Report of the Statistician.* Springfield: State of Illinois, 1942.
Illinois Department of Public Welfare. *Annual Report of the Statistician.* Springfield: State of Illinois, 1922–1938.

——. *Dedication of Oakdale: State Reformatory for Women.* Springfield, Ill.: Schnepp and Barnes Printers, 1932.

——. *Statistical Review of Prisons, Reformatories, and Correctional Schools.* Springfield: Illinois Department of Public Welfare, 1939.

——. *Statistical Review of State Prisons and Correctional Schools.* Springfield: Illinois Department of Public Welfare, 1940.

Illinois General Assembly. *Report of the Joint Committee of Investigation into Affairs of the Illinois State Penitentiary.* Springfield, Ill.: Illinois Journal Printing Office, 1872.

——. *Report of the Senate Vice Committee.* Springfield, Ill.: n.p., 1916.

Illinois General Assembly Commission to Visit and Examine State Institutions, Penal Division. *Report of the Penal Division of the Legislative Commission to Visit and Examine State Institutions.* Springfield, Ill.: The Commission, 1953–1963 (biennially).

Illinois General Assembly Commission to Visit and Examine State Institutions, Subcommittee on Penal Institutions. *Report of the Subcommittee on Penal Institutions of the Legislative Commission to Visit and Examine State Institutions.* Springfield, Ill.: The Commission, 1965–1978 (biennially).

Illinois Prison Inquiry Commission. *The Prison System in Illinois: A Report to the Governor.* Springfield: State of Illinois, 1937.

Immarigeon, Russ, and Meda Chesney-Lind. *Women's Prisons: Overcrowded and Overused.* San Francisco: National Council on Crime and Delinquency, 1992.

Ireland, Robert. "Frenzied and Fallen Females: Women and Sexual Dishonor." *Journal of Women's History* 3 (1992): 95–117.

Jacobs, James B. "The Stateville Counselors: Symbol of Reform in Search of a Role." *Social Service Review* 50 (1976): 138–47.

——. *Stateville: The Penitentiary in Mass Society.* Chicago: University of Chicago Press, 1977.

"John L. Whitman: Dreamer and Doer." *Journal of Criminal Law and Criminology* 18 (May 1927): 5–10.

Jones, Ann. *Women Who Kill.* New York: Fawcett Crest, 1980.

Kamerling, Henry L. "Too Much Time for the Crime I Done: Race, Ethnicity, and the Politics of Punishment in Illinois and South Carolina, 1865–1900." Ph.D. dissertation, University of Illinois at Urbana-Champaign, 1998.

Kantrowitz, Nathan. *Close Control: Managing a Maximum Security Prison.* New York: Harrow and Heston, 1996.

Kavanaugh, Marcus. *The Criminal and His Allies.* Indianapolis: Bobbs-Merrill, 1928.

Kellor, Frances A. "Psychological and Environmental Study of Women Criminals." *American Journal of Sociology* 5 (1900): 527–43, 671–83.

Kevles, Daniel J. *In the Name of Eugenics: Genetics and the Uses of Human Heredity,* 2nd ed. Cambridge: Cambridge University Press, 1995.

Klein, Charlotte Ruth. "Success and Failure on Parole: A Study of 160 Girls Paroled from the State Training School at Geneva, Illinois." Master's thesis, University of Chicago, 1935.

Klein, Dorie. "The Etiology of Female Crime: A Review of the Literature." In *The Female Offender,* ed. Laura Crites, 5–32. Lexington, Mass.: Lexington Books, 1976.

Knupfer, Anne Meis. *Reform and Resistance: Gender, Delinquency, and America's First Juvenile Court.* New York: Routledge, 2001.

Kremer, Gary R. "Strangers to Domestic Virtue: Nineteenth-Century Women in the Missouri Prison." *Missouri Historical Review* 84 (1990): 293–310.

Krohn, Marvin D., James P. Curry, and Shirley Nelson-Kilger. "Is Chivalry Dead? An Analysis of Changes in Police Dispositions of Males and Females." *Criminology* 21 (1983): 417–47.

Kruttschnitt, Candace. "Respectable Women and the Law." *Sociological Quarterly* 23 (1983): 221–34.

——. "Social Status and Sentences of Female Offenders." *Law and Society Review* 15 (1980–81): 247–62.

Laberge, Danielle. "Women's Criminality, Criminal Women, Criminalized Women? Questions in and for a Feminist Perspective." *Journal of Human Justice* 2 (1991): 37–56.

Lane, Roger. *Murder in America: A History.* Columbus: Ohio State University Press, 1997.

———. *Roots of Violence in Black Philadelphia, 1860–1900.* Cambridge, Mass.: Harvard University Press, 1986.

———. *Violent Death in the City: Suicide, Accident, and Murder in Nineteenth-Century Philadelphia.* Cambridge, Mass.: Harvard University Press, 1979.

Lane, Winthrop D. "The Illinois Prison Riots." *The Survey* 66 (1931): 94.

———. "Prisons Where Trouble May Come." *The Survey* 64 (1930): 399–401.

Langan, Patrick A. *Race of Prisoners Admitted to State and Federal Institutions, 1926–86.* Washington, D.C.: Government Printing Office (Bureau of Justice Statistics Publication), May 1991.

Larson, John A., and Herman M. Alder. "Lie Detection Tests with Prisoners: A Preliminary Communication." *Institution Quarterly* 16 (1925): 118–19.

Lathrop, Reverend S. G. *Crime and Its Punishment and Life in the Penitentiary.* Springfield, Ill.: n.p., 1866.

Laws of the State of Illinois. Springfield, Ill.: n.p., 1867, 1887, 1889, 1895, 1899, 1939.

League of Women Voters of Illinois. *Women in Prison.* Chicago, Ill.: League of Women Voters, 1973 (mimeograph).

Lekkerkerker, Eugenia C. *Reformatories for Women in the United States.* Gronigen, Netherlands: J. B. Wolters, 1931.

Leonard, Eileen B. *Women, Crime, and Society: A Critique of Criminology Theory.* New York: Longman, 1982.

Lerner, Gerda. "The Lady and the Mill Girl: Changes in the Status of Women in the Age of Jackson." *Mid-Continental American Studies Journal* 10 (1969): 5–15.

Lewis, Diane K. "Black Women Offenders and Criminal Justice: Some Theoretical Considerations." In *Comparing Female and Male Offenders,* ed. Marguerite Q. Warren, 89–105. Beverly Hills, Calif.: Sage, 1981.

Lewis, Elizabeth H. "Service of Dedication at Illinois State Reformatory for Women." *Welfare Bulletin* 33 (1942): 1–4.

Lewis, W. David. *From Newgate to Dannemora: The Rise of the Penitentiary in New York, 1796–1848.* Ithaca, N.Y.: Cornell University Press, 1965.

Lightner, David L. *Asylum, Prison, and Poorhouse: The Writings and Reform Work of Dorothea Dix in Illinois.* Carbondale: Southern Illinois University Press, 1999.

Lombroso, Cesare, and William Ferrero. *The Female Offender.* 1895. Reprint, New York: D. Appleton and Co., 1900.

Lunbeck, Elizabeth. *The Psychiatric Persuasion: Knowledge, Gender, and Power in Modern America.* Princeton, N.J.: Princeton University Press, 1994.

MacChesney, Nathan. "Race Development by Legislation." *Institution Quarterly* 4 (1913): 62–75.

McClellan, Dorothy S. "Disparity in the Discipline of Male and Female Inmates in Texas Prisons." *Women and Criminal Justice* 5 (1994): 71–97.

MacCormick, Austin H., and Paul W. Garrett. *Handbook of American Prisons.* New York: G. P. Putnam's Sons, 1926.

———. *Handbook of American Prisons and Reformatories.* New York: National Society of Penal Information, 1929.

McKelvey, Blake. *American Prisons: A History of Good Intentions.* 1936. Reprint, Montclair, N.J.: Patterson Smith, 1977.

Mann, Coramae Richey. "Black Female Homicide in the United States." *Journal of Interpersonal Violence* 5 (1990): 176–201.

———. *When Women Kill.* Albany: State University of New York Press, 1996.

Martin, Walter B. "Behavior Study of Criminals." *Welfare Magazine* 18 (1927): 1580–85.

Melossi, Dario, and Massimo Pavarini. *The Prison and the Factory: Origins of the Penitentiary System.* London: Macmillan, 1981.

Merriam, Charles E. "Findings and Recommendations of the Chicago Council Committee on Crime." *Journal of the American Institute of Criminal Law and Criminology* 6 (1915): 345–62.

Miller, Sally M. *From Prairie to Prison: The Life of Social Activist Kate Richards O'Hare*. Columbia: University of Missouri Press, 1993.

Monahan, Florence. "Separate Penal and Reformatory Institutions for Women." *Women's City Club Bulletin* 15 (1925): 135–6.

———. *Women in Crime*. New York: Washburn, 1941.

Morris, Allison. *Women, Crime and Criminal Justice*. Oxford: Basil Blackwell, 1987.

Morris, Norval, and David J. Rothman, eds. *The Oxford History of the Prison: The Practice of Punishment in Western Society*. New York: Oxford University Press, 1995.

Morton, Patricia. *Disfigured Images: The Historical Assault on Afro-American Women*. New York: Greenwood Press, 1991.

Muraskin, William A. "The Social-Control Theory in American History: A Critique." *Journal of Social History* 9 (1976): 559–69.

Naffine, Ngaire. *Female Crime*. Sydney, Australia: Allen & Unwin, 1987.

Nagel, Ilene H., and John Hagan. "Gender and Crime: Offense Patterns and Criminal Court Sanctions." In *Crime and Justice: An Annual Review of Research*, vol. 4, ed. Michael Tonry and Norval Morris, 91–144. Chicago: University of Chicago Press, 1983.

Norton, Mary Beth. "Gender, Crime, and Community in Seventeenth-Century Maryland." In *The Transformation of Early American History: Society, Authority, and Ideology*, ed. James A. Henretta, Michael Kammen, and Stanley N. Katz, 123–50. New York: Alfred A. Knopf, 1991.

Obitko, Mary Ellen. "Custodians of a House of Resistance: Black Women Respond to Slavery." In *Black Women in American History: From Colonial Times through the Nineteenth Century*, ed. Darlene Clark Hine, 985–98. New York: Carson, 1990.

O'Brien, Patricia. *The Promise of Punishment: Prisons in Nineteenth-Century France*. Princeton, N.J.: Princeton University Press, 1982.

Odem, Mary E. *Delinquent Daughters: Protecting and Policing Adolescent Female Sexuality in the United States, 1885–1920*. Chapel Hill: University of North Carolina Press, 1995.

Ordahl, George, and Louise Ordahl. "A Study of 49 Female Convicts." *Journal of Delinquency* 2 (1917): 331–51.

Ordahl, Louise E. "A Study of Girls at Geneva." *Institution Quarterly* 9 (1918): 56–60.

Otis, Margaret A. "Perversion Not Commonly Noted." *Journal of Abnormal Psychology* 8 (1913): 112–14.

Parker, Ian, Eugenie Georgaca, David Harper, Terence McLaughlin, and Mark Stowell-Smith, eds. *Deconstructing Psychopathology*. London: Sage, 1995.

Peck, Mary G. "Race Betterment." *Welfare Magazine* 18 (1927): 1477–82.

Petersilia, Joan. *Racial Disparities in the Criminal Justice System*. Santa Monica, Calif.: Rand, 1983.

Phelps, Margaret Dorsey. "Idled Outside, Overworked Inside: The Political Economy of Prison Labor during Depressions in Chicago, 1871–1897." Ph.D. dissertation, University of Iowa, 1992.

Pisciotti, Alexander W. *Benevolent Repression: Social Control and the American Reformatory-Prison Movement*. New York: New York University Press, 1994.

———. "Corrections, Society, and Social Control in America: A Metahistorical Review of the Literature." *Criminal Justice History: An International Annual* 2 (1981): 109–30.

———. "A House Divided: Penal Reform at the Illinois State Reformatory, 1891–1915." *Crime and Delinquency* 37 (1991): 167–85.

Platt, Anthony M. "Rethinking and Unthinking 'Social Control.'" In *Inequality, Crime, and Social Control*, ed. George S. Bridges and Martha A. Myers, 72–79. San Francisco: Westview, 1994.

Pollak, Otto. *The Criminality of Women*. New York: A.S. Barnes & Co., 1950.

Pollock, Joycelyn M. *Criminal Women*. Cincinnati: Anderson, 1999.

——. *Sex and Supervision: Guarding Male and Female Inmates.* Westport, Conn.: Greenwood Press, 1990.

Pollock-Byrne, Joycelyn M. *Women, Prison, and Crime.* Belmont, Calif.: Wadsworth, 1990.

Potter, Ellen C. "Women in Correctional Institutions." In *1933 Annual Proceedings of the Annual Congress of the National Prison Association,* 101–13. Indianapolis: W. B. Burford, 1933.

Price, Barbara R., and Natalie J. Sokolff, eds. *The Criminal Justice System and Women.* New York: Clark Boardman, 1982.

Purcell-Guild, June. "Study of One Hundred and Thirty-One Delinquent Girls Held at the Juvenile Detention Home in Chicago, 1917." *Journal of the American Institute of Criminal Law and Criminology* 10 (1919): 441–76.

Rafter, Nicole Hahn. "Chastising the Unchaste: Social Control Functions of a Woman's Reformatory, 1894–1931." In *Social Control and the State: Historical and Comparative Essays,* ed. Stanley Cohen and Andrew Scull, 288–311. Oxford: Martin Robertson, 1983.

——. *Creating Born Criminals.* Urbana: University of Illinois Press, 1997.

——. "Criminal Anthropology in the United States." *Criminology* 30 (1992): 525–45.

——. "Gender, Prisons, and Prison History." *Social Science History* 9 (1985): 233–47.

——. "Hard Times: Custodial Prisons for Women and the Example of the New York State Prison for Women at Auburn, 1893–1933." In *Judge, Lawyer, Victim, Thief: Women, Gender Roles, and Criminal Justice,* ed. Nicole Hahn Rafter and Elizabeth A. Stanko, 237–60. Boston: Northeastern University Press, 1982.

——. *Partial Justice: Women, Prisons, and Social Control,* 2nd ed. New Brunswick, N.J.: Transaction, 1990.

——. "Prisons for Women, 1790–1980." *Crime and Justice: An Annual Review of Research* 5 (1984): 129–181.

Ragen, Joseph E. *The Devil Stoned: The History of an Institution.* Unpublished manuscript. Circa 1960. Joseph E. Ragen Collection, Box 4, TS, p. 175. Illinois State Historical Library, Springfield.

Reagan, Leslie J. "'About to Meet Her Maker'": Women, Doctors, Dying Declarations, and the State's Investigation of Abortion, Chicago, 1867–1940." *Journal of American History* 77 (1991): 1239–64.

——. *When Abortion Was a Crime: Women, Medicine, and Law in the United States, 1867–1973.* Berkeley: University of California Press, 1997.

"Record, 1878 May 16–17 Testimony before the Commissioners of the Illinois State Penitentiary on the Inhuman Treatment of Prisoners." Handwritten transcript. Regenstein Library, University of Chicago, Special Collections, Box 1.

Reeves, Margaret. *Training Schools for Delinquent Girls.* New York: Russell Sage Foundation, 1929.

Rennie, Ysabel. *The Search for Criminal Man: A Conceptual History of the Dangerous Offender.* Massachusetts: Lexington, 1978.

Robb, George. "Circle in Crinoline: Domestic Poisonings in Victorian England." *Journal of Family History* 22 (1997): 176–90.

Robert, Jeanne. "The Care of Women in State Prisons." *The American Review of Reviews* 44 (1911): 76–84.

Roberts, Virginia Culin. "The Women Was Too Tough." *Journal of Arizona History* (1985): 395–413.

Robinson, Frederick W. *Female Life in Prison, by a Prison Matron.* London: Hurst and Blackett, 1862.

Rolison, Garry L. "Toward an Integrated Theory of Female Criminality and Incarceration." In *Women Prisoners: A Forgotten Population,* ed. Beverly R. Fletcher, Lynda D. Shaver, and Dreama G. Moon, 135–146. Westport, Conn.: Praeger, 1993.

Rothman, David J. *Conscience and Convenience: The Asylum and Its Alternatives in Progressive America.* Boston: Little, Brown, and Co., 1980.

———. "Perfecting the Prison: United States, 1780–1865." In *The Oxford History of the Prison: The Practice of Punishment in Western Society*, ed. Norval Morris and David J. Rothman, 111–30. New York: Oxford University Press, 1995.

———. "Social Control: The Uses and Abuses of the Concept in the History of Incarceration." In *Social Control and the State*, ed. Stanley Cohen and Andrew Scull, 106–117. New York: St. Martin's Press, 1983.

Rules for the Government of Officers and Employees of the Southern Illinois Penitentiary. St. Louis: Globe-Democrat Job Printing Co., 1879.

Sanders, Wiley B. "The History and Administration of the State Prisons of Illinois." Ph.D. dissertation, University of Chicago, 1929.

Schlossman, Steven. *Love and the American Delinquent: The Theory and Practice of 'Progressive' Juvenile Justice, 1825–1920*. Chicago: University of Chicago Press, 1977.

Schweber, Claudine. "Beauty Marks and Blemishes: The Coed Prison as a Microcosm of an Integrated Society." *The Prison Journal* 64 (1985): 3–15.

Siegfried, Michael Lee. "Crime and the Institutionalization of the Penitentiary in Illinois 1818–1841: A Study in Penal Change." Ph.D. dissertation, Southern Illinois University at Carbondale, 1992.

Smart, Carol. "The Female Offender: Reality or Myth?" In *The Criminal Justice System and Women*, ed. Barbara R. Price and Natalie J. Sokoloff, 105–116. New York: Clark Boardman, 1982.

———. *Women, Crime, and Criminology: A Feminist Critique*. London: Routledge & Kegan Paul, 1976.

Smith, Daniel Scott. "Family Limitation, Sexual Control, and Domestic Feminism in Victorian America." In *Clio's Consciousness Raised: New Perspectives on the History of Women*, ed. Mary Hartman and Lois Banner, 119–36. New York: Octagon, 1974.

Smith, Douglas A., Christy Visher, and Laura A. Davidson. "Equity and Discretionary Justice: The Influence of Race on Police Arrest Decisions." *Journal of Criminal Law and Criminology* 75 (1984): 234–49.

Smith-Rosenberg, Carroll. "Beauty, the Beast, and the Militant Woman: A Case Study in Sex Roles and Social Stress in Jacksonian America." *American Quarterly* 23 (1971): 562–584.

———. *Disorderly Conduct: Visions of Gender in Victorian America*. New York: Oxford University Press, 1985.

Smith-Rosenberg, Carroll, and Charles Rosenburg. "The Female Animal: Medical and Biological Views of Women and Her Role in Nineteenth-Century America." *Feminist Studies* 1 (1973): 40–57.

Spaulding, Edith R. *An Experimental Study of Psychopathic Delinquent Women*. 1923. Reprint, Montclair, N.J.: Patterson Smith, 1969.

Spear, Allen H. *Black Chicago: The Making of a Negro Ghetto, 1880–1920*. Chicago: University of Chicago Press, 1967.

Spohn, Cassia, John Gruhl, and Susan Welch. "The Impact of Ethnicity and Gender of Defendants on the Decision to Reject or Dismiss Felony Charges." *Criminology* 25 (1987): 175–91.

Spohn, Cassia, John Gruhl, and Susan Welch. "Women Defendants in Court: The Interactions between Sex and Race in Convicting and Sentencing." *Social Science Quarterly* 66 (1985): 178–185.

Spohn, Cassia, and J. Spears. "Gender and Case Processing Decisions: A Comparison of Case Outcomes for Male and Female Defendants Charged with Violent Felonies." *Women and Criminal Justice* 8 (1997): 29–59.

Stage, Sarah, and Virginia B. Vincenti, ed. *Rethinking Home Economics: Women and the History of a Profession*. Ithaca, N.Y.: Cornell University Press, 1997.

State of Illinois. *The Prison System in Illinois: A Report to the Governor*. Springfield: State of Illinois, 1937.

Steffensmeier, Darrell, John Kramer, and Cathy Streifel. "Gender and Imprisonment Decisions." *Criminology* 31 (1993): 411–46.

Steinberg, Allen. *The Transformation of Criminal Justice: Philadelphia 1800–1880.* Chapel Hill: University of North Carolina Press, 1989.

Sterns, Carol Z., and Peter N. Stearns. "Victorian Sexuality: Can Historians Do Better?" *Journal of Social History* 18 (1984–85): 626–33.

Stone, Esther H. "Plea for an Early Commitment to Correctional Institutions of Delinquent Children." *Institution Quarterly* 9 (1918): 64–67.

Strickland, Kathleen G. "Correctional Institutions for Women in the United States." Ph.D. dissertation, Syracuse University, 1967.

Takagi, Paul. "Revising Liberal Conceptions of Penal Reform: A Bibliographic Overview." *Crime and Social Justice* 5 (1976): 60–65.

Takagi, Paul, and Tony Platt, ed. *Punishment and Penal Discipline: Essays on the Prison and the Prisoner's Movement.* San Francisco: Crime and Social Justice Associates, 1980.

Taylor, Ian. *Crime, Capitalism, and Community: Three Essays in Socialist Criminology.* Toronto, Ont.: Butterworths, 1983.

Temin, Carolyn Engel. "Discriminatory Sentencing of Women Offenders: The Argument for ERA in a Nutshell." In *The Female Offender,* ed. Laura Crites, 49–66. Lexington: D. C. Heath Co., 1976.

Thornton, Alice. "The Pound of Flesh." *Atlantic Monthly* 135 (1925): 433–46 and 611–23.

Tilendis, Albert. "The Prison Labor Problem in Illinois." Ph.D. dissertation, University of Illinois at Urbana, 1941.

Tulchin, Simon. *Intelligence and Crime: A Study of Penitentiary and Reformatory Offenders.* Chicago: University of Chicago Press, 1939.

Tuttle, William M. *Race Riot: Chicago in the Red Summer of 1919,* 2nd ed. Urbana: University of Illinois Press, 1996.

U.S. Department of Commerce, Bureau of the Census. *Prisoners, 1923.* Washington, D.C.: Government Printing Office, 1926.

U.S. Department of Justice, Bureau of Justice Statistics. *Bulletin: State and Federal Prisoners, 1925–1985.* Washington, D.C.: Government Printing Office, 1986.

———. *Special Report: Prison Rule Violators.* Washington, D.C.: Government Printing Office, 1989.

———. *Special Report: Women in Prison.* Washington, D.C.: Government Printing Office, 1994.

———. *Special Report: Women Offenders.* Washington, D.C.: Government Printing Office, 1999.

———. *Bulletin: Prison and Jail Inmates at Midyear 2000.* Washington, D.C.: Government Printing Office, 2001.

U.S. Department of the Interior, Census Office. *Reports of the Thirteenth Census: Population.* Vol. 2. Washington, D.C., Government Printing Office, 1913.

U.S. Superintendent of the Census. *Statistical View of the United States.* Washington, D.C.: A. O. P. Nicholson, 1854.

Victor, Sarah M. *The Life Story of Sarah M. Victor.* Cleveland, Oh.: Williams, 1887.

Visher, Christy A. "Gender, Police Arrest Decision, and Notions of Chivalry." *Criminology* 21 (1983): 5–28.

Waite, Robert. "Necessary to Isolate the Female Prisoners: Women Convicts and the Women's Ward at the Old Idaho Penitentiary." *Idaho Yesterdays* 29 (1985): 2–13.

Walker, Samuel. "Origins of the Contemporary Criminal Justice Paradigm: The American Bar Foundation Survey, 1953–1969." *Justice Quarterly* 9 (1992): 201–30.

———. *Popular Justice: A History of American Criminal Justice.* New York: Oxford University Press, 1998.

———. *Taming the System: The Control of Discretion in Criminal Justice, 1950–1990.* New York: Oxford University Press, 1993.

Walker, Samuel, Cassia Spohn, and Miriam Deleone. *The Color of Justice: Race, Ethnicity, and Crime in America.* Belmont, Calif.: Wadsworth, 1996.

Ward, David A., and Gene G. Kassebaum. *Women's Prisons: Sex and Social Structure.* Chicago: Aldine-Atherton, 1965.

Weidensall, Jean. *The Mentality of the Criminal Woman*. Baltimore: Warwick & Work, 1916.

Weisheit, Ralph. "Female Homicide Offenders: Trends over Time in an Institutionalized Population." *Justice Quarterly* 1 (1984): 471–89.

Weiss, Robert, "Humanitarianism, Labor Exploitation, or Social Control? A Critical Survey of Theory and Research on the Origin and Development of Prisons." *Social History* 12 (1987): 331–50.

Welter, Barbara. "The Cult of True Womanhood: 1820–1860." *American Quarterly* 18 (1966): 151–74.

Wetmore, Sidney W. *Behind the Bars: Life and Times in Joliet Prison*. Chicago: Ottaway, 1883.

———. *Behind the Bars at Joliet: A Peep at a Prison, Its History, and Its Mysteries*. Joliet, Ill.: J. O. Gorman and Co., 1892.

———. "Fantastic Photos: The Joliet Penal Colony." *New York Illustrated American* (1890).

———. Typed notes for slideshow presentations. Wetmore Collection. Chicago Historical Society, Manuscript Division.

Whitman, John L. "Illinois Parole Law: Method and Results of Administration." *Journal of Criminal Law and Criminology* 11 (1920): 375–85.

———. "The Progressive Merit System: A Treatise on Prison Management." *Institution Quarterly* 12 (1921): 33–55.

Wickersham Commission. *Report on Penal Institutions, Probation, and Parole*. 1931. Reprint, Montclair, N.J.: Patterson Smith, 1968.

Wilbanks, William. "Are Females Treated More Leniently by the Criminal Justice System?" *Justice Quarterly* 3 (1986): 517–29.

Will County Historical Society. *A Pictorial History of Will County*. Vol. 2. Joliet, Ill.: Will County Historical Publications, 1975.

Willrich, Michael. "The Two Percent Solution: Eugenic Jurisprudence and Socialization of American Law, 1900–1930." *Law and History Review* 16 (1998): 63–111.

Wines, Enoch C. *The State of Prisons and of Child-Saving Institutions in the Civilized World*. Cambridge, Mass.: John Wilson and Son, 1880.

Wines, Frederick Howard. *Report on Crime, Pauperism, and Benevolence . . . at the Eleventh Census: 1890*. Washington, D.C.: Government Printing Office, 1895.

———. *Report on the Defective, Dependent, and Delinquent Classes . . . As Returned at the Tenth Census: 1880*. Washington, D.C.: Government Printing Office, 1888.

Wolloch, Nancy. *Women and the American Experience*. Boston: McGraw Hill, 2000.

Worrall, Anne. *Offending Women: Female Lawbreakers and the Criminal Justice System*. London: Routledge & Kegan Paul, 1990.

Worthington, George E., and Ruth Topping. *Specialized Courts Dealing with Sex Delinquency: A Study of the Procedures in Chicago, Boston, Philadelphia, and New York*. 1923. Reprint, Montclair, N.J.: Patterson Smith, 1969.

Wright, Richard A. "From Vamps to Tramps to Teases and Flirts: Stereotypes of Women in Criminology Textbooks, 1956 to 1965 and 1981 to 1990." *Journal of Criminal Justice Education* 3 (1992): 223–36.

Young, Vernetta D. "Gender Expectations and Their Impact on Black Female Offenders and Victims." *Justice Quarterly* 3 (1986): 305–28.

Zedner, Lucia. "Wayward Sisters: The Prison for Women." In *The Oxford History of the Prison: The Practice of Punishment in Western Society*, ed. Norval Morris and David J. Rothman, 328–65. New York: Oxford University Press, 1995.

———. *Women, Crime, and Custody in Victorian England*. Oxford: Oxford University Press, 1991.

———. "Women, Crime, and Penal Responses: A Historical Account." In *Crime and Justice: An Annual Review of Research*, vol. 14, ed. Michael Tonry, 307–62. Chicago: University of Chicago Press, 1991.

INDEX

DATE DUE

APR 3 0 2003

DEMCO, INC. 38-2931